Contemporary Youth Activism

Contemporary Youth Activism

Advancing Social Justice in the United States

Jerusha Conner and Sonia M. Rosen, Editors

PRAEGER™

An Imprint of ABC-CLIO, LLC

Santa Barbara, California • Denver, Colorado

Library of Congress Cataloging-in-Publication Data

Names: Conner, Jerusha Osberg, editor. | Rosen, Sonia M., editor.
Title: Contemporary youth activism : advancing social justice in the United
    States / Jerusha Conner and Sonia M. Rosen, editors.
Description: Santa Barbara, California: Praeger, [2016] | Includes index.
Identifiers: LCCN 2016019569 (print) | LCCN 2016031039 (ebook) |
    ISBN 9781440842122 (alk. paper) | ISBN 9781440842139 (ebook)
Subjects: LCSH: Youth—Political activity—United States. | Social justice—
    United States. | Community leadership—United States. | Community
    development—United States.
Classification: LCC HQ799.2.P6 C664 2016 (print) | LCC HQ799.2.P6
    (ebook) | DDC 320.40835—dc23
LC record available at https://lccn.loc.gov/2016019569

ISBN: 978-1-4408-4212-2
EISBN: 978-1-4408-4213-9

20 19 18 17 16   1 2 3 4 5

This book is also available as an eBook.

Praeger
An Imprint of ABC-CLIO, LLC

ABC-CLIO, LLC
130 Cremona Drive, P.O. Box 1911
Santa Barbara, California 93116-1911
www.abc-clio.com

This book is printed on acid-free paper ∞
Manufactured in the United States of America

Contents

PART IV CONCLUSION

Acknowledgments

It has been our privilege to work alongside and learn from the contributors to this volume and the inspiring youth activists they discuss. We thank them for their important contributions. We also gratefully acknowledge Edward Fierros and Graciela Slesaransky-Poe for supporting this project. Jessica Gribble has been a steadfast guide and constant champion, and we greatly appreciate all she has done to shepherd this book to publication. Kelly Monahan deserves our particular gratitude for her tireless work and uncompromising attention to detail. Finally, we offer heartfelt thanks to our families, Austin and Samer, Curtis, Coco, Kiki, Nadim, and the little person we can't wait to meet for putting up with us as we completed this project. Your unwavering love, patience, and support as we worked late nights and weekends were immensely sustaining throughout this process.

1

Introduction

Jerusha Conner and Sonia M. Rosen

At the present moment in the United States, youth activism is highly visible. The spring of 2015 saw a resurgence of marches, peaceful protests, and demonstrations across the nation, as Black youth joined with adults to assert that Black Lives Matter and to call for an end to the aggressive policing of Black and Brown bodies. Die-ins occurred on many college and high school campuses. In the fall of 2015, using a range of tactics from old-fashioned sit-ins and hunger strikes to new media campaigns, students from various universities and colleges forced administrators to engage in long-overdue conversations about institutionalized racism and sexism, to change policies, to revise curricula, and to reconsider building names. With the support of their coach, student athletes at the University of Missouri stood in solidarity with fellow student activists, calling for an increase in the hiring of Black faculty members and the creation of a comprehensive racial awareness and inclusion curriculum, among other demands. The football players' refusal to participate in revenue-generating games until the president of the university resigned garnered national headlines and triggered an outpouring of support from other students across the country.

High school students, too, have staged dramatic walkouts over the past couple of years to protest policies and practices that disproportionately affect low-income students of color, including funding cuts to education, violent treatment at the hands of school resource officers, and high-stakes testing regimes that narrow the curriculum and punish students. Youth from the United States have also assumed roles in international campaigns and social justice movements; they were actively involved in the demonstrations surrounding the climate talks in Paris in December 2015, and they have joined with youth from more than 100 other nation-states in U.N.-sponsored programs and events, such as the United Nations Economic and Social Council Youth Forum held in New York in February 2016.

Of course, not all activism is highly visible, and much of the work of activists occurs behind the scenes. Nonetheless, the ongoing conversations activists have pursued with local, state, and federal decision makers have led to significant changes in recent years in such areas as Title IX reporting and compliance (Brodsky, this volume), Deferred Action for Childhood Arrivals and Deferred Action for Parents of Americans and Lawful Permanent Residents (Negrón-Gonzales, this volume), and school-level student disciplinary policies (Fernández, Kirshner, & Lewis, this volume).

The years 2015–2016 seem to mark an important turning point in this history of youth activism in the United States. This book explores the significance of the current moment by examining the strategies, struggles, and successes of some recent cases of contemporary youth activism and synthesizing broad lessons from the field. In an effort to capture the vastness and complexity of the work young people are doing to effect social change, we chose to highlight diverse examples of youth activism that span a range of social identities, geographic regions, and issue areas. The chapters that follow offer insight into how young people engage in activism and how their participation transforms them and their communities, functioning as a formidable force in the U.S. social and political landscape. In the remainder of this introduction, we frame this examination by unpacking our terms. What do we mean by *youth*? How are we defining *activism*? How do we understand the *contemporary* moment in the United States? We then offer an overview of the scope, structure, and central arguments of the book and preview the chapters and essays to come.

WHAT IS YOUTH ACTIVISM?

In this volume, we offer many examples that we situate under the umbrella term "activism," a term that is frequently invoked in mainstream media and scholarly literature but rarely defined. Sherrod (2006) defines activism broadly as "action for social change" (p. 2), claiming that activism encompasses a wide range of practices intended to challenge and change existing social institutions. Others have echoed this definition, referring to "struggles for social justice" (Taft, 2011, p. 3) and the transformation of civil society (Kirshner, 2015) to describe what activists do. With these conceptions in mind, we understand activism as acts that challenge the status quo and seek to reconfigure asymmetrical power relations. Activism involves undermining structures that privilege particular social actors and marginalize others, and it seeks to include in decision-making structures and processes those whose voices have been systematically muted. It paves pathways for inclusion, access, and equity.

In a democracy, activism is one of countless ways that stakeholders exert agency. Kennelly (2011) recognizes activism as a "mode of democratic engagement with the public sphere" (p. 133); as Gallay and colleagues point out in this volume, activists can simultaneously challenge and redefine our notion of the public sphere. As we elaborate below, in a neoliberal context, grassroots activism can be interpreted as "troublemaking" rather than the constructive actions of good citizens (Kennelly, 2011). However, the cases presented in this book support Sherrod's (2006) claim that activism is one of many possible forms of good citizenship:

> Whereas commitment to the rule of law is an aspect of being a good citizen, a society that is "ruled by the people," as should be true of any democracy, also depends on citizens who make informed judgments, who at times object to policies and even disobey unjust laws, as they have in many movements for social justice. This is activism. Good behavior may be one aspect of citizenship, but so is activism or taking action to improve the nation-state, which is frequently not considered good behavior. (p. 2)

In some cases, the authors in this volume demonstrate that activism may be the only effective method of interrupting the systemic violence perpetrated by the nation-state itself.

Though activism encompasses a broad range of behaviors, in the last few decades the term "youth organizing" has been used to refer to particular forms of activism that tend to be formally institutionalized and are thus sustainable across generations of youth activists (for a more in-depth discussion of this topic, see Braxton, this volume). Organizing efforts like these seek to mobilize youth toward meaningful social change, and they simultaneously work to support young people's needs and develop their leadership capacity (Delgado & Staples, 2008). These youth organizers favor forms of activism that promote sustained engagement and offer infrastructure and intergenerational support rather than the more spontaneous, less tightly knit approaches that characterized the various antiglobalization activists who protested in Seattle and Quebec City in the late 1990s or the 2014 Occupy movement. Recently, we have seen the rise of momentum-based organizing work in the form of the Black Lives Matter movement, a well-coordinated network of local groups whose social and organizational configuration sits somewhere between institutionalized organizing and the antiglobalization and Occupy movement examples (Braxton, this volume; Dohrn & Ayers, this volume).

Importantly, we have sought to showcase a range of examples of *grassroots* activism—activism that emerges from the ground up, engaging people who genuinely feel inspired by a cause and come to the work on their own volition. We view this type of activism as having a markedly different effect from what is commonly referred to as "astroturf activism," or activism that is prompted and paid for by outside organizations that then publicize these mobilizations in ways that deceptively make them appear to be examples of grassroots organizing. Often, astroturf activism involves organizations paying people to come to political rallies or institutions requiring their employees to attend a protest (Au & Ferrare, 2015b). In contrast, grassroots activism derives its support from communities and positions people from marginalized groups to assert collective agency in ways that would be impossible if they were merely acting alone. When young people engage in this grassroots work, activism becomes "a way of rethinking youth within youth's own paradigm" (Quijada, 2008, p. 209).

Even the term "youth," which is used throughout this book, is vague and inconsistently defined in the broader literature. "Youth" can signify a narrow or wide age range; it has been employed to refer to all adolescents, children below the legal age of consent, or even a mix of children and young adults. The category of youth is a social construct whose meaning varies widely depending on cultural and historical context. In any society, categorizations of childhood are shaped by the roles people of different ages are expected to play, as well as the institutions that structure those roles, all of which change significantly over time. In the contemporary United States, childhood and adolescence are understood as a period of less social and economic responsibility than adulthood, and those ages are defined by our legal system (e.g., "minors" are under age 18) and by social institutions, such as K–12 schools and higher education institutions (Flanagan & Syvertsen, 2006). Moreover, adults have, historically, demonstrated ambivalence toward youth: We create protections for children and, at the same time, we leave them in precarious social and economic circumstances. We see young people as a future in which to invest, yet we dehumanize them in the present and rarely envision them as stakeholders with valuable contributions (Ginwright & Cammarota, 2006). In the face of adult ambivalence, the terminology used to describe this population carries political weight. Bishop (2015) explains, "Youth is itself a political term, one that recognizes the power of young people not as 'kids' to be controlled and 'children' to be quieted but as growing adults who possess the capacity to be leaders in the present" (p. 2). With this assertion in mind, we consciously employ the term "youth activism" to acknowledge the numerous ways young people—especially youth of color, low-income youth, young women, and LGBTQ youth—have mobilized to exert collective power in the face of the intersectional oppressions they face daily.

In this volume, we define youth broadly, including individuals ages 12–24 and possibly even beyond that range. Some of the chapters present stories of middle and high school–aged youth whose organizing has manifested as part of established youth organizing groups and other youth-serving organizations, whereas other chapters highlight the efforts of university students whose organizing has happened within and across campuses. Almost all of these examples demonstrate the intergenerational nature of this work, a theme that emerges repeatedly in literature on youth activism (Braxton, Buford, & Marasigan, 2013; Delgado & Staples, 2008). In intergenerational organizing spaces, youth and adults are able to reimagine the divisions between them, challenging our constructions of youth and the social roles we attribute to young people. In this sense, the very act of resisting injustice repositions young people and undermines and redefines the category of youth (Quijada, 2008).

A UNIQUE MOMENT FOR YOUTH ACTIVISTS

Having unpacked the terms "youth" and "activism" as they will be used throughout this book, we now turn to the term "contemporary" and consider what is unique about the present moment. Defining this moment, however, first requires turning to the past. The literature on youth activism regularly reminds us that youth activism is not new; a frequent refrain states that youth have long been at the forefront of struggles for social change. As Boren (2001) argues, "Throughout history, students have catalyzed local education reform, transformed national political structures, and in more than a few instances, spurred coups d'état" (p. 3). In the early 19th century, teenage girls in the United States organized and led labor union strikes, and as early as 1937, the Southern Negro Youth Congress organized protests against segregation and police brutality (Light, 2015). Certainly, it is important to continue to trace youths' leadership in social movements and to situate today's examples of youth activism within the long and storied history of youths' efforts to bring about a more just and peaceful world. However, we argue that contemporary youth activism merits attention not just because of the rich tradition it is advancing, but also because of the unique set of circumstances and social conditions to which it is responding today.

The Neoliberal Context for Youth in the United States

Neoliberalism. Today, wealth disparities in the United States are at an all-time high and growing numbers of U.S. residents live in extreme poverty, with incomes 50% lower than the national poverty threshold (Moller, Nielsen, & Alderson, 2009). Those living in extreme poverty include more than seven million children and youth, or roughly 10% of the population under age 18 (Annie E. Casey Foundation, 2015). Scholars have linked the increasing consolidation of wealth and the tattering of social safety nets for the poor to a rise in neoliberal policies and ideologies over the last 40 years. Neoliberalism has been defined by Lipman (2011) as

> an ensemble of economic and social policies, forms of governance, and discourses and ideologies that promote self-interest, unrestricted flows of capital, deep reductions in the cost of labor, and sharp retrenchment of the public sphere. Neoliberals champion the privatization of social goods and the withdrawal of the government from provision of social welfare. (p. 6)

Neoliberalism advances market solutions to public problems and seeks to create new competitive markets, while shrinking the role of government. This approach privileges the rich, who are positioned to take advantage of these new markets, while further dispossessing the poor, who might have otherwise benefited from government-run social programs. As Au and Ferrare (2015a) explain, neoliberalism "redistributes resources, social and economic goods, wealth and power upwards to those individuals, communities, and corporations already benefiting from high concentrations of wealth . . . simultaneous[ly] restrict[ing] access to those same resources and opportunities for those already on the bottom" (p. 3). This redistribution and restriction serve to restructure both the economy and the state "in line with individual self-interest and at a cost to commitments to collective well-being" (Au & Ferrare, 2015a, p. 3).

Some scholars connect the rise of the neoliberal state to an increase in state violence (Lipman, 2011; Tuck, 2011). This violence is particularly directed against poor people, people of color, and recent immigrants, who under neoliberalism are blamed for the conditions in which they live. Forms of state violence include direct violence, such as harassment by the police and police killing of unarmed Black men; Immigration and Customs Enforcement raids; detention, deportation, and Department of Children and Family Services practices that break up families; the disproportionate numbers of school-based arrests of youth of color; and mandatory sentencing laws and court decisions that result in stiffer penalties and harsher sentences for Black and Brown offenders than for white offenders. State violence can also include symbolic, structural, and more subtle forms of violence, such as the lack of access poor people have to quality educational opportunities, affordable housing, decent jobs, healthy food, and clean environments. Hanchard (2015) argues,

> legacies of racial regimes in societies where disproportionately high levels of unemployment and incarceration rates, poor education, spatial segregation and capricious doses of state violence structure the conditions of

marginality, . . . [make] violence against these populations not only plausible, but banal.

Hanchard's examples point to the hegemony of neoliberal state violence—a reality that the public has been conditioned to either ignore completely or view as normal and justified.

The effects of neoliberalism for youth.   Neoliberalism affects youth by (re)shaping the institutions that most touch their lives and by narrowing the pathways they can use to navigate these institutions. Under neoliberalism, the educational, criminal justice, health care, and immigration systems have all seen a rise in privatization as well as a shift from *"government* by elected state bodies . . . to *governance* by experts and managers" (Lipman, 2011, p. 13). In each of these arenas, government has either given way to or cleared the way for private companies, opening up new markets for competition and profiteering. Typically, the entrepreneurs who have entered these new marketplaces have found ways to make money, while further marginalizing and isolating the poor. For low-income young people, the effects have been particularly devastating.

In education policy, the growing prominence of high-stakes testing as a tool for holding students, teachers, and schools accountable has been a boon to publishers and testing companies, even as it has served to stigmatize, penalize, and further erode educational opportunity for youth in the lowest socioeconomic brackets. One prominent textbook manufacturing company, Pearson, for example, makes $4 billion annually from its North American education division, much of which comes through no-bid "public contracts and public subsidies—including at least $98.5 million in tax credits from six states" (Simon, 2015). Meanwhile, as Broussard (2014) documents, underfunded school districts, like the School District of Philadelphia, simply cannot afford to buy the textbooks that are produced by the very same companies that manufacture and grade the tests. As a result, students in the least well-resourced schools—predominantly Black and Latino students and English language learners—will never be prepared to perform at the same level on these tests as students in more affluent districts. Nonetheless, under federal and state policy, low-performing schools are shamed and castigated for this manufactured failure and subjected to escalating sanctions, such as firing at least half of the teachers and the principal, handing the governance of the school over to a charter management organization, or closing the school entirely, displacing the students. Such "disruption" is often hailed by a new class of "edupreneurs," from high-technology companies to charter management organizations, all seeking to capitalize on the poor test scores of students in underresourced schools. The new industry, spawned by high-stakes testing, has resulted not in rich, engaging, real-world curricula that promote critical thinking and curiosity, but in tightly scripted lessons and computer-based programming, narrowly focused on test preparation, drilling, and remediation (Yee, 2015). It has also resulted in high push-out rates for students who are either perceived as most detrimental to a school's bottom line (Heilig & Darling-Hammond, 2008) or who can no longer tolerate the indignities of such an educational experience (Tuck, 2011).

Neoliberal education policy intersects with policing practices in low-income communities of color to further limit opportunities for youth, funneling many into what is commonly referred to as the school-to-prison pipeline or what Fernández et al. (this volume) call the "school-to-prison nexus." Students in charter schools and "low-performing" public schools are especially subject to excessive surveillance and harsh discipline policies. For example, New Orleans, the first city in the United States to have a fully charterized system of education, has one of the highest incarceration rates in the world, with "the majority of youth arrestees coming from low-income backgrounds" (Marshall, 2012, p. 14). The emergence and rise of the prison-industrial complex (Whitehead, 2012) and private detention centers that profit from keeping immigrants detained (Golash-Boza, 2009) have also disproportionately impacted low-income youth of color, undocumented youth, and their families.

In addition to shaping institutions like the education and criminal justice systems, neoliberalism has influenced the content and nature of after-school programs and opportunities for youth. As Kwon (2013) explains, the move from the welfare state to the neoliberal state was accompanied by a shift in the rhetoric and emphasis of after-school programming from kid-fixing to youth-empowering. Programs designed to help youth avoid problems, such as drug use, gang involvement, or teen pregnancy, fell out of favor in the 1990s and early 2000s and were replaced by programs designed to build youths' developmental assets, such as their latent leadership skills, resilience and grit, or cultural competence. The language of empowerment, and the positive youth development framework that gave rise to it, were promulgated by foundations and nonprofit organizations (sometimes referred to as the nonprofit industrial complex [Smith, 2007]) interested in helping communities improve themselves in the wake of government retrenchment. The empowerment perspective calls on youth to take responsibility for themselves and others, challenging them to become productive citizens who work to fix the problems in their communities. This framework places the burden on youth to generate community-based alternatives to fraying social safety nets and reduced government-sponsored social service programs, to call for different policies, and to hold governments accountable for addressing their needs— even though they cannot vote. Kwon (2013) argues that the nonprofitization of youth after-school programming, including the nonprofitization of youth activism, must be understood as a technology of the neoliberal state, which deploys civil society to manage and control youth by enlisting them to fix their own problems. The state only steps back in when youth show an unwillingness to accept such responsibility. Indeed, according to Kwon (2013), young people's failure to participate enthusiastically and voluntarily in existing after-school programs "justifies state intervention and legitimates young people's criminalization" (p. 9).

Other scholars agree with and extend Kwon's (2013) notion that neoliberalism frames youth narrowly as either "good" after-school program participants who are involved in their own development and empowerment or as "bad" nonparticipants, who merit state surveillance, control, and intervention. Kennelly (2011), for example, asserts that the ideal youth citizen in a neoliberal state engages in worthwhile, often consumer-driven community service projects, not intended to subvert the status quo; whereas youth who critique or challenge state actions are constructed as "bad activists." She continues:

> It is no coincidence that the former is highly reconcilable with the neoliberal model of the self-perfecting citizen, through its relentless focus on the individual benefits that accrue to someone performing this version of activism (e.g., an endorphin rush) and its focus on individualized consumption as the path to social change. (pp. 51–52)

Kennelly uses the example of Free the Children to illustrate this model. She recounts a speech by one of the founders in which he reiterated the personal benefits of becoming involved in efforts to address poverty and suggested that young people could make a difference by buying his book and a T-shirt with the organization's logo: Me to We.

Another example of neoliberal-sanctioned, consumer-based youth activism comes from the case of Kony 2012. This campaign, orchestrated by the nonprofit organization Invisible Children, encouraged young people to watch a video describing the atrocities committed by African warlord Joseph Kony, circulate it virally, and purchase an "action kit" for $30, which contained a T-shirt, bracelets, posters, and stickers—material intended to help youth increase awareness of Kony and build political pressure to take action against him. More than 500,000 action kits were sold, and demand quickly outstripped supply. The overall significance and impact of this campaign continue to be debated (Fung & Shkabatur, 2015). Invisible Children came under harsh criticism for its presentation of "a world where the individual, voluntary and one time actions of consumers are an easy solution to the complex problems of developing countries and global health issues" (Larson, 2012); however, few politicians and media personalities critiqued the more than half a million youth who participated in some fashion in the campaign, and many news stories celebrated the young Kony 2012 activists for becoming engaged beyond slacktivism (Fung & Shkabatur, 2015).

In contrast to consumer activism, forms of activism that involve youth outwardly defying the neoliberal state are quickly condemned by pundits and policymakers. Such was the case in Baltimore in the spring of 2015, when a young Black man named Freddie Gray died while in police custody and outraged youth responded by walking out of their schools, taking to the streets, and raising their voices in anger (Glum, 2015). During a continuation of this protest later that evening, a small number of protesters launched bottles and bricks toward police officers in response to provocation by a police force decked out in riot gear. The mayor of Baltimore, President Obama, and many media personalities were quick to denounce these youth as "thugs" (Bradner, 2015). In response, the National Guard was deployed, armed with tear gas and rubber bullets to control the protesters, and a strict curfew was instituted (Myers & Dishneau, 2015). A mother who was caught on camera whacking her son for being involved in a protest, while shooing him away from the scene, was heralded by many as "mom of the year" (Whitaker & Snell, 2016).

These analyses illuminate how the neoliberal state constructs and constrains youth by reconfiguring power relations and narrowing publicly acceptable roles for young people. Although such neoliberal formulations have "severely limited the potential of oppositional political activism in the contemporary moment" (Kwon, 2013, p. 5), the challenges contemporary youth activists mount to these social constructions, the policies that perpetuate them, and the neoliberal state itself are significant and worthy of scholarly and popular attention.

NEOLIBERALISM AND YOUTH ACTIVISM: THE SCOPE OF THIS BOOK

Neoliberalism has become the dominant ideology in the United States; however, it is not totalizing, and contemporary youth activists have found ways to speak back to its logic and to dispute the narrow roles it offers them. This book is a collection of examples that show how, why, and to what effect youth are countering neoliberal policies and perspectives, putting forward alternative solutions to the problems that matter most to them, asserting their rights to democratic participation, and advancing social justice.

Although we include several chapters that take a wide-angle view of youth activism, all of the issue-based cases in this volume focus on contemporary youth activists responding in some way to the context of neoliberalism—even though they might not use this language explicitly. We deliberately chose this set of cases because at the same time that they represent different struggles and different arenas in which neoliberalism is manifest, they also collectively represent the constellation of issue areas that form the core of youth activism in the present moment in the United States. In fact, contemporary youth activists understand the links among these core issue areas, and they appreciate the importance of working together across the lines that typically divide them, whether those lines are geographic, identity-based, or thematic. For example, after the fatal shooting of 17-year-old Michael Brown by a police officer in Ferguson, Missouri, in the summer of 2014, local organizers invited the executive director from the Philadelphia Student Union, a youth organizing group known primarily for its work on education reform, to help them train youth leaders and strategize a response to police brutality and the criminalization of young Black males.

Intersecting issues and transcended boundaries are also distinguishing features of the biannual Free Minds, Free People conference, which "brings together teachers, high school and college students, researchers, parents and community-based activists/educators from across the country to build a movement to develop and promote education as a tool for liberation" (Free Minds, Free People, 2015). Workshops and assemblies examine such diverse topics as media sexism, health disparities and inequalities, criminal justice reform and the school-to-prison pipeline, and the Black Lives Matter movement. At the center, connecting all of these presentations, is a framework that

> place[s] education injustice and mis-education into a context of national and international attacks on communities of color and low-income communities—an assault that includes poverty, incarceration, theft of resources, exploitation of workers, displacement, state-sanctioned violence, and genocide. (Free Minds, Free People, 2015)

A similar framework animated the Funders' Collaborative for Youth Organizing's (FCYO) first annual Youth Power Convening, held November 13–14, 2015, in Durham, North Carolina. At this event, 150 representatives from different youth organizing groups across the country came together to develop "new models, tools and tactics for social justice"; to "better understand each other across differences and form stronger connections"; and to formulate "new and expanded consciousness and new visions for the world we want and need." The program for this convening acknowledged, "There is a growing analysis of the impact of state violence across all of our communities. This moment brings opportunities" (Funders' Collaborative on Youth Organizing, n.d.). Although the groups participating in this convening focused on different core issues, ranging from immigration to criminal justice and police accountability, they found common purpose in their definition and critique of state violence, especially as it targets low-income youth of color and as it draws its legitimacy from neoliberalism.

There are many movements and cases of youth activism that we do not profile in this book because they do not involve youth in confronting neoliberalism. Some youth activists may work on issues that are unrelated or peripheral to the core set of issues discussed above. For example, groups engaged in right to life and anti-abortion activism do not participate in either the Free Minds, Free People conference or FCYO events, such as the Youth Power Convening. In fact, policies that legislate and limit what women may do with their bodies may be seen as a form of the very state violence that the youth participating in these events sought to critique and challenge.

We also acknowledge that there are youth activists who actively embrace neoliberal viewpoints and seek to advance market solutions to social problems. For example, Students for Education Reform (SFER) focuses on training first-generation college students to serve as "community organizers," who work at the state level to accelerate a particular brand of education reform that prioritizes accountability and school choice, including the expansion of charter schools. The chair of SFER's board of directors is the "Chief Growth Officer" for a prominent charter management organization, KIPP. SFER's advocacy for charter schools, the use of high-stakes testing data, and teacher accountability schemes align it with the corporate education reform movement, a neoliberal approach to privatize public education, and its close financial and political ties to corporate reformers make it a prime example of the kind of astroturf activism we mentioned above (Au & Ferrare, 2015b). SFER—and other examples of youth activists who claim the mantle of social justice but who promote policies aligned with privatization—are not included as cases in this volume because they are not participating in the broader conversations among youth activists about the problems with neoliberal and market-based approaches, their implications for youth and for society, and alternative paradigms. In what follows, we give a brief overview of the chapters to come, situating them within this larger conversation.

OVERVIEW OF CHAPTERS

The 18 chapters of the book are organized around three main themes, which collectively advance the argument that contemporary youth activism stands to strengthen U.S. society as much as it might benefit the individual participants and the institutions they are working to change. Part I offers a historical perspective on youth activism in the United States, followed by chapters that present recent examples of contemporary youth activism (CYA) for social justice, drawn from a range of contexts and issue areas. The second and third sections analyze the individual, institutional, and ideological effects of CYA, arguing that youth activism works to promote change at three levels: self, systems, and the broader society. Part 2 focuses on the ways in which involvement in youth activism impacts youth, while Part 3 explores how youth activism results in tangible changes to practice, policy, power structures, and paradigms.

Part 1, "The Landscape of Contemporary Youth Activism," opens with an essay by Beatrice Galdamez, a youth activist involved in the Youth Organizing Institute in Durham, North Carolina, who reflects on first becoming involved in activism, links this work to the legacies of Ella Baker and other important civil rights leaders, and describes the impulse to continue to fight for the rights of others, particularly LGBTQ youth. Chapter 2 offers an overview of contemporary youth activism, situating it in a broader historical trajectory of young people's resistance movements. From his unique vantage point as a former youth activist and current executive director of the Funders' Collaborative for Youth Organizing, Eric Braxton traces the rise of contemporary youth organizing in the early 1990s and describes key approaches, features, and trends in this maturing field. Mark Warren and Luke Aubry Kupscznk extend this analysis by exploring the differences between locally rooted youth organizing campaigns and broad-based social movements, as they consider whether we are witnessing the birth of a new youth justice movement—a movement that expands beyond youth organizing groups and includes adults as well as young people. In Chapter 4, we unpack the meaning of a frequently used term in the youth organizing literature, "youth-led," and offer a framework for conceptualizing youth leadership within organizations and institutions. In Chapters 5–7, the authors introduce various ways of conceptualizing the sociopolitical context in which young people are mobilizing for justice. Chapter 5, by Bernardine Dohrn and William Ayers, focuses on the Black Lives Matter movement, locating it within the long history of civil rights activism in the United States in response to institutional racism and state violence. Jesica Siham Fernández, Ben Kirshner, and Deana G. Lewis further this discussion of state violence in Chapter 6 by examining a specific instantiation of the criminalization of Black and Brown youth through their analysis of how youth activists are challenging the school-to-prison nexus and advancing alternative disciplinary practices, such as restorative justice. Part 1 concludes with Chapter 7, in which Erin Gallay, John Lupinacci, Carolina S. Sarmiento, Constance A. Flanagan, and Ethan Lowenstein introduce the historical image of the commons not just as a way to conceptualize youth engagement in environmental justice activism and anti-eco-racism efforts, but also as a way to understand the broader social justice goals and commitments of youth activists.

Part 2, "How Youth Activism Supports Youth," leads with an essay by Jamia Brown, a high school youth activist from New Orleans. In this piece, she reflects on how being an activist has shaped her identity. In Chapter 8, John Rogers and Veronica Terriquez extend Brown's analysis as they examine the implications of formative experiences with activism for young people's identity development. Rogers and Terriquez's data on the academic and civic trajectories of former youth organizers demonstrate the longer-term benefits of involvement in activism during high school. The subsequent three chapters take up the issues of relationships and social capital in relation to youth development. In Chapter 9, Kira J. Baker-Doyle examines how youth participatory action research sets the stage for youth to use relationships with different kinds of social actors to accrue social capital and come to see themselves as engaged civic actors. In Chapter 10, Barbara Ferman and Natalia Smirnov consider how young people are empowered by producing media for social change. They illustrate how this process enables youth to develop important skills and build relationships with one another and with key allies, ultimately providing youth with opportunities to contribute to public discourse about issues that affect their lives. Continuing this focus on storytelling and the sharing of counternarratives, in Chapter 11 Julia Daniel and Michelle Renée Valladares describe ways that young Black women and Black gender-queer youth activists have created spaces to tell their own stories, which help them heal from and challenge gender-based oppression and exclusion within and outside of their movement work. Parissa J. Ballard and Emily J. Ozer address the themes of health and well-being in Chapter 12, considering the potential of activism to have both positive and detrimental effects on young people's well-being. This section closes with Alexandra Brodsky's compelling account in Chapter 13 of the nationwide fight to end sexual assault on college campuses. Brodsky presents a complex picture of the benefits she and other activists derived from their work in this area and the unique vulnerabilities that survivors of sexual assault experience as activists.

Part 3, "How Youth Activism Strengthens Society," begins with an essay by Janelle Astorga-Ramos about her experience as an organizer in New Mexico, working on campaigns that changed policy in the areas of reproductive justice and educational equity. This essay sets the stage for a number of thoughtful explorations of the impacts that youth activists can have on policy, practice, and discourse. Chapters 14 and 15 showcase the efforts of undocumented immigrant youth activists from Tucson, Arizona—the DREAMers—and Asian immigrant student activists from Philadelphia, Pennsylvania, respectively. In Chapter 14, Genevieve Negrón-Gonzalez explores the power of civil disobedience for particularly vulnerable youth as a means of altering political discourse and public perception of undocumented immigrants, even though these youth did not succeed in making the immediate policy changes they sought. Conversely, Mary Yee's account in Chapter 15 of Asian immigrant high school students' struggle to feel safe in their schools demonstrates that in some arenas, young people's activism can achieve important legal changes and affect districtwide policies. Similarly, in Chapter 16, Rachel Gunther describes an "inside-out" model in which youth activists strategize from within existing school institutions to effect systemwide changes and amplify student voice over the long term. Chapter 17, authored by Brett G. Stoudt, Caitlin Cahill, Darian X, Kimberly Belmonte, Selma Djokovic, Jose Lopez, Amanda Matles, Adilka Pimentel, and María Elena Torre, tells the story of an intergenerational group of researchers in New York City whose research and activism around the controversial stop-and-frisk policy posed a significant public challenge to the police narrative about Black and Brown communities and resulted in concrete policy changes. Chapters 18 and 19 highlight campaigns led by university students. In Chapter 18, Jessica Ann Solyom details Native American student organizing to address the campuswide silencing, exclusion, and racist depictions of Native Americans, as well as the university's systematic failure to uphold its stated commitments to Native American students. She analyzes the way media shapes narratives and demonstrates the importance of youth activists' efforts to shift dominant narratives about Native American resistance. Finally, in Chapter 19, Joe Curnow and Allyson Gross explore how student activists involved in fossil fuel divestment campaigns on various North American campuses have developed a deep intersectional analysis of divestment and reinvestment that extends beyond economic considerations to include issues of colonialism and institutional racism and opens up new possibilities for working in solidarity with frontline communities.

At a time when neoliberal paradigms position young people as either empowered consumers or deviants requiring state intervention (Giroux, 2009), it is vital to understand how today's youth are pushing back, challenging these constructions, and advancing new possibilities for both their institutions and themselves. This book examines the latest developments in the field of contemporary youth activism and documents the myriad ways in which youth activists are effecting social change and experiencing personal change. The chapters show that as youth activists take public, political action in a range of intersecting issue areas, they are shifting their own developmental pathways, shaping public policy, and shaking up traditional paradigms. Overall, this book reveals how youth activists around the United States are working across issues and connecting communities to build a progressive, leader-full movement for social justice that promises to reimagine and remake American democracy.

REFERENCES

Annie E. Casey Foundation. (2015). Kids Count Data [Data file]. Retrieved from http://datacenter.kidscount.org/

Au, W., & Ferrare, J. J. (2015a). Introduction: Neoliberalism, social networks, and the new governance of education. In W. Au & J. J. Ferrare (Eds.), *Mapping corporate education reform* (pp. 1–22). New York: Routledge.

Au, W., & Ferrare, J. J. (2015b). Other people's policy: Wealthy elites and charter school reform in Washington state. In *Mapping corporate education reform: Power and policy networks in the neoliberal state* (pp. 147–164). New York: Routledge.

Bishop, E. (2015). *Becoming activist: Critical literacy and youth organizing.* New York: Peter Lang.

Boren, M. E. (2001). *Student resistance: A history of the unruly subject.* New York: Routledge.

Bradner, E. (2015, April 28). Obama: "No excuse" for violence in Baltimore. *CNN.* Retrieved from http://www.cnn.com/2015/04/28/politics/obama-baltimore-violent -protests/

Braxton, E., Buford, W., & Marasigan, L. (2013). *National Field Scan.* New York: Funders' Collaborative on Youth Organizing.

Broussard, M. (2014, July 15). Why poor schools can't win at standardized testing. *Atlantic Monthly.* Retrieved from http://www.theatlantic.com/features/archive /2014/07/why-poor-schools-cant-win-at-standardized-testing/374287/

Delgado, M., & Staples, L. (2008). *Youth-led community organizing: Theory and action.* New York: Oxford University Press.

Flanagan, C. A., & Syvertsen, A. K. (2006). Youth as a social construct and social actor. In L. R. Sherrod, C. A. Flanagan, R. Kassimir, & A. K. Syvertsen (Eds.), *Youth activism: An international encyclopedia* (Vol. 1, pp. 11–19). Westport, CT: Greenwood Press.

Free Minds, Free People. (2015). Call for proposals. Retrieved from http://www .nycore.org/2010/11/free-minds-free-people-call-for-proposals/

Funders' Collaborative on Youth Organizing. (n.d.). Youth power convening. Retrieved from http://fcyo.org/

Fung, A., & Shkabatur, J. (2015). Viral engagement: Fast, cheap, and broad but good for democracy? In D. Allen & J. S. Light (Eds.), *From voice to influence: Understanding citizenship in the digital age* (pp. 155–177). Chicago, IL: University of Chicago Press.

Ginwright, S., & Cammarota, J. (2006). Introduction. In S. Ginwright, P. Noguera, & J. Cammarota (Eds.), *Beyond resistance!: Youth activism and community change: New democratic possibilities for practice and policy for America's youth* (pp. xiii–xxii). New York: Routledge Taylor and Francis Group.

Giroux, H. A. (2009). *Youth in a suspect society.* New York: Palgrave Macmillan.

Glum, J. (2015, April 29). Baltimore youths protest Freddie Gray's death with student-led march to city hall. *IB Times.* Retrieved from http://www.ibtimes.com/baltimore -youths-protest-freddie-grays-death-student-led-march-city-hall-1902462

Golash-Boza, T. (2009). A confluence of interests in immigration enforcement: How politicians, the media, and corporations profit from immigration policies destined to fail. *Sociology Compass, 3,* 1–12. http://dx.doi.org/10.1111/j.1751-9020.2008.00192.x

Hanchard, M. (2015, June 9). State violence against black and brown youth. *Huffington Post.* Retrieved from http://www.huffingtonpost.com/michael-hanchard/state -violence-against-black-and-brown-youth_b_7000210.html

Heilig, J. V., & Darling-Hammond, L. (2008). Accountability Texas-style: The progress and learning of urban minority students in a high-stakes testing context. *Educational Evaluation and Policy Analysis, 30,* 75–110. http://doi.org/10.3102/016 2373708317689

Kennelly, J. (2011). *Citizen youth: Culture, activism, and agency in a neoliberal era.* New York: Palgrave Macmillan.

Kirshner, B. (2015). *Youth activism in an era of education inequality.* New York: NYU Press.

Kwon, S. A. (2013). *Uncivil youth: Race, activism, and affirmative governmentality.* Durham, NC: Duke University Press.

Larson, P. S. (2012). Kony 2012: Public service or shameless self promotion? Retrieved from http://peterslarson.com/2012/03/10/kony2012-public-service-or -shameless-self-promotion/

Light, J. L. (2015). Putting our conversation in context: Youth, old media and political participation 1800–1971. In D. Allen & J. L. Light (Eds.), *From voice to influence: Understanding citizenship in the digital age* (pp. 19–33). Chicago, IL: University of Chicago Press.

Lipman, P. (2011). *The new political economy of urban education: Neoliberalism, race, and the right to the city.* New York: Routledge.

Marshall, A. (2012). *Countering youth incarceration: Community strategies in New Orleans and Cape Town.* San Francisco, CA: University of San Francisco Press.

Moller, S., Nielsen, F., & Alderson, A. S. (2009). Changing patterns of income inequality in U.S. counties, 1970–2000. *American Journal of Sociology, 114,* 1037–1101. http://dx.doi.org/10.1086/595943

Myers, A. L., & Dishneau, D. (2015, April 29). Police clash with Baltimore protesters for a second night. *Associated Press.* Retrieved from http://www.apnewsarchive .com/2015/Police_clash_with_Baltimore_protesters_for_a_second_night/id-53ee 1c04ca12437196f2c76bdcd30885

Quijada, D. A. (2008). Marginalization, identity formation, and empowerment: Youth's struggles for self and social justice. In N. Dolby & F. Rizvi (Eds.), *Youth moves* (pp. 207–220). New York: Routledge.

Sherrod, L. R. (2006). Youth activism and civic engagement. In L. R. Sherrod, C. A. Flanagan, R. Kassimir, & A. K. Syvertsen (Eds.), *Youth activism: An international encyclopedia* (Vol. 1, pp. 2–10). Westport, CT: Greenwood Press.

Simon, S. (2015, February 10). No profit left behind. *Politico.* Retrieved from http:// www.politico.com/story/2015/02/pearson-education-115026_Page3.html

Smith, A. (2007). Introduction: The revolution will not be funded. In INCITE! Women of Color Against Violence (Ed.), *The revolution will not be funded: Beyond the non-profit industrial complex* (pp. 1–18). Cambridge, MA: South End Press.

Taft, J. K. (2011). *Rebel girls: Youth activism and social change across the Americas.* New York: NYU Press.

Tuck, E. (2011). *Urban youth and school pushout.* New York: Routledge.

Whitaker, T. R., & Snell, C. L. (2016). Parenting while powerless: Consequences of "the talk." *Journal of Human Behavior in the Social Environment, 26*(3–4), 303–309. http://dx.doi.org/10.1080/10911359.2015.1127736

Whitehead, J. W. (2012, April 10). Jailing Americans for profit: The rise of the prison industrial complex. Retrieved from https://www.rutherford.org/publications _resources/john_whiteheads_commentary/jailing_americans_for_profit_the_rise _of_the_prison_industrial_complex

Yee, M. (2015). What English language learners have to say about NCLB. In J. Conner, R. Ebby-Rosin, & A. S. Brown (Eds.), *Speak up and speak out: Student voice in American educational policy* (Vol. 114, pp. 19–38). New York: Teachers College Record.

Part I

The Landscape of Contemporary
Youth Activism

Introduction

Contemporary youth activism is the product of a strong tradition of youth leadership and participation in movements for social change. It is a proclamation that circumstances are untenable. It fills the gaps left by widespread adult complacence. It is a mounting of power by social actors who have been systematically stripped of political agency. It is a response to neoliberal policies that commodify youth and privatize the public support system on which marginalized young people and their families rely, and it is a resistance to state violence and a reclamation of public space.

This section features a historical overview of youth activism, complicating our vision of a contemporary youth justice movement and clarifying what it means for young people to create such a movement. The chapters here examine features of contemporary youth activism and the metaphors that define youth resistance. In doing so, they pose key questions about how youth activists negotiate their relationships with adult movement actors and remain affected by histories of violence and connected to legacies of struggle. Together, the authors in this section explore the relationship between historical context and youth action, taking up the notion of place as a defining contextual feature of youth activism. They describe the structures of oppression connected to particular geographies, demonstrate the capacity of youth to transcend place as a means of disrupting these oppressive structures, and challenge the neoliberal understanding of places as private commodities. The overarching argument of this section is that contemporary youth activism borrows from and builds on a long legacy of young people's involvement in social justice movements. However, the chapters here demonstrate that youth activists are also working innovatively to respond to new manifestations of injustice and navigate complex new social, economic, and political realities.

Opening Youth Essay

Beatrice Galdamez

Before activism, I didn't have a clear vision of what was really going on around me. I grew up in a low-income home in a Latin American community, where I learned what a woman was "supposed" to act like, and what a man had to do. The product of generations of oppressive traditions funneled into me, twisting me into something others wanted. I didn't have opinions of my own, because I was taught adults knew better. I felt that I was trapped in a mold others created for me, but I never fell into these roles that easily. I was a tomboy who loved getting messy and played rough with the boys. Barbie, Bratz, or any glamorous kind of toy was never really that appealing to me. Cooking and cleaning seemed like something that had to be done, though. I felt that I was helping my mother when I did it, so I never really minded. Because I never fit into my societal role, I was constantly reminded of who I was "supposed" to be, if not by my family, by the schools I attended, or television. I knew I didn't fit into the classic roles, and I allowed it to bother me to the point that I stopped speaking. I just observed everything around me.

When I entered middle school, it was no change. Everything I had been taught forced me to do nothing but observe. Through observing I finally learned that everything was not as black and white as I was told. Thoughts and feeling I had kept to myself all those years were finally being heard and expressed. They were not confident, but they definitely grew more and more power behind them every time I spoke.

Eventually I found myself recommended to attend the Youth Organizing Institute's 2012 Freedom School. It was a space where I could share my opinions and develop them without fear of being judged. I had the opportunity to learn about multiple systems of oppressions and how they exist within our society. I found groups of people I could identify with and was able to connect more with my own culture. Soon, I was able to discover different parts of myself that had been repressed for so long.

Activism is a big part of who I am and has expanded my knowledge and confidence in things I couldn't even begin to fathom on my own before. I was finally allowing myself to express the feeling I had been denied for so long. I want to give that or create that kind of space for other people. I want to defend those who still have to remain silent for their own safety.

Being a part of the Freedom School program introduced me to what's possible when young people organize for change. In particular, I learned about Ella Baker who fought to uplift the leadership of young people. She believed in strong people, in young people, and in our society's ability to change. She is a part of the legacy that I fight in. There are many others like her who have come before me who have fought against injustice and for a better world. They have taught me lessons about what it means to fight and to defend my community. My activism is a continuation of their work and legacy.

Today, I fight to create a community where differences do not influence who gets treated better. I fight for a community where people of color don't have to constantly worry about whether their experience with the police is going to be their last; where LGBTQ youth don't have to worry about how others will respond to how they express themselves in friendships and relationships; where all youth can live free from fear, and able to live and breathe. As an activist, I don't just fight for myself—I fight for everyone who wants to be able to live their full selves.

2

Youth Leadership for Social Justice: Past and Present

Eric Braxton

From the movement for black lives, to the DREAMers, to efforts to end the school-to-prison pipeline, the last few years have seen youth-led social movements capture public attention, change dominant narratives, and win significant policy changes. The leadership of young people in social movements, however, is nothing new. From the movement for women's suffrage to the civil rights movement, to the current moment, the leadership of young people has always been central to social movements. Because of their relative lack of financial and familial commitments and less accumulated conditioning to accept the status quo, young people have a willingness to take risks and an inherent sense of justice that has allowed them to play central roles in many movements. While young people's leadership has always been central, the forms of youth activism have changed throughout history in relation to their sociopolitical context, resource availability, and technology. This chapter will look briefly at historic forms of youth activism, discuss the development of the youth organizing field in the 1990s and early 2000s, explore new and emerging forms of youth activism in the present moment, and conclude with thoughts on the prospects for transformative youth power in the coming years.

YOUTH ACTIVISM IN HISTORY

Young people have been involved in activism in the United States at least since the 19th century, when student governments at universities and high schools became common. During this period, young people also played critical roles in labor organizing, the movement to abolish slavery, and the movement for women's suffrage by organizing strikes and protests and making up a significant part of the membership of several organizations. In the early 1900s, for the first time, childhood began to be viewed as a separate and distinct phase of life with a need for extensive adult supervision (Kwon, 2013). This resulted in the formation of a new set of youth organizations such as the Boy Scouts and Campfire Girls. In addition, organizations like Junior Citizens organized young people to participate in mock government activities and sometimes enter real politics as well. Much of the youth activism in this period occurred under adult supervision, but there were also significant instances of autonomous youth activism including child labor strikes, rent strikes, and organizing among students in historically black colleges (Light, 2015).

Light (2015) describes the 1950s as being marked by a "peer oriented youth culture that would rebel against adults" (p. 26). Many new youth organizations formed in this period. The National Student League supported strikers and opposed war. The American Youth Congress issued the Declaration of the Rights of American Youth and won passage of the American Youth Act to support youth programs. The Southern Negro Youth Congress engaged in militant racial justice organizing, while young people in the Congress of Racial Equity led some of the first antisegregation sit-ins (Light, 2015). In 1959, Bayard Rustin, who had been involved in the Young Communist League, led a youth march for school integration in Washington, D.C.

The dramatic social movements of the 1960s were largely led by young people. The Children's Crusade in Birmingham, Alabama, in 1963, with Birmingham commissioner of public safety Bull Connor turning dogs and fire-hoses on hundreds of protesting schoolchildren, gained national attention for the growing demand for civil rights. Students for a Democratic Society, the Student Nonviolent Coordinating Committee, the Black Panthers, as well as feminist and gay rights movements all drew their leadership from young people. All of this activism from young people resulted in a reduction of the voting age from 21 to 18 in 1971 (Hosang, 2003). There was a clear generation gap between young activists and the older generation, but as Hosang (2003) notes, leaders "rarely posed their demands as 'youth' concerns per se, perhaps in spite of the era's mantra to 'never trust anyone over 30'" (p. 3).

THE RISE OF THE YOUTH ORGANIZING FIELD

In the 1990s, a new set of youth organizing groups began cropping up across the country. These groups were often responding to antiyouth policies. As sociologist Mike Males (1999) has documented, the conservative backlash of the 1980s and 1990s included an intense scapegoating of young people of color. Many white Americans felt threatened by the quickly growing population of young people of color. According to Hosang (2003),

Curfew laws and anti-gang taskforces proliferated. Clinton's 1994 crime bill allowed more juveniles to be tried as adults, and 41 states followed suit with their own versions of this policy. A 1996 Newsweek headline story titled "Superpredators Arrive" posed the policy question of the day: "Should we cage the new breed of vicious kids?" . . . Parental consent laws limiting abortion access for young women proliferated. California voters attempted to block undocumented immigrant students from public school. (pp. 4–5)

Youth organizing groups began forming to respond directly to these anti-youth policies. The tone of these organizations was different from that of past generations of youth activists in that many were organizing as young people against specific attacks on young people. In California, young people fought against a ballot initiative that would allow more young people to be tried as adults. In San Francisco and Oakland, ballot initiatives were passed dedicating funding for youth programs. Boston young people won reduced-price public transit for students. In Philadelphia, young people fought for adequate school funding.

Out of these struggles, new organizations and a new paradigm for youth work were born. According to Listen, Inc. (2003),

The field of youth organizing is the outgrowth of three important elements: the legacy of traditional organizing models, particularly those informed by Saul Alinsky; the progressive social movements of the 1960s and 1970s; and the rise of positive youth development. (p. 4)

Saul Alinsky is often considered a founder of community organizing based on the organizing model he developed in Chicago in the 1950s. From Alinsky's community organizing tradition, these new youth organizing groups learned how to build a membership, identify issues, analyze power, and escalate pressure on power holders. The Alinsky organizing tradition, however, focused on pragmatic politics and stayed away from ideological political analysis or significant focus on race, class, and gender. Therefore, these new youth organizing groups, who were primarily based in communities of color, drew a great deal of inspiration from the social movements of the 1960s and 1970s, including the civil rights, Black and Brown power, Chicano, feminist, and gay rights movements. From these movements, they learned to lead with a critical analysis of race, class, and gender.

In the 1980s, youth workers began developing a critique of traditional youth programs operating from a deficit model that treated young people as problems to be solved and pathologized their behavior. In response, the field of positive youth development, with its focus on providing opportunities that help young people develop their skills and competencies, was born. Youth organizers incorporated many of these principles into their work, but they also took them a step further, recognizing that not only did young people have skills and assets, but they also could use those assets to build power to address root causes of inequity in their communities (Listen, Inc., 2003).

Though there are many differences among youth organizing groups, there are at least five common features. First, most of these groups employ a community organizing approach based on recruiting a membership from a defined constituency, identifying issues of concern, and organizing campaigns focused on policy changes. For the majority of youth organizing groups, middle and high school students of color are the primary constituency. Second, most groups incorporate intensive political education, helping young people connect the issues in their communities to broader issues of race, class, and gender oppression. Third, nearly all youth organizing groups have formal leadership development programs that support young people in developing concrete leadership skills such as public speaking, negotiation, and working with the media. Finally, many youth organizing groups, either formally or informally, offer academic and social and emotional supports to their members.

The growth and development of the youth organizing field is something that I have personally watched and participated in over the last 20 years. After graduating from high school in 1994, I helped found an organization called the Philadelphia Student Union and spent 12 years organizing high school students in Philadelphia for educational justice. During this time, the Student Union grew from a small group of young people eating pizza together on Saturdays to a critical force for educational justice in Philadelphia. For the last three years, I have served as the executive director of the Funders' Collaborative on Youth Organizing (FCYO), an organization that brings funders and youth organizers together to increase resources for youth organizing groups and strengthen the national youth organizing field.

In our 2013 National Youth Organizing Field Scan, the FCYO recognized nearly 180 youth organizing groups across the country. While these groups are most common in the big cities on the coasts, there are growing numbers in the South and Midwest. The most common issues around which these groups organize are education reform, community and neighborhood development, health, immigrant rights, and gender (Braxton, Buford, & Marasigan, 2013).

Over the last 20 years, these new youth organizing groups have grown and matured in many important ways. First, what was once a scattered and disconnected set of organizations has grown into a definable field with established best practices, regular opportunities for groups to share learning, networks, and intermediary institutions. Twenty years ago, new organizations mostly had to invent their models, curricula, and campaigns on their own.

Now there are many opportunities for groups to learn from successful existing practices such as conferences and published toolkits.

Additionally, organizations have increased their scale, power, and ability to win meaningful victories. In the 1990s, many groups were organizing campaigns for small changes in individual schools and communities. At the Student Union our first campaigns were aimed at making sure students had textbooks. Now more organizations are winning significant city and statewide victories that improve the lives of thousands of people. For example, a coalition of youth organizing groups in Los Angeles including Inner City Struggle, Community Coalition, and Californians for Justice recently won passage of a groundbreaking policy that ensured college preparatory curriculum for all students in Los Angeles. In Colorado, Padres Y Jovenes Unidos won a statewide bill addressing racial disparities in suspension rates. The FCYO did an analysis of policy over the last three years and found of the 84 reported victories that youth organizing groups identified, 80% made impacts at a community level or larger scale (i.e., city, state, multistate, national). Only 17 victories were limited to affecting a singular entity such as one school, hospital, or neighborhood. The remaining victories were largely school district, citywide wins, and state victories. The most prominent national victory was the implementation of the Deferred Action for Childhood Arrivals program, which granted legal status to young immigrants who came to this country as minors (Braxton et al., 2013).

One way that youth organizing groups have increased their power is by incorporating voter engagement into their work. In the past, many youth organizing groups focused on issue-based organizing and stayed away from elections, but in our 2013 field scan FCYO found that 41% of youth organizing groups were engaging in nonpartisan voter engagement work and 25% were interested in getting involved (Braxton et al., 2013). While most voter engagement programs have young people doing their canvassing, youth organizing groups have the unique advantage of being able to engage a pool of young leaders who have been involved in year-round campaigns. These young people can talk to infrequent voters from their own communities in a way that is unparalleled. Youth organizing groups that have incorporated voter engagement into their overall theory of change have found it to be an effective way to increase their power. As political parties struggle to reach the growing population of young people of color, there is an opportunity for youth organizing groups to play an important role (Lee & Wechsler, 2015).

Another important factor has been the growth of alliances and coalitions. In our field scan, FCYO found that the majority of youth organizing groups were participating in state and national coalitions such as the Alliance for Educational Justice, Dignity in Schools Campaign, or the Community Justice Network for Youth. This coalition-building has been an important way for local organizations to impact state and national policy and to learn from successful local campaigns (Braxton et al., 2013).

In addition, organizations have increased their focus on partnerships with adults. In the 1990s, young organizers were responding to antiyouth policies and often focused on building a youth-led movement. Today, there is more recognition that young people are part of whole communities and a focus on building strong youth leadership in a multigenerational social justice movement (Braxton et al., 2013).

Finally, many youth organizing groups have increased their ability to support young people's holistic needs. While youth organizing was heavily influenced by youth development, in the 1990s there was less emphasis on providing young leaders with social, emotional, and academic services than there is today. Some groups saw services as less radical than the organizing that was central to their work. In recent years, however, more youth organizing groups have recognized that if they want to support young people to become lifelong leaders, they also need to support some of their basic needs. Through a combination of formal and informal services and partnerships with other agencies, youth organizing groups have increased their focus on this area, and the results have been impressive. A multiyear study by the University of California–Los Angeles and the University of Southern California found that youth organizing alumni were significantly more likely to attend a four-year college when compared to young people from similar backgrounds (Rogers & Terriquez, this volume).

One clear example of the impact of youth organizing has been in the area of school discipline policy. A few years ago, the prevailing trend was for stricter discipline policies and more school police and metal detectors. Over the last 10 years, youth organizing groups, in partnership with legal and advocacy organizations, have fundamentally transformed the common sense on school discipline. They have raised national attention to the issues of racial disparities in suspensions and the school-to-prison pipeline (Fernández, Kirshner, & Lewis, this volume). Young people have pressured dozens of school districts to pass new student discipline policies to address these disparities. Restorative justice approaches to discipline have expanded. Congress has even held hearings on the issue, with youth organizing groups providing critical testimony.

THE CURRENT YOUTH ACTIVIST LANDSCAPE

The FCYO has typically used the term *youth organizing* to describe a specific organizational form: local nonprofit organizations working with young people of color, ages 13 to 18, organizing local policy campaigns and conducting political education. This form grew dramatically during the 1990s and 2000s. It is important to note, however, that in the last few years some of the most dynamic social justice work happening with young people and young adults has emerged outside of the typical boundaries of the youth organizing field. This work has resulted in a landscape of youth activism that is changing rapidly.

Some of this change is due to changing political conditions. The youth organizing groups of the 1990s were responding to particular attacks on young people of color. While those attacks have certainly not ended, they exist within a context of overall attacks on the working class and communities of color. This context has included attacks on unions, public schools, and voting rights, as well as growing mass incarceration and increasing battles over immigration.

Another factor in this changing landscape has been the way that new technology has allowed flashpoint incidents to rapidly grow into social movements. The killing of unarmed black people at the hands of police is, unfortunately, not a new phenomenon. However, the response from young black people and the way they have used social media to connect, communicate, and organize has helped make the Movement for Black Lives one of the most powerful movements of the last 30 years.

The last two years have seen a dramatic rise in activism among Black young people in response to violence from police (Dohrn & Ayers, this volume). This new generation of Black organizers has innovated in some important ways including incorporating a focus on love and healing; lifting up the leadership of Black women and lesbian, gay, bisexual, and trans people; and developing mechanisms to support rapid response after dramatic incidents like the killing of unarmed Black people by police. This movement has established space for people to be "unapologetically black" and created a powerful opportunity to finish the unfinished business of the civil rights movement.

It is also important to note that there are two distinct, but complementary organizing approaches being used by youth activist organizations. Most youth organizing groups have employed a structure-based organizing model focused on building strong organizations that can consistently mobilize a defined constituency and put pressure on decision makers to win incremental policy victories. In contrast, some newer organizations are using a momentum-based organizing model, which emphasizes taking advantage of opportunities to build mass movements. These momentum-based organizations are less focused on mobilizing a defined group of leaders to achieve policy change and more focused on using tactics that can politicize and engage large numbers of people (Aronoff, 2014).

The FCYO recently conducted an analysis of major forms of youth activism in the current moment. In addition to the groups organizing middle and high school students of color that are described above, we identified five additional forms of youth activism. (See Table 2.1.) I will briefly describe the

Table 2.1. Youth Activist Landscape Summary

	Adolescence (13–18) Key Institutions: Schools, Juvenile Justice System, Foster Care		Young Adulthood (17–25) Key Institutions: Colleges and Universities, Employers			
	Youth Civic Engagement and Leadership	Middle and High School Age Youth Organizing	Young Adult Social Justice Organizing	Campus-Based Organizing	Civic Engagement and Advocacy/Policy	Young Worker Organizing
Common Model Features	• Civic education in schools • Service learning • Participatory action research	• Focus on low-income young people and young people of color • Focus on ages 13–18 • Structure-based organizing model • Mostly small local grassroots organizations • Young adult staff play support, ally, and mentor roles • Popular/political education and leadership development • Integration of youth development supports	• Focus on ages 17–25 or 18–30 • Momentum-based organizing • Intensive use of social media • Integrated on- and offline • Intersectional analysis • Radical political analysis • Mix of campus- and community-based organization • Decentralized leadership	• Based on college campuses • Primarily organized around student issues	• Young adult base • Intensive voter engagement • Policy advocacy • Progressive political analysis	• Organizing of fast-food, restaurant, and retail workers • Often led by or in partnership with labor unions

Examples					
• Generation Citizen, National • Youth Leadership Institute, CA • Mikva Challenge, IL	• Inner City Struggle, CA • Padres Y Jovenes Unidos, CO • Youth United for Change, PA • SouthWest Organizing Project, NM • Power U Center for Social Change, FL • Make the Road NY, NY • FIERCE, NY	• United We Dream, National • Dream Defenders, FL • Ohio Student Association, OH • BYP 100, National • Millennial Activists United, MO • Get Equal, National	• United States Student Association, National • Generation Progress, National • Responsible Endowment Coalition, National • Student Power Networks, National • Student Divestment Network, National • Roosevelt Campus Network, National	• Young Invincibles, National • Bus Federation, National • Advocates for Youth, National • NAACP Youth and Student, National • Young People For (YP4), National	• Fight for 15, National • SEIU Millennial Project, National

first four and then delve more deeply into the fifth. It is important to note that such a categorization has limitations. Many organizations span multiple categories and others are not easily categorized. Nonetheless, we have found it to be useful in understanding the current landscape of youth organizing.

The first category is *Youth Civic Engagement and Leadership*. Groups in this category engage in civic education in schools, service learning, and participatory action research with middle and high school students. They may not be building a base or running ongoing campaigns, but they often have good access to city government, school districts, and other institutions, and more examples of partnerships between civic engagement and youth organizing groups are emerging. These partnerships utilize an inside-outside strategy that takes advantage of the institutional access of the civic engagement groups and the power and independence of the youth organizing groups. This category includes groups like Generation Citizen and the Mikva Challenge, which do civic education and participatory action research in schools and led the effort in New York City to establish a youth council in every city department.

The second category is *Campus-Based Organizing*. Groups in this category primarily organize students on college campuses, often mainly around student issues such as college access and affordability and student debt. National associations like the United States Student Association have been a major training ground for progressive leaders. Identity-based groups on campuses like Movimiento Estudiantil Chicano de Aztlán (MEChA), Black Student Unions, and LGBT student groups have often been a key home and training place for youth organizers. Organizing in community colleges has been growing with support from places like the Rappaport Foundation. The last few years have seen dynamic organizing around issues like student debt, climate justice (Curnow & Gross, this volume), sexual violence on campus (Brodsky, this volume), and reproductive justice (Astorga-Ramos, this volume).

The next category is *Civic Engagement and Advocacy/Policy*. These are groups that may do less base building or deep leadership development but do engage young people in voter engagement and issue advocacy. There are a few variations in this category. Some groups offer internships and training, like Young People for the American Way and Wellstone Action. Some focus on policy advocacy, like the Young Invincibles, which has organized young adults around issues including health care reform. Some groups have become skilled at mass voter engagement, like the Buss Federation. There are also important national identity- and issue-based advocacy groups like the NAACP Youth and Student division or Advocates for Youth, which organize young people and young adults around reproductive justice and sexual health.

A fourth category is *Young Worker Organizing*. Much of the growing organizing of fast-food, retail, and restaurant workers is focused on young workers. This work is often led by labor unions. Fight for Fifteen has raised the issue of increasing the minimum wage across the country. The SEIU Millennial Program has organized young workers and supported the development of up and coming labor leaders. There are several examples of collaboration between young worker organizing and other social justice issues. For example, several key leaders in the Ferguson uprising had been involved in young worker organizing. Throughout history, connections between organized labor and other social movements have been critical because labor unions have been the largest and most independently funded working-class organizations. Strengthening these ties is vital to building a strong progressive infrastructure.

The final category is *Young Adult Social Justice Organizing*. Given the amount of recent activity in this area, it warrants some added attention. These groups are mainly organizing young people ages 17–25 or 30, often with a focus on young people of color. Many of these groups utilize social media, focus attention on their branding, and combine on- and offline organizing. As opposed to the structure-based organizing of many organizing groups today, many of these groups use a momentum-based organizing strategy that focuses on capitalizing on flashpoints and movement moments (such as the killings of Michael Brown in Ferguson and Freddie Gray in Baltimore) to build a mass movement rather than deep work with smaller groups of individual leaders and incremental victories. Many of these groups have some form of decentralized leadership. For some of these groups, youth is the leading identity. For many, such as Black Lives Matter, it is not. In addition, many Young Adult Social Justice groups emphasize an intersectional analysis that links race, class, gender, and other forms of oppression. For example, United We Dream, the national network of undocumented young immigrants, has made connections between immigration and LGBT issues, while Black Lives Matter has raised the leadership and experiences of queer black women (Dohrn & Ayers, this volume). Intersectionality has been important in lifting up the leadership of people who have been marginalized in past social justice struggles (such as women in the struggle for racial justice), understanding how multiple oppressions reinforce one another (such as racism and sexism), and in building an analysis that recognizes that in order to end one form of oppression, all oppression must be ended.

There are several common variations within Young Adult Social Justice organizations. There are national organizations like Black Youth Project 100, Million Hoodies Movement for Justice, and United We Dream. There are local or statewide organizations like Dream Defenders in Florida and the Ohio Student Association. There are also new and emerging groups, many of which come out of hot spots like Ferguson and Baltimore where police killings events have radicalized young people. In contrast to most contemporary youth organizing groups, some of these newer organizations operate as informal networks and some are not registered nonprofit organizations.

Young Adult Social Justice groups have many strengths. Because of their use of social media and a momentum-based approach, they have commonly been effective at mass mobilization and emergency response. The focus on branding has often attracted media coverage, which has also helped these groups shift the narrative on issues like immigration and mass incarceration. Many of these groups have been able to reach young people who have been radicalized by significant events and, in contrast to more formal membership organizations, they have created network structures that allow young people to stay engaged as they move in and out of various organizations.

CONCLUSION

The last year has seen young people take major leadership on a variety of issues. With young people of color as the fastest-growing part of the population, this demographic shift in the United States creates an opportunity for them to shape the future. Demography, however, is not destiny. There are ongoing attempts to limit the power of young people of color through tactics such as voter suppression and mass incarceration.

Taking advantage of this opportunity will require several strategies. First, momentum- and structure-based organizing approaches both offer important opportunities to engage young people. There is a need both for organizations that can support intensive leadership development and policy campaigns as well as formations that can generate transformative national movements. There is great potential to create opportunities for these different kinds of organizations to work together and learn from each other.

Recent movement moments have politicized hundreds of thousands of young people, and there is a need for organizations that can engage them in sustained ways, support their development, and win meaningful local campaigns. Ensuring that these moments result in real, transformative change will require continued direct action and mass mobilization along with campaigns for clear policy changes. It will also require moving from a place of opposition to an attempt to build the independent political power needed to govern. This will require bold experiments to expand scale and principled strategies for engaging with the political system. Different organizations will specialize in different parts of this process, but powerful movements need to develop all of these muscles.

Identifying the financial resources to support young leaders will be an ongoing challenge. In recent years, youth organizing groups have relied heavily on foundation funding and the ever-changing priorities in philanthropy have created ebbs and flows of resources. A recent decrease in foundation funding for youth organizing created major challenges for many organizations. Long-term sustainability will require that youth organizing develop a more stable base of support among foundations by demonstrating an ability to meet the needs of different kinds of funders, including youth development funders, community foundations, social justice funders, and issue-based funders. A growing recognition among social justice funders that investment in youth leadership is critical to both the present and future is creating some reason for optimism. In addition, youth organizations will need to develop stronger support from nonfoundation sources, including individual donors and labor unions.

While always present, the roles of young people in social movements have shifted throughout history. At times, youth has been a leading identity. At other times, young people have provided key leadership on a variety of issues. Movements may not always identify as youth movements, but for any social justice sector to be successful, supporting the active participation and leadership of young people is essential both for the development of future leaders and for engaging the most active, energetic, and creative part of society. Strong and lasting movements require that young people have autonomous space to utilize their creativity and create their own demands and tactics while simultaneously building strong alliances with adults.

Across the country, young people are once again demonstrating their willingness to take risks and stand up for justice. There are many diverse strands at this moment. The challenge is to unite them into a coherent movement that allows cooperation and coordination, while enabling each to play to its strengths.

REFERENCES

Aronoff, K. (2014, August 24). Mastering movements—An interview with immigrant rights activist Carlos Saavedra. *Waging Nonviolence*. Retrieved from http://wagingnonviolence.org/2014/08/mastering-movements-interview-carlos-saavedra/

Braxton, E., Buford, W., & Marasigan, L. (2013). *2013 national field scan: The state of the field of youth organizing*. New York: Funders Collaborative on Youth Organizing.

Hosang, D. (2003). Youth and community organizing today. *Occasional Papers Series on Youth Organizing, 2*. New York: Funders Collaborative on Youth Organizing.

Kwon, S. A. (2013). *Uncivil youth: Race, activism, and affirmative governmentality*. Durham, NC: Duke University Press.

Lee, E. Y., & Wechsler, S. (2015). *Now or never: The fight for the millennial generation*. Retrieved from http://fcyo.org/media/docs/6684_NoworNeverFinal.pdf

Light, J. S. (2015). Putting our conversation in context: Youth, old media, and political participation, 1800–1971. In D. Allen & J. S. Light (Eds.), *From voice to influence: Understanding citizenship in a digital age* (pp. 19–33). Chicago: University of Chicago Press.

Listen, Inc. (2003). An emerging model for working with youth. *Occasional Papers Series on Youth Organizing, 1.* New York: Funders Collaborative on Youth Organizing.

Males, M. (1999). *Framing youth: 10 myths about the next generation.* Monroe, ME: Common Courage Press.

3

The Emergence of a Youth Justice Movement in the United States

Mark R. Warren and Luke Aubry Kupscznk

Over the past 20 years, the United States has seen a rise in collective action by young people seeking community, institutional, and political change. Young people are working together to stop police harassment and killings, end the school-to-prison pipeline, expand funding for summer jobs, improve transportation services, address environmental injustice, and in many other ways address a range of issues they face in their lives (Checkoway & Richards-Schuster, 2006; Delgado & Staples, 2008; Ginwright, Noguera, & Cammarota, 2006; Warren, Mira, & Nikundiwe, 2008). The focus of this collective action is typically local; but groups are increasingly working together at state and national levels as well. These efforts are part of a long tradition of young people playing important, sometimes leading roles in movements for social change, as they did in the civil rights movement (Carson, 1981; Clay, 2012).

Much of the scholarship on this growing phenomenon has focused on one type of activism called youth organizing. Youth organizing has been defined as an approach that "trains young people in community organizing and advocacy and helps them use these skills to alter power relations and create meaningful institutional change in their communities" (Ginwright, 2003, p. 2). Youth who participate in this field are typically teenagers of color from low-income communities and usually enrolled in secondary school; we follow this age definition of youth. Most research in this area has taken a case-study approach, focusing on the experiences of young people in youth organizing groups, in order to document and analyze organizing processes and their impacts (e.g., Conner, Zaino, & Scarola, 2013; Mediratta, Shah, & McAlister, 2009). Some survey data have begun to show the impact of participation in youth organizing on young people's development (Cheadle et al., 2001; Franklin, 2014) and later civic engagement (Rogers, Mediratta, & Shah, 2012; Rogers & Terriquez, this volume). This focus has enabled scholars and other researchers to describe and sometimes measure the effects of organizing in many dimensions including policy change, the operations of public institutions like schools, and the effects of participation on young people and their communities (Warren, Mapp, & Community Organizing and School Reform Project, 2011).

Youth organizing is typically discussed as taking place in locally based organizing groups. The Funders' Collaborative on Youth Organizing identifies three types of these organizing groups (Braxton, Buford, & Marasigan, 2013). Some young people participate in groups that are solely devoted to youth organizing and typically describe themselves as youth-led, adult-supported organizations. Others participate in youth organizing programs within community organizations that also work with adults. Finally, young people are sometimes involved in organizing efforts that are intergenerational, where youth and adults organize together within a single effort. All three types of organizations are typically locally based, either concentrating their efforts in one neighborhood or operating citywide. One survey estimated that there were more than 180 organizations focused on youth organizing active in 2013, although many more organizations may incorporate youth organizing in some way (Braxton et al., 2013).

We believe, however, that a broader youth justice movement has been emerging, which includes, but is not limited to, these kinds of organizing groups. We see youth organizing groups as part of a larger array of actors that includes critical educators, youth development programs, and legal and advocacy organizations, among others that are working for *youth justice*. In other words, an array of groups is working to address the structural and cultural processes that oppress youth—particularly low-income youth of color—and to engage them in collective action for their own liberation.

Moreover, these actors and groups are increasingly working together at local, state, and national levels. These activists, together and on their own, may focus on different issues, as mentioned earlier, but they all target pieces of an interlocking system of oppression that they and other young people face. This intersectionality—the interrelationship of racism, classism, sexism, and other forms of oppression—and the increasing connections between organizing groups and other actors, suggests to us the emergence of a youth justice movement in the United States. Indeed, many youth organizers have been talking in movement-building terms for a while (e.g., James & McGillicuddy, 2001), but scholarship for the most part has not conceptualized the field this way.

We consider this issue first by discussing the extent to which youth share a common identity and culture(s) of resistance—as these provide a foundation for the emergence of a movement. Next, we discuss the relationship between youth organizing—as a form of community organizing—and social movements, and argue that youth organizing constitutes part of a broader, emerging youth justice movement. We then explore the injustices youth activists and organizers are responding to and how "youth justice" might be defined. Finally, we describe the range of groups participating in the movement and the growth of broader alliances that characterize an emerging movement.

YOUTH IDENTITY AND CULTURES OF RESISTANCE

A youth justice movement supposes that "youth" is an actionable social category and that the youth captured therein share a common identity. We know that some youth organizers identify as part of a youth justice movement (Warren et al., 2014). However, we do not yet know the extent to which this identification is broadly shared—in part because few researchers have used a movement lens to study this kind of activism (for exceptions, see Clay, 2012; Curnow & Gross, this volume; and Movement Strategy Center & FCYO, 2011), and therefore the issue has been underinvestigated.

Part of the basis for a common "youth" identity is the recognition of cultural identities and practices shared by many young people. We believe that youth of color in particular have a foundation for a shared cultural identity that is already serving as a basis for resistance to oppression as young people. Hip-hop is arguably the central cultural form through which a culture of resistance is expressed (Clay, 2012). Hip-hop culture is a complex phenomenon with highly commercialized aspects, while other traditions speak out about the oppressive conditions facing young people of color (Cohen, 2010; Malone & Martinez, 2014). According to Clay (2012), hip-hop music "acts as a base for social protest among today's youth, in much the same ways that rhythm and blues, early rock and roll, and folk music did for youth activists in the 1960s" (p. 93). Artists like Tupac Shakur, arguably the most influential rapper and poet for many young people of color, serve as a voice for youth who face oppression. His vision of an urban life of discrimination and resistance resonates past his death with both young people of color and other fans of hip-hop. Music also provides an organizing tool to draw young people to events that involve hip-hop music, poetry slams, and rap-battles as preludes to activism (Clay, 2012; Duncan-Andrade, 2007, 2009).

Hip-hop culture sometimes directly connects past civil rights activism to contemporary culture and concerns among young people. Rap artists like Dead Prez emulate the Black Panthers and other civil rights heroes, linking them to current youth activism. Russell Simmons, the co-founder of Def Jam Recordings, founded the Hip-Hop Summit Action Network (HSAN) in 2001 to mobilize the hip-hop vote (Clay, 2012). While running the risk of minimizing their influence, people like Martin Luther King Jr., Fannie Lou Hamer, Huey Newton, Dolores Huerta, Malcolm X, Angela Davis, and Che

Guevara have been commoditized in film, poster, fashion, and popular history. The ubiquitous presence of images like T-shirts that say "Free Angela" among young people in hip-hop culture signals an awareness of discrimination and an affinity with resistance.

Hip-hop culture is the dominant, but not the only musical or cultural form expressed by young people. Other subcultures of young people exhibit different forms of cultural expression. For example, many Latino youth follow rock, garage, or punk musical and cultural genres (Avant-Mier, 2010). Some of these cultural practices, like spoken word performances (Rabaka, 2013), can also serve as cultures of resistance and become part of social movement activity. For example, Café Teatro Batey Urbano in Chicago engages youth in a variety of cultural forms of expression that connect them to community history and activism (Flores-González, Rodriguez, & Rodriguez-Muniz, 2006). Meanwhile, across the nation (and world) young women are lashing out against adult officials who have told them to avoid rape by "not dressing like sluts." These young feminists have hijacked the term and started the "slutwalk" movement, in which young women march while holding signs that protest the blaming of women and girls for the actions of men (Stampler, 2011).

COMMUNITY ORGANIZING AND SOCIAL MOVEMENTS

By social movement in this context, we mean collective action on the part of oppressed or marginalized people, on the basis of shared identity, to build power to win changes in government policy and public attitudes that advance the cause of social justice. There are many definitions of social movements that emphasize various aspects of this complex phenomenon. Ours is a slightly more focused definition, derived from Sidney Tarrow (1998), who defines social movements as "collective challenges [to elites, authorities, other groups or cultural codes] by people with common purposes and solidarity in sustained interactions with elites, opponents and authorities" (p. 4). Movements transform unequal power arrangements in part by demanding recognition, voice, and participation. Social movements challenge stereotypes held against marginalized groups and in this way create shifts in cultural attitudes and public discourse. Successful movements seek allies and work to build a larger societal consensus for change. In this way movements build power but also appeal to the hearts and change the minds of the majority. By putting forward a concrete agenda for change and a vision for a more just and equitable society, movements create change in dominant discourses and cultural patterns (Giugno, McAdam, & Tilly, 1999).

A long argument in the community organizing world, however, has contrasted community organizing with social movements. Saul Alinsky (1962), the so-called "father" of community organizing in the United States, argued strongly against ideology and for more pragmatic forms of political action (Fisher, 1994). He saw community organizing as a way for poor people to build power and claim a seat at the table alongside the interest groups and civic associations of the more affluent. The network he founded, the Industrial Areas Foundation (IAF), still today contrasts its approach to organizing with that of social movements, criticizing movements as ephemeral and enabled by charismatic leaders (Shirley, 1997). Instead, the IAF says it seeks to build long-lasting organizations in which ordinary people learn to do the regular work of politics.

Central to this debate is the distinction between institutional and extrainstitutional forms of political action. The "normal" institutional actions of interest groups and civic associations include lobbying, voter education and mobilization, and contributions to the campaigns of political candidates. Movements, however, are often described as using extrainstitutional forms of actions, such as demonstrations, marches, sit-ins, and nonviolent civil disobedience (Tarrow, 2011). Movements work for policy change (as in institutional politics), but they also try to shift public attitudes and cultural patterns (Giugno et al., 1999).

In some ways, though, the contrast between community organizing and movement building has created a false polarity. Community organizing has never fallen easily into either of these categories, but sits between the poles of institutional and extrainstitutional forms of political action, using either or both practices when seen as necessary. Moreover, community organizing groups do deep cultural work: they engage a wide array of cultural practices including those of religious faith (Warren, 2001; Wood, 2002), help people craft a narrative of their struggle as just (Ganz, 2010), and attempt to change public discourse and dominant norms about subordinated groups (Warren et al., 2011). More recently, organizing groups are increasingly interested in forming broader alliances and explicitly thinking in movement terms (Wood, Partridge, & Fulton, 2012).

Within the world of community organizing, we would argue that youth organizing has more of a movement quality than adult organizing. Young people are often more likely than adults to take militant, extrainstitutional forms of action (Carson, 1981). Moreover, as noted above, youth organizing typically features a more explicit engagement of cultural forms like hip-hop music and art (Clay, 2012). Finally, we have some evidence that, compared to adults, young people more easily step out of organizational forms of identity and more readily adopt a movement identity (Warren et al., 2014).

Based upon these considerations, we consider locally based community and youth organizing to be potentially part of social movement activity, not a distinctly different form of collective action. Historically, in fact, local organizing has been considered to be foundational to the emergence of movements, as in the civil rights movement (Payne, 1995). Social movements, however, suggest combined efforts by an array of actors and extralocal forms of activity, usually at the national (and sometimes global) level. To the extent that organizing and other youth justice activity remain fragmented and isolated at local levels, then no movement exists.

As we detail below, however, youth organizers are increasingly finding ways to ally with a range of other actors who are trying to advance the cause of youth justice. They are working across localities and state lines to build the greater power necessary to combat systems of oppression such as the school-to-prison pipeline (Mediratta, 2012; Warren, 2014). We therefore argue that a social movement has been emerging, one that we characterize as a youth justice movement. This movement features collective action by young people that attempts to transform the social, cultural, and political institutions that oppress them. It is broader than organizing in that it encompasses multiple sources of change and support, including critical education, advocacy, media, and culture.

ADULTISM AND YOUTH INJUSTICE

The emergence of a youth justice movement responds to the discrimination youth confront in society and, in particular, to the multiple and interconnected systems of oppression faced by low-income youth of color. Youth face adultism, that is, prejudice and discrimination against them specifically as youth (Bell, 1995; Fletcher, 2013; Males, 2006). By adultism, we mean the devaluing of the ideas and participation of young people that denies them voice and agency in the issues and institutions that shape their lives. Indeed, we live in an era that negates the positive agency of young people. Adultism dominates youth-adult interactions as adults often treat youth with a deficit orientation, assuming their voice and participation lack significant value. The media have contributed to a discriminatory image of youth. From Generation X's grunge-slackers, to the depiction of young, black drug-runners in HBO's *The Wire*, to the common view of Millennials as lazy and unemployed by choice, the media have promoted negative perceptions of young people (Adams-Bass, Stevenson, & Kotzin, 2014; Guastaferro, 2013; Males, 2006).

While adultism affects all youth, it impacts low-income youth of color especially deeply, with youth of color demonized as predatory, dangerous, and undeserving of help (Youth Speak Out Coalition & Zimmerman, 2007). Meanwhile, the broader public discourse pathologizes youth of color, especially urban African American youth (Cohen, 2010; Gordon, 2009). Marginalized youth have become scapegoats as they are often blamed for societal problems like teen pregnancy, gangs, violence, drug and alcohol abuse, and poverty. Those young people not seen as corrupt or violent are often objectified as "precious resources" in need of protection, rather than as positive agents of change (Gordon, 2009, p. 8).

Too often, youth delinquency is understood as a biological, physiological, or cognitive reality, divorcing youth from the realities of their history, community, and culture (Gordon, 2009). In reality, the shaming of youth has been accompanied by divestments in public education, social welfare, and community resources—while spending has increased on prisons and juvenile detention facilities, as drug and immigration laws criminalize youth of color (Youth Speak Out Coalition & Zimmerman, 2007). In addition to overrepresentation in the juvenile and adult justice systems, youth of color tend to vote less often, have fewer civic participation opportunities, participate in community service less frequently, fall behind in academic, social, and economic achievement, and are overrepresented in the lowest performing schools (Kirshner & Ginwright, 2012; Rogers et al., 2012).

Indeed, low-income youth of color face both cultural and structural forms of oppression along multiple dimensions including race, class, gender, sexual orientation, and immigration status, as well as age. It could be argued that low-income youth of color face a profound crisis today. In many large cities, less than half of black and Latino young people graduate from high school with their peers (Orfield, Losen, Wald, & Swanson, 2004; Sum, Khatiwada, & McLaughlin, 2009). Fully two-thirds of black young men without a high school degree will end up in prison at some point in their lives (Western & Pettit, 2010). Indeed, at any one time, one-third of all black men without a high school degree are in prison or jail. Girls of color also face discrimination—they are more likely, for example, to receive punitive discipline in schools—forms of oppression that consign many to lives of poverty and physical insecurity (Crenshaw, 2015). Meanwhile, undocumented youth are denied access to higher education and face lifetimes of low-wage and insecure employment (Chavez, Soriano, & Oliverez, 2007).

There is an interconnected set of issues that stretches across our educational, economic, cultural, and criminal justice institutions that condemn many young people to lives of poverty, violence, and incarceration (Warren, 2014). The connection between educational failure and incarceration has come to be known as the school-to-prison pipeline (Bahena, Cooc, Currie-Rubin, Kuttner, & Ng, 2012; Fernández, Kirshner, & Lewis, this volume), which captures a key part of this system. However, the systemic nature of youth oppression has multiple and complex institutional interconnections. Newer scholarship on structural racism has shown how patterns of residential segregation connect to educational underfinancing and economic disinvestment to produce conditions of concentrated disadvantage that profoundly limit access to a wide range of opportunities for children of color in low-income communities (Bonilla-Silva, 2001; powell, 2007).

DEFINING YOUTH JUSTICE

In response to adultism and interlocking systems of oppression, young people are increasingly organizing to assert their voice, demand respect, and build power for themselves as youth, that is, they are building a movement for youth justice. Heretofore, the term *youth justice* has referred to the effort to create reform in the juvenile justice system for young people (see, for example, Campaign for Youth Justice, 2007). However, we believe that the concept of youth justice broadly reflects the goals and practices of the actors and groups named earlier. The youth justice movement, as we define it, seeks fair treatment and access to resources and opportunities so that young people can develop into active and productive members of their communities and reach their human potential. It seeks respect for young people and meaningful participation by young people in social and political life. In this way, it challenges adultism and the structures of injustice faced by young people on multiple dimensions and calls for policies and practices that support their full development. The youth justice movement seeks to develop young people as critical thinkers and agents of change for themselves and their communities.

The emerging youth justice movement is a fluid phenomenon, as are many social movements, and does not exist isolated from broader social justice initiatives. When young people are involved in youth-only organizing groups of the type we discuss above, they eventually "age out" as they turn 18 or graduate from high school; many become connected to other movements during this time and move on to participate in these efforts as they enter adulthood (Terriquez, 2014). Indeed, one of the goals of youth organizing groups is often to cultivate a commitment to social justice among youth participants so that they will continue to participate in social justice and community activism after they "graduate" from these groups (Ginwright, 2010).

In many cases, young people participate in social movements or issue-based alliances with adults (Braxton et al., 2013). For example, youth have played a prominent role in the movement against the school-to-prison pipeline (Fernández et al., this volume; Mediratta, 2012). High school–aged youth have also played an important role in the immigrant rights movement, joining college-aged and other young people in creating the DREAMers movement (Nicholls, 2013; Terriquez, Rogers, Vargas, & Patler, 2013). In this and other cases, such as work for immigrant rights, environmental justice, or LGBTQ rights, youth work may be considered the "youth wing" of a larger movement (Milkman & Terriquez, 2012). In intergenerational groups or overlapping movements as well as youth-only groups, however, youth bring their own perspective to issues such as environmental justice, immigrant rights, transportation reform and equity, and mandatory minimum prison sentences. In all these formations, we see a common commitment by young activists to youth justice, that is, that any campaign includes a focus on issues that concern youth and provides young people with an opportunity to express their voice and command a share of leadership (Nicholls, 2013; Torres-Fleming, Valdes, & Pillai, 2010).

A BROADER FIELD OF YOUTH JUSTICE ACTIVISM

As noted above, we find that youth organizing groups typically work in a larger youth justice field composed of a diverse set of actors, including activist-oriented youth development or service programs, critical education and leadership development programs, and advocacy organizations. In this section, we catalog several examples of key actors in the youth justice movement. This catalog shows that this field is much broader than youth organizing groups, although interconnected with them. Despite attempts to categorize these organizations, the lines drawn to distinguish and define them are sometimes blurry. Some youth development organizations teach about systems of oppression, while many critical education programs attempt to involve young people in activism. We consider all of these groups to be part of the youth justice movement if they contribute in some way to helping young people develop their capacity to understand systems of oppression, assert youth voice, and take collective action to improve their lives.

In Boston, for example, the City School offers a summer leadership institute and after-school programs that combine social justice–oriented, critical education with internships in social change, typically in partnership with youth organizing groups. In addition to working with these organizations, it offers mentorship programs that encourage young people to become leaders in business, government, and nonprofit sectors. Its programs span a wide range of issues, from environmental justice to education reform, and aim to develop youths' capacities for leadership not only during their teen years but also into adulthood. The City School does not practice organizing itself, but it is intertwined with organizing groups and sees itself as a key part of a larger youth justice movement (Kirschenbaum, 2014; Warren et al., 2014).

The field in Boston also includes the hybrid Boston Student Advisory Council (BSAC), which is a joint project of Boston Public Schools and Youth on Board, a youth organizing intermediary affiliated with Youth Build, a youth development organization (see Gunther, this volume). BSAC organizes young people around education issues but also has an official student representative on the Boston School Committee (BSAC, 2015). Youth in BSAC have organized to revise the school district's code of conduct and pilot restorative justice in schools and have developed an innovative app to inform students of their rights. Finally, a number of teachers in Boston engage students in youth participatory action research projects or service learning programs that connect to youth organizing. Some of these teachers are part of the Boston Teachers Activist Group, which works closely with youth organizing groups across the city (TAG Boston, 2015).

In fact, teachers and youth organizers across the country are increasingly joining forces to combine youth participatory action research with critical education and youth justice activism (Cammarota & Fine, 2008). These efforts often feature a diverse array of actors and actions. For example, the Mexican American Studies Program (MAS) in Tucson, Arizona, combined critical education, Chicano/a cultural studies classes, student and teacher–led social research, teacher professional development, and parent and community involvement to educate and empower Mexican American high school students (Cammarota, Romero, & Stovall, 2014; Gómez & Jiménez-Silva, 2012). When the state school board threatened the program in 2011, students in MAS organized to occupy the school board meeting and delay the vote. When this resulted in violent actions by police officers, SWAT team members, and immigration enforcement officers against the peaceful protesters, a group of teachers and students filed suit against the law banning MAS classes in the U.S. District Court. MAS began as an education program; yet youth came to organize within the program and undertook many actions, including a march to the state capitol, to save it (Acosta & Mir, 2012).

The emerging movement for youth justice also includes adult allies in legal advocacy and support organizations. The Children's Defense Fund, for example, sponsors a variety of initiatives including a Freedom School summer camp and after-school program, youth advocacy training, a Black Community Crusade for Children, and a campaign against what it calls the cradle to prison pipeline (Children's Defense Fund, 2015). The Children's Defense Fund began in 1969 as an extension of the Washington Research Project, a law firm concerned with federal programs for low-income families. Since then, it has sought improved public policy by monitoring the effects of federal and state policies on children and families. The Children's Defense Fund is connected to youth organizing efforts via partnerships and community-based programs, as well as efforts to develop youth as leaders in their communities.

Intermediaries like the Advancement Project have also played critical supportive roles for youth organizing groups working on issues like the school-to-prison pipeline (STPP) and for movement building more broadly (Advancement Project, 2015). The Advancement Project is a racial justice organization that combines legal, communications, and policy strategies and partners with community organizations to advance movement building. It has helped organizations conduct youth participatory action research projects that support organizing efforts in places like Denver and Philadelphia. Additionally, it has sponsored action camps in which hundreds of young people received training in STPP organizing and were connected to parents, teachers, community activists, and other organizers. These camps played an important role in connecting young people and their organizations across the country—strengthening evolving national alliances and coalitions.

We are witness to an even larger array of actors in youth justice than are captured here. Some of these actors participate in movement activities directly, such as adults in schools and churches that work to involve young people in education and organizing. In addition to high school teachers who engage their students in youth participatory action research through the classroom, program staff in churches have helped young people develop a more activist approach to their youth groups with many increasingly involved with faith-based organizing networks (Cammarota & Fine, 2008; Wood et al., 2012). Others are movement allies, such as those in philanthropic foundations or other nonprofit organizations that support youth justice organizing (Braxton et al., 2013). From this point of view, the lens of youth organizing seems too narrow to capture the potential and dynamics of what can be better understood as an emerging youth justice movement field.

ALLIANCES AND COALITIONS

The broad array of groups working with or on behalf of youth that we have just described is increasingly combining efforts at local, state, and national levels. Some researchers have highlighted the alliance work of youth organizing groups at the local level (Mediratta et al., 2009). However, little attention has been paid to the connections being made across localities. These new connections and alliances at multiple levels suggest the further emergence of a youth justice movement.

At the local level, many cities have seen the rise of alliances that bring together youth organizing and other groups working for youth justice. Many of these are short-term alliances where groups come together around an issue campaign. But some groups have forged longer-term relationships and have succeeded in sustaining these alliances and building power for significant change. In Chicago, youth of color from six community organizations formed Voices of Youth in Chicago Education, which calls itself a "youth organizing collaborative for education and racial justice"; its members have worked together for nearly 10 years (VOYCE, 2015, para. 1). Grants from an array of private foundations have helped VOYCE work to stop widespread school closings and keep young people of color in neighborhood schools, reduce high-stakes standardized testing, fund the hiring of 600 additional teaching positions, increase the length of the school day, provide music classes, and install a new discipline code ending automatic suspensions and stressing restorative justice (Christens, Collura, Kopish, & Varvodic, 2014). Not content to work within separate organizations, VOYCE is committed to "building a multi-racial, city-wide cohort of youth leaders" (VOYCE, 2015, para. 3).

In New York City, three youth organizations, Sistas and Brothas United, Make the Road by Walking, and Youth on the Move/Mothers on the Move came together in 2004 to form the Urban Youth Collaborative in order to bring young people's voice to school reform in the city (Mediratta, 2006). They organized for better counseling and academic programs to help more students attend college and advocated for cleaner and safer schools. They went on to expand their alliance with new youth organizing groups and organized against the school-to-prison pipeline and to oppose school closings with strategies to improve struggling schools (Urban Youth Collaborative, 2015). Youth leaders in the groups have pushed for the creation of this kind of long-term alliance to expand the power of individual groups to confront the city's vast Department of Education.

Youth justice groups are also increasingly engaged in state-level coalitions. In Massachusetts, the Youth Jobs Coalition, formed in 2009, connects 40 youth and community groups across the state. It pursues an annual campaign each year to lobby for state funding for youth jobs. In 2011 it mobilized more than 1,000 young people and won an additional $9 million in the state allocation for youth jobs (Warren et al., 2014). In California, Californians for Justice campaigns at the district level for reforms in school discipline, college access, healthy schools, environmental justice, and community improvements; in addition, each of its district-level student teams comes together to advocate for state-level change as well. Its victories range from winning a district initiative for cleaner school bathrooms in Long Beach, to reversing school budget cuts at the state level (Rogers & Terriquez, 2013). In Colorado, Denver-based Padres y Jovenes Unidos spearheaded the building of a statewide coalition that won passage of a Smart School Discipline Law by the General Assembly in 2012 that limits referrals of students to law enforcement and reduces racial disparities in school discipline, requiring local school districts to rewrite their discipline codes (Gonzalez, 2014).

Twenty youth organizing groups across the country have come together to form the Alliance for Educational Justice (AEJ) at the national level. AEJ delivered proposals to Congress and the president regarding the Elementary and Secondary Education Act and organized on Tax Day, April 15, 2010, to demand more school funding, using rallies, press conferences, and street theater. AEJ has also worked with the Young People's Project of the Algebra Project and other groups to support a constitutional amendment for the right to a quality education, an idea first promoted by Bob Moses (Perry, Moses, Wynne, Cortes, & Delpit, 2010).

In addition, AEJ and a large number of youth justice groups have worked together in a variety of groupings around the school-to-prison pipeline

(STPP), including supporting the regional and national Action Camps sponsored by the Advancement Project, where hundreds of young people, parents, and other local leaders received week-long training in organizing against the STPP (Mediratta, 2012). Many of these youth organizing groups are part of the Dignity in Schools Campaign (DSC), which consists of youth and adults and of multiple stakeholders—parent organizing groups like CADRE in Los Angeles and civil rights and legal advocacy groups like the NAACP Legal Defense and Education Fund—that is, the kinds of organizations mentioned above in describing the variety of the youth justice field. This broader alliance was instrumental in pushing the U.S. Departments of Education and Justice to issue joint guidelines to school districts warning against excessive and racially inequitable school discipline practices and encouraging districts to adopt more positive behavioral and restorative justice alternatives (U.S. Department of Education, 2014).

AEJ and DSC are designed to undertake national action when possible, but they also work to support and strengthen local organizing. By participating in national actions, young people become stronger local leaders. They also have the experiences and make the connections that help them to feel part of a larger youth justice movement (Warren et al., 2014). Increasingly, local groups are searching for ways for young people to connect and learn from one another as well as from adults in a broader social justice movement (Ginwright, 2010). For example, local groups sent hundreds of youth leaders to the U.S Social Forums in Atlanta and Detroit where they connected to one another and with adult organizers and activists seeking transformational change. Widespread use of social media has expanded the possibilities for young people to remain connected after developing face-to-face relationships in national meetings like action camps, social forums, and protest marches (Cohen & Kahne, 2012).

There are a growing number of examples, like the school-to-prison pipeline space and the U.S. Social Forum, that suggest the existence of a much larger field of intersectional and cross-generational movement activity beyond locally based youth organizing groups. Increasingly, young people interconnect with these movements and cross-fertilize ideas, strategies, and tactics. Cristina Beltrán (2015) argues that the DREAMers movement, for example, has "appropriated strategies of visibility developed during the gay rights movement and has chosen to 'come out' and openly declare their undocumented status" (p. 80). She suggests that social media have allowed undocumented youth to create a "queered" or rival public space in which they could express "more complex and sophisticated conceptions of loyalty, legality, migration, sexuality, and patriotism than those typically offered by politicians, pundits, and other political elites" (p. 82). In other words, the DREAMers have not only borrowed strategies from the successes of the gay rights movement, but also a language and worldview that encourages the public-space legitimacy of formerly illegitimate actors (Beltrán, 2015). We believe that scholarship on youth activism needs to focus on the emergence of these examples of a larger, intersectional movement toward youth justice, like the school-to-prison pipeline and the DREAMers.

AN EMERGING MOVEMENT IN A BROADER SOCIAL JUSTICE FIELD

The youth justice movement may be best understood at this point as a nascent or emerging movement. Social movement scholars typically study movements once they are fully formed and their existence is self-evident (Blee & Currier, 2005). In fact, scholars have been hard pressed to identify clear criteria for when a movement exists. However, we believe we have offered strong evidence that a youth justice movement has been emerging, one that includes the activities of youth organizing groups but encompasses a broader field of groups seeking justice for youth. Young people in these groups are drawing upon shared cultural resources to respond to their oppression as young people. They are increasingly connecting beyond their individual groups to create emerging movement structures including alliances at local, state, and national levels. Through these structures they are demanding voice and participation to transform adultist power relationships and win concrete improvements in their lives across a range of salient issues.

The emerging youth justice movement contains a diverse set of overlapping phenomena that do not currently coalesce into a single unified movement. However, this is typical at the stage of movement emergence (Diani, 2013). Moreover, even fully formed movements usually consist of multiple and overlapping networks and organizations, which both cooperate and sometimes conflict or compete with one another (Morris, 1984).

It remains to be seen—and studied—if the recent attempts at alliance building will lead to the fuller emergence of a movement. One critical question concerns the financial resources necessary to build and sustain a movement. Youth justice groups tend to be small and underfunded. A 2010 survey of youth organizing groups found that more than 75% of their funding came from private foundations and that they had experienced a decline in such funding in the recent period (Braxton et al., 2013; Torres-Fleming et al., 2010). Many foundations have shifted their grant making to support strategic priorities that they set, rather than projects defined by youth participants. More broadly, foundations may be hesitant to support the political demands of youth justice groups (Kwon, 2013).

Another important question concerns the power and sustainability of a movement consisting of people who will "age out" at a certain point in their lives. This issue is related to funding because youth justice groups often receive grants from foundations to work with young people who are secondary school age. When young people "graduate" from the programs around the age of 18, what structures exist to connect these alumni to broader movements? In some places like California with an expansive social movement infrastructure, many youth activists become connected to other social movements like the labor or immigrant rights movements (Terriquez, 2014). In many if not most places, however, few structures exist that directly connect alumni to continued participation in movements for social justice (Ginwright, 2010). This situation may be changing with the recent advent of the Black Lives Matter movement, especially if that movement develops the capacity for sustained organizing.

Many other questions remain to be explored. Can people who lack the right to vote exert sufficient power to create transformative change? Since the youth justice movement alone cannot transform the institutions that oppress youth, what will be the relationship of the youth movement to other social movements? More broadly, will the cause of youth justice acquire sufficient allies in a country that has so devalued young people? Yet it is precisely by recognizing collective action by young people and their allies as an emerging youth justice movement that we are challenged to investigate these and other questions.

ACKNOWLEDGMENTS

We would like to thank Najma Nazy'at, Seth Kirshenbaum, and David Jenkins who helped shape our thinking about youth justice and a youth justice movement. We would also like to thank Sandeep Jani, Elena Dowin Kennedy, Perri Leviss, Matthew Poirier, Kimberly Williams, and Lindsay Morgia, with whom conversations about youth organizing in Boston also contributed to our thinking. Finally, we would like to thank Veronica Terriquez, in particular, as well as Paul Kuttner for very helpful comments on earlier versions of this chapter. Please send all correspondence to mark.warren@umb.edu.

REFERENCES

Acosta, C., & Mir, A. (2012). Empowering young people to be critical thinkers: The Mexican American Studies Program in Tucson. *VUE: Voices in Urban Education*, 34, 15–27. Retrieved from http://annenberginstitute.org/

Adams-Bass, V. N., Stevenson, H. C., & Kotzin, D. S. (2014). Measuring the meaning of black media stereotypes and their relationship to the racial identity, black history knowledge, and racial socialization of African American youth. *Journal of Black Studies*, 45(5), 367–395. http://dx.doi.org/10.1177/0021934714530396

Advancement Project. (2015). *Ending the schoolhouse to jailhouse track*. Retrieved from http://www.advancementproject.org/

Alinsky, S. D. (1962). *Citizen participation and community organization in planning and urban renewal*. Chicago: Industrial Areas Foundation.

Avant-Mier, R. (2010). *Rock the nation: Latin/o identities and the Latin rock diaspora*. London: Continuum International.

Bahena, S. A., Cooc, N., Currie-Rubin, R., Kuttner, P., & Ng, M. (Eds.). (2012). *Disrupting the school-to-prison pipeline*. Cambridge: Harvard Educational Review.

Bell, J. (1995). *Understanding adultism: A key to developing positive youth-adult relationships*. Somerville, MA: YouthBuild USA.

Beltrán, C. (2015). "Undocumented, unafraid, and unapologetic": DREAM activists, immigrant politics, and the queering of democracy. In D. Allen & J. Light (Eds.), *From voice to influence: Understanding citizenship in a digital age* (pp. 80–104). Chicago: University of Chicago Press.

Blee, K. M., & Currier, A. (2005). Character building: The dynamics of emerging social movement groups. *Mobilization: An International Quarterly, 10*(1), 129–144. Retrieved from http://mobilizationjournal.org/

Bonilla-Silva, E. (2001). *White supremacy and racism in the post–civil rights era*. Boulder, CO: Lynne Rienner.

Braxton, E., Buford, W., & Marasigan, L. (2013). *2013 national field scan*. New York: Funders Collaborative on Youth Organizing.

BSAC. (2015). Boston Student Advisory Council. *Youth on Board*. Retrieved from http://www.youthonboard.org/-!bsac/c1duk

Cammarota, J., & Fine, M. (Eds.). (2008). *Revolutionizing education: Youth Participatory Action Research in motion*. New York: Routledge.

Cammarota, J., Romero, A., & Stovall, D. (2014). *Raza studies: The public option for educational revolution*. Tucson, AZ: University of Arizona Press.

Campaign for Youth Justice. (2007, March). The consequences aren't minor: The impact of trying youth as adults and strategies for reform. *A Campaign for Youth Justice Report*. Retrieved from http://www.campaignforyouthjustice.org/

Carson, C. (1981). *In struggle: SNCC and the black awakening of the 1960s*. Cambridge: Harvard University Press.

Chavez, M. L., Soriano, M., & Oliverez, P. (2007). Undocumented students' access to college: The American dream denied. *Latino Studies, 5*(2), 254–263. http://dx.doi.org/10.1057/palgrave.lst.8600255

Cheadle, A., Wagner, E., Walls, M., Diehr, P., Bell, M., Anderman, C., . . . & Neckerman, H. (2001). The effect of neighborhood-based community organizing: Results from the Seattle Minority Youth Health Project. *Health Services Research, 36*(4), 671–689. Retrieved from http://www.ncbi.nlm.nih.gov/pubmed/11508634

Checkoway, B., & Richards-Schuster, K. (2006). Youth participation for educational reform in low-income communities of color. In S. Ginwright, P. Noguera, & J. Cammarota (Eds.), *Beyond resistance: Youth activism and community change* (pp. 319–332). New York: Routledge.

Children's Defense Fund. (2015). *Cradle to Prison Pipeline campaign*. Washington, DC: Author. Retrieved from http://www.childrensdefense.org/

Christens, B. D., Collura, J. J., Kopish, M. A., & Varvodic, M. (2014). Youth organizing for school and neighborhood improvement. In K. L. Petterson & R. M. Silverman (Eds.), *Schools and urban revitalization: Rethinking institutions and community development* (pp. 151–166). New York: Routledge.

Clay, A. (2012). *The hip hop generation fights back: Youth, activism, and post–civil rights politics*. New York: NYU Press.

Cohen, C. J. (2010). *Democracy remixed: Black youth and the future of American politics*. New York: Oxford University Press.

Cohen, C. J., & Kahne, J. (2012). *Participatory politics: New media and youth political action*. Oakland, CA: Youth and Participatory Politics Research Network.

Conner, J., Zaino, K., & Scarola, E. (2013). "Very Powerful Voices": The influence of youth organizing on educational policy in Philadelphia. *Educational Policy, 27*(3), 560–588. http://dx.doi.org/10.1177/0895904812454001

Crenshaw, K. W. (2015). *Black girls matter: Pushed out, overpoliced, and underprotected*. New York: African American Policy Forum.

Delgado, M., & Staples, L. (2008). *Youth-led community organizing: Theory and action*. New York: Oxford University Press.

Diani, M. (2013). Organizational fields and social movement dynamics: Dynamics, mechanisms and processes. In J. van Stekelenburg, C. Roggeband, & B. Klandermans (Eds.), *The future of social movement research* (pp. 145–168). Minneapolis: University of Minnesota Press.

Duncan-Andrade, J. M. R. (2007). Urban youth and the counter-narration of inequality. *Transforming Anthropology, 15*(1), 26–37. http://dx.doi.org/10.1525/tran.2007.15.1.26

Duncan-Andrade, J. M. R. (2009). Note to educators: Hope required when growing roses in concrete. *Harvard Educational Review, 79*(2), 181–194. http://dx.doi.org/10.17763/haer.79.2.nu3436017730384w

Fisher, R. (1994). *Let the people decide: Neighborhood organizing in America* (Updated ed.). New York: Twayne.

Fletcher, A. (2013). *Ending discrimination against young people*. Olympia, WA: CommonAction.

Flores-González, N., Rodriguez, M., & Rodriguez-Muniz, M. (2006). From hip hop to humanization: Batey Urbano as a space for Latino youth culture and community action. In S. Ginwright, P. Noguera, & J. Cammarota (Eds.), *Beyond resistance: Youth activism and community change* (pp. 175–196). New York: Routledge.

Franklin, S. (2014). Race, class, and community organizing in support of economic justice initiatives in the twenty-first century. *Community Development Journal, 49*(2), 181–197. http://dx.doi.org/10.1093/cdj/bst035

Ganz, M. (2010). Leading change: Leadership, organization, and social movements. In N. Nohria & R. Khurana (Eds.), *Handbook of leadership theory and practice* (pp. 527–568). Boston: Harvard Business School Press.

Ginwright, S. (2003). *Youth organizing: Expanding possibilities for youth development*. New York: Funders Collaborative on Youth Organizing. Retrieved from www.fcyo.org/Papers_no3_n3.qxd.pdf

Ginwright, S. (2010). *Building a pipeline for justice: Understanding youth organizing and the leadership pipeline*. New York: Funders' Collaborative on Youth Organizing.

Ginwright, S., Noguera, P., & Cammarota, J. (2006). *Beyond resistance! Youth resistance and community change: New democratic possibilities for practice and policy for America's youth*. New York: Routledge.

Giugno, M., McAdam, D., & Tilly, C. (Eds.). (1999). *How social movements matter*. Minneapolis, MN: University of Minnesota Press.

Gómez, C., & Jiménez-Silva, M. (2012). Mexican American studies: The historical legitimacy of an educational program. *Association of Mexican-American Educators Journal, 6*(1), 15–23. Retrieved from http://eric.ed.gov/?id=EJ995428

Gonzalez, T. (2014). Socializing schools: Addressing racial disparities in discipline through restorative justice. In D. J. Losen (Ed.), *Closing the discipline gap: Equitable remedies for excessive exclusion* (pp. 151–165). New York: Teachers College Press.

Gordon, H. R. (2009). *We fight to win: Inequality and the politics of youth activism*. New Brunswick, NJ: Rutgers University Press.

Guastaferro, W. P. (2013). Crime, the media, and constructions of reality: Using HBO's The Wire as a frame of reference. *College Student Journal, 47*(2), 264–270. Retrieved from http://search.proquest.com/docview/1416788840?accountid=14853

James, T., & McGillicuddy, K (2001). Building youth movements for community change. *The Nonprofit Quarterly, 8*(4), 1–3. Retrieved from http://racialequity tools.org/resourcefiles/james1.pdf

Kirschenbaum, S. (2014) *Interview*. Boston, MA.

Kirshner, B., & Ginwright, S. (2012). Youth organizing as a developmental context for African American and Latino adolescents. *Child Development Perspectives, 6*(3), 288–294. http://dx.doi.org/10.1111/j.1750-8606.2012.00243.x

Kwon, S. A. (2013). *Uncivil youth: Race, activism, and affirmative governmentality*. Durham, NC: Duke University Press.

Males, M. (2006). Youth policy and institutional change. In S. Ginwright, P. Noguera, & J. Cammarota (Eds.), *Beyond resistance: Youth activism and community change* (pp. 301–318). New York: Routledge.

Malone, C., & Martinez Jr., G. (Eds.). (2014). *The organic globalizer: Hip hop, political development, and movement culture*. New York: Bloomsbury.

Mediratta, K. (2006). A rising movement. *National Civic Review, 95*(1), 15–22. http://dx.doi.org/10.1002/ncr.126

Mediratta, K. (2012). Grassroots organizing and the school-to-prison pipeline: The emerging national movement to roll back zero tolerance discipline policies in U.S. public schools. In S. A. Bahena, N. Cooc, R. Currie-Rubin, P. Kuttner, & M. Ng (Eds.), *Disrupting the school to prison pipeline* (pp. 211–236). Cambridge: Harvard Educational Review.

Mediratta, K., Shah, S., & McAlister, S. (2009). *Community organizing for stronger schools: Strategies and successes*. Cambridge: Harvard Education Press.

Milkman, R., & Terriquez, V. (2012). "We are the ones who are out in front": Women's leadership in the immigrant rights movement. *Feminist Studies, 38*(3), 723–752. Retrieved from http://www.jstor.org/stable/23720205

Morris, A. D. (1984). *The origins of the civil rights movement: Black communities organizing for change*. New York: Free Press.

Movement Strategy Center & FCYO (2011). *Looking forward: Youth leading the way to a sustainable planet: Lessons learned from the ReGenerations project*. Brooklyn, NY: Funders' Collborative on Youth Organizing.

Nicholls, W. J. (2013). *The DREAMers: How the undocumented youth movement transformed the immigrant rights debate*. Stanford, CA: Stanford University Press.

Orfield, G., Losen, D., Wald, J., & Swanson, C. B. (2004). *Losing our future: How minority youth are being left behind by the graduation rate crisis*. Cambridge, MA: The Civil Rights Project at Harvard University.

Payne, C. M. (1995). *I've got the light of freedom: The organizing tradition and the Mississippi freedom struggle*. Berkeley: University of California Press.

Perry, T., Moses, R. P., Wynne, J. T., Cortes, E., & Delpit, L. D. (2010). *Quality education as a constitutional right: Creating a grassroots movement to transform public schools*. Boston: Beacon Press.

powell, j. a. (2007). Structural racism and spatial Jim Crow. In R. D. Bullard (Ed.), *The black metropolis in the twenty-first century: Race, power and the politics of place* (pp. 41–65). Lanham, MD: Rowman & Littlefield.

Rabaka, R. (2013). *The hip hop movement: From R&B and the civil rights movement to rap and the hip hop generation*. Lanham, MD: Lexington Books.

Rogers, J., Mediratta, K., & Shah, S. (2012). Building power, learning democracy: Youth organizing as a site of civic development. *Review of Research in Education*, 36(1), 43–66. http://dx.doi.org/10.3102/0091732X11422328

Rogers, J., & Terriquez, V. (2013). *Learning to lead: The impact of youth organizing on the educational and civic trajectories of low-income youth*. Los Angeles: UCLA, Institute for Democracy, Education, and Access.

Shirley, D. (1997). *Community organizing for urban school reform*. Austin: University of Texas Press.

Stampler, L. (2011, April 20). SlutWalks sweep the nation. *Huffington Post*. Retrieved from http://www.huffingtonpost.com/2011/04/20/slutwalk-united-states-city_n_851725.html

Sum, A., Khatiwada, I., & McLaughlin, J. (2009). *The consequences of dropping out of high school*. Boston, MA: Northeastern University Center for Labor Market Studies.

TAG Boston. (2015). Our beliefs. *Teacher Activist Group Boston*. Retrieved from http://tagboston.org/about/

Tarrow, S. G. (1998). *Power in movement: Social movements and contentious politics* (2nd ed.). Cambridge: Cambridge University Press.

Tarrow, S. G. (2011). *Power in movement: Social movements and contentious politics* (3rd ed.). Cambridge: Cambridge University Press.

Terriquez, V. (2014). Training young activists: Grassroots organizing and youths' civic and political trajectories. *Sociological Perspectives*, 58(2), 223–242. http://dx.doi.org/10.1177/0731121414556473

Terriquez, V., Rogers, J., Vargas, A., & Patler, C. (2013). *Powerful learning: The impact of CHIRLA's Wise Up! on members' educational and civic pathways*. Los Angeles: UCLA Institute for Democracy, Education and Action.

Torres-Fleming, A., Valdes, P., & Pillai, S. (2010). *2010 youth organizing field scan*. New York: Funders' Collaborative on Youth Organizing.

Urban Youth Collaborative. (2015). *Ending the school-to-prison pipeline*. Retrieved from http://www.urbanyouthcollaborative.org/

U.S. Department of Education. (2014). *Guiding principles: A resource guide for improving school climate and discipline*. Washington, D.C.: U.S. Department of Education.

VOYCE. (2015). About us. *Voices of Chicago youth*. Retrieved from http://voyce project.org/

Warren, M. R. (2001). *Dry bones rattling: Community building to revitalize American democracy*. Princeton: Princeton University Press.

Warren, M. R. (2014). Transforming public education: The need for an educational justice movement. *New England Journal of Public Policy, 26*(1), 1–17. Retrieved from http://scholarworks.umb.edu/nejpp/vol26/iss1/11/

Warren, M. R., Jani, S., Kennedy, E. D., Kupscznk, L., Leviss, P., Poirrier, M., & Williams, K. (2014). *"We want to create our own history": Youth power and leadership in the Boston Youth Justice Movement 2005–2008*. Boston, MA: University of Massachusetts Boston.

Warren, M. R., Mapp, K. L., & Community Organizing and School Reform Project. (2011). *A match on dry grass: Community organizing as a catalyst for school reform*. New York: Oxford University Press.

Warren, M. R., Mira, M., & Nikundiwe, T. (2008). Youth organizing: From youth development to school reform. *New Directions in Youth Development, 2008*(117), 27–42, http://dx.doi.org/10.1002/yd.245

Western, B., & Pettit, B. (2010). Incarceration and social inequality. *Daedalus, 139*(3), 8–19. http://dx.doi.org/10.1162/DAED_a_00019

Wood, R. L. (2002). *Faith in action: Religion, race and democratic organizing in America*. Chicago: University of Chicago Press.

Wood, R. L., Partridge, K., & Fulton, B. (2012). *Building bridges, building power: Developments in institution-based community organizing*. Jericho, NY: Interfaith Funders.

Youth Speak Out Coalition, & Zimmerman, K. (2007). Making space, making change: Models for youth-led social change organizations. *Children Youth and Environments, 17*(2), 298–314. Retrieved from http://www.jstor.org/stable/10.7721/chilyoutenvi.17.2.0298

4

Conceptualizing Youth Activists' Leadership: A Multidimensional Framework

Sonia M. Rosen and Jerusha Conner

As youth activism has extended its reach in the past two decades to engage middle- and high school–aged youth (Braxton, this volume), questions have arisen about what exactly is the role of young people in driving the vision, structure, and strategies of their youth organizing groups. A product of this shift is the circulation of new terminology around youth leadership. One term, "youth-led," is ubiquitous in discussions of youth activism yet defined inconsistently. In practice, the term is at the center of disputes around whose voices are actually expressed when young people rise up to demand justice and equity in their schools and communities. In these circumstances, policy-makers and the media have been known to call the term "youth-led" into question, claiming that youth are manipulated by the adult staff members in their organizations. Youth organizing groups and other youth organizations frequently respond that adults are merely present in those groups to lend support and facilitate young people's access to adult domains (Conner, 2015). In short, the term "youth-led" is at the heart of an important discursive struggle around who is driving the work of youth activism and youth political engagement. In examining what "youth-led" means and how it is negotiated in practice, this chapter illuminates what is at stake for these organizations and programs, for the youth they engage, and for the field of youth activism when one of its most common adjectives is imprecisely defined.

In a recent field scan of youth organizing groups, Braxton, Buford, and Marasigan (2013) found that increasingly adults are playing important roles in these organizations. Of the 111 organizations they sampled, only 24% met their criteria for being youth-led, meaning that youth "provided leadership for the design, implementation, and evaluation of organizing campaigns as well as the management of the organization" (p. 15). They explain the trend toward intergenerational organizing and collaboration with adult allies by observing, "There is a growing recognition that low-income young people and young people of color are part of whole communities and that to achieve the kinds of changes desired, people of all ages must organize together" (p. 6). In Chapter 2 of this book, Eric Braxton makes a distinction between activism that engages adolescents and activism that involves primarily young adults. Though the term *youth-led* has generally been employed by groups that mobilize adolescents, the framework we offer here could also be applied to young adult activist groups based on intergenerational models.

The trend of increasing adult presence in youth organizing groups has coincided with the growing influence of these organizations. Perhaps not coincidentally, then, some adult onlookers have expressed skepticism about the roles adults play in youth organizing. Policymakers and other civic leaders who have been the targets of organizing campaigns have raised questions about what exactly youth-led means, and some point to the strength of the adult presence within these organizations as a reason to disregard them and their demands (Conner, 2015). The external reputations of youth organizing groups and the potential potency of their work, then, appear to hinge partially on how they interpret, enact, and communicate youth leadership. Additionally, these groups' internal capacity to build a pipeline of critically engaged civic actors is tightly connected to their implementation of youth leadership. If youth are to assume future roles as civic leaders, they need to develop clear understandings of what leadership entails. Moreover, these groups are part of a larger youth justice movement that is built around expressions of youth identity and that uses a range of strategies to resist the array of injustices that intersect to constrain the lives of the most vulnerable youth (Warren & Kupscznk, this volume). In this context, it is useful for both youth activists and adult outsiders to have a strong grasp of the roles youth can play in their local organizing efforts.

Researchers can help advance the goals of youth activists by generating greater conceptual clarity and consensus around the meaning and use of buzzwords, like youth-led, which are applied with ease by insiders but often viewed suspiciously by outsiders. In this chapter, we offer a conceptual framework for negotiating the meaning of "youth-led." We are guided by the fundamental question of whether or not there is a meaningful distinction to be drawn between youth-led and youth-run, and, if so, what such a distinction accomplishes.

LITERATURE REVIEW

Defining "Youth-Led"

In the field of youth organizing, the term "youth-led" remains poorly defined, yet it is used frequently by both researchers and practitioners to describe a wide variety of practices and organizational configurations. Delgado and Staples (2008) explain that leadership models can be placed on a continuum defined by the power young people are able to assert in organizing groups. They identify four models of "youth power in community organizing": adult-led with youth participation, adult-led with youth as limited partners, youth-adult collaborative partnership, and youth-led with adult allies. They use broad strokes to explain the youth-led model, which is the focus of their book, as one in which "youth are in charge and adults play supportive roles as needed and defined by youth" (p. 70). This continuum offers a helpful starting point for considering degrees of power sharing between youth and adults; however, it does not clarify *how* youth power and control may manifest within an organization. Although the cut-and-dried aspect of this definition holds appeal, we seek to complicate it by examining what exactly it is that youth are "in charge" of and how they assert this authority.

Like Delgado and Staples (2008), Zimmerman (2007) presents a spectrum of youth leadership that charts youth organizing based on "the degree to which youth are empowered to participate and lead" (p. 301). Her spectrum ranges from organizations in which youth are positioned as clients on the one end to organizations that are youth-led on the other. Importantly, she makes a key distinction among youth-driven organizations, youth-run organizations, and youth-led organizations, defining them as follows:

> Youth driven: Youth have substantive, meaningful roles in leadership positions, including governance and programming
> Youth run: Youth fill a majority of staff positions and manage the day-to-day operations of the organization
> Youth led: Youth are in all major leadership roles, including executive director, and have majority membership on boards of directors, with appropriate support from adult allies (p. 301)

In this framework, the action of leadership is conceptualized primarily in terms of governance, and only a subset of organizational members are viewed as leaders.

In contrast, theorists who discuss distributed leadership and collectivist leadership view leadership differently. Work in these areas envisions leadership as embodied in relationships and expressed through a variety of actions that support the culture, vision, and work of an organization in purposeful and constructive ways (Rosen, 2016; Spillane, Halverson, & Diamond, 2001). For instance, in his discussion of youth-led participatory action research, London (2007) introduces a matrix that locates youth-led organizations and projects along two axes. The vertical axis describes the degree to which youth have authority over decision making, and the horizontal axis measures how included they are across the different stages of a project. This matrix, then, helps us describe the parameters around youth participation. Similarly, Rosen (2016) explores the myriad manifestations of youth leadership in a youth-led organization. She claims that a "collectivist" approach to youth leadership emerges as young people develop leadership capacity among their peers, participate in decision making, and represent their youth organizing group to outsiders. In this sense, leadership is embodied by members across the organization who may participate in a range of ways. This conception reflects the notion of collectivism as a "leaderful" not "leaderless" endeavor (Smith & Glidden, 2012). Still, this research has not helped to define and explain adult roles in youth-led organizations.

In fact, although some theorists specify clear roles for adults in their definitions of youth-led (e.g., Delgado & Staples, 2008), others leave out adults altogether (e.g., Braxton et al., 2013). For example, Gavrielides (2015) defines youth-led organizations as those "that organically and on a day-to-day basis allow both their internal and external affairs to be run and scrutinized by young people" (p. 428). The omission of specified roles for adults in such conceptualizations can lead to uncertainty as to whether or not adults are even involved in the organization and, if so, how.

Several researchers have looked explicitly at adult roles in youth organizing and youth-led participatory action research (Larson et al., 2004; Mitra, 2005; O'Donoghue & Strobel, 2007). Kirshner (2008), for example, examines how adults support young people in learning the skills and practices of organizing. His analysis of adults' influence on youth organizers' learning is framed as an example of guided participation, which "emphasizes how adults help to structure children's developmental trajectories and also the active participation by children in these processes" (p. 62).

In a study of another youth organizing group, Larson and Hansen (2005) found that adults provided youth with training experiences; scaffolded their participation by assisting with the actual work, supporting youth ownership, and encouraging evaluation of their campaigns; and cultivated a culture and community of social change and strategic thinking. However we think about the complex and contrasting ways in which adults can interact with and support youth activism work, it is important to acknowledge that adult allies who want to foster a youth-led organizational culture must strike a delicate balance between principled involvement and noninvolvement (Kirshner, 2008).

(Youth) Leadership in Social Movements

Social movement theorists have studied the roles and functions of leaders (Goldstone, 2001), styles and types of leaders (Barker, Johnson, & Lavalette, 2001; Eichler, 1977), the relationships between leaders and organizational structures (Ganz, 2000), and the relationships between leadership and social change outcomes (Campbell, 2005). The strategies, frames, and decision-making processes of social movement leaders have been well documented; nonetheless, several scholars contend that leadership in social movements has been undertheorized (Aminzade, Goldstone, & Perry, 2001; Barker et al., 2001; Campbell, 2005; Morris & Staggenborg, 2007).

Particularly striking is the lack of attention to youth leadership in social movements, even though student leaders were instrumental in the civil rights movement (Carson, 1981; Clay, 2012) and the antiwar movements of the 1960s. Furthermore, youth are at the forefront of many of today's social movements, including struggles for immigration reform, LGBTQ rights, climate justice, educational equity, reform of the policing and criminal justice system, and women's rights, among others, as many chapters in this volume attest.

Warren and Kupscznk (this volume) argue that as they work together at state and national levels, youth are leading a new movement for youth justice: "In response to adultism and interlocking systems of oppression, young people are increasingly organizing to assert their voice, demand respect, and build power for themselves as youth, that is, they are building a movement for *youth justice*." Warren and Kupscznk identify many questions about this emergent movement, but a key question concerns the role and manifestations of leadership as the movement evolves, particularly as young leaders "age out" of their identities as youth.

A FRAMEWORK FOR YOUTH LEADERSHIP

Our theoretical framework unpacks and integrates current definitions of youth-led in the literature, each of which seems to foreground a slightly different aspect of leadership, while also incorporating additional considerations that have received relatively short shrift in the research base. We weave together strands drawn from literature on youth organizing and organizational theory.

In this framework, we build on Delgado and Staples's (2008), Zimmerman's (2007), and Braxton and colleagues' (2013) notions of "youth-led" in order to more thoroughly explore and describe the organizational dimensions in which this practice may manifest. Delgado and Staples's (2008) definition focuses on youth being "in charge" (p. 70), whereas Zimmerman's (2007) definition considers governance structures and the formal authority vested in the youth for internal decision making and the actual running of organizations. In contrast, Braxton and colleagues' (2013) definition emphasizes the central work of the organization, such as the organizing campaigns and day-to-day management. Together, these definitions draw attention to the importance of examining how youth in youth-led organizations accept and enact their responsibility for the main work of the organization and for organizational health and functioning.

In synthesizing these extant definitions, however, we identified what we saw as two shortcomings in the field. First, much of the literature on youth-led organizations ignores important questions about organizational culture, such as what is central, distinctive, and enduring about the organization (Brown, Dacin, Pratt, & Whetten, 2006) and how those features are negotiated by various internal actors over time. Organizational decision making is not simply a matter of management and operations; it also encompasses long-term vision and strategy as well as organizational identity and culture. Leadership must occur in all these domains.

Second, the term "youth-led" may emphasize traditional expressions of leadership, neglecting other ways in which young people can assume agentive roles within organizations, as they express responsibility not just for the organization and the work, but also to one another. Relationship building is fundamental to the success of organizing campaigns as well as broader social movements, because relationships between movement participants are the foundations for trust and can help participants feel connected to key collective identities (Goodwin, Jasper, & Polletta, 2007).

Based on these observations, we propose a new framework, which suggests that youth-led organizations are those in which youth feel and express responsibility to one another, to the core work of the organization, and to the organization itself through their involvement in running the day-to-day management of the organization, designing and implementing the core programming activities or campaigns, and shaping and reshaping the organization's culture and vision. (See Figure 4.1.) Day-to-day management refers to the work of keeping the organization running. This work may entail such tasks as pursuing funding, managing hiring, recruiting new members, coordinating staff and leadership development, and taking on administrative duties such as paying the bills and doing payroll. In a youth organizing group, the core work encompasses both leadership development activities, including political education, and organizing campaigns. Expressing responsibility for the organizational culture and vision entails safeguarding, sustaining, and sometimes redefining what is central, distinctive, and enduring about the organization (Brown et al., 2006).

We do not propose this framework as a checklist or an evaluation tool, but as a way of conceptualizing and describing the variety of ways in which youth leadership can manifest in a youth-led organization. This framework sets us up to explore the many forms of participation available to and enacted by various sets of organizational actors within a youth-led organization.

At the same time, we want to account for the complexity and nuance of these manifestations, so we frame each of the boxes in Figure 4.1 as

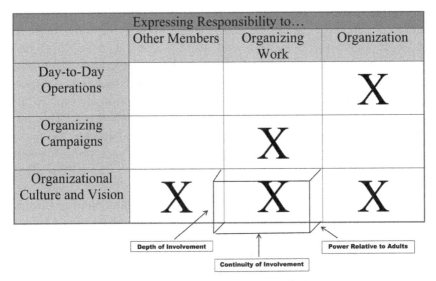

Figure 4.1. Manifestations of Youth Leadership in Youth Organizing.

three-dimensional bins. The three dimensions take into consideration the power and authority of youth relative to adults in this area; the depth of youths' involvement; and the continuity of their involvement in this arena over time. By depth of involvement we mean how *much* responsibility they are taking on, and by continuity of involvement, we consider *how often and consistently* they are enacting these roles. Again, however, we offer this three-dimensional framework not as a gauge for assessing the extent to which an organization is or is not youth-led, but as a lens for recognizing and understanding the negotiations of youth leadership in youth-led organizations.

METHODS

Our theoretical framework is supported by both extant literature and qualitative research we have conducted on the Philadelphia Student Union (PSU). PSU is a nonprofit youth organizing group that aims to mobilize high school students to effect systemic change in Philadelphia's public schools. At the time of our research, PSU had chapters in comprehensive neighborhood schools and specialized magnet schools; however, members hailed from around the city, and most were Black students from low-income communities and severely underresourced neighborhood schools. At the time of this research, PSU had a staff of five paid adults, with such titles as Executive Director, Curriculum Coordinator, and Director of Finance and Operations.

PSU was founded in 1995 by a group of students who were dissatisfied with the quality of education they and their peers were receiving. Since that time, the organization has grown to engage thousands of youth in its political education curriculum, its young men's and young women's support groups, its media programs, and its organizing work. During our studies of PSU, members met on Saturdays for political education workshops around such topics as "the spiral of oppression," "the ideal school," and "capitalism and consumerism." On Wednesday evenings, a Youth Leadership Team would meet to discuss and plan for ongoing campaigns and new strategic initiatives. PSU doors were also open during the week after school for youth to hang out, get homework help, use the computers, or engage in the organizing work. Members worked throughout the week to produce content for the organization's blog, biannual newsletter, and weekly radio show.

Over the last two decades, PSU has pursued campaigns around such issues as promoting small schools, securing full and fair funding for public education, revising school discipline policies, and combating privatization efforts. It has worked in coalition with adult, youth, and intergenerational organizing groups in the city and on the national stage. It has established a reputation as one of the most long-standing and well-regarded contemporary youth organizing groups in the country.

To illustrate our claims in this chapter, we draw on data collected as part of three separate studies of PSU conducted between the years 2008 and 2013. Our data include 50 interviews with members, staff, and alumni; observations of PSU meetings, events, and actions totaling more than 85 hours; and PSU artifacts such as curricular materials, student-produced radio programs, and newsletters. Interviews were conducted individually, following a semistructured protocol. They lasted between 45 and 90 minutes and took place at PSU headquarters, at a park or coffee shop chosen by the respondent, or in a few cases over the phone. All interviews were digitally recorded and transcribed. Field notes were taken during and occasionally immediately after observations of PSU functions. Each author assumed the role of a participant observer during these moments, working to support the organization's goals and activities.

Throughout data collection, we remained mindful of our positioning as adults, academics, and middle-class women who bring certain privilege and power to a site where most of the participants are low-income Brown and Black youth. We worked deliberately to build relationships of trust with our study participants, to support the work of PSU, and to ensure our work would be useful to the organization. Such an approach is consistent with feminist methodologies, which contend that "research should be emancipatory" (Hammersley & Atkinson, 2007, p. 14) and change oppressive realities. We operated from a place of belief in PSU and its members with the intention of being respectful, and ultimately acting as allies, to these individuals and their work.

Acknowledging our positionality as researchers and monitoring our subjectivity as it shaped data collection and analysis helped us to understand and represent our findings as social constructions. At the same time, we sought ways to strengthen the validity of our findings. By interviewing staff as well as current and former youth members, observing diverse PSU events, and examining PSU artifacts, we were able to triangulate our data sources, a key strategy for enhancing validity in qualitative research (Golafshani, 2003; Hammersley & Atkinson, 2007). Finally, by working together, we were able to check, complicate, and validate each other's interpretations, until we arrived at shared understandings.

YOUTH LEADERSHIP IN THE PHILADELPHIA STUDENT UNION

When applied to our data, our theoretical framework illuminates various ways in which leadership is negotiated by youth and adults in a youth-led organization. Negotiations between youth and adults can be understood as ways in which organizational insiders hold one another accountable in order to support young people's psychosocial development and advance the social justice goals of the organization. This accountability emerged in how PSU's adult staff and youth members felt and expressed a sense of responsibility to other organizational insiders, to the organization as a whole, and, more broadly, to the work of youth organizing. We view these domains of negotiation as important categories that can help researchers, youth organizers, and funders recognize how organizations can be youth-led. For the sake of simplicity, we begin by illustrating bins diagonally, starting from the top right and going toward the bottom left of the matrix (Figure 4.1). However, in our final example, we demonstrate how youth in our studies expressed leadership in ways that fit into the entire bottom row of bins.

Expressing Responsibility to the Organization

We found several instances in which youth expressed their sense of responsibility to the organization by participating in the running of the organization. Although PSU relied on individuals, usually adults, to pursue funding, manage hiring, recruit new members, plan fundraising and other events, coordinate staff and leadership development, and take on administrative duties such as paying the bills and doing payroll, the organization was intentional about making room for youth in these activities, as students' schedules and interests allowed. As one staff member explained, PSU staff sought to include students' voices, especially around internal issues regarding the work:

That isn't to say that . . . it's perfect, but there's been a progression towards more inclusion of young people in terms of those internal moves
and decisions. . . . We're honest about our youth leadership; we don't
want that to be hot air.

Nevertheless, as another staff member pointed out, "There's a certain
amount of just keeping an organization going . . . that falls to staff." This staff
member explained that adults end up doing some of the background work in
order to enable students to engage in more substantive political organizing.

Though the students' role in some administrative functions was minimal,
they took part in hiring committees, contributed to fundraising efforts, and
were instrumental to planning retreats and leadership trainings, such as their
annual week-long series of summer leadership development workshops. Of
her involvement in staff hiring, one alumna recalled, "I went to one of the
staff hiring meetings and all of the meetings were facilitated by a student and
real decisions took place in those meetings." Another alumna described the
key role her peers played at a fundraising event:

> We had a fundraiser last year; a bunch of people were there. . . . Some
> one tapped the mic like, "We were gonna have some students, a whole
> bunch of students who were going to speak about PSU and their experi
> ences. . . ." And a couple of them came up and they were really nice.
> And then [Henry][1] got up there, and he broke into this outrageous
> speech; I mean it was just crazy. And the highlight of his speech was at
> the very end, to paraphrase, he said something like, "When I die, before
> my last breath, I hope that when a new life comes in, I hope that they'll
> have a quality education" or something to that effect, and everybody
> was just like "Wow!" And that set the stage, and it was a really good
> moment.

Indeed, this respondent identified that moment as the most memorable
experience she had had in PSU, as it showcased the power of youth voice, the
centrality of youth voice to PSU's identity, and PSU members' commitment
to the issue of educational equity.

While funding is one critical factor that keeps a nonprofit organization like
PSU running, another is having a steady membership base and having strong
content in which to engage them. One alumnus recounted his contributions
to the organization's curriculum development and membership recruitment:

> I was actually one of the student facilitators for the student leadership
> that we did for [our summer student recruitment retreat]. I remember
> coming into the office and working with other students and staff to

create workshops. . . . We created all of the workshops that we did at [the retreat] that year, as we continue to do now. A lot of those workshops are still being used. Me and [Crystal] actually created the racism workshop that we're still using in our curriculum today and that was from the first year of [the summer retreat].

By demonstrating leadership in hiring decisions, fundraising efforts, curricular development, and new member recruitment, PSU youth made important contributions not just to the immediate, but also to the long-term health and functioning of the organization. In these ways, youth kept the organization running. All of the above examples vary with respect to the youths' depth of involvement, the continuity of their involvement in that effort over time, and how their contribution was negotiated with (or without) adults in PSU, but each showcases youth stepping up to assume and express responsibility for the organization in a key way.

Negotiations around organizational management took into account high school students' limited time and schedule constraints, as well as the need to develop technical expertise for certain kinds of tasks (such as administering payroll). As such, students were involved in the management tasks that had the biggest impact on the long-term direction of the organization, while taking a more involved role in other aspects of the organization. In this sense, PSU *was* partially youth-run, with youth leadership emerging in key areas of organizational management.

Expressing Responsibility to the Organizing Work

The nature of PSU's work is to respond strategically to inequitable circumstances. Youth and adults engage in negotiations around when to respond, how to respond, what kinds of initiatives to put in place, and which allies to seek. Negotiations around these issues happened frequently in meetings, which were usually led by youth, as one student member's account of a youth leadership team meeting makes clear. She reported that those meetings, which "were facilitated by a student," entailed "deciding what campaign we were going to take on that year, deciding what tactics we were going to pursue, deciding what skit we were going to do at the early-on protest." Another student member described the youth leadership team meetings as a collective, shared undertaking:

The first thing we do, it's sort of a backwards process. . . . First, we figure out our agenda, and then we pick our facilitator. Somebody facilitates the agenda making, and then we pick our facilitator for that day. Then everybody just adds things to the agenda that should be on there.

Normally, we start with report backs from the different chapters, from radio squad, from video squad, from soundtrack, from newsletter, from open mic, if they have anything going on, and just all of the different programs. If there were any meetings in the past week, they report back. Normally, we'll talk about how the last Saturday [citywide] meeting went and what the next Saturday meeting is going to be and the up-coming meetings that are coming up that week or any things coming down the road. Sometimes we'll do fundamental strategizing if that's something that can't be handled in a Saturday meeting for whatever reason. Anything that's sort of general direction of the organization and sort of turn-around time [that] has to be [figured out] before next Satur-day. We sort of handle all those things.

Significant in this student's account of the youth leadership team meetings is the use of the word "we." Notably absent in his account is any mention of adult leaders or facilitators; however, adults did sometimes facilitate meetings when they were chosen by the students to take on this role.

As the above quotation also indicates, the youth leadership team meetings set the stage for Saturday citywide meetings. The citywide meetings were times when all youth members could engage in ongoing strategizing around specific campaigns. An adult staff member affirmed that when it comes to questions of strategy, such as, "Who should we talk to? Who would be more strategic: the Teachers Union or [the superintendent]? . . . Students drive those kinds of decisions." He went on to explain that in PSU students take an active role in the work, noting an example of a citywide meeting in which "students came up with a phone script and a press release for an upcoming action."

Further corroborating the enduring quality of such youth leadership in PSU, an alumna from many years prior recalled that one of the key things she learned from her involvement in PSU "was really how much planning went into [the actions] and how much behind the scenes work you really have to do." She detailed the mobilization efforts, coordination among chant leaders, placard developments, and media strategy that went into planning a march. When asked how much of this "behind the scenes work" was orchestrated by students, rather than adults, she responded,

When I came into it, I really couldn't tell. It wasn't like we would sit around and they would tell us, "This is what we're going to do." That was not at all the case. It was very much, "OK, we want to have a rally. What do we need?" It was more like they were the facilitator of the conversation as opposed to the dictator of what was going to happen. We came up with chants; we made posters; we would make sure that there was press releases about it; we would make sure that everything was getting done. Even if an adult staff member was leading it in terms of "OK, I have this assigned project that I have to do," all of the students did the work. They [adults] were more like checkers; they were making sure that we were on the right path and that we thought about everything, and when we didn't think about something, yes, they were there to guide us.

In terms of the organizing work, adults offered support and suggestions, but their advice was not always followed. For example, one alumna recalled the year she and her peers decided to focus on securing passes to make transportation to and from school more affordable for students, despite the serious reservations expressed by the adult leaders.

People brought up different ideas and we brainstormed different problems we wanted to look at in the city. Finally, we decided to get free school tokens for all students. [It was] the least popular choice but the one everybody agreed was important. . . . I remember [the executive director] said this was a terrible idea for a campaign: "It's not going to be a good campaign and we have to do this the rest of the year.". . . It wasn't a good idea to select that as our campaign; we didn't win, and it was a lame year for PSU. But [the executive director] saw it as a bad idea and he let us do it; he didn't take control of our decision, and we failed, and then we lived to fight another fight. So that's an example of [adults] backing off.

A later executive director of PSU demonstrated a similar deference to students during the development and enactment of organizing campaigns. One member described her as someone who was "able to step back and trust that things will be OK, or she has the discipline to say, 'No, I can't make this decision [for you],' even if she knows what the best decision is." With respect to the political organizing in which PSU engaged, it is clear that youth were firmly in charge, feeling and demonstrating leadership over the design, implementation, and evaluation of the actions and campaign strategies.

Expressing Responsibility to One Another

Across several generations of alumni, a common phrase used to describe PSU and its members is "like family." Interview participants were quick to point out the importance and intimacy of the relationships they forged with other members through "intense" political education workshops that deal with heady issues, young men's and women's support groups, weekend retreats, and dramatic, highly charged actions. In fact, internal relationship building is a central part of PSU's work and its identity, and this relationship building can be understood as a leadership task.

Our data make clear that members and staff supporting one another became a distinctive characteristic of PSU's culture. This support was bidirectional, flowing not just from adults to youth, but also from youth to adults. For example, one adult staff member recalled that when he was first hired, he had to rely on students as well as other staff to help him learn the ropes. It was not enough to be entrusted with an important job, though he certainly appreciated the trust that these others had in him. He explained,

> The trust needs to be back-stopped by the support that PSU staff and students give me, which, if there are things I need help with or there are things that are challenging to me, I can always rely on other staff and student organizers, the youth leadership team, to really support me in whatever it is that is challenging. So I'd say that those two things are the reason why I've been able to do the job that I've done so far.

This adult staff member recognized the support of youth leaders as instrumental to his own effectiveness as a leader in PSU.

However, by far the most common examples of support that we witnessed were between student members. One instance, captured in an observation of a summer media training, is particularly useful in illustrating how youth leadership is expressed across the bins in the bottom row of our framework (Figure 4.1). This interaction happened between two students, Mike and Terrance. Mike was a longtime PSU member who had been heavily involved in media production during his years as a youth organizer. He had just graduated from high school and was readying himself to attend college in the fall. However, before leaving Philadelphia he felt it was important to help facilitate (along with one adult staff member) the annual media training to assist less experienced members become the new producers and hosts of On Blast!, PSU's youth-produced radio program. Terrance was a newer member who had only recently become heavily involved in PSU. He struggled academically and had been working hard to avoid disciplinary infractions at school. As part of their several weeks'–long training, the incoming radio team was tasked with producing their own segments on key issues having to do with the PSU-led Campaign for Nonviolent Schools (CNS), all of which would be aired near the end of the summer.

As part of his segment, Terrance needed to interview an administrator at his high school. He struggled with how to contact the person, what to say over the phone, and how to leave a professional voicemail message. However, he was not left to flounder; rather, Mike stepped in to coach him through the whole process. Mike talked with Terrance before the call, helping him think of the words to use. He stood next to Terrance through several failed attempts at leaving an appropriate message and helped Terrance gather the courage to call back after each one. Terrance asked Mike questions, and Mike became a guide, offering him both practical knowledge about how to talk with a school administrator and the encouragement he needed to get over his fear of reaching out to a person with significant institutional power. In return, Terrance overcame his fears and put in the intellectual and emotional effort to contribute his segment to the CNS campaign. In doing so, he was also tacitly committing to being a long-term member of the PSU radio team. These commitments speak to deep involvement in the sense that both Mike and Terrance were taking on meaningful long-term responsibility within PSU.

What is particularly interesting about this story is the way it illustrates Mike's and Terrance's roles in shaping the organization as both of them solidified and performed their commitment to the work of PSU. In this story, each one was expressing responsibility to each other, to other PSU members, to the work, and to the organization as a whole, which allowed them to further PSU's organizing work and strengthen the organizational culture and vision. How a youth organizing group functions and what it becomes are dependent on its members. Radio production was a site for youth members and the adult staff member to hold the organizational vision. At the same time, the above example of Mike and Terrance demonstrates that this work involved an ongoing creation and re-creation of organizational identity that manifested as youth "stepped up" to produce media that would serve to shape PSU's public image and "stepped back" to support their peers in participating in the work and culture of the organization.

DISCUSSION

Our analysis conceptualizes organizational leadership in terms of how different internal stakeholders participate and negotiate their work toward the three key goals of keeping the organization running, furthering its core work, and shaping its culture and vision. The framework we propose, which we have represented in a matrix that includes responsibilities and organizational dimensions, can help us to pay attention to the complex ways in which youth leadership manifests in established youth activist organizations that are designed to mobilize youth over the short- and long-term, what Braxton (this volume) calls a structure-based organizing model.

By focusing on PSU as one case of youth-led organizing, we present these findings to illustrate how researchers and practitioners might use this framework to better understand how youth leadership is enacted in youth-led organizing groups. In this particular case, we have demonstrated that youth leadership was strongest—that is, PSU members had the deepest and most continuous involvement and the most power relative to adults—in the second and third rows of the model. Youth were instrumental in determining and carrying out organizing campaigns, and they took a central role in shaping PSU's culture and vision. As campaign participants, they expressed clear responsibility to the organizing work, developing and engaging the public around collective action frames, which highlight themes of injustice, identify the perpetrators of injustice, and serve to mobilize groups of people against these individual or institutional targets. And it was in expressing responsibility to one another, to the work, and to the organization as a whole that these young people determined the trajectory and culture of the organization, enacting and shaping the beliefs, values, and underlying assumptions that are so central to the very notion of organizational culture (Schein, 2010). Though members were involved in day-to-day management activities, this was not the focus of their leadership. Using our framework, then, we might claim that PSU youth showed deep, continuous, and powerful leadership along the bottom row of the matrix and in the middle box in the second row, but their involvement was not as deep or continuous in the right-hand box in the top row of the matrix. Viewing youth members' leadership in this way gives us a much more specific, clearer picture of *how* PSU is youth-led (and, truly, a more accurate understanding of PSU as an organization) than if we relied on the term youth-led as the only descriptor available to us to characterize the way PSU members assert agency both within and on behalf of the organization.

This framework contributes to advancing understandings and theorizing about leadership in the field of youth organizing. The literature on youth organizing tends to rely on relatively undefined terminology around organizational leadership. In this field, some scholars draw distinctions between youth-led and youth-run organizations (e.g., Zimmerman, 2007), while others equate youth leadership with organizational management. Gavrielides (2015), for example, defines youth-led organizations as those that are run by youth. In the literature, different definitions of youth-led exist, but, most often, the term is used without precise specification as to its meaning. Our framework attempts to move the field toward greater clarity, specificity, and consensus about the various dimensions and instantiations of youth leadership in a youth-led organization.

The framework we propose in this chapter has practical as well as theoretical significance. We can use this framework to describe organizations in terms of *how* they are youth-led and what role adults play, rather than simply focusing on *whether or not* they are youth-led. Our framework, then, enables us to explore the many types of decisions that are made in organizations, including those pertaining to management and operations, the core organizing work, long-term vision and strategy, and organizational identity and culture.

It encourages consideration of the various ways in which decisions might be made and the many forms of participation available to and enacted by various sets of organizational actors. It also helps us to recognize the many ways in which young people can be considered agentive, as they engage and assume responsibility for one another, the organization, and the work.

Our framework also shows that youth leadership can take many different forms, some of which are sustained and others of which are momentary enactments; some of which entail deep involvement and others of which entail less demanding investments of time, thought, and training; some of which are negotiated with adults, and others of which simply happen. Understanding this variation is important to understanding the full complexity of organizational youth leadership in practice.

CONCLUSION

We began this analysis with a seemingly simple question about whether a useful distinction could be drawn between youth-led and youth-run organizations. After reviewing the literature and data from our case study of PSU, we have come not to an easy answer, but to a better appreciation of the complexity of the ways in which youth leadership manifests and is negotiated. We understand that youth leadership in the day-to-day management and running of an organization can take many forms and can vary along a number of dimensions. Meanwhile, youths' involvement in other domains of activity, notably the core work of the organization and the stewardship of the organization's culture and vision, can have major implications for organizational health, functioning, and broader social impact. Any clear, bright defining line that could be drawn, then, between youth-led and youth-run organizations starts to blur; nonetheless, accounting for youth involvement and leadership in the major strategic decisions of the organization (from hiring to actions) is important because it may determine the degree to which outsider adults take youth organizers seriously instead of dismissing them as puppets whose agenda and messaging are adult-controlled. Problematizing the distinction between youth-led and youth-run also helps us to think critically about how we can maximize opportunities for young people's agentive participation in a range of different kinds of youth organizations by recognizing that negotiations between youth and adults can happen in ways that still privilege and empower young people.

As with any study, the present work is not without limitations. It is important to acknowledge that our proposed framework was developed using data from only one organization. Therefore, we recognize that it may need to be expanded as other organizations are considered. Future research can build on this work by testing, extending, or complicating the propositions of our framework by applying it to different "youth-led" organizations around the world, working on different issue areas, with different constituents, and within different cultural settings. Another interesting line of inquiry for future research would focus on the dynamics of youth-led initiatives that are situated within adult-led institutions, such as a government agency–based youth council or school-based youth organizing chapters, youth-led participatory action research projects, or student voice efforts. What are the differences in how youth leadership manifests in an autonomous youth-led organization and in a youth-led project or initiative embedded in a context that is traditionally controlled by adults? We also need more research that examines how youth leadership unfolds in social movements and in momentum-based organizing models. With different structures and hierarchies in momentum-based organizing, our framework may not adequately capture the shape and quality of youth leadership in this type of activism.

Though questions remain, we contend that, as a starting point, this framework has tremendous explanatory power. This volume contains numerous examples of structure-based organizing work that relies on the leadership of youth activists, and our framework offers a glimpse into the nuanced ways such activists express their leadership, as well as how organizations establish the space and support for youth members to engage as leaders with one another, the organizing work, and the organization as a whole.

NOTE

1. We have assigned pseudonyms to all PSU members and staff mentioned in this chapter. In some cases, we have also changed identifying information in order to protect the privacy of our participants and other affiliated parties.

REFERENCES

Aminzade, R. R., Goldstone, J. A., & Perry, E. J. (2001). Leadership dynamics and the dynamics of contention. In R. R. Aminzade, J. A. Goldstone, D. McAdam, E. J. Perry, W. H. Sewell Jr., S. Tarrow, & C. Tilly (Eds.), *Silence and voice in the study of contentious politics* (pp. 126–154). Cambridge, MA: Cambridge University Press.

Barker, C., Johnson, A., & Lavalette, M. (2001). Leadership matters: An introduction. In C. Barker, A. Johnson, & M. Lavalette (Eds.), *Leadership in social movements* (pp. 1–23). Manchester: Manchester University Press.

Braxton, E., Buford, W., & Marasigan, L. (2013). *National Field Scan*. New York: Funders' Collaborative on Youth Organizing.

Brown, T. J., Dacin, P. A., Pratt, M. G., & Whetten, D. A. (2006). Identity, intended image, construed image, and reputation: An interdisciplinary framework and suggested terminology. *Journal of the Academy of Marketing Science, 34*(2), 99–106. http://dx.doi.org/10.1177/0092070305284969

Campbell, J. L. (2005). Where do we stand? In G. F. Davis, D. McAdam, W. R. Scott, & M. N. Zald (Eds.), *Social movements and organization theory* (pp. 41–68). Cambridge, MA: Cambridge University Press.

Carson, C. (1981). *In struggle: SNCC and the black awakening of the 1960s.* Cambridge, MA: Harvard University Press.

Clay, A. (2012). *The hip hop generation fights back: Youth, activism, and post–civil rights politics.* New York: NYU Press.

Conner, J. (2015). Pawns or power players: The grounds on which adults dismiss or defend youth organizers. *Journal of Youth Studies, 19*(3), 403–420. http://dx.doi.org /10.1080/13676261.2015.1083958

Delgado, M., & Staples, L. (2008). *Youth-led community organizing: Theory and action.* New York: Oxford University Press.

Eichler, M. (1977). Leadership in social movements. *Sociological Inquiry, 47*(2), 99–107. http://dx.doi.org/10.1111/j.1475-682X.1977.tb00783.x

Ganz, M. (2000). Resources and resourcefulness: Strategic capacity in the unionization of California agriculture: 1959–1966. *American Journal of Sociology, 105*(4), 1003–1062. http://dx.doi.org/10.1086/210398

Gavrielides, T. (2015). Moving beyond a "frail" democracy: A youth-led youth studies. In P. Kelly & A. Kamp (Eds.), *A critical youth studies for the 21st century* (pp. 426–443). Leiden: Brill.

Golafshani, N. (2003). Understanding reliability and validity in qualitative research. *The Qualitative Report, 8*(4), 597–607.

Goldstone, J. A. (2001). Toward a fourth generation of revolutionary theory. *Annual Review of Political Science, 4,* 139–187. http://dx.doi.org/10.1146/annurev.polisci .4.1.139

Goodwin, J., Jasper, J. M., & Polletta, F. (2007). Emotional dimensions of social movements. In D. A. Snow, S. A. Soule, & H. Kriesi (Eds.), *The Blackwell companion to social movements* (pp. 413–432). Malden, MA: Blackwell Publishing.

Hammersley, M., & Atkinson, P. (2007). *Ethnography: Principles and practice* (3rd ed.). New York: Routledge.

Kirshner, B. (2008). Guided participation in youth activism: Facilitation, apprenticeship, and joint work. *Journal of the Learning Sciences, 17*(1), 60–101. http://dx.doi .org/10.1080/10508400701793190

Larson, R., & Hansen, D. (2005). The development of strategic thinking: Learning to impact human systems in a youth activism program. *Human Development, 48,* 327–349. http://dx.doi.org/10.1159/000088251

Larson, R., Jarrett, R., Hansen, D., Pierce, N., Sullivan, P., Walker, K., . . . Woods, D. (2004). Organized youth activities as contexts of positive development. In P. A. Linley, S. Joseph, & M. E. P. Seligman (Eds.), *Positive psychology in practice* (pp. 540–560). New York: Wiley.

London, J. K. (2007). Power and pitfalls of youth participation in community-based action research. *Children, Youth and Environments, 17*(2), 406–432.

Mitra, D. (2005). Adults advising youth: Leading while getting out the way. *Educational Administration Quarterly, 41,* 520–553. http://dx.doi.org/10.1177/00131 61X04269620

Morris, A. D., & Staggenborg, S. (2007). Leadership in social movements. In D. A. Snow, S. A. Soule, & H. Kriesi (Eds.), *The Blackwell companion to social movements* (pp. 171–196). Malden, MA: Blackwell Publishing.

O'Donoghue, J. L., & Strobel, K. R. (2007). Directivity and freedom: Adult support of activism among urban youth. *American Behavioral Scientist, 51*(3), 465–485. http://dx.doi.org/10.1177/0002764207306071

Rosen, S. M. (2016). Identity performance and collectivist leadership in the Philadelphia Student Union. *International Journal of Leadership in Education: Theory and Practice, 19*(2), 224–240. http://dx.doi.org/10.1080/13603124.2014.954628

Schein, E. H. (2010). *Organizational culture and leadership* (4th ed.). San Francisco, CA: Jossey-Bass.

Smith, J., & Glidden, B. (2012). Occupy Pittsburgh and the challenges of participatory democracy. *Social Movement Studies, 11*(3–4), 288–294. http://dx.doi.org/10.1080/14742837.2012.704182

Spillane, J. P., Halverson, R., & Diamond, J. B. (2001). Investigating school leadership practice: A distributed perspective. *Educational Researcher, 30*(3), 23–28. http://dx.doi.org/10.3102/0013189X030003023

Zimmerman, K. (2007). Making space, making change: Models for youth-led social organizations. *Children, Youth and Environments, 17*(2), 298–314.

5

Young, Gifted, and Black: Black Lives Matter!

Bernardine Dohrn and William Ayers

In 1964, Nina Simone recorded "To Be Young, Gifted, and Black." The song still resonates today. In 2015, young Black people dramatically reframed the serial killing of Black youth, naming, documenting, exposing, and challenging state violence: the visible and undeniable militarized police occupation of Black communities, the impunity with which police murder Black young (and not so young) people, and the institutionalized White supremacy embodied in the carceral police state. Black Lives Matter! exploded into public consciousness as a radical, national social movement, but it did not fall fully formed from the sky.

In the wake of the assassination of Trayvon Martin in 2012 and his killer's 2013 acquittal, three savvy young Black women, Alicia Garza, Patrice Cullers, and Opal Tometi, experienced in labor, immigrant rights, and social justice organizing, conceived of #BlackLivesMatter as a mobilizing tool (Black Lives Matter, n.d.), and this proved to be one critical root in a gathering storm. Youth from coast to coast had been organizing for years around a range of racial justice issues, demanding work on living wages, immigrant rights, voting rights, adequate schools and educational opportunities, and an end to street harassment, stop-and-frisk, and mass incarceration. This emerging movement had been energized by grounded, community-based leaders/organizers rather than charismatic or hierarchical leaders; it is not leaderless but "leader-full," in the words of Patrice Cullers (Martin, 2015, para. 7). The movement, operating through a Black queer lens and embracing an antiauthoritarian politics and a Black feminist approach to organizing (that is, African American, womanist-powered, and gender/gay/lesbian/trans inclusive), welcomed street theater, arts interventions, demonstrations, die-ins, and light brigades and, at its heart, required community organizing.

This movement-in-the-making, brought to life decisively by determined African American youth, is rising up in neighborhoods and streets across the land, mobilized to reset the justice/equality agenda for this political moment, increasingly networked and deeply engaged in local organizing: Ferguson Action, Black Youth Project 100 (BYP 100), Dream Defenders, Hands Up United, Assata's Daughters, Justice League NYC, Critical Resistance, Radical Brownies, Dignity and Power Now, Malcolm X Grassroots Collective, Crunk Feminist Collective, We Charge Genocide, BlackOUT Collective, Project NIA, Columbia Prison Divest, the Baltimore Algebra Project, and more. By late 2015, there were 23 Black Lives Matter! chapters in the United States, Canada, and Ghana.

Black Lives Matter! youth, accessible and collaborative, seek the widest participation and represent an open expression of the full range of community grievances and common dreams. Sparked by the additional police killings of Michael Brown in Ferguson, Missouri, and then Eric Garner on Staten Island—and the subsequent official findings in late 2014 that no one outside of the victims themselves bore any responsibility for their deaths—the movement blew open a vast public space for organizing, education, activism, and dialogue.

This violent assault on Black youth is nothing new—there is no documented national spike in police violence. In fact, despite widespread criminal law data collection, there has been no U.S. tracking of police shooting deaths. Black deaths at the hands of the state have been tacitly accepted for decades as routine by the mainstream media and most White Americans, but today this practice has been made visible and undeniable: a moment to open our eyes, to insist that Black youth not be denied their childhoods, to listen, to see the connections, and to act up.

Tamir Rice, a 12-year-old out frolicking in a city park, was set upon and immediately shot dead by Cleveland police who described him as "menacing" and "in an adult body" (Schultz, 2015, para. 2); Rekia Boyd, an unarmed 22-year-old Black woman, was shot in the head and killed in 2012 by off-duty Chicago police detective Dante Servin, who was acquitted in April 2015; Michael Brown, 18 years old, was murdered by a policeman who described him as unstoppable, like "Hulk Hogan" (Cave, 2014, para. 1), his body defiled and left to lie in the summer street for hours; Sandra Bland, a 28-year-old Black woman, was stopped for "failing to signal when changing lanes" by Texas trooper Brian Encinia, who ordered her to put out her cigarette, pulled her out of her car, and threatened Bland with a taser: "I will light you up"— Bland was found dead in a Waller County jail cell three days later (Ohlheiser & Phillip, 2015); Eric Garner was confronted for participating in the informal economy by selling "loosies," put into a choke hold and piled on by New York City police officers, and then recorded desperately pleading, "I can't breathe, I can't breathe," until he lost consciousness and died (Murray, Burke, Marcius, & Parascandola, 2014, para. 2); the police murder of unarmed

Samuel DuBose during a traffic stop was caught on camera in Cincinnati, Ohio (Meyer, 2015); Laquan McDonald, a 17-year-old Black youth, was shot 16 times by a cop on the streets of Chicago in October 2014. These murders became the egregious and recognizable emblems of police occupation and official state terror and plunder. The world is being offered a high-level education and some essential clarity on U.S. racism and oppression, the links between racial injustice and economic exploitation, and the correlation of a violent military system abroad and a colonial militarized police practice at home.

After Trayvon Martin's death, a gesture of outrage and solidarity spread across the land, and people of goodwill donned hoodies (Million Hoodies, n.d.). After Michael Brown's murder, justice-seeking people said, "Hands up, don't shoot!" After Eric Garner was choked to death, they chanted, "I can't breathe!" And the cohering, crystallizing sentiment has become a simple phrase with massive implications pointing toward profound and radical changes: Black Lives Matter!

There are no excuses for the White-dominated "public" ignorance about the serial killing of unarmed Black people, especially youth, at the hands of militarized, aggressive, and racially biased police forces; we know many of their names, and we should learn all of them: Trayvon Martin, Amadou Diallo, Timothy Stansbury, Tamir Rice, Rekia Boyd, John Crawford, Alex Nieto, Aura Rosser, Eleanor Bumpurs, Oscar Grant, Walter Scott, Sean Bell, Fred Hampton, Victor Steen, Timothy Russell, Sandra Bland, Mark Clark, Orlando Barlow, Aaron Cambell . . . It does not end. We know, too, that African Americans are twice as likely to be arrested and four times more likely to have force used against them while being arrested than Whites (Kerby, 2012); we know that Black people are much more likely to die at the hands of police than are Whites (Lee, 2014). We know that the criminal justice system is driven by federal policy and that court and jail systems from Ferguson to Chicago and from Baltimore to San Francisco are run on money squeezed from poor people through a system of civil as well as criminal harassment and peonage. We know that state violence is deployed selectively and systematically. We know all these things, and it is past time for large numbers of White people to wake up to reality and act out; silent recognition is complicity. As Nina Simone sang, "Can't you see it? Can't you feel it?" (Simone, 1964).

We also know that when the federal levees failed in New Orleans in 2005, it was not only that the segregated Black areas were hardest hit but also that police repeatedly fired on unarmed Black people and abandoned those confined in jails and those in the stadium fleeing the flooding (Thompson, McCarthy, & Maggi, 2009). We know that the massive shuttering of public schools in Chicago under orders from the mayor were those schools serving Black families and neighborhoods (Younge, 2013). We know that Black babies die at more than twice the rate of White babies in the first months of life (CDC, 2015). We know that there are more African American men in prison, on probation, or parole today than were enslaved in 1850 and that on any given day tens of thousands of men, overwhelmingly Black and Latino, are incarcerated in the torturous condition known as solitary confinement. We know that in the past 20 years, the amount states have spent on prisons has risen six times the rate spent on higher education. And we know that Troy Davis was executed by the state of Georgia in 2011 in spite of overwhelming evidence of his innocence (Innocence Project, 2011). Each of these hard examples is an expression of White supremacy right now, today. And the continuing youth-led movements unfolding from coast to coast are an auspicious and powerful response.

CHARACTERISTICS OF YOUTH MOVEMENTS: YOUTH ACT COLLECTIVELY, TAKE RISKS, AND REJECT ADULT HYPOCRISY

In our lifetimes, young people here and across the globe have risen up to challenge and change the world again and again: from Little Rock to Birmingham, Soweto to Tiananmen, Palestine to Chiapas, Wounded Knee to Tunisia. *To be sure, youth did not remain alone in these struggles, but they were the ones who sparked the uprisings against vicious, repressive power.* In the past decade, we witnessed the Arab Spring, Occupy, and dazzling social movements for LGBTQ rights, urgent climate justice, immigrant justice, trans justice, peace movement, resurgent labor rights, and reproductive rights. It is the youth who reject taken-for-granted injustices, and in this moment it is young people who are providing the insight and inspiration as catalysts, activists, and organizers.

With their radical impulse to revolt, a spirit of hopefulness and possibility, and their laser-like insights into the hypocrisies of the adult world, youth are propelled to break the rules, resist collectively, and reimagine another world. They look at the status quo as unnatural and immoral—a state of emergency for the downtrodden, the marginalized, the exploited, and the oppressed. Inspired by the courage and determination of Ferguson youth, young people across the nation exercised their stubborn agency and walked out of schools, marched on police stations and city halls, sat in, died in, blocked highways and bridges— becoming the fresh, searing force for equality, racial justice, and dignity.

Black youth were not unaware of the risks they were taking by challenging police power and violence. In fact, young people were painfully and brutally aware of the police targeting of Black youth as well as the pervasive institutionalized devaluing of Black lives in the United States.

The moral activism of the Black Lives Matter! movement—angry and loving—not only illustrates the brilliance and clarity of young people who were also catalysts for protest by high school and college students, adults and elders, communities and labor—an example of class solidarity with more privileged college students, where racial profiling remains routine—but also flies in the face of popular currency that children and youth are passive and disengaged, less competent, less thoughtful, less wise, and more dangerous than adults. The continuing reality of young people as social actors stands in opposition to official policies of silencing students, suppressing, searching, drug testing, expelling, and punishing our youth, depriving them of an education, and denying their creativity and their right to be heard.

If we look carefully, we can see that young Black activists are showing us once again what it means to step into history as subjects, not objects, as central actors willing to pursue their own interests; as they search for root causes and develop a broader analysis, they expose patterns and institutional expressions, not a few miscarriages of justice in a normally fair system, nor a couple of bad apples in an otherwise healthy barrel, nor a bit of bigotry in a "postracial" America. State-sanctioned police violence is one pillar of White supremacy, an evil that transforms over time and in changing conditions but maintains a singular function that lies at the heart of our history—the violently enforced superexploitation of an intentionally stigmatized group of people. These activists are challenging a system not attuned to their needs, or the needs of their communities, as they devise methods and means to upend it.

CONTEXT AND MEANING

After 250 years of legal slavery, 90 years of legally enforced Jim Crow, 60 years of "separate but equal," 35 years of official state-sanctioned redlining, 45 years of federal policy to militarize the police, and 30 years of mass incarceration, Black people are still deemed a criminal class by the predominantly White ruling class, and Black lives are still seen as expendable. It is worth harvesting our history: Harriet Tubman was a criminal, and so were Nat Turner and Denmark Vesey, Rosa Parks and Martin Luther King Jr., Malcolm X and Marcus Garvey, Angela Davis, Bayard Rustin, and James Forman.

Frederick Douglass opened a talk to abolitionists by noting that he was appearing before them with a stolen body—his own. He famously gave an angry and stirring speech in 1852 to the Anti Slavery Sewing Society in Rochester, New York, called "What to the Slave Is Your 4th of July?" In 2015, one passage rings with particular urgency:

> Whether we turn to the declarations of the past, or to the professions of the present, the conduct of the nation seems equally hideous and revolting. America is false to the past, false to the present, and solemnly binds herself to be false to the future. (Douglass, 1852, para. 5)

Recognizing the full humanity of Black people once meant urgently fighting to end the North Atlantic slave trade, and every White person who was conscious and humane joined that fight. The battle to abolish slavery altogether drew the next generation of freedom fighters, and it bears noting that the heart of the abolitionist movement was the insurgent acts (self-liberation, or running away; arson, vandalism, and violence; uprisings large and small) of the enslaved people themselves—and that the resistance was led by the young; overwhelmingly fugitives from slavery were between 13 and 29 years old (Franklin & Schweninger, 1999). Now we are all certain we would have been abolitionists, of course, but we are living here and now, not there and then. The long and noble struggle against American apartheid achieved its greatest victories decades ago, and again, it's easy enough to celebrate the civil rights movement and to declare proudly which side you're on in that great upheaval. But that settles nothing for now. These milestones and partial victories did not defeat the system of White supremacy and colonial exploitation. That work lies ahead. What is to be done?

Today's freedom movement is gathering energy and insight, focus, and direction from the streets, from the wisdom of youth, and from the experiences of community people right now. It is a fight against police violence and the colonial-like occupation of communities of color replete with surveillance cameras on every corner and military weapons in the hands of even small-town police. It is a fight against the so-called war on drugs, aggressive "broken windows" interventions, confrontational stop-and-frisk, racial profiling, and repeated identity checks. It is a fight against the mass incarceration of Black people and the enveloping paradigm of punishment, the unnatural disaster of prisons springing up like weeds in every corner of the American landscape, hostile, resilient, and resistant, a carceral system powered by its own self-justifying internal logic and mechanisms, a vast prison-industrial gulag with a distinct racial caste, an engulfing and transforming system choking folks and communities to death, harming future common possibilities of work, housing, and education, burdening families and entire communities who have loved ones in prison, on probation or parole.

The struggle today is also in part a fight for decent public schools for all people, schools that serve rather than punish, that open rather than close down options and choices, and that are built on a deep embrace of our common humanity and the fullest recognition of the dignity and value of each human being. The 20th-century campaigns against segregation in schools—a struggle aimed at equal access to resources—is (and must be declared) an intentional failure. What we have now is a system and policies that allow the existence of one set of meagerly funded schools for the descendants of formerly enslaved people that are walled off from generously funded schools available to the children of moderately wealthy White people, a curriculum for relatively privileged Whites that allows initiative and invention, and a curriculum of control and testing that force-feeds children of color a steady diet of obedience and passivity.

The Fifteenth Amendment to the U.S. Constitution, ratified in 1870 at the height of radical Black Reconstruction, stated, "The right of citizens of the United States to vote shall not be denied or abridged by the United States or by any State on account of race, color, or previous condition of servitude" (U.S. Const., Amend. XV). This was a powerful victory brought about by decades of slave rebellions; abolitionist actions; the self-activity, resistance, general strike, and flight of enslaved people; and finally a great Civil War, or the War of Liberation, a reminder—and we need to be reminded in good times as well as bad—of another provocative and incendiary statement from the incomparable Frederick Douglass (1857): "Power concedes nothing without a demand; it never has and it never will" (para. 43).

By the end of the Civil War and Reconstruction, the economic, military, and legal powers of White supremacy were institutionalized by a range of harsh economic policies, voting exclusion, and restrictive new criminal laws, status offenses (loitering, jaywalking, curfews), and legal punishments, enforced by a mass campaign of terror against recently liberated Black people. The rising political power of the Ku Klux Klan, the sheriffs and the courts, lynchings, death sentences, and the seizure of Black-owned land were the components of official terror. White supremacy reasserted itself with a vengeance.

When it comes to today's agenda of voter suppression of communities of color, the poor, recent immigrant populations and young people, the Prison Nation, all-out protection for Wall Street predators, police impunity, and cuts in government services, the agenda of the powerful remains consistent: White power and the power of the corporate elite continually reassert themselves.

White supremacy has been intertwined with the capitalist system of predation and profit, and bigotry flows directly from that system as both explanation and justification. The system spawns prejudice, not the other way around—bigotry is not the cause of institutional racism but its result. Slavery built the country, and theories of inferiority and superiority justified that massive exploitation, a brutal and unprecedented crime against humanity. The source of Jim Crow segregation for decades and racial inequality today is not mean ideas but harsh reality: Black folks are structurally cast down and pushed out in order that the powerful can exploit and plunder them. It has been a triumph of capitalism to offer a range of privileges to White people that encourage poor and working White people to identify more with the most powerful than with poor and ordinary working Black people.

Americans typically use the word racism to mean two quite different things: on the one hand, racial prejudice or backward ideas and, on the other hand, institutional enforcement of systemic racial hierarchies. So media commentators happily label Donald Sterling and Cliven Bundy and Donald Trump as racists because of their ignorant bigotry and explicitly racist remarks, and anyone who is a bit more careful in speech and personal behavior is magically off the hook, but this is a conceptual mistake. The Wall Street moguls who engineered the vast plundering of Black wealth in the 2008 collapse practice a form of White supremacy that Cliven Bundy could not even dream of. Donald Sterling's vast real estate dealings were more far-reaching and harmful to African Americans than his ignorant comments.

While activism in the Black Lives Matter! movement is reaching new heights, the truths of colonial state repression are not new. The power of the state has always been in the business of violence: inventing and stockpiling weapons, training thousands to wield them, invading, conquering, occupying—violence is as American as cherry pie, deep in the DNA of a nation founded on theft, the genocidal conquest of indigenous peoples, and the enslavement of Africans. For First Nations people, the genocidal and colonizing nature of U.S. expansion and terror included its own distinctive character (see Dunbar-Ortiz, 2014), and here, too, the unspoken acceptance of White privilege—this (patently false) sense of superiority, this agreement to take on cultivated fear, this silence in the face of violent subjugation of others—is the shame and the disgraceful bargain that formed the nation.

The young organizers of the Student Nonviolent Coordinating Committee (SNCC) asserted 50 years ago that their freedom would not wait until the ideas in a White man's head change; they said that they needed power over their own lives so this White man, whatever his mentality, could not harm them. We can ponder whether the killings of Black people by armed enforcers are symptoms of a criminal justice system not working or whether they are evidence that the system is working exactly as intended. An edifice of laws has inscribed the supremacy of private property, the power of the 1%, the privileges of White people, and the regime of repression and control for subject peoples. There is a false equivalency that suggests that a police officer shot by someone mentally deranged or someone committing a crime is the same as an armed agent of the state killing innocent Black and Brown people with impunity. When we speak of state violence, we are not trying to get these agents to unlearn racism. Policing power in the hands of the community—community safety through community control—would spell the end of police as a colonizing force.

STATE DENIAL OF THE RIGHTS OF YOUNG PEOPLE AND THE CRIMINALIZATION OF BLACK YOUTH

Think of young people's loss of rights in just the past three decades. Youth have had their freedom of speech suppressed through laws, regulations, and

U.S. Supreme Court decisions. As students, young people have their speech, clothing, and banners censored and suppressed. School newspapers, email, texting communications, and graduation speeches are regulated, criminalized, and suppressed. Books are banned. There is relentless persecution and violence against queer and trans youth. High school locker searches and mandatory drug testing regimes are sanctioned without reasonable suspicion or due process. Schools are the frequent site of police interrogation of young people, with the participation of school officials and personnel. In each of these domains, it is thoroughly documented that Black youth and youth of color face the harshest consequences.

The right to an education has been massively eroded by unjust funding practices, privatization schemes, and the use of zero tolerance policies. Enormous rule books and elaborate codes of conduct were created to sanction school punishments, police presence in schools, school-based arrests, and suspension and expulsion practices. This transformation of the school landscape into a place of surveillance and fear, identification and searches, policing and cameras began and accelerated in the mid-1990s with the racist campaign against so-called youth "super-predators." Notable White academics who initiated that sensationalist campaign against Black youth, sparked by the now-discredited Central Park jogger case (where five young Black and Latino youth were called a "wolf pack" and "super-predators," tried and convicted of the rape and attempted murder of a White Wall Street broker who was running in Central Park, in a sensationalized and explicitly racialized case—but where decades later the five were exonerated when the actual attacker was identified) (Burns, Burns, & McMahon, 2012), were successful in creating a climate of fear and in transforming existing juvenile justice laws into harsher crime legislation, in effect "adultifying" punishment for youthful transgressions. Add the invention of police gang databases, gang "terrorism" laws, and gang and gun "enhancement" sentencing, the prosecution of children as sexual "predators," and their inclusion in mandatory sex registry statutes in every state, and a picture of the pervasive criminalization of youth of color becomes clear.

This severe and rapid criminalization of "normal" adolescent behavior is stunning. And just like the rest of U.S. crime and justice practice, the above rules, laws, policies, and practices against youth both in school and on the streets are highly racialized: in every category of accelerated harshness toward youth, each regulation, rule, and law is enforced disproportionately against young Blacks. This is true from police stopping, frisking, and questioning Black youth to arrest, from filing of delinquency petitions or criminal charges to prosecuting, from detention to incarceration; from sentencing to confinement, probation, parole, and violation. Fully 75% of youth who are locked up are confined for nonviolent offenses. Racial and ethnic disparities are unconscionable, but the naked racial disproportion of who is arrested, beaten, and killed characterizes the entire youth justice system.[1]

Children and youth, in fact, are whole persons with full human and constitutional rights and with energy, capacity, and willful agency. They are inevitably an active part of their time and place, their culture and community, their race, class, and ethnicity, and their extended families. Simultaneously, they may also be more vulnerable, more easily manipulated and used by adults, such that they must be, to the extent possible, protected, sheltered, and insulated from serious harm, both from their own impulses and from adults who might prey upon them or use youth for their own purposes. This is why human rights activists, for example, advocate for children to be protected from the harshest consequences of war, from hazardous labor, and from family violence.

Of course, young people are not yet fully adults; but what kind of a person is a child? In considering children as social actors, this contradiction is worthy of continuing deliberation and nuance. How can society heed this paradox—rights versus protections—and tilt toward children as bearers of rights while taking the responsibility for providing youth with equal access, due process, constitutional rights, economic rights, and human rights? Are youth not right to see the adult world as compromised, duplicitous, and—worst of all—indifferent to the state violence, dangerous neighborhoods, and suffering all around them?

Children were acknowledged as constitutional persons almost 50 years ago in the landmark U.S. Supreme Court case of *In re Gault* (1967). Yet with the subsequent repressive waves to restrict their active whole personhoods, as described above, U.S. courts and legislators have shrunk the constitutional rights of children by constricting or eliminating their rights to speech and expression, association, action, education, privacy, health care, due process, equal protection, and liberty. This has been done in the name of either protecting them and "saving" them from themselves or by constructing some children as larger-than-life monsters, wolf packs, and gangs out to rob, rape, and even kill (White) adults. Consequently, specific populations of children are seen as dangerous and capable of destroying civilization.

The diabolical invention of the 1990s youth predator by law enforcement, academics, and the mass media resulted in the harsh criminalization of youth of color—subjecting them to arrests, incarceration, trials in adult criminal courts, and extreme sentencing. The profound echo of young Black men as "super-predators" would arise again with the Ferguson grand jury testimony of White officer Darren Wilson, who saw in Michael Brown someone enormous, looming up and becoming larger even after being stalked and shot by Wilson six times.

"*It* looks like a demon [emphasis added]," Wilson told the grand jury (Cave, 2014).

At its best, contemporary analysis of children and adolescents recognizes the dialectical nature of youth: being and becoming, categorically less culpable than adults, and with enhanced prospects for recovery, rehabilitation, and "attaining a mature understanding of [one's] humanity" (Bouchard, 2011, p. 272). Diminished culpability is not, however, the same as lesser competence or capacity. Culpability is commonly misunderstood, and current professional discourse about adolescent development research, because it is about Black youth and the criminal justice system, frequently and easily collapses into language of lesser adolescent *competence*, ignoring the imperative of youth—and particularly Black youth—to be engaged in moral direct action amid struggles for social justice.

Thus, we see the insufferable know-it-all lecturing to the Black Lives Matter! organizers by pundits and older former activists, to youth in the front line of the struggle, urging them to have explicit leadership, state their goals, and stick to legal and moderate tactics and strategies.

In this light, one may ask why two older White radicals write about Black Lives Matter! youth in this volume. For us, this thrilling movement toward justice and dignity is yet another generous challenge to Whites: to live a practice of challenging White supremacy in all its forms, to take responsibility for organizing Whites against racism—as women, as queers and trans, as workers and migrants, as teachers and nurses, as artists and prisoners, as neighbors and people who are homeless—facing up to and confronting state violence against Black youth. It is our responsibility to speak up and to act out in solidarity, as allies, but also as activists who can repudiate structural and personal White superiority, over and over again.

BLACK LIVES MATTER!: TRANSFORMING THE POSSIBLE

The story of the August 9, 2014, police killing of Michael Brown stayed in the news because the Black young people (and adults) in Ferguson refused to leave the streets. And although the protests there and nationally were the broadest and most sustained radical coalitions in decades, the protesters themselves were largely young, Black, queer, poor, working-class, secular, women, and trans.

The young people of Ferguson did not back down in the face of a highly militarized small-town police force armed with federally funded Kevlar helmets, assault-friendly gas masks, combat gloves and kneepads, woodland marine pattern utility trousers, tactical body-armor vests, some 120 to 180 rounds for each shooter, semiautomatic pistols attached to their thighs, disposable handcuff restraints hanging from their vests, close-quarter-battle receivers for their M4 carbine rifles, Advanced Combat Optical Gunsights, flash-bangs or flash grenades, 37-mm tear-gas canisters, "pepper balls," rubber bullets, wooden and beanbag projectiles, a BEARCAT G3 Mine Resistant Ambush Protected (MRAP) vehicle, a Long Range Acoustic Device (LRAD), and an MD Helicopter 500 Series (Rubin, 2014).

This military-grade weaponry was not about riot control during the long months leading up to the grand jury verdict in the murder of Michael Brown. It was the menacing and terrorizing arsenal of White supremacy and racial oppression. The fierce, unarmed, and highly disciplined young people who dared to stand up against this militarized police violence are responsible for revealing to the public that the war-making hardware, paid for by our tax dollars, is coming home to police forces for use against the Black, Latino, and indigenous communities and to patrol U.S. borders.

Created in the crucible of Black Lives Matter! is a new generation of young African American organizers and activists with experience in strategy development, tactics, decision making under pressure, coalition building, and clarity about long-range radical goals, about their vision. They are savvy and wise, filled with love and caring for one another and for everyone who has suffered the terror of police violence: youth, their families, and loved ones; allied people of color and trans and LGBTQ youth; native and Palestinian people; victims of police violence and whole communities. They have traveled to the Palestinian West Bank and to international law bodies in Geneva. They are inviting White people to come along.

All of this indicates a vibrant transformation of the possible. Police torture and killing of African Americans is visible, no longer background normal, as Black youth resist being branded as criminals at birth. Their resistance is communal, shared, and collective.

Youth, and Black youth will be catalysts for the revolutionary struggles; youth will initiate and hold the space for an intergenerational movement of agricultural and domestic workers, artists, and communities of resistance. And in remaking the world in their own interest and in the interests of the Black poor, they can make a world fit for all people.

Can we hold the moment? Do we have the knowledge that young people are capable of seeing and seizing what most adults cannot imagine? In the uncertainty and complexity of civil strife and disciplined rebellion, shall we see children and young people capable of being agents of their own liberation?

This is the challenge.

ACKNOWLEDGMENTS

Portions of this chapter are adapted from Dohrn, B. (2015, March 4). Youth Resistance Unleashed. *Portside*. Retrieved from http://portside.org /2015-03-18/youth-resistance-unleashed

NOTE

1. See the W. Haywood Burns Institute website for a state-by-state analysis of the racial disproportion of youth justice punishment: www.burnsinstitute.com

REFERENCES

Black Lives Matter. (n.d.). About the Black Lives Matter network. Retrieved from http://blacklivesmatter.com

Bouchard, M. R. (2011). *A user's guide to your mind: How to win in love & get along with each other* (Vol. 2). Bloomington, IN: iUniverse.

Burns, K., Burns, S., & McMahon, D. (Directors). (2012). *The Central Park five* [Motion picture]. USA: Florentine Films and WETA.

Cave, D. (2014, November 25). Officer Darren Wilson's Grand Jury testimony in Ferguson, Mo., shooting. *New York Times*. Retrieved from http://www.nytimes.com

Center for Disease Control and Prevention. (2015). Infant mortality. Retrieved from http://www.cdc.gov

Douglass, F. (1852, July 5). What to the slave is your 4th of July? University of Rochester Frederick Douglass Project. Retrieved from http://rbscp.lib.rochester.edu

Douglass, F. (1857, August 3). West India emancipation. University of Rochester Frederick Douglass Project. Retrieved from http://rbscp.lib.rochester.edu

Dunbar-Ortiz, R. (2014). *An indigenous peoples' history of the United States*. Boston: Beacon Press.

Franklin, J. H., & Schweninger, L. (1999). *Runaway slaves: Rebels on the plantation*. New York: Oxford University Press.

Innocence Project. (2011, September 21). Troy Davis executed in Georgia despite substantial evidence pointing to innocence. Retrieved from http://www.innocenceproject.org

In re Gault, 387 U.S. 1, 20 (S. Ct. 1967).

Kerby, S. (2012, March 13). The top 10 most startling facts about people of color and criminal justice in the United States: A look at the racial disparities inherent in our nation's criminal-justice system. *Center for American Progress*. Retrieved from https://www.americanprogress.org

Lee, J. (2014, September 10). Here's the data that shows cops kill Black people at a higher rate than White people. *Mother Jones*. Retrieved from http://www.motherjones.com

Martin, M. (2015, July 11). The #BlackLivesMatter movement: Marches and tweets for healing. *Michel Martin, Going There. NPR*. Retrieved from http://www.npr.org

Meyer, R. (2015, July 29). Body-camera footage gets an officer indicted for murder. *The Atlantic*. Retrieved from http://www.theatlantic.com

Million Hoodies. (n.d.). About. *Million Hoodies Movement for Justice*. Retrieved from http://millionhoodies.net

Murray, K., Burke, K., Marcius, C. R., & Parascandola, R. (2014, July 18). Staten Island man dies after NYPD cop puts him in chokehold. *New York Daily News*. Updated 2014, December 3. Retrieved from http://www.nydailynews.com

Ohlheiser, A., & Phillip, A. (2015, July 22). "I will light you up!": Texas officer threatened Sandra Bland with taser during traffic stop. *Washington Post*. Retrieved from www.washingtonpost.com

Rubin, L. J. (2014, August 20). A former Marine explains all the weapons of war being used by police in Ferguson. *The Nation*. Retrieved from http://www.thenation.com

Schultz, C. (2015, February 23). A city of two tales: The Justice Department says Cleveland is in crisis; the city's Black mayor and police chief say the opposite. Who's right? *Politico Magazine*. Retrieved from http://www.politico.com

Simone, N. (1964). Mississippi goddam. On *Nina Tre in Concert*. New York: Philips Records.

Thompson, A. C., McCarthy, B., & Maggi, L. (2009, December 12). New Orleans Police Department shootings after Katrina under scrutiny. *Times-Picayune*. Updated 2010, August 5. Retrieved from http://www.nola.com

U.S. Const., amend. XV.

Younge, G. (2013, March 27). Chicago Teachers Union plans mass demonstration against school closings. *The Guardian*. Retrieved from http://www.theguardian.com

6

Strategies for Systemic Change: Youth Community Organizing to Disrupt the School-to-Prison Nexus

Jesica Siham Fernández, Ben Kirshner, and Deana G. Lewis

The school disciplinary landscape across the United States changed significantly through the enactment of policies that criminalize students' behaviors during the 1990s and 2000s. Schools began to involve the police and criminal legal system in school disciplinary issues that used to be handled by school administrators. This shift led youth of Color[1] to increasingly come into contact with the juvenile legal system through school suspensions, expulsions, and referrals to alternative schools—what we characterize as the school-to-prison nexus.

Conceptualizing the school-to-prison pipeline as a nexus, or interlocking system of power over youth, allows us to understand how the criminalization of youth is a systemic problem that demands structural change and interventions across multiple levels of analysis and settings, including local schools, school districts, police departments, and state policies. Although important research has documented the ways that Black and Latino youth are referred to the juvenile legal system through punitive school policies, there has been less attention to the actions youth are taking to critique and dismantle these policies. Youth community organizing (YCO) against the school-to-prison nexus represents an arena of youth activism that deserves further attention and analysis. In this chapter, we define YCO as groups that create spaces for young people to think critically about their everyday social conditions, identify root causes of social problems, and build political power and voice to create policy solutions and change in their communities (Ginwright, Noguera, & Cammarota, 2006; Kirshner, 2015; Watts, Griffith, & Abdul-Adil, 1999).

To illustrate young people's role in YCO to disrupt the school-to-prison nexus, this chapter draws on two campaigns. We focus on the Solutions Not Suspensions (Coleman Advocates/Y-MAC, San Francisco) and the End the School to Jail Track (S2J) (Padres & Jóvenes Unidos, Denver) campaigns in order to highlight differences and similarities across each YCO site. We describe each campaign in relation to the YCO, as well as the leadership of young people in employing three strategies—problematization/ denaturalization, testimony, and community accountability—to win their campaigns. Each campaign was organized to address practices and/or policies associated with the school-to-prison nexus. In Coleman Advocates, Y-MAC mobilized students, educators, community members, and board of education officials in a campaign to replace zero tolerance policies in schools with restorative justice practices, while at Padres & Jóvenes Unidos, the youth membership, Jóvenes Unidos, implemented legislative polices to hold school districts and police departments accountable to behavior prevention strategies to reduce student exposure to the criminal legal system. The strategies that characterize each campaign address different, yet related aspects of a systemic problem: the racialized criminalization of youth in schools.

Through specific examples of intergenerational and youth-centered organizing, we posit these campaigns are models of contemporary youth activism because they constitute part of a broader social movement to address issues of racial and education justice in schools. Our goal is to demonstrate the strategies youth employed to successfully drive grassroots campaigns to disrupt the school-to-prison nexus.

THE SCHOOL-TO-PRISON NEXUS

The school-to-prison nexus is an interlocking system that disciplines, punishes, and forces youth out of schools and into the legal system through a network of institutions, policies, practices, and ideologies (Hartnett, 2011; Kim, Losen, & Hewitt, 2010; Meiners & Winn, 2010; Morris, 2012; Winn & Behizadeh, 2011). These institutions include schools, law enforcement agencies, and social service agencies that seemingly work in collusion to disenfranchise youth of Color. The ideologies that fuel these practices in schools are informed by the criminalization of young people of Color, specifically Black and Latino youth (Fenning & Rose, 2007; Noguera, 2003; Wallace, Goodkind, Wallace, & Bachman, 2008). Although young people are "tracked" into a criminal legal system, the process does not necessarily follow a linear trajectory or pipeline. In effect, several interlocking practices of power and oppression intersect to create a "nexus" that locks youth out of education, economic, health, and social opportunities.

Zero Tolerance Policies

Discourses on the school-to-prison nexus center on a number of punitive disciplinary policies that criminalize young people. Among these are zero tolerance policies, which originated in 1994 when the U.S. Congress passed the Gun-Free Schools Act (GFSA), which required states that received federal money for their schools, or local educational agencies (LEAs), to institute state laws that required LEAs to expel a student for one year if she or he brought a weapon to school[2] (Skiba et al., 2006). As part of the reauthorization of the Elementary and Secondary Education Act (ESEA), the law was meant to keep schools safe for their participants by imposing harsh penalties for those who broke the law and the loss of funding for states and LEAs that did not comply with the law. Although the federal government allowed states to include an exception for the "chief administering officer" of the LEA to review expulsion cases individually, the GFSA was straightforward in its requirements and consequences for not fulfilling those expectations (Office of Safe & Drug Free Schools, 2013).

States instituted yet more strict mandates by passing laws that not only banned firearms, as defined by the federal government, but also other weapons that could cause bodily harm and drugs or other substances (Kim et al., 2010; Skiba & Peterson, 2000). Skiba and Peterson (2000) argue that these rules expanded to student behaviors that might be perceived as potential weapons or threats to the social order of schooling.

Since the early 2000s students, educators, and researchers began to notice a problem with zero tolerance approaches. First, students were sent to the police for offenses that in past eras would have been handled by a principal. The Advancement Project (2005) documented the most egregious of these: a 10-year-old handcuffed and brought to the police station for bringing scissors to school; a 7-year-old brought to the county jail because he hit a classmate, teacher, and principal; a 14-year-old girl arrested and charged with battery for pouring chocolate milk over a classmate's head. Considering these events, the Annie E. Casey Foundation reports that there was a 72% increase in referrals to juvenile detention facilities from 1985 to 1995, despite the fact that less than one-third of the youth in custody had been charged with violent acts (Hoytt, Schiraldi, Smith, & Ziedenberg, 2002).

Referrals to the police were disproportionately levied against students of Color, mostly African American and Latino, who were already at a disadvantage due to the lack of resources available in their low-income city schools and communities (Sughrue, 2003; Wald & Losen, 2003). Among youth with no prior detentions who were charged with the same offenses, African Americans were six times and Latinos three times more likely than white youth to be incarcerated (Hoytt et al., 2002). White youth represented 71% of the youth arrested for crimes nationwide but only 37% of youth committed to juvenile prisons (Shollenberger, 2013).

Zero tolerance policies have profound implications on young people's futures, especially their academic trajectories (Casella, 2003; Gregory, Skiba, & Noguera, 2010; Sughrue, 2003). The proliferation of zero tolerance policies, coupled with the lack of resources in certain communities, makes schools physically and psychologically unsafe for youth (Winn & Behizadeh, 2011). Moreover, referrals to the police from school created a record for students that could track them into future unemployment. Such experiences can have a destructive impact on youths' well-being, education, employment, and future civic participation. In many states, for example, serving time in prison leads to a permanent loss of voting rights. Michelle Alexander (2010), a civil rights attorney, calls this the "new Jim Crow" wherein racialized social categories are replaced with prison-time status, thereby leading to the systematic and legalized disenfranchisement of a whole class of people, who are mostly African American and Latino. Zero tolerance policies are not a constructive solution, nor do these policies support students' academic thriving. In fact, these policies do the opposite, pushing more youth of Color into the criminal legal system (Blake, Butler, Lewis, & Darensbourg, 2011).

School-Based Alternatives to Zero-Tolerance Policies

Restorative practices in schools are one alternative to zero tolerance policies that have gained currency in ending the school-to-prison nexus (Payne & Welch, 2015; Stinchcomb, Bazemore, & Riestenberg, 2006). The goal of restorative practices, or more specifically restorative *justice* practices, is to provide individual youth with support and resources for them to learn to develop the social and emotional skills to cope with and work through their stressors. Positive Behavioral Interventions and Supports (PBIS) are one example of restorative practices. Such programs are aimed at changing the behaviors and emotional response of young people who are undergoing difficult experiences (Bradshaw, Koth, Bevans, Ialongo, & Leaf, 2008). PBIS focus on resolving conflicts through collaboration and dialogue among all involved. Some aspects that characterize restorative justice practices include conflict resolution strategies, such as finding a positive solution to an issue, deescalating conflicts, and avoiding victim blaming and punitive punishments such as suspensions (Mendez & Knopf, 2003; Payne & Welch, 2015; Stinchcomb et al., 2006).

Restorative justice practices provide an alternative solution to the police presence in schools, while encouraging constructive and supportive dialogues between students and teachers. Some restorative justice practices demonstrate successful outcomes (Mendez & Knopf, 2003; Payne & Welch, 2015), however, these programs must be developed and sustained over time to best support youth. Equally important is ensuring that teachers and school staff have access to the skills and resources to engage, communicate, and respond to youths' needs. Implementing practices like these across school districts nationwide requires young people as well as multiple constituencies coming together to create awareness and structural change.

In the next sections, we highlight three strategies youth employed to lead successful YCO campaigns to disrupt the school-to-prison nexus. First, young people in YCO *problematized* and *denaturalized* their social conditions in schools in order to develop a sociopolitical consciousness of the racialized schooling experiences that have systematically disenfranchised youth of Color by pushing them out of schools and into the criminal legal system. Second, through the use of *testimonios* (testimonies), youth organizers created greater awareness of zero tolerance policies in schools and the disproportionate impact these policies have on students of Color, thereby garnering the collective power of youth, community members, and school officials in support of their campaign. Third, youth organizers implemented strategies of *community accountability* to hold school districts and police departments accountable to implementing restorative justice practices in schools. Before discussing these strategies further, we must first describe the context of our study, specifically the two YCOs that served as sites for the campaigns that are the focus of this chapter.

YOUTH COMMUNITY ORGANIZING TO END THE SCHOOL-TO-PRISON NEXUS

Study Background: International Study on Youth Organizing

The two campaigns we discuss in this chapter were led by organizations that took part in a larger study that investigated seven youth community organizations in four different countries: Northern Ireland (1 site), the Republic of Ireland (1 site), South Africa (1 site), and the United States (4 sites).[3] Data collection across all sites began in 2012 and continued until 2015. The first and third authors were local ethnographers in San Francisco and Chicago, respectively, for three years. Over this time period, local ethnographers wrote field notes, conducted semistructured interviews with youth and YCO staff, administered surveys, and collected digital artifacts, videos, documents, and photographs. Periodically, local ethnographers completed analytic memos, higher inference observations, site profiles, and detailed descriptions of the organizational structure of their sites. For the purposes of this chapter, the case study narratives of the sites relied on an examination of the field notes, interviews, and artifacts.

In the United States, all sites worked directly with youth on issues that were impacting their education experiences. Although the issues varied from place to place, most youth across these YCOs prioritized issues related to education justice and affiliated with the Alliance for Educational Justice (AEJ), a nationwide coalition of intergenerational youth organizing for educational justice. The two organizations we focus on in this chapter developed campaigns to end the school-to-prison pipeline.

Youth Community Organizations (YCO)

Coleman Advocates for Children & Youth (San Francisco, California).   As a multiracial, member-led community organization in the heart of San Francisco, Coleman Advocates for Children & Youth has been in existence since 1975. Over its institutional career, Coleman has followed a grassroots community organizing approach toward social change, advocacy, and leadership development. Coleman has gained national recognition for its efforts to bring justice and equity to youth, families, and communities in the city by asserting that the people most affected by a problem must be the ones who determine and fight for the solutions. Through this approach, Coleman has won many victories for San Francisco's communities. It has built strong coalitions among community members, activists, advocacy groups, and local power holders and boasts a track record of successful campaigns focused on economic and education justice.

The unique organizational structure of Coleman allows for its constituents to organize separate, yet interconnected campaigns. Coleman's organizing model consists of adults and youth planning and leading separate campaigns yet working collectively and intergenerationally on issues that concern the wider community. Work is led by three distinct groups: Parents Making a Change (P-MAC), Youth Making a Change (Y-MAC), and Students Making a Change (S-MAC). Y-MAC tends to orient strongly toward high school youth and ensuring that young people in San Francisco can access equal opportunities in K–12 education, higher education, employment, and quality of life. S-MAC focuses on the political education of college students in order to mobilize them to make demands for education equity and changes at the college level.

Within Coleman, Y-MAC led the Solutions Not Suspensions (SNS) campaign, which focused on "ending the school-to-prison nexus by implementing Restorative Justice Practices in schools, along with Positive Behavioral Interventions and Supports (PBIS) in San Francisco's public schools" (Coleman Advocates, 2013). The campaign was primarily led by Y-MAC with the support of the wider Coleman Advocates community. Data from California echo national data about the school-to-prison nexus. For example, during the time period of this study, African American students represented less than 10% of the student body in San Francisco schools but made up more than 50% of the suspension rate (Coleman Advocates, 2013). Under the subjective category of "willful defiance," students could be suspended for minor issues, such as forgetting their textbook, leaving their hat on during class, or engaging in nonconforming classroom behaviors, like failing to raise their hands before speaking. Willful defiance suspensions made up nearly 42% of all suspensions in California and 37% of all San Francisco Unified School District (SFUSD) suspensions.

Padres & Jóvenes Unidos (PJU) (Denver, Colorado). Located in Denver, Colorado, Padres & Jóvenes Unidos is a multigenerational, multiracial, member-led organization that is committed to organizing efforts on racial justice, immigrant rights, quality health care, civic engagement, and educational excellence for all people. Founded in 1992 by a group of parents who organized to remove a principal at a local Denver school because he had punished elementary-age students for speaking Spanish by forcing them to eat their lunches on the cafeteria floor, PJU has been active in organizing movements for social and racial justice. The strong presence of young people, and their desire to have their voice and needs heard within PJU, led to the development of a subgroup called Jóvenes Unidos. Since 2000, Jóvenes Unidos has developed youth-centered campaigns that focus on various issues disproportionally affecting young people in Denver's public school (DPS) system. Among the issues Padres & Jóvenes Unidos advocate for are immigrant student rights and ending the school-to-jail track.

When we began our ethnographic work, the End the School to Jail Track (S2J) campaign had been in operation for more than five years and was beginning to see victories. Yet, the youth membership, Jóvenes Unidos, recognized that they needed to implement a significant piece of legislation called the Smart School Discipline Law (SSDL) (House Bill 1345, Senate Bill 46).[4] This state-level law required schools to improve their student behavior prevention strategies to reduce student exposure to the criminal legal system. The legislation constituted part of the broader S2J campaign that sought to end the disproportionate rate of suspension in DPS.

According to an accountability report released by PJU for the 2013–2014 academic year, Black students were six times more likely than white students to be suspended from schools. Students of Color, especially African American, Latino, and Native American students, were more likely to be suspended, expelled, and referred to law enforcement compared to white students. Although all school districts are required to improve and increase their data collection methods to account for various forms of disciplinary actions and the racial composition of students who were disproportionately being affected, Jóvenes Unidos recognized that in addition to holding schools accountable, police departments also had to be held accountable. Over the course of the S2J campaign, a Memorandum of Understanding between DPS and the Denver Police Department was implemented to further ensure that students would not be disciplined and criminalized for behaviors that school administrators could resolve.

STRATEGIES IN YCO CAMPAIGNS TO END THE SCHOOL-TO-PRISON NEXUS

Problematizing and Denaturalizing Schooling Experiences

Two interconnected practices we identified in our study of YCO campaigns to end the school-to-prison nexus included what Freire (1970) terms problematizing and denaturalizing the social world. Problematizing is a strategy employed to critically analyze one's social condition and role in the society. This is then complemented by a process of denaturalizing, which involves deconstructing oppressive social circumstances by recognizing that social problems are embedded within institutional structures that have been rendered normal, or "the ways things are," but can actually be changed.

One activity that demonstrates how Y-MAC (Coleman Advocates) youth engaged in a practice of problematizing and denaturalizing their schooling experiences included an activity in which young people were asked to visually demonstrate with drawn symbols and images what "institutional oppression" means to them. In these field notes, we documented the conversations that unfolded as youth shared with one another what they had drawn to represent institutional oppression:

[Jalissa][5] (Filipina American, Y-MAC organizer) and [Tamara] (Samoan American, Y-MAC organizer) discussed the three different types of "oppression: institutional, internalized, and interpersonal." [Tamara] stated, "Institutional oppression is the power of one or some institutions taking over another institution." [Jalissa] agreed and mentioned school as an example. [Gloria] (African American, Y-MAC organizer) added that school districts run the schools, and the state and government run the school district. [Khalil] (African American, adult staff) agreed and stated that the system worked in such a way that "one would not [be] able to know or determine who is responsible because the system is set up to work together to oppress or make people do something." [Khalil], (African American, adult staff) shared that one time he and his friends were hanging out, and the security guard came up to them and told them "we were rolling too deep." When he said this, [Roxanna] (African & Filipina American, Y-MAC organizer) spoke out loud that a similar experience happened to her and her friends the other day. [Khalil] acknowledged [Roxanna's] comment and added that the setting was meant to "put surveillance on people that look like they're up to no good." He continued by saying that, "the system is set up to make you feel that you've done something bad when you haven't; it criminalizes you without a crime." (6/6/2013)

As demonstrated in these field notes, Y-MAC youth—Jalissa, Tamara, Gloria, and Roxanna—and an adult ally and Coleman staff member, Khalil, engaged in a problematizing and denaturalizing process. Two Y-MAC leaders, Jalissa and Tamara, began by posing three different forms of oppression, which were further discussed and contextualized through examples offered by Gloria, Khalil, and Roxanna. The concept-defining process allowed youth to share and discuss among themselves how they understood and experienced institutionalized oppression. Jalissa mentioned schools as an example, and Gloria echoed her remarks by adding that schools are part of a broader structure that links them to the school district, the state, and the government. Khalil offered an example of being "policed" by security guards, which thus served to validate Roxanna's experience and the subsequent remarks made by Tamara. By critically reflecting and discussing institutionalized oppression, Y-MAC youth were able to see their experiences in school as stemming from systems of oppression.

Conversations such as this served as powerful discursive tools to denaturalize youths' lived experiences that were constructed as normal and unchangeable. Similar to Y-MAC, Jóvenes Unidos youth engaged in problematizing and denaturalizing practices. Jóvenes Unidos youth often discussed the goals of the S2J campaign in relation to their schooling experiences. Employing a denaturalizing strategy toward zero tolerance policies that disproportionately targeted students of Color, Santiago, a Latino youth organizer, offered the following explanation to the local ethnographer when asked to discuss the goals of the S2J campaign:

The purpose of the [S2J] campaign is for students to be equal in schools. Police officers at our schools—Right now students are getting tickets and ending up in court, even doing jail time for a minor offense that could be solved within school. So a student is getting tickets for jacking in a bathroom stall, or talking back to a teacher. They're [students] getting tickets for that, when back in the day that was just like giving detention, or cleaning the school after school. Right now, it can be taken to another level! So that's why we try to get police officers out of schools. Also to have equality in our schools, since white students, Anglo students, are preferred in schools right now—It's the black or brown students who make a [problem] in school, but if a white student also does it, the white student wouldn't get punished as the brown or black student. (12/1/2012)

Santiago drew a historical comparison ("back in the day") as a way to make the familiar policing practices strange. Santiago explained his experience of racialized practices in his school and argued they were unjust and in need of change. Engaging Santiago and other who were most affected by punitive disciplinary policies in the S2J campaign was a necessary strategy that afforded him an opportunity to make a change. By problematizing and denaturalizing his schooling experience, Santiago was able to participate in the S2J campaign and experience his social conditions being systematically changed and transformed. Like Santiago, other youth who participated in campaigns to end the school-to-prison nexus discussed their schooling experiences in relation to structural problems in order to build collective power to support their movement.

In most cases, the problematizing and denaturalizing strategies, which often began with a question that served as a trigger to elicit a reaction, led youth to reflect and participate in critical dialogues with one another about their schooling experiences (Freire, 1970). These critical dialogues were a crucial strategy and starting point for engaging young people in YCO. In effect, youth participated in a discourse that framed their experiences not as isolated events or personal failings, but as collective experiences of racialized punishment and oppression in schools. The sharing of each other's experiences via critical dialogues within internal YCO meetings was just a starting point for efforts to build collective power in public settings.

Building Collective Power Through Testimony

Words in the form of stories, or *testimonios*[6] (testimonies), have great power to effect change (Cammarota & Ginwright, 2007; Delgado Bernal, Burciaga, & Flores Carmona, 2012). In our study, we observed the ways that testimonies afforded youth an opportunity to voice their lived experiences and critiques of the failing education system, while simultaneously allowing them to build collective power and awareness of the issues they were facing in schools.

Y-MAC, for example, with support from Coleman Advocates, organized a community-wide event that served as a catalyst to generate awareness about the disproportionate suspension rates in San Francisco's schools and the impact of zero tolerance policies on students, specifically Black and Latino youth. The event brought together young people, students, educators, activists, and community members who were concerned and eager to get involved in disrupting the school-to-prison nexus.

At the launching event, the goals of the SNS campaign were introduced along with a list of demands made by young people affected by punitive disciplinary schooling practices. Young people took an active role at this first event by sharing their testimonies and highlighting the impact of zero tolerance policies. Itzel, a Y-MAC member, was among the first youth to share her testimony at a SNS campaign event:

[Itzel] (Latina, Y-MAC organizer) came up to the front of the room, and introduced herself as a 10th grader at [Costanoa] (high school). She began to share her testimony of a time when she was suspended for eating another student's cupcakes. She mentioned that the next day she went to school, she was called into the principal's office and told to leave the school because she was suspended. [Itzel] didn't know that she had been suspended because no one had followed a protocol to call her or inform her of the suspension. [Itzel] added that she felt "stupid and embarrassed" as if she didn't "belong at school." [. . .] The room became silent as [Itzel] sobbed, and [Keanu] called out "Deep breath [Itzel]! You got this!" Soon thereafter [Itzel] turned around and continued to talk in a much stronger tone about her anger and frustration. [Itzel] mentioned that she didn't want to go to school because everyone, teachers and students alike, would label her as a "bad student." She added, "School didn't teach me anything; I didn't see the point in going to school." [Itzel] exclaimed, "Suspensions don't teach anything! Suspensions are just about unfair treatment!" She began to unpack this point by talking about the demographics in her high school; how the majority of the students were white or Asian American and she was among the very few Latina students who, on account of her race, was viewed as "a trouble student with no future." After several suspensions [Itzel] remarked that she didn't see the point in school so she stopped going, and began to believe that she really wasn't a good student. [Itzel] concluded by stating: "Schools need to change their policies and treatment of students, otherwise they risk pushing them out of schools and into prisons." (10/29/2013)

Itzel's testimony demonstrates the impact of zero tolerance policies on students' perceptions of themselves and their academic aspirations. Her story shows how such policies create oppressive environments where students begin to internalize deficit and disempowering narratives about themselves, such that they begin to see themselves as "bad students." Through zero tolerance policies, youth like Itzel are given the implicit message that school is not a place for them.

Itzel, like other youth who participated in the SNS campaign, saw her schooling experience in relation to a much broader structural problem: the racialized criminalization of students. Itzel's explicit testimony led her to re-live the moment, such that it evoked feelings of anger and frustration, which made salient her passion to change an education system that had failed her and many students. Seeing her school as an oppressive institution that denied her opportunities in education, she directed her difficult emotions into organ-izing and mobilizing youth to speak about experiences when their rights to an education, and to be treated with dignity and respect, were being violated.

With Itzel's testimony setting the tone and urgency of the SNS campaign, many other actions followed. Among these were disseminating information through community flyers, the Internet, and school clubs, as well as organiz-ing listening sessions, rallies, and meetings with school officials. Community flyers included images of Y-MAC youth with their testimonies on the school-to-prison nexus serving as a powerful strategy to generate greater youth pres-ence and involvement in the SNS campaign. Quotations from students talked about the impact of these policies on their identities and aspirations. As one flyer quoted:

Kicking kids out of school without ever looking at what is really going on with us—that just makes things worse. It's like saying "We don't care about you or whether you succeed in life. You are just a problem we want to get rid of." (First year high school student, Y-MAC organizer)

The voices of young people like Itzel and Roxanna were central in mobiliz-ing constituents, as well as encouraging other youth to speak up, stand in soli-darity, and build their collective power in a movement to reform the disciplinary policies in the SFUSD.

The presence of young people in the SNS campaign demonstrated to school officials and stakeholders that young people, despite being pushed out of schools, were indeed committed to their education: an education rooted in values of equity, democracy, and social justice. Y-MAC members were at the forefront of the campaign, advocating for safe alternatives to zero tolerance policies; however, they were not alone in their organizing. Several other YCOs across the nation were also engaged in similar efforts to disrupt the school-to-prison nexus. Among them was Padres & Jóvenes Unidos' cam-paign to End the School to Jail Track (S2J), a campaign that illustrates the third strategy: community accountability.

Community Accountability to Sustain Systemic Change

Community accountability is a term that describes the practices and pro-cedures in place that hold constituents and stakeholders accountable to the goals, objectives, and needs of the community (Stovall, 2006). For example, even after winning important legislative achievements or new policies, groups need to monitor public agencies for compliance and quality implementation. In this case, the community constituents were students in public schools, and practices involved ongoing report-back accountability meetings where youth organizers shared their concerns and made demands to eliminate the criminalization of youth. We draw from the S2J campaign led by youth organizers at Padres & Jóvenes Unidos to demonstrate community accountability, specifically the procedures they implemented to keep Denver's public schools and the police department "in check" after undergoing a shift from zero tolerance policies to restorative justice practices.

The S2J campaign involved young people playing a significant role as leaders and advocates for reducing disciplinary actions against students of Color. Similar to Y-MAC youth in the SNS campaign, Padres & Jóvenes Unidos worked tirelessly to organize and lead meetings with important school officials who recognized the value of restorative justice practices. To demonstrate the role of youth organizers in implementing community accountability, we offer the following field notes from the early stages of the campaign. At this stage, PJU youth were being told that they could not be part of the negotiation of the intergovernmental agreement (IGA); however, youth organizers insisted on having a meeting with DPS officials to have their voices heard and needs meet:

The meeting began with [Yury's] (Latina, youth organizer) welcome, "I'd like to thank you for having us here. We're going to do introductions and what we're looking forward to in this meeting. My name is [Yury]. I'm looking forward to a mutual agreement." [Elliot] (school official) interrupts, "If you're a student, would you be willing to say what school you're at?" [Yury] responds, "I go to [Seaside Academy]." [Luis] (Latino, adult staff) followed, "Buenas tardes (good afternoon), I'm [Luis], a graduate of [Uptown] (high school), and I'm here to support and come to an agreement just like [Yury]." [Santiago], [Lorena], [Maritza], [Faye], [Yvonne], [Chela], and [Joanna] introduced themselves as student leaders, organizers and supporters of the PJU's efforts to end the school to jail track. [Kathy] and [Jared], staff attorneys with the Advancement Project, introduced themselves. [Jared] mentioned, "We work with grassroots organizations across the country. We're a civil rights racial justice group working to end the prison-school pipeline." School officials then introduced themselves, including a school psychologist and the DPS Executive Director of Student Services. All of them stated their support for ending the racial disproportionality in school punishment. With an emphasis in her voice, Yvonne stated, "We want to acknowledge the good work by DPS for its holistic approach, and for eliminating [school] expulsions. However, we think improvements must be made." [Yury] and [Faye] take turns reading their list of demands. [Yvonne] adds, "Before a student is disciplined, he or she must be notified of restorative justice. The school must assist. We want to highlight the help that the district will give to all students." She then shifts the tone of the conversation by sharing her testimony: "I was a freshman at [Uptown] when they showed us changes to the disciplinary policy. The teachers didn't know what to do with it so each teacher made her own version of it. Not every [student] was treated equally. So what we did was we made both of these policies into this one, which is going to be more effective and treat students equally." [Yvonne] gives examples of how one teacher could think a problem was one level, and a different teacher could think it's a different level of offense. [Santiago] adds, "This is important because it aligns with the state law (SSDL). This policy review will include: student enrollment, average classroom size, bully prevention programs, drop-out rates, conduct violations, and student demographics." [Chela] mentions, "I'm doing the SRO (school resource officer) data. We want to look at the SROs doing investigations, ticket issues, race/ethnicity, and the schools where it happens." (10/25/2012)

Youth organizers from PJU, such as Yvonne, Yury, Santiago, Joanna, and Faye, became adept at "holding their own" in high-stakes encounters with administrators. Equipped with knowledge of disciplinary policies, restorative justice practices, and a plan for collecting data on student disciplinary procedures, youth organizers built alliances with school officials and policymakers. The preparation in which youth organizers engaged, such as delegating and rehearsing roles, familiarizing themselves with the policies, and setting clear goals to help the campaign move forward, was a common practice. This was especially useful once at the meeting, in which a series of conversations unfolded in regard to the demands Jóvenes Unidos was organizing to implement to keep DPS accountable. Community accountability was therefore reflected in Padres & Jóvenes Unidos' commitment to ensuring that young people not only interact directly with power-holders and policymakers, but that they participate effectively and forcefully in keeping DPS and DPD accountable to all students. This meeting, however, was neither the first nor the last, but rather one in a series of subsequent and continuous meetings between PJU, DPS, and DPD.

Ten months after their meeting with DPS, Jóvenes Unidos called for another meeting to discuss the inclusion of youth and community voice in the creation of an IGA or a memorandum of understanding (MOU) between DPS and DPD (8/17/2013). The demands Jóvenes Unidos voiced encompassed several interrelated objectives, such as limiting police presence in schools, implementing restorative justice practices, and creating greater transparency of student disciplinary procedures and records.

The goal was to disrupt the traditional roles of SROs by forcing the DPS and DPD to consider alternative strategies to police presence in schools, especially in regard to student disciplinary procedures. In placing the responsibility of student disciplinary procedures back on school administration, Jóvenes Unidos created a promising IGA to reduce and eliminate zero tolerance policies and police presence in schools. In effect, youth organizers argued their case for why community input in the MOU could reduce education inequalities and racial disparities and keep students out of the criminal justice system. Thus, when the MOU was passed in 2013 by the Denver City Council, the final IGA document contained many of the edits suggested by youth organizers and PJU members. It was a victory for the youth, parents of students, and concerned community members who participated in the process.

Summary

Y-MAC and PJU made three strategies—problematization and denaturalization, testimony, and community accountability—central to their efforts to engage youth in dismantling the school-to-prison nexus. Padres & Jóvenes Unidos' S2J campaign was one of the first in the country to win local and statewide victories, and it paved the way for other YCOs, like Coleman Advocates, to implement similar campaigns. In fact, Jóvenes Unidos youth organizers were part of a contingent that met with the U.S. secretary of education to propose and discuss federal reforms to school discipline policies. Both YCOs have been nationally recognized for leading the way in dismantling the school-to-prison pipeline.

CONCLUSION

The school-to-prison nexus grew out of zero tolerance policies in schools and racialized disciplinary practices associated with the "new Jim Crow" (Alexander, 2010). Although we focused on the local features of campaigns in San Francisco and Denver, we also see evidence that these campaigns were part of a broader national movement to end the school-to-prison nexus.

We mean this in two ways. First, there was some coordination and strategy across Coleman Advocates and Padres & Jóvenes Unidos. The two YCOs were part of the Alliance for Education Justice (AEJ); several youth organizers in Y-MAC and Jóvenes Unidos attended trainings and nationwide gatherings sponsored by AEJ. In the latter part of our field study, these organizations also became involved in the national Dignity in Schools Campaign (DSC) as well

as in a series of regional Action Camps coordinated by the Advancement Project. Through these networks and field-building activities, youth convened
periodically to discuss local campaigns, build coalitions, and share strategies
and resources to help other YCOs lead their own local or regional campaigns.
At the same time, the organizational structure of each group followed a local
grassroots approach to organizing. The privileging of local organizing made it
possible to target the specific issues in each school district; however, the communication across YCOs enabled youth organizers to adopt effective levers for
policy change, such as the implementation of restorative justice practices and
the creation of IGAs between school districts and police departments.

Second, we propose thinking of these campaigns as part of a national
movement that presaged the emergence of the Black Lives Matter (BLM)
grassroots organizing movement to end police violence. Although charting
the relationship between BLM and the YCO campaigns is for another study,
we trace a connection in the substantive practices and human experiences
that animated BLM and the campaigns to end the school-to-prison nexus.
There may also be evidence that some of the key BLM organizers developed
certain strategies and organizing skills through working to end the school-to-
prison pipeline in prior years.

Implications for Contemporary Youth Organizing

In effect, the United States is in the midst of a pivotal turning point on
ending the violence against and criminalization of young people of Color.
Movements like BLM are but one example of the many interrelated social
movements to end the systematic violence against and criminalization of
youth of Color. The campaigns to end the school-to-prison nexus are connected to broader social movements like BLM because such campaigns have
the potential to raise the consciousness of young people of Color and their
communities who will not stand for injustice. Youth activism has created
critical spaces for youth to support one another, engage in social actions, and
grow in their leadership within their schools and communities (Ginwright
et al., 2006; Kirshner, 2015).

Thus, in this chapter we offered a perspective on youth community organizing, specifically the collective power of youth in employing problematizing/
denaturalizing, testimonies, and community accountability strategies. In doing so, we centered the voices and experiences of youth activists who are at
the front lines of an ongoing struggle to not only reform, but also transform
and revolutionize the structure of the education and criminal legal system in
a way that honors, respects, and treats with dignity the lives of all youth. We
offered a small glimpse of the strategies youth organizers employed in the context of successfully driving campaigns to end the school-to-prison nexus.

One chapter cannot do justice to the multitude of YCO practices, strategies, efforts, and voices that went into making these campaigns successful and part of a nationwide movement to end the criminalization of young people. However, this chapter, in conversation with several other accounts of youth activism, aims to shift how we think about systemic change by situating grassroots organizing at the intersections of local campaigns and nationwide movements. Indeed, education and racial justice in schools and in the criminal legal system are possible when youth community organizing and activism transgress the boundaries of education, practice, and policy to create systemic changes that revolutionize the lives of young people.

ACKNOWLEDGMENTS

We thank Dr. Rod Watts and Dr. Rashida Govan for their support and collaboration on the International Study of Youth Organizing. Many thanks to the youth community organizations who participated in this study, as well as thanks to Erik Dutilly for his contributions to earlier versions of this chapter. Funding in support of this study was provided by Atlantic Philanthropies and the California Endowment.

NOTES

1. In aligning our work with feminists scholars like Hurtado (1996) and MacKinnon (1982), we choose to capitalize the word *Color* because it refers to "a heritage, an experience, a cultural and personal identity, the meaning of which becomes specifically stigmatic and/or glorious and/or ordinary under specific social conditions" (MacKinnon, 1982, p. 516). In a U.S. context, Color is therefore understood to refer to people's experiences and social positioning as distinct from whiteness and race-based privileges.

2. There is an exception in the law that allows students to bring a firearm to school if it is "lawfully stored inside a locked vehicle on school property, or if it is for activities approved and authorized by the local educational agency" (Office of Safe & Drug-Free Schools, 2013).

3. Roderick Watts, a professor at the City University of New York, was principal investigator of the study. Ben Kirshner, second author on this paper, was co–principal investigator. For more information about the study please see www.research2action .net

4. More details on the legislation can be accessed via the report "Lessons in Racial Justice Movement Building: Dismantling the School-to-Prison Pipeline in Colorado" (2012) (http://b.3cdn.net/advancement/ad2cf09c7de156e4d2_b9m6i8ubh.pdf), published by Padres & Jóvenes Unidos and the Advancement Project.

5. All names have been changed to pseudonyms to maintain the confidentiality of our respondents; however, to honor the achievements of each YCO and the campaign, we refer to each one by their actual name.

6. *Testimonio* is a practice and a method of conveying experiences and speaking against oppression and injustice. Rooted in Latin American oral cultures, *testimonio* privileges the narrative of personal experience as a source of both knowledge and political power for claiming rights and working toward social change (Delgado Bernal et al., 2012).

REFERENCES

Advancement Project. (2005). *Education on lockdown: The schoolhouse to jailhouse track.* Washington, DC: Advancement Project.

Alexander, M. (2010). *The new Jim Crow: Mass incarceration in the age of colorblindness.* New York, NY: New Press.

Blake, J., Butler, B., Lewis, C., & Darensbourg, A. (2011). Unmasking the inequitable discipline experiences of urban Black girls: Implications for urban educational stakeholders. *Urban Review, 43*(1), 90–106. http://dx.doi.org/10.1007/s11256-009-0148-8

Bradshaw, C. P., Koth, C. W., Bevans, K. B., Ialongo, N., & Leaf, P. J. (2008). The impact of school-wide Positive Behavioral Interventions and Supports (PBIS) on the organizational health of elementary schools. *School Psychology Quarterly, 23*(4), 462–473. http://dx.doi.org/10.1037/a0012883

Cammarota, J., & Ginwright, S. (2007). "Today we march, tomorrow we vote": Youth transforming despair into social justice. *Journal of Educational Foundations, 21*(1/2), 3–8. Retrieved from http://ic.galegroup.com/

Casella, R. (2003). Zero tolerance policy in schools: Rationale, consequences, and alternatives. *Teachers College Record, 105*(5), 872–892. http://dx.doi.org/10.1111/1467-9620.00271

Coleman Advocates. (2013). *Coleman Advocates for children and youth: Solutions not suspensions.* Dignity in Schools. Retrieved from http://www.dignityinschools.org/sites/default/files/SanFranciscoSummaryResolution.pdf

Delgado Bernal, D., Burciaga, R., & Flores Carmona, J. (2012). Chicana/Latina testimonios: Mapping the methodological, pedagogical, and political. *Equity & Excellence in Education, 45*(3), 363–372. http://dx.doi.org/10.1080/10665684.2012.698149

Fenning, P., & Rose, J. (2007). Overrepresentation of African American students in exclusionary discipline: The role of school policy. *Urban Education, 42*(6), 536–559. http://dx.doi.org/10.1177/0042085907305039

Freire, P. (1970). *Pedagogy of the oppressed.* New York, NY: Continuum.

Ginwright, S. A., Noguera, P., & Cammarota, J. (2006). *Beyond resistance!: Youth activism and community change: New democratic possibilities for practice and policy for America's youth.* New York, NY: Routledge.

Gregory, A., Skiba, R. J., & Noguera, P. A. (2010). The achievement gap and the discipline gap: Two sides of the same coin? *Educational Researcher, 39*(1), 59–68. http://dx.doi.org/10.3102/0013189X09357621

Hartnett, S. J. (Ed.). (2011). *Challenging the prison-industrial complex: Activism, arts, and educational alternatives.* Champaign, IL: University of Illinois Press.

Hoytt, E. H., Schiraldi, V., Smith, B. V., & Ziedenberg, J. (2002). *Reducing racial disparities in juvenile detention. Pathways to juvenile detention reform.* The Annie E.

Casey Foundation. Retrieved from http://www.aecf.org/m/resourcedoc/aecf -Pathways8reducingracialdisparities-2001.pdf

Hurtado, A. (1996). *The color of privilege: Three blasphemies on race and feminism.* Ann Arbor, MI: University of Michigan Press.

Kim, C., Losen, D, & Hewitt, D. (2010). *The school-to-prison pipeline structuring legal reform.* New York, NY: New York University.

Kirshner, B. (2015). *Youth activism in an era of education inequality.* New York, NY: NYU Press.

MacKinnon, C. A. (1982). Feminism, Marxism, method, and the state: An agenda for theory. *Signs,* 515–544.

Meiners, E. R., & Winn, M. T. (2010). Resisting the school to prison pipeline: The practice to build abolition democracies. *Race, Ethnicity and Education, 13*(3), 271–276. http://dx.doi.org/10.1080/13613324.2010.500832

Mendez, L. M. R., & Knopf, H. M. (2003). Who gets suspended from school and why: A demographic analysis of schools and disciplinary infractions in a large school district. *Education and Treatment of Children, 26*(1), 30–51. Retrieved from http://eric.ed.gov/?id=EJ678680

Morris, M. (2012). *Race, gender, and the school-to-prison pipeline: Expanding our discussion to include black girls.* Schott Foundation for Public Education. Retrieved from http://schottfoundation.org/resources/race-gender-and-school-prison-pipe line-expanding-our-discussion-include-black-girls.

Noguera, P. (2003). Schools, prisons, and social implications of punishment: Rethinking disciplinary practices. *Theory into Practice, 42*(4), 341–350. http://dx.doi .org/10.1207/s15430421tip4204_12

Office of Safe & Drug Free Schools. (2013). Guidance concerning state and local responsibilities under the Gun-Free Schools Act. U.S. Department of Education. Retrieved from http://www2.ed.gov/programs/dvpformula/gfsaguid03.doc

Payne, A. A., & Welch, K. (2015). Restorative justice in schools: The influence of race on restorative discipline. *Youth & Society, 47*(4), 539–564. http://dx.doi.org /10.1177/0044118X12473125

Shollenberger, T. L. (2013). Racial disparities in school suspension and subsequent outcomes: Evidence from the National Longitudinal Survey of Youth 1997. In D. J. Losen (Ed.), *Closing the school discipline gap: Research for policymakers.* New York, NY: Teachers College Press.

Skiba, R., & Peterson, R. L. (2000). School discipline at a crossroads: From zero tolerance to early response. *Exceptional Children, 66*(3), 335–396. http://dx.doi.org /10.1177/001440290006600305

Skiba, R., Reynolds, C. R., Graham, S., Sheras, P., Conoley, J. C., & Garcia-Vasquez, E. (2006). *Are zero tolerance policies effective in the schools? An evidentiary review and recommendations.* Washington, DC: American Psychological Association.

Stinchcomb, J. B., Bazemore, G., & Riestenberg, N. (2006). Beyond zero tolerance restoring justice in secondary schools. *Youth Violence and Juvenile Justice, 4*(2), 123–147. http://dx.doi.org/10.1177/1541204006286287

Stovall, D. (2006). From hunger strike to high school: Youth development, social justice and school formation. In S. Ginwright, P. Noguera, & J. Cammarota (Eds.),

Beyond resistance: Youth activism and community change (pp. 97–110). New York, NY: Routledge.

Sughrue, J. A. (2003). Zero tolerance for children: Two wrongs do not make a right. *Educational Administration Quarterly, 39*(2), 238–258. http://dx.doi.org/10.1177/00 13161X03251154

Wald, J., & Losen, D. J. (2003). Defining and redirecting a school-to-prison pipeline [Special issue]. *New Directions for Youth Development, 2003*(99), 9–5. http://dx.doi .org/10.1002/yd.51

Wallace Jr., J. M., Goodkind, S., Wallace, C. M., & Bachman, J. G. (2008). Racial, ethnic, and gender differences in school discipline among US high school students: 1991–2005. *Negro Educational Review, 59*(1–2), 47. Retrieved from http:// www.ncbi.nlm.nih.gov

Watts, R. J., Griffith, D. M., & Abdul-Adil, J. (1999). Sociopolitical development as an antidote for oppression—theory and action. *American Journal of Community Psychology, 27*, 255–271. http://dx.doi.org/10.1023/A:1022839818873

Winn, M. T., & Behizadeh, N. (2011). The right to be literate: Literacy, education, and the school-to-prison pipeline. *Review of Research in Education, 35*(1), 147–173. http://dx.doi.org/10.3102/0091732X10387395

7

Youth Environmental Stewardship and Activism for the Environmental Commons

Erin Gallay, John Lupinacci, Carolina S. Sarmiento, Constance A. Flanagan, and Ethan Lowenstein

Environmental issues are arguably the biggest *civic* challenge facing younger generations. Because of the effects of a changing global climate, basic human needs such as water access and availability will be compromised, and many believe that wars will be waged over what will become a scarce and critical resource (Solomon, 2010). It is commonly agreed that environmental issues represent enduring challenges to the way people live their lives. Human populations cannot continue to use resources and produce waste without paying attention to the maximum limits the earth can sustain. Instead, we will have to alter our activities to respect and remain within the biological limits of the earth (Wapner, 1996). Unless we do this, environmental degradation will continue to greatly threaten the quality and even the very existence of life on earth.

Global climate change alone compels that we change how we interact with our environment and our communities, lowering our carbon footprint and changing what we have come to accept as normal consumption behavior. It also forces us to face questions of social justice because people will have to bear unequal burdens from the lasting effects of a changing climate, with some facing displacement, famine, disease, and war. Those populations that have contributed the least in greenhouse gases will likely experience the worst impacts (Samson, Berteaux, McGill, & Humphries, 2011). People of color and low-income communities are the most vulnerable to the predicted negative impacts; power asymmetries based on gender, class, ethnicity, and race will all influence people's capacities to minimize and adjust to those impacts (Adger, Paavola, & Huq, 2006). Given this social justice imperative, and because younger generations will be the ones most affected by environmental degradation, youth activism on environmental issues takes on an increased significance. It will be critical to develop the younger generation's understanding of environmental issues as collective action problems in which they and fellow citizens are stakeholders.

In this chapter we discuss the *environmental commons* as a space for youth activism. We use the term to refer to communities of interdependence—humans with other living things—and to public space where people, including young people, gather and engage in civic affairs. Our particular focus is on the intersection of social and environmental justice action that links human interdependence with other living things. We argue that this important nexus is a space ripe for youth civic engagement in part because an understanding of the commons, and the sense of responsibility and care that accompanies it, compels one to notice and respond to the injustice that exists in one's community.

We start with a definition of the environmental commons and its inherent intersectionality, highlighting the potential to bring a social justice approach to youth-led environmental organizing and action. In order to set the stage for understanding the current context to our argument of the intersectionality of youth environmental commons activism, we then discuss the historical separation of social and environmental issues, critiques of discriminatory practice in the environmental movement in the United States, and the emergence of environmental justice in response. Next, we delve more deeply into the connections between youth organizing and environmental justice and relay four examples that support our argument and illustrate youth environmental activism and organizing around the commons in the United States. These examples emphasize how young activists recognize the intersectional ways they are affected by enclosing the commons, transform public discourse to retain access to public space, mobilize communities through culturally relevant forms, and lay claim to the commons with cross-generational work.

THE ENVIRONMENTAL COMMONS AND ITS POTENTIAL FOR SOCIAL JUSTICE EDUCATION AND ACTION: AN INTERSECTION OF SOCIAL JUSTICE AND LOCAL ENVIRONMENTAL ISSUES

The commons is a concept that connects humans to one another and to a larger world, encompassing ideas of the common good, community, and ecological and cultural responsibility that have implications for how we live (Flanagan & Gallay, 2014; Martusewicz, Edmundson, & Lupinacci, 2015). Originally referring to the way communities managed shared land in medieval Europe (Anderies & Janssen, 2013), the commons came to mean the natural areas and assets—water, earth, and air—and cultural and societal resources, such as arts, information, traditions, and public spaces and institutions, that were shared and could be utilized by all. For example, fisheries and shared grazing land were important commons in the mid-19th century whereas today this may include parks and the Internet.

The intersection of social and environmental justice can be traced to the times in history when these natural areas were enclosed and access was limited. Most famously, this occurred in England, where enclosure of common land had been taking place since the time of the Tudors, but increased dramatically between the mid-18th and 19th centuries (Rosenman, n.d.). Enclosure of these lands was a form of privatization and a major injustice insofar as access to common land was essential to the poor for growing food, grazing animals, collecting firewood, and hunting game. Enclosure meant that access was cut off, effectively ignoring traditional rights to common land and prioritizing private property (Swineheart, 2013). Similarly, enclosure of land, forest, and water resources were colonial policies in India, Asia, Africa, and North and South America that increased during the industrial revolution when the natural resource supply needed for industry was appropriated (Shiva, Jafri, Bedi, & Holla-Bhar, 1997).

Whenever these public resources have been privatized, social issues of elitism, privilege, and discrimination have been coupled with issues of environmental justice. Enclosure of these commons today includes the privatization of water, the patenting and modification of seeds, and the sale of mineral and energy rights in combination with extraction practices that release toxic pollution into the atmospheric and hydrologic systems. The pattern is repeated: what was once held by the many and recognized as a vital and fundamental aspect of one's right to exist is taken over in the interest of a few.

In this chapter we refer to "the commons" as the natural areas and systems that we all share and for which we are all responsible, including the environmental systems and areas on which life depends; the public spaces and settings where we gather and negotiate how we want to live together; and the culture, values, and beliefs that hold a people or a polity together. The commons is an expansive definition of the spaces where we form relationships and group identities and develop feelings of social responsibility for one another. It includes the social and ecological assets that are accessible to all and bind us to one another in a community (Flanagan & Gallay, 2014; Martusewicz et al., 2015). These commons serve to help young people understand the world as interdependent and understand the need for people to engage in what Harry Boyte (2011) has called public work, in order to make the world better.

In using the terms environment and environmental commons, we are not referring to nature or wilderness as an entity apart from people. Instead, the environment is the everyday ecology of local communities where people live interdependently with everything and everyone around them. Identification with and activism on behalf of the environmental commons is relevant to youth in urban, suburban, and rural communities because the quality of their lives is inextricably linked to the local ecology and the health of other living things in that local place. Consequently, environmental commons work raises intersecting issues of justice.

For example, the degradation of the natural world and widening social inequalities are both founded in the capitalist ideal of accumulation (Klein, 2014). The accumulation of wealth exacerbates inequalities and contributes to environmental degradation via such things as resource depletion, pollution, and climate change. A focus on the local environment is tied to race and class because of the inequities in power that underlie policies and practices such as locating environmental hazards in low-income and ethnic minority communities. There is a confluence of economic and environmental injustice, with environmental burdens and poverty going hand in hand. The lower a person's income, the more likely it is that she or he will be exposed to toxins and suffer from diseases caused by environmental factors and the less likely she or he is to have easy access to healthy food or live in a community with safe outdoor spaces (Grist, 2006). In short, racism and classism are key factors in environmental oppression because environmental degradation disproportionately affects low-income and ethnic minority groups.

Youth environmental commons activism addresses the interconnections between issues of justice and the systems of oppression that create them. It focuses questions in terms of everyday life and asks that we look at the places where the environment and access to opportunity intersect.

RACE AND CLASS IN THE ENVIRONMENTAL MOVEMENT: ENVIRONMENTAL DISCRIMINATION AND JUSTICE

Environmental issues have not always been recognized as obviously intersecting with social justice issues. In particular, before the 1960s, leaders of the environmental protection movement in the United States did not pay attention to the commonalities between environmental concerns and other social justice issues. In fact, criticisms leveled at the environmental movement have included its failure to reflect on which groups benefit from its campaigns and whose issues are ignored (Pezzullo & Sandler, 2007).

The environmental movement in the United States began in the late 1800s largely as conservation, in response to unchecked exploitation of natural areas and resources during the 19th century. Conservation was framed as management of natural resources for future human consumption. But even this consumption was limited to a narrow audience. It was the white, primarily male, middle and wealthy classes that profited from new regulations as they pursued the sport of hunting. At the same time, it was the poor who suffered from new prohibitions that restricted their means of hunting and fishing for subsistence. By requiring the purchase of licenses and putting restrictions on where, when, and with what equipment people could hunt and fish, governments protected wildlife for use in sport, cutting off those who depended on it for their livelihood and survival (Taylor & Klingle, 2006). The same power-based policies are evident today in, for example, conflicts between government and indigenous populations, when environmental policies and regulations threaten traditional fishing practices while favoring commercial fisheries.

Prejudice, stereotyping, and discriminatory policies also were part of preservation efforts that lobbied for the preservation of nature for its inherent value (Dunlap & Mertig, 1991). Preserving wilderness as a place separate and away from humans was at the heart of the establishment of the national parks. However, creating these parks apart from humans meant displacing native peoples from their homes and sacred spaces. In the name of preservation, Native Americans were forcibly removed from their lands (Taylor & Klingle, 2006).

Even when environmental preservation was done in order to benefit the public at large and urban poor in particular, public parks and spaces that were meant to function as a commons were enclosed at the behest of the elite class. For example, Central Park in New York was created by reformer Frederick Olmsted to better the lives of all urban residents and to amend class inequalities. Instead, his parks gentrified neighborhoods, pushing the people intended as beneficiaries away from these open spaces through higher property pricing, new discriminatory restrictions, and incidents of harassment (Taylor & Klingle, 2006). Even today, such ostensibly public spaces like parks and natural areas are often enclosed and policed through restrictions on their use, such as those imposed by vagrancy laws. Consequently, they are no longer truly public spaces or commons where people from diverse backgrounds can gather.

Historically, wealth and power have determined who had access to natural spaces and resources and, conversely, who was subjected to pollution and environmental degradation in their communities. Today it is still typically minority communities that bear the brunt of the impact of environmental degradation and pollution. Waste disposal, toxic manufacturing, and other land use practices that compromise human and environmental health are disproportionately located in minority communities (Bullard, 2002). It was these facets of environmental discrimination that led to the development of the environmental justice movement.

By the late 20th century, the environmental movement was still led largely by middle-class white men and came under critique for primarily supporting the interests of this constituency (Pezzullo & Sandler, 2007) and rarely paying attention to issues that transcended lines of race and class. Part of this critique was that certain places, commonly wilderness areas, were protected, while other places, typically more urban areas, were ignored by large environmental organizations that were seen as special interests valuing nature over people. Because they attended to issues such as endangered species but ignored urban pollution, they were critiqued for being detached from the concerns of minority, working-class, and low-income communities.

The environmental justice movement emerged amid these critiques of the racism, classism, and limited agenda of mainstream environmental groups. A field dedicated to justice in the distribution of goods and resources and in decision making about environmental issues (Pezzullo & Sandler, 2007), environmental justice has mobilized people from blue-collar and ethnic minority backgrounds to demand more attention to connections between environmental and human health (Dunlap & Mertig, 1991).

Environmental justice work continues to highlight how destructive environmental practices, such as the locating of industrial toxic disposal sites, occur disproportionately in or near low-income communities and communities of color. By recognizing the intersectional impacts and causes of destructive environmental practices as interrelated with social justice issues, this movement emphasizes that solutions to one issue are inextricably linked to the other issues and their solutions. And this social justice framework emphasizes the fact that the environmental effects of human choices have a disproportionate impact on groups with the least power, especially affecting young women and children. Robert Bullard (2002), the leading scholar on environmental racism in North America, writes that environmental degradation is much more likely to be experienced by peoples who have also been systematically excluded and exploited economically.

A major aspect of this violence borne by communities of color that regularly goes unacknowledged by privileged—often white—communities is the alarming levels of toxicity in soil, air, and water. Much of this toxicity is the result of the disposal of hazardous waste in or near indigenous communities and in neighborhoods populated primarily by poor people of color. As just one example of this environmental racism, in Los Angeles County, hazardous waste, treatment, and storage facilities were found to be disproportionately located in areas where African Americans and Latinos live (Boer, Pastor, Sadd, & Snyder, 1997).

YOUNG ACTIVISTS' INTERPRETATION OF AND MOBILIZATION AROUND THE COMMONS

In this section, we discuss examples of youth activism that illustrate particular aspects of our theory about the environmental commons. Specifically, these examples illustrate how young people are identifying the connections between injustice based on race and class and those in power over decisions about the environmental commons; insisting on their right to assembly in public space and objecting to restrictions on their access to the environmental commons; using community-centered cultural forms to mobilize people around the notion of the commons; and learning how to work cross-generationally to lay claim to the commons.

Increasingly, young people are becoming a voice in the environmental justice movement, often stemming from the fact that they have felt the negative impacts of discriminatory systems that contribute to environmental degradation in their communities. A recent report focusing on youth organizing and environmental justice (Quiroz-Martinez, Wu, & Zimmerman, 2005) highlights the intersectional analysis that is a key feature of both, which attend to issues of race, class, gender, age, and interrelated causes of injustice. The authors point out that young people are organizing around integrated concerns about their communities and environment in a holistic way, in part, due to efforts to build movement sustainability and critiques of older organizing models. For example, the need for community recreation areas may lead to land reclamation and public green space initiatives; solutions to the lack of fresh and healthy food sources in an economically depressed community may include creating urban gardens, advocating for farm projects, and planning grocery initiatives. As Quiroz-Martinez et al. (2005) write:

> In many communities, the connection between the health of the land and the health of the community is essential and deep. While some of the work that youth environmental justice groups are doing looks like environmental stewardship and conservation projects on the surface, its roots are deeply tied to cultural survival and self-determination. (p. 30)

RECOGNIZING THE INTERSECTIONAL EFFECTS OF RESTRICTING THE COMMONS: YOUNG ACTIVISTS ORGANIZING AROUND THE CONNECTIONS OF RACE, CLASS, AND ENVIRONMENTAL OPPRESSION

The connections between environmental justice and systemic racism and classism for families of color can be seen in an example from Detroit, Michigan. In 1986 the city constructed the largest municipal trash incinerator in the world, burning 4,000 tons of garbage every day in a process that converts waste into electricity (Zero Waste Detroit, n.d.). The incinerator ravages the local neighborhoods with toxic pollution linked to high asthma rates and other illnesses. Today, Detroit has higher rates of respiratory illness than the rest of the State of Michigan. Children living near the incinerator are hospitalized three times more often than the state average for asthma, and Detroit's death rates among children with asthma are twice the state's average (Wasilevich, Lyon-Callo, Rafferty, & Dombkowski, 2008).

Young people in Detroit, like those involved in the East Michigan Environmental Action Council's (EMEAC's) Stand Up Speak Out! (SUSO) and Young Educator Alliance (YEA) are actively fighting against social and environmental injustices such as the incinerator. Their work illustrates an awareness of the intersections of class, race, and environmental justice. These youth also understand the interdependence of the health of their community and the political choice of the environmental racism affecting their communities. They are resisting the enclosure of the commons through collective action and power.

SUSO is an outreach and advocacy arm of EMEAC that engages youth and families in Detroit to advocate for environmental justice for Southeast Michigan. SUSO works with urban youth to influence policy changes for a zero-waste Detroit that include shutting down the city's massive incinerator and campaigning for anti-idling (a major cause of lead poisoning) policies for commercial vehicles.

A part of SUSO, the YEA seeks to provide a "pipeline for community activism" by fostering the development of young activists learning "to identify injustices, place them in a historical context, and propose alternatives that involve community input, community organizing, and/or advocacy" (East Michigan Environmental Action Council, 2015, para. 4). Youth working with EMEAC address food security and environmental justice issues in Detroit, building community organizing skills and preparing to restore and reshape their communities in keeping with the wants and needs of neighborhood residents (Smith, 2015). These young people analyze and collectively address environmental issues that are affecting their communities, engendering a sense of community responsibility and efficacy.

Young people in the YEA are learning to lead discussions and facilitate dialogues that raise consciousness and lead to political empowerment (Smith, 2015). Through Feed 1 Teach 1 events, YEA members lead conversations with community participants about an issue Detroit is facing and collectively come up with solutions to address it. During one event, the YEA engaged community members in a dialogue about gentrification. The Cass Corridor area in Detroit, where EMEAC is located, is experiencing gentrification, or as one YEA member put it, "the displacement of native lower and working class communities that takes place when new development in an area results in an increase in daily living expenses, which in turn makes the area unaffordable for the original residents and business owners" (Frye, 2013, para. 2). During this event, the YEA worked with community members to explore solutions that reverse gentrification and advocate for equality (Frye, 2013).

This example showcases what Smith (2015) contends are youth in the YEA exercising "their 'right to the city'" (p. 483). He outlines how these young people are acquiring the skills to become citizen activists while working to create inclusive and equitable neighborhoods that welcome new residents without displacing others. The right to the city was first outlined by Henri Lefebvre (1996) as a demand for "a transformed and renewed right to urban life" (p. 158) and expanded upon by David Harvey (2008):

> The right to the city is far more than the individual liberty to access urban resources: it is a right to change ourselves by changing the city. It is, moreover, a common rather than an individual right since this transformation inevitably depends upon the exercise of a collective power to reshape the processes of urbanization. (p. 23)

In their resistance to gentrification, the young people in the YEA are also resisting enclosure of the commons. Much like Frederick Olmsted's parks were enclosed, so too are cities, as gentrification favors the right to private property and an elite class who can afford that property. Young people in the YEA are fighting against a right to the city that is restricted to the economic and political elite who are shaping these spaces to their benefit. Like David Harvey, they are calling for a democratization of that right to the city, so that common people are not driven from their neighborhoods.

THE RIGHT TO ASSEMBLY: YOUNG ACTIVISTS RESISTING THE ENCLOSURE OF THE COMMONS

In Santa Ana, California, young people are addressing issues of the commons by organizing to shape their environment and the policies that impact their neighborhoods and their everyday inhabitance of the city. In a city that's almost 80% Latino, youth have been central in organizing efforts around issues that disproportionately impact immigrants such as the lack of public space, parks, and affordable housing for low-income families and the criminalization of immigrant communities. From civil disobedience to stopping deportations, youth-led organizations such as Resistencia, Autonomia, Igualidad, lideraZgo (RAIZ) and the Orange County Immigrant Youth United (OCIYU) are challenging the local city council and its commitment to the immigrant community.

In particular, they are challenging the surveillance and restrictions on their right to assemble and use public space that are the result of a 2014 gang injunction. That injunction requires police departments to label youth as criminal gang members based on how they dress, with whom they affiliate, and other behaviors. Behavioral restrictions often include standing in certain areas of the neighborhood, socializing with other youth who are "known gang members," being outside past 10:00 p.m., blocking a passageway, and standing in front of a mural. If family members are on the gang injunction list, they cannot associate with one another. All of these restrictions serve to limit the youths' constitutional right of assembly. Local youth, their families, and organizers are fighting to be kept off the gang injunction list, which limits their actions and documents them as gang members.

In fact, the gang injunction is like a modern-day Enclosure Act,[1] containing the environmental commons as a space for the public to gather by delineating a certain area as a "safety zone" where behavior is subsequently policed and monitored. To fight this policy, youth have organized protests and rallies to call out the injustices, as well as community events such as film screenings that bring together neighbors to present a different face to the area. For example, in collaboration with a local cultural center, more than 100 people came together for a screening of Selma, which elicited a discussion of the injustices people of color continue to face and the unity necessary to fight those injustices. Consistent with the observations of Quiroz-Martinez et al. (2005), these youth organizers are using culture to "reach the hearts of community members" and "inspire dialogue around divisive topics" (p. 36).

In order to influence the direction of development policies in Santa Ana, youth have also taken a central leadership role in the Santa Ana Collaborative for Responsible Development (SACReD), a coalition that includes neighborhood residents, community-based organizations, labor, and business owners. In response to a strong feeling of exclusion from public processes, SACReD and its youth membership passed a Sunshine Ordinance, increasing transparency, accountability, and participation measures in the planning process. In addition, they increased park access for residents through a joint-use plan with the Santa Ana School District, and led the way in research and development of restorative justice programs for Santa Ana youth.

Santa Ana youth coming together around immigration policy, gang injunctions, and responsible development is an example of how youth are responding to local policies that shape the relationships they have with their neighborhood and environment. Through their responses, young people are not only changing policy but also ensuring youth have a serious voice in decision making. In the SACReD example, youth are challenging the practices of governance and changing the planning process to be more inclusive of youth and immigrant working communities. In the case of the immigrant rights organizing efforts, youth are challenging the role of immigration officials and the police department in the governance of their own neighborhoods and struggling to take back some of the power to claim their identities, shaping what it means to be Mexican and immigrant in Santa Ana.

MOBILIZING FOR THE COMMONS: YOUNG ACTIVISTS USING COMMUNITY-CENTERED CULTURE

Aspects of the cultural commons can support stewardship of social justice and environmental sustainability, helping young people develop a critical and ethical awareness, and responsibility for the environmental commons. One example for many urban youth around the globe politically mobilizing as activists is hip-hop. As a political form of art and means of storytelling and teaching rooted in Afro-centric traditions, hip-hop engages youth in: (1) emceeing (rapping), (2) deejaying (DJ mixing), (3) breaking (dancing), (4) writing (graffiti), and (5) sharing knowledge (teaching and learning). While hip-hop is influencing youth movements globally, the intersection of urban youth culture and environmental justice in the United States can be illustrated in the work of the hip-hop youth organization called Grind for the Green (G4G). G4G is in Oakland, California, where residents of neighborhoods such as West Oakland have a life expectancy that is 10 years lower than in the nearby, more affluent Berkeley hills area (Dyson, 2008).

G4G aims to responsibly mobilize youth of color into the environmental movement, a population that traditional approaches to environmental activism has historically left disengaged and underrepresented (Harris, n.d.). Striving to address the shortfall of the environmental justice movement to reach urban youth in culturally relevant ways, G4G works to connect environmental literacy with real-world life experiences, mixing art, activism, social justice, and the environment.

As Quiroz-Martinez et al. (2005) found, innovative cultural work is a key strategy for environmental justice in youth organizing and leadership development. Arts and culture are used to engage young people, build community, and reach out to community members. G4G does this by working through social media networks and grassroots organizing to coordinate and host musical events. It employs music and culture to "empower young people with information and knowledge necessary to make informed decisions and take action in their communities" (Idealist, n.d., para. 1). Youth function as program leaders because G4G has found that young people are best at making connections between their lifestyle choices and the impacts of these choices on the environment (Harris, n.d.).

In this way, G4G is addressing a critically important aspect of understanding the commons. By emphasizing the impacts of lifestyle choices on the environment, the organization develops in the young participants an awareness of the effects of their actions on others, including the natural world. G4G follows five principles for mobilizing a youth activist group: "reconnection to the earth, eco-literacy, leadership development, new media, and cultural relevancy" (Florez & Gokaldas, 2010, p. 22). G4G created and hosted the first ever solar powered hip-hop concert, mobilizing youth, their families, and hip-hop fans and artists with environmental activist groups, organizing the community to take action against environmental racism in the Bay Area (Arnold, 2009). In addition to organizing hip-hop events as a platform for engaging more than 1,500 inner city youth, G4G has employed 25 youth in green jobs staffing the very events that are produced by youth. Efforts to educate and mobilize youth into environmental activism intimately connected with social justice are increasing because of community actions like the concerts organized by G4G and the role such events play in educating the community.

These examples of youth activism on behalf of the environmental commons have showcased youth working to address issues of importance to them, on their own time, as part of community-based organizations. Because public education is actively being privatized and, we would argue, enclosed, it is easier for youth to organize as activists in after-school and out of school programs and efforts. Nonetheless, it is often in schools that young people have some of their earliest experiences of building community, where they are exposed to policies and practices that affect their lives and form the foundations of their political identities, and where they become actors in the polity (Flanagan & Gallay, 2014). Schools are settings where young people can learn their place in the social order but also learn to question it, a prerequisite for activism. In the next example, we highlight an activism model of place-based stewardship education that is rooted in schools and combines learning in class with community-based actions to address social and environmental justice issues affecting the local commons.

INTENTIONAL ACTIVISM IN FORMAL EDUCATION: YOUNG ACTIVISTS' CROSS-GENERATIONAL STRATEGIES IN LAYING CLAIM TO THE ENVIRONMENTAL COMMONS

Place-based education uses the local community and environment as starting points for study as young people solve community issues through experiential hands-on learning. The term *place-based stewardship education* (PBSE) as used here distinguishes efforts focusing on the relationship between humans and the natural environment and action(s) that benefit the local environment. The PBSE efforts of groups like the Southeast Michigan Stewardship (SEMIS) Coalition offer examples of what schools and communities are doing to prepare students for the environmental challenges of the coming decades and to resist the enclosure of the commons. These efforts are exemplified by the students at one of the sites in the SEMIS Coalition, the Detroit Institute of Technology (DIT) at Cody High School, where Detroit youth have been active in shaping their communities and molding their neighborhoods into their vision for Detroit.

The DIT Cody/Rouge neighborhood on the west side of Detroit faces serious social and ecological challenges. Students at DIT, as is common for urban youth in marginalized communities, feel they are often not seen and are accustomed to being ignored (Lowenstein et al., in press). Yet, as several of the students comment, they are committed to being the "voice of the students at our school, and for the community." They are aware that they are activists, working for change in their school community and in the lives of those they love (Lowenstein et al., in press). It is in part their PBSE efforts at DIT that help them to gain this sense of power as agents of change.

Through PBSE, SEMIS helps students engage in work with community partners to identify local environmental issues impacting their communities and take action to address them. One such project saw DIT students working with the Detroit-based Youth Energy Squad, connecting issues of safety and energy savings with broader issues of climate change. The students helped people in the community learn how to interpret their utility bills so that they could save money and energy and weatherized close to 1,000 homes in the neighborhood. Taking their message to a larger audience, the DIT students led workshops at local and statewide events, teaching others to perform energy audits, implement efficiency upgrades, and become more efficient energy users.

These students at DIT are part of a commons-based culture that includes mechanisms for the intergenerational sharing of knowledge and peer teaching and support. In their PBSE efforts, students and teachers work with community-based organizations and other community members outside of school, establishing intergenerational connections and learning together. These close partnerships create a sense of generativity, that is, a commitment to protecting the commons for future generations. In addition, as part of the cultural commons, wisdom and learning are passed within and between generations, shared as part of the set of knowledge, skills, and beliefs that help make up a community. This commons-based culture is perhaps most apparent in the Cody Youth Ambassadors (YAs), DIT students who act as leaders for their peers and community.

Working with a group of community partners, the YAs have established a yearly ritual called Re-Creation Day when hundreds of community members converge on the school to meet student-articulated needs for increased safety, building beautification, and care for the environment. YAs work closely with community partners to organize their efforts and lead the charge in recruiting and engaging community members in creating community gardens, artwork on nearby abandoned buildings, and outdoor learning spaces.

The YAs are also influencing the educational opportunities of their peers by co-creating a PBSE curriculum in which all ninth graders take part. This curriculum focuses on adopting a section of Rouge Park and the Rouge River close to their school. As part of this curriculum, the students have started taking actions that connect the built environment with environmental health, including creating a bio-swale near their school to reduce surface water runoff and lessen pollution reaching the waterway. In addition, the YAs have taken their responsibility as experts on their school and neighborhood beyond education and into the realm of advocacy. They began by presenting at local and state events to spread the word about their work and the needs of their community, then led public advocacy efforts, tackling issues of transportation, inequitable school funding, and crumbling infrastructure and arguing how these compromise students' success.

DIT students share what they have learned with peers and adults in the community, extending their commitment to the environmental commons and inviting fellow community members to join the efforts. This intergenerational sharing of knowledge helps to challenge the exclusionary idea that expertise is limited to those with advanced degrees and in positions of power or that wisdom is passed only from elders to youth. As Quiroz-Martinez et al. (2005) found in youth organizing and environmental justice, experts are not limited to scientists, policymakers, and government officials, but rather include young people and other community members.

When youth are recognized as experts by the public and become conscious of their own expertise on environmental conditions and the politics underlying them, their leadership and commitment help to challenge the conventional wisdom that the health of people and the environment should be left to trained scientists, technicians, and elected officials. When youth are seen and see themselves as experts, they also challenge a "free rider" mentality, that is, that everyday citizens can ignore environmental problems because "more knowledgeable experts" will take care of the issues. With their expertise comes an implied responsibility and an expectation to work toward solutions. This sense of responsibility and of the need for collective action is exemplified in the words of one DIT student: "Don't just go to people with power, go to the citizens. The more citizens, the people are together, the more power we have" (Gallay, 2016).

By intentionally creating spaces in schools for students to become activists, PBSE organizations like the SEMIS Coalition are giving young people the chance to actively participate in democracy. Through these types of PBSE projects, students develop identities as community members who assume responsibilities for the commons that bind them to other members of their communities. They become environmental citizens and agents for social change.

BUILDING A THEORY OF YOUTH ACTIVISM FOR THE ENVIRONMENTAL COMMONS

We have argued that environmental degradation and climate change are the most pressing civic challenges facing younger generations. The cumulative impact of the unjust consumption choices of wealthy and powerful people and nations will be borne by younger generations. Furthermore, those lifestyle choices have exacted and will continue to exact a disproportionate cost on the poor nations and people who neither enjoyed the benefits nor had a voice in the decisions that created the problems.

In facing these challenges youth will have to be skilled at problem solving that recognizes the interrelationship between environmental and social justice and involved in the decision-making process on matters that affect their communities—they have to be organizers and activists in their communities. Youth activism and engagement in stewardship of the commons focuses on the potential of young people to take collective action on an issue of public consequence in their local community. And the model of an environmental commons emphasizes that (1) the resources that sustain healthy lives belong to all people; (2) the public spaces where people assemble are rights of all people; and (3) privatizing those resources and spaces or denying access is unjust.

But youth engagement in organizing for the environmental commons does not happen out of thin air. Instead it happens out of polluted air, that is, in response to an issue that is affecting the youth and their community directly. In light of the disproportionate burden of environmental degradation on the health of poor communities and the marginalization of their voices in public space and, historically, in environmental discourse, we have highlighted four examples of ways youth are interpreting and mobilizing around the commons. As we have argued, these examples illustrate how young activists employ organizing strategies that reflect the intersectional ways they are affected by the enclosure of the commons, alter public discourse to retain access to public space, use culturally relevant forms to mobilize people around the notion of the commons, and use cross-generational strategies to lay claim to the commons.

Our specific examples illustrate how young people are organizing around integrated concerns about their communities and environment. The intersectional analysis motivating and informing the young people's action is a political education for the youth involved both in terms of power dynamics and their capacities to be experts leading their communities. Taken together, the four cases demonstrate how environmental commons organizing helps young people to see the intersection of social justice and environmental issues, honors their cultural claims and voices, and nurtures their expertise and leadership.

The work of the youth in EMEAC's SUSO and YEA illustrates an awareness of the intersections of class, race, and environmental oppression and an understanding of how the health of their community is affected by the political choice to locate an incinerator in their back yard. These activists show

how action for the environmental commons raises basic questions about justice in terms of the access, availability, and use of resources, unequal contributions to environmental degradation, and the burdens of the impact of human
lifestyles. Because issues of the environmental commons consider a social justice framework in the environmental impacts of human choices, they can
focus on the disproportionate effect of these impacts on the most vulnerable
groups with the least power.

As Quiroz-Martinez et al. (2005) note, social and environmental justice go
hand in hand for many communities. As members of the Southwest Network for
Environmental and Economic Justice stated, "They are tightly interrelated . . .
when our communities are confronted with issues of environmental racism, gentrification, etc. it impacts us as families. Our grandparents, parents, uncles, aunts,
children and community overall are impacted" (Quiroz-Martinez et al., 2005, p.
6). This connection is seen in the EMEAC youth organizing community dialogues around gentrification, arguing, like their sisters and brothers in Santa
Ana, that the city belongs to all of the people.

Indeed, that is the claim to public space and the right to assembly called
for in the work of the Santa Ana groups, RAIZ, SACReD, and the OCIYU.
This example of youth activism illustrates the historical struggle of people
resisting the enclosure of the commons by the wealthy and powerful. By applying the environmental commons lens to this struggle, we point out that
the constitutional right to assembly in public space is being denied, in this
case to immigrants, through gang injunction orders and police surveillance.

As Santa Ana youth ensure their voices are heard and demand inclusion
in the planning process of their city, they take back their power and exercise
their rights as citizens in a democracy. After participating in these types of
actions for the environmental commons, young people from diverse backgrounds express an awareness of themselves as civic actors who, in partnership with others, can address public problems and effect change that benefits
their communities (Gallay, Marckini-Polk, Schroeder, & Flanagan, in press).
It is through such collaborative actions that young people develop ideas about
their role in the commons and beliefs about the larger common good.

It is also collaborative action in the cultural commons that enables people
to shape their future together, forging their vision for civil society, as highlighted in the work of G4G. G4G showcases how urban youth, and especially
youth of color, who have not been as readily engaged as their peers in mainstream environmental activism, can develop a voice for their communities
and environments through culturally relevant mediums. Via art linked with
activism for social and environmental justice, youth in G4G are developing
an awareness of how human choices affect each other and the environment.

When young people are engaged in work on the environmental commons,
they learn about the impact of humans on the environment and increase

their awareness of positive and negative consequences of human actions (Gallay et al., in press). Pro-environmental behavior is associated with awareness of one's interdependence with other people and species (Bamberg & Moser, 2007), and research with adults shows that feelings of interdependence with the environmental community are correlated with motivations and actions to protect that larger community (Bamberg & Moser, 2007). Likewise, environmental action is correlated with generativity in parents and adolescents as both adolescents and adults are more likely to engage in pro-environmental behavior if they are cognizant of the impact of their actions on future generations (Pratt, Norris, Alisat, & Bisson, 2013).

In fact, environmental issues raise intergenerational questions of social justice because actions in the present affect lives in the future. In the DIT example we see that youth environmental commons activism can influence feelings of generativity because it engages diverse intergenerational voices and perspectives. In this way, environmental commons activism offers the opportunity for adults to pass on important experience as elders to future leaders in the community. Through such intergenerational encounters over common concerns, youth should become aware that their own actions in the present have consequences for generations that come after them.

As exemplified in the words of the students at DIT, environmental commons activism also spurs an understanding of the need for collective action and responsibility. Like other civic issues, an understanding of and commitment to the environmental commons do not happen by default and do not occur in private. They develop through relationships and collaborative action with others around issues of common concern. As Elinor Ostrom (1998, 2010) and colleagues demonstrated, isolated individuals may consider only their own interests and consequently overconsume the environmental commons, but when people work together they are more likely to see how their self-interest is intertwined with that of the group and work to protect these commons.

When individuals see their fate as intertwined with that of a group, they are prepared to assume responsibility for the welfare of that group. By extension, we would argue that identification with the commons occurs when people realize that their fates are intertwined with the fates of others—humans as well as other species—and that this realization motivates actions to preserve the commons.

Finally, we argue that a focus on the environmental commons expands the notion of civic engagement beyond a narrow framework of electoral politics where youth, by virtue of their age, are not serious voices. The young people in the examples from Detroit and California are creating meaningful change in their communities, altering power relations, raising consciousness, and helping their communities become politically empowered. Age is not a prerequisite for taking action, and the actions of these young people to preserve the commons are not preparatory for their future as democratic citizens, but are affecting their communities now. Youths' voices and actions matter in the here and now, both because of the effects on their communities and because of the cumulative impact of environmental choices. It is critical that younger generations have a voice on issues that concern the future of life on earth, as it is their futures that are at stake.

ACKNOWLEDGMENTS

We thank the Spencer Foundation for providing support for the environmental commons work in the SEMIS project discussed in this chapter.

NOTE

1. The Enclosure Acts were a series of Acts of Parliament in the United Kingdom that (between the 17th and 20th centuries) created legal private property rights to lands that were previously considered common.

REFERENCES

Adger, W. N., Paavola, J., & Huq, S. (2006). Toward justice in adaptation to climate change. In W. N. Adger, J. Paavola, S. Huq, & M. J. Mace. (Eds.), *Fairness in adaptation to climate change* (pp. 1–19). Cambridge, MA: MIT Press.

Anderies, J. M., & Janssen, M. A. (2013). *Sustaining the commons.* Tempe, AZ: Center for the Study of Institutional Diversity, Arizona State University.

Arnold, E. (2009). The greening of hip-hop: Urban youth address climate change and sustainability. *Race, Poverty & the Environment, 16*(2), 82–83.

Bamberg, S., & Moser, G. (2007). Twenty years after Hines, Hungerford, and Tomera: A new meta-analysis of psycho-social determinants of pro-environmental behavior. *Journal of Environmental Psychology, 27*(1), 14–25. http://dx.doi.org/10.1016/j.jenvp.2006.12.002

Boer, J. T., Pastor, M., Sadd, J., & Snyder, L. (1997). Is there environmental racism? The demographics of hazardous waste in Los Angeles County. *Social Science Quarterly, 78*(4), 793–810.

Boyte, H. C. (2011). Constructive politics as public work: Organizing the literature. *Political Theory, 39*(5), 630–660. http://dx.doi.org/10.1177/0090591711413747

Bullard, R. D. (2002, July 2). *Poverty, pollution and environmental racism: Strategies for building healthy and sustainable communities.* Paper presented at the NBEJN Environmental Racism Forum World Summit on Sustainable Development Global Forum, Johannesburg, South Africa.

Dunlap, R. E., & Mertig, A. G. (1991). The evolution of the U.S. environmental movement from 1970 to 1990: An overview. *Society and Natural Resources, 4*(3), 209–218. http://dx.doi.org/10.1080/08941929109380755

Dyson, K. (2008, October 10). *Grind for the green* [Video file]. Retrieved from https://www.youtube.com/watch?v=c6tt9iOox84

East Michigan Environmental Action Council (EMEAC). (2015, April). Stand up speak out. Retrieved from http://www.emeac.org/2012/04/stand-up-speak-out.html

Flanagan, C., & Gallay, E. (2014). Adolescents' theories of the commons. In J. B. Benson (Series Ed.), *Advances in child development and behavior: Vol. 46* (pp. 33–55). http://dx.doi.org/10.1016/B978-0-12-800285-8.00002-9

Florez, I., & Gokaldas, V. (2010). Youth activists revitalize EJ movement. *Race, Poverty, & the Environment. 17*(2), 21–23. Retrieved from http://reimaginerpe.org/17-2/Florez

Frye, N. (2013, May). Tackling controversy in harmony. *East Michigan Environmental Action Council.* Retrieved from http://www.emeac.org/2013/05/tackling-controversy-in-harmony.html

Gallay, E. (2016). Students' commitments to the commons: Civic learning in Eco-Justice Place-based Stewardship Education. Masters Thesis. Eastern Michigan University.

Gallay, E., Marckini-Polk, L, Schroeder, B., & Flanagan, C. (in press). Place-based rural stewardship education: Engendering an identification with the local commons. *Peabody Journal of Education.*

Grist. (2006, February 14). Introducing a seven-week series on the intersection of economic and ecological survival. *Grist.* Retrieved from http://grist.org/article/pate/

Harris, Z. (n.d.). *Grind for the green | Zakiya Harris.* Retrieved from www.zakiyaharris.com/book/grind-for-the-green/

Harvey, D. (2008). The right to the city. *New Left Review, 53*, 23–40.

Idealist. (n.d.). *Grind for the green.* Retrieved from http://www.idealist.org.view/nonprofit/tGWCJnW2z95P/

Klein, N. (2014). *This changes everything: Capitalism vs. the climate.* New York, NY: Simon & Schuster.

Lefebvre, H. (1996). *Writings on cities.* Cambridge, MA: Blackwell.

Lowenstein, E., Voelker, L., Sylvester, J., Roundtree, A., Harris, K., Segrist, C., & Nielsen, R. (in press). Fostering youth leadership in urban place-based education. *Green Teacher.*

Martusewicz, R. A., Edmundson, J., & Lupinacci, J. (2015). *EcoJustice education: Toward diverse, democratic, and sustainable communities* (2nd ed.). New York, NY: Routledge.

Ostrom, E. L. (1998). A behavioral approach to the rational choice theory of collective action. Presidential Address, American Political Science Association, 1997, *American Political Science Review, 92*(1), 1–22. http://dx.doi.org/10.2307/2585925

Ostrom, E. (2010). Beyond markets and states: Polycentric governance of complex economic systems. *American Economic Review, 100*(3), 641–672. http://dx.doi.org/10.1257/aer.100.3.641

Pezzullo, P. C., & Sandler, R. (2007). Introduction: Revisiting the environmental justice challenge to environmentalism. In R. Sandler & P. C. Pezzullo (Eds.), *Environmental justice and environmentalism: The social justice challenge to the environmental movement* (pp. 1–24). Cambridge, MA: MIT Press.

Pratt, M. W., Norris, J. E., Alisat, S., & Bisson, E. (2013). Earth mothers (and fathers): Examining generativity and environmental concerns in adolescents and their parents. *Journal of Moral Education, 42*(1), 12–27. http://dx.doi.org/10.1080/03057240.2012.714751

Quiroz-Martinez, J., Wu, D. Pei, & Zimmerman, K. (2005). *ReGeneration: Young people shaping environmental justice.* Oakland, CA: Movement Strategy Center.

Rosenman, E. (n.d.). On enclosure acts and the commons. *BRANCH: Britain, Representation and Nineteenth-Century History.* Retrieved from http://www.branchcollec tive.org/?ps_articles=ellen-rosenman-on-enclosure-acts-and-the-commons

Samson, J., Berteaux, D., McGill, B., & Humphries, M. (2011). Geographic disparities and moral hazards in the predicted impacts of climate change on human populations. *Global Ecology and Biogeography, 20*(4), 532–544. http://dx.doi.org/10.1111/j.1466-8238.2010.00632.x

Shiva, V., Jafri, A. H., Bedi, G., & Holla-Bhar, R. (1997). *The enclosure and recovery of the commons: Biodiversity, indigenous knowledge, and intellectual property rights.* New Dehli: Research Foundation for Science, Technology, and Ecology.

Smith, G. A. (2015). Community organizing, schools, and the right to the city. *Environmental Education Research, 21*(3), 478–490. http://dx.doi.org/10.1080/13504622.2014.996207

Solomon, S. (2010). *Water: The epic struggle for wealth, power, and civilization.* New York, NY: HarperCollins.

Swineheart, T. (2013). The real history of the commons and today's environmental crisis. *UTNE Reader.* Retrieved from http://www.utne.com./environment/history-of-the-commons-zm0z13mjzbla.aspx?PageId=3#ArticleContent

Taylor, J. E., & Klingle, M. (2006, March 6). Environmentalism's elitist tinge has roots in the movement's history. *Grist.* Retrieved from http://grist.org/article/klingle/

Wapner, K. (1996). *Environmental activism and world civic politics.* Albany, NY: State University of New York.

Wasilevich, E. A., Lyon-Callo, S., Rafferty, A., & Dombkowski, K. (2008). Detroit—The epicenter of asthma burden. In *Epidemiology of asthma in Michigan*: Bureau of Epidemiology, Michigan Department of Community Health.

Zero Waste Detroit. (n.d). Detroit incinerator. *Zero Waste Detroit.* Retrieved from http://zerowastedetroit.org/our-work/detroit-incinerator

Part II

How Youth Activism Supports Youth

Introduction

Youth derive numerous short-term and long-term benefits from their work as activists. When youth are framed as active agents in a neoliberal context, it is either as consumers—those who buy or use products or services marketed by the private sector—or as nonparticipating deviants—those who are not furthering state interests by participating in established market structures. In some cases, such as in privatized criminal justice or educational institutions, youth play the role of commodities—those who are, themselves, the products of market-based, privatized public service providers. In these roles, youth agency and voice either take the form of consumer "choices" or are completely nonexistent, and youth are valued only for their profit potential. In contrast, activism humanizes youth, offering them the chance to contribute to their social context and equipping them with the civic dispositions and skills that position them as social actors.

As is evident in the following chapters, youth activists pose a challenge to the passivity that characterizes the neoliberal subject by engaging in storytelling, research, media production, policy advocacy, and other activities that allow them to produce counternarratives that re-create the vision of young people in the public imagination. Whereas in a neoliberal state subjects can assert agency only through consumption, youth activists assert agency by speaking up and speaking back to structures of power. In the process, youth develop the social capital necessary to facilitate action and process and heal from trauma, benefits that are also inherent challenges to neoliberal subjectivity. The chapters in this section collectively advance the argument that engagement in activism benefits youth; however, some authors complicate this claim by acknowledging the potential of activism to undermine young people's well-being. All the authors in this section cite empirical examples to explore how engaging in activism influences young people. The chapters here touch on a range of intertwined domains of influence, including the development of academic and leadership skills, civic dispositions, and civic knowledge; the broadening and strengthening of social networks; individual sociopolitical development; enhanced wellness; and opportunities for healing and intersectional identity work.

Opening Youth Essay

Jamia Brown

Being asked to write about what being an activist means to me and how it has affected me has caused me to actually go back to the root of what it was that made me want to start organizing. I wanted to know who I was and find myself.

To me, the most important thing that you should keep in mind while being an activist is the most obvious, yet one of the most complex ideas ever—identity. It is one of the many things that I have learned how to embrace and that I should appreciate because it will always be there, whether I like it or not, claim it or am ashamed. I had to face the realities of being Black in America, which is a struggle, yet is still beautiful. The beauty is in the minds and faces that make a revolution that is long overdue and much needed.

As the co-facilitator of the Rethink Organizing Collective (the ROC), my job is to plan and facilitate weekly political education meetings, plan and support actions, and maintain relationships with the 20 ROC members. Being an activist who wants to start this long overdue and much needed revolution to me is summed up in the words of Assata Shakur: "It is our duty to fight for freedom. It is our duty to win. We must love and support each other. We have nothing to lose but our chains." I feel that these are the words the collective must keep in mind. Even in my toughest times and when I feel that it isn't worth it, I remember these words, keeping in mind that I need to show solidarity with the people with whom I share the same risks. I think that this is the most beautiful part of the duty and the process of dismantling systems and institutions of oppression.

Being an activist, I have become aware of who it is that I am and what I think liberation feels and looks like.

Learning who you are comes along with getting to know the people around you, which I feel is an important skill especially when you are trying to get what is better and beneficial for those people. I have met many other young people with dope personalities and beautiful minds that are filled with amazing ideas and visions. Ideas and visions that are similar to mine and make me feel that I am not the only person who's observing the oppression, struggle, and ongoing war between my people and society that not many know is taking place. The values of these young people and adult supporters have made me feel that I have a second family. In this case, this family told me that I do have a voice, that it matters, and they will always listen.

With the family that I have in Rethink (I have been with them since I was 13), I have learned essential skills and many lessons that help me grow as an organizer and a person in general. I have taken notice of these skills and lessons in the most recent months in particular, being that I have begun my high school career at a predominantly white institution. An institution that constantly reminds me that I will never catch a break as a young Black girl. Especially a young Black girl who's "woke" and knows when she's being oppressed, yet is still proud of the features, identities, and characteristics that they are oppressing me about.

I'm a student trying to resist "schooling" while chasing a liberatory education. Being a student at my school, I have learned what I call "Black girl lessons," something that will stay with me for the rest of my life when dealing with patriarchy and white supremacy, which is something that I have to deal with every day, not just as an organizer but as a colored girl in America. Many times I feel alone because I am surrounded by people whom I can't relate to and who know nothing about what I am talking about when I say "the struggle." But the only thing this has done is motivate me even more as an organizer. Knowing this, I have learned to see microaggressions that portray Black women like me as angry and hypersensitive in almost every situation when we are just passionate and concerned about issues that we have every right to care about. I see these portrayals and I walk right past them. They can miss me with all the ways they try to diminish who I am or scare me into not speaking up. Many Black women are in fear of being portrayed in this negative way, but being in an environment that can be oppressive, I have learned not to be maladaptive and to actually speak up. I'm not exactly applauded when I do so, but I don't need to be. And I know they will never give me or my people credit when it's due.

With other young Black girls and people of color who do organizing, I feel as if I have a whole army behind me, and they can't take us down all at once when we come together. Especially since we intimidate them just by being here, knowing that we matter and that a struggle is actually taking place. That is the epitome of what Assata Shakur was saying to her partner. And I also think that is the epitome of what being an activist is and what it means to me.

This is for all the colored girls.
"It is our duty to fight for freedom!"
Yours in Struggle,
Jamia Brown
Rethinker

8

"It Shaped Who I Am as a Person": Youth Organizing and the Educational and Civic Trajectories of Low-Income Youth

John Rogers and Veronica Terriquez

Twenty-five-year-old Raymond Garcia[1] is a young man with a bright future. He holds a bachelor's degree from the University of California and is employed full time at a nonprofit organization working to improve the South Los Angeles neighborhood in which he grew up. Raymond loves "connecting to people and hearing people's stories." He also has an appreciation for history and political affairs. Raymond is particularly interested in issues such as immigration and economic development that affect his family and his community. He believes that he, in concert with other members of his community, can impact such issues through the ballot box and by sharing concerns with public officials.

Raymond's future did not seem so promising as he entered ninth grade. "When I started high school," he now remembers, "it was kind of like a bet to see when I was going to drop out." His sister and brother both dropped out of the same high school a few years before, as did most of their classmates. Of those who did graduate, few were ready for a four-year university. Only about 5% of each entering ninth-grade class matriculated into a university four years later.

Wanting something different for himself, Raymond listened attentively when an organizer with the Community Coalition came to one of his classes recruiting new members. Raymond was drawn to the idea of doing "something to change" his school, so, along with a couple of his friends, he began to attend workshops at the Community Coalition's offices. There, speakers came to talk about the civil rights movement, the Chicano movement, and social justice. He recalls these talks as "an eye opener . . . [they] made me look at things that I was already kind of looking at, but look at them totally differently." Raymond began having regular discussions with other members of the Community Coalition about big issues such as "Who has power? Why don't we have power? And what do we need to do to get power?" Over time, Raymond became a member of the Community Coalition's high school organizing committee. He recruited new members and led meetings. Together, he and other youth members initiated a campaign to expand access to college preparatory classes in neighborhood schools.

As Raymond participated in collective efforts to improve conditions in his school and across the district, he also benefited from academic support and guidance at the Community Coalition. The Community Coalition provided Raymond with an SAT prep class and offered help with his college application. Staff from the Community Coalition even brought Raymond to UCLA to present his insights about organizing to students in the Department of Social Welfare. Raymond remembers the sense of empowerment that came with telling these graduate students "about the subject they're learning in books." By the time he enrolled in college, Raymond knew he too wanted to study social work, and he felt he had the knowledge and social networks necessary for success.

Raymond's membership in a youth organizing group while he was in high school influenced profoundly who he has become as a young adult—his sense of self, his educational success, and his civic commitments and practices. This chapter takes up the question of whether Raymond's experience is idiosyncratic or characteristic of a broader pattern. Comparing the experiences of 410 young adults who were members of California youth organizing (YO) groups while in high school to those of a representative sample of young adults who never participated in youth organizing, we investigate the extent to which participation in youth organizing has a positive effect on educational and civic trajectories. We also demonstrate how involvement in YO groups during high school corresponds with movement along these trajectories.

The central finding of this chapter is that YO alumni are far more likely than comparable peers across California to enroll in four-year colleges and universities and engage in various civic activities in early adulthood. We also identify a number of learning opportunities and developmental supports associated with youth organizing that are related to college attendance and to robust forms of civic engagement in early adulthood.

Our chapter proceeds in five sections. Section one presents a rationale for examining the impact of youth organizing on the development of young adults, describing both the rapid growth of YO groups in recent years as well as efforts to study this emerging field. Section two discusses the methods we used to investigate the impact of youth organizing, our YO alumni sample, and the groups that these young adults participate in while in high school.

The findings of the study are presented in sections three (on educational attainment) and four (on civic engagement). Our concluding section points to implications of the study.

YOUTH ORGANIZING AND THE DEVELOPMENT OF YOUNG ADULTS

Youth organizing is a process for developing "within a neighborhood or community a base of young people committed to altering power relationships and creating meaningful institutional change" (Sullivan, Edwards, Johnson, & McGillicuddy, 2003, p. 9). Members are generally high school–age youth living in low-income communities and communities of color. YO groups attract new members through peer-to-peer outreach and the promise of addressing problems in their daily lives. Interested youth attend youth-led meetings and "popular education" activities at their school or a community-based site. These gatherings offer young people a welcoming environment, food, and academic and social supports. Over time, youth members take on leadership roles and participate in campaigns to effect social change. By creating a context in which youth practice politics, YO groups promote both community improvement and youth development (Ginwright & Cammarota, 2007; Rogers, Mediratta, & Shah, 2012).

While there have been numerous instances of youth activism throughout American history, the current practice and structure of youth organizing has emerged over the last three decades. YO groups began to form in urban centers during the late 1980s and early 1990s against the backdrop of growing economic inequality, disinvestment in social programs, and dramatic increases in incarceration rates (Rogers et al., 2012; Warren, Mira, & Nikundiwe, 2008). In response, many activists sought to bring young people together in campaigns to advance alternative policies and insert the voices of low-income youth of color into the public sphere. Over time, youth and adult allies developed ongoing structures to sustain organizing projects after the campaigns ended. Nonprofit community-based organizations were established that provided groups with a meeting place, stable staff, and capacity to secure more resources and develop longer-term strategies.

YO groups have grown in size and influence in recent decades (Warren et al., 2008). While there was only a spattering of YO groups active in the late 1980s, hundreds of such organizations existed by the early 2000s (Endo, 2002). These groups generally include core members who participate in activities several times a week, as well as active members who participate in workshops and actions throughout the year.

As youth organizing has grown, the field has attracted the attention of educational researchers interested in its potential for advancing educational reform (Torres-Fleming, Valdes, & Pillai, 2010). A good deal of research has documented how YO groups shape the understandings of policymakers and effect change in local and state policy and institutional practice (Mediratta, Shaw, & McAlister, 2009; Warren & Mapp, 2011). For example, successful youth organizing campaigns in Los Angeles have shaped policies on the location of new schools, the rigor of high school graduation requirements, and school discipline (Rogers & Morrell, 2010).

A number of researchers also have examined youth organizing as a context for learning and development (Kirshner, 2009; Larson & Hansen, 2005). Many YO groups embody practices associated with powerful learning—they are voluntary organizations, critical in orientation, focused on real-world problems, and committed to development (Rogers et al., 2012). Researchers have found that participants in youth organizing acquire knowledge and skills necessary for participation in civic life (Watkins, Larson, & Sullivan, 2007). Participation in youth organizing also forges civic commitments and enhances young people's sense of agency (Ginwright & James, 2002; Shah, 2011; Taines, 2012).

Many researchers have hypothesized that experiences with youth organizing in high school will shape development into adulthood, but there has been little empirical evidence to date. Some research suggests that members of YO groups believe that their participation will influence their future behavior. Shah (2011) found that a strong majority of high school–age members of YO groups reported that their experience in organizing not only has led them to take more rigorous academic courses and achieve better grades, but also forged higher educational aspirations for the future. The youth members in Shah's study also reported that they planned to remain civically engaged as young adults.

Beyond self-reported plans for the future, there has been little research linking youth organizing experiences during high school with young adult beliefs and behaviors. Perhaps the best example is Conner's (2011) case study of 25 former participants of one youth organizing group in Philadelphia. Her interviews suggest that many of the young adults still draw upon the critical thinking, interpersonal, communication, and introspective skills that they first forged in the context of youth organizing while in high school. Conner's study illuminates how early experiences in one organizing group shape identities over time, but it does not delineate a causal relationship between involvement in youth organizing and the educational and civic outcomes of its members.

While the value of youth organizing as a strategy for political change has been well established, the evidence to date has been more limited on the value of youth organizing for the long-term development of its members. It thus is important to understand how experiences with youth organizing during high school shape the pathways members follow as they enter adulthood. That understanding is the purpose of this current study.

DATA AND METHODS

We draw on survey and semistructured data from the California Young Adult Study (CYAS) to examine how high school YO groups shape the postsecondary educational and civic trajectories of their members in early adulthood. We primarily rely on information drawn from two distinct samples of 18- to 26-year-olds who attended school in California before the age of 17.

The first sample includes a group of 2,200 young adults who participated in a phone survey between April and August 2011. This sample was generated through random digit dialing of landline and cell phones in California, with an oversampling of landlines located in high-poverty census tracts. (We refer to this group as the "general population.") When sampling weights are applied, this group is representative of California's 18- to 26-year-old population, excluding international students and first-generation immigrants. Following the survey administration, researchers conducted 174 in-depth interviews in 2011–2012 with survey participants largely residing in the greater San Francisco and Los Angeles metropolitan areas.

The second sample comes from alumni rosters of eight California community-based organizations that engage high school students in youth organizing activities. Four of the groups are based in the greater San Francisco Bay Area: Asian Youth Promoting Advocacy and Leadership (AYPAL), Youth Making a Change (Y-MAC) of Coleman Youth Advocates, Youth Together, and Youth United for Community Action (YUCA). Three are located in Los Angeles: Coalition for Humane Immigrant Rights of Los Angeles' (CHIRLA) Wise Up!, the Community Coalition's South Central Youth Empowered through Action (SCYEA), and InnerCity Struggle. The final group, Californians for Justice (CFJ), is a statewide network with youth organizing sites in Fresno, Long Beach, Oakland, and San Jose. All eight of these groups have engaged young people in organizing activities for a decade or longer. We surveyed 410 young adults who had been members of these eight groups while they were in high school. Members of these organizations generally attended a weekly meeting, often held at school sites. They also participated throughout the year in occasional workshops and became deeply engaged in political action in the context of shorter-term campaigns. We refer to this group of former members as "YO" alumni. Our research team also conducted in-person semistructured interviews with 84 of the alumni who had participated in the survey.

Both the general population and YO alumni were administered the same survey, which included more than 170 questions regarding past and current educational experiences, employment history, and participation in various civic engagement opportunities. The survey also asked respondents about their demographic and other personal and family background characteristics.[2] The follow-up interviews explored young adults' early family life, activities during high school, and educational, civic, and employment experiences following high school. Interviews with alumni of YO groups probed respondents' entry into organizing, the nature of their participation, and the effects of membership on their knowledge, skills, and identity.

Fully transcribed interviews were initially coded into broad topical categories and then recoded inductively based on emerging themes, with an eye toward identifying how YO groups orient their members toward college and future civic participation. We use semistructured interview data from the YO alumni to help us identify how the unique practices of YO groups shape members' postsecondary educational attainment and civic participation in young adulthood.

In addition to the surveys and interviews with young adults, we conducted interviews with eight staff or former staff from the eight YO groups that are represented in the study. The interviews provided contextual information on the organizations—the demographics and size of the membership, educational and civic activities, and recent campaigns. We also explored how members are recruited and retained and how and under what circumstances they take on leadership roles.

This large data set allows us to (1) roughly compare the trajectories of young adults who participated in youth organizing while in high school with those who did not; and (2) illuminate key conditions for youth development in the organizing groups.

Comparing the general population sample and the YO alumni sample is a complex undertaking given potential problems stemming from selection bias and differences in sampling methodology (for further discussion see Terriquez, 2014). Survey data are cross-sectional and cannot account for self-selection into YO groups. Additionally, the YO sample is based on all available records of 18- to 26-year-olds who participated in eight groups during high school, while the general population sample is based on stratified random sampling. There is no perfect methodology for dealing with selection biases and differences in sampling methodology. In this chapter, we simply use descriptive statistics to generally compare the two samples along demographics, postsecondary educational outcomes, and civic participation.

As demonstrated in Table 8.1, YO alumni are on average slightly younger and more likely to be female than the general population. The eight YO groups in this study disproportionately serve nonwhite, immigrant, and low-income youth. More specifically, almost all YO alumni are Latino, African American, or Asian American. Only 1% of the organizing alumni identified

Table 8.1. Demographics and High School Achievement

	Youth Organizing Alumni	CA General Population
Average Age	20.6	21.3
Gender		
Male	36%	52%
Female	64%	48%
Race		
Latino	58%	44%
White	1%	35%
Asian/Pacific Islander	23%	11%
Black	11%	6%
Other	7%	4%
Immigrant Generation		
1.5 generation	27%	16%
2nd generation	55%	38%
3rd generation+	19%	46%
U.S. Citizen	82%	92%
Low-Income Family Background	88%	38%
H.S. Academic Achievement		
Received mostly As & Bs	54%	47%
Still in High School/Recent Graduates	23%	13%

as white, compared with 35% of California's young adult population. Similarly, the organizing alumni are substantially more likely to be 1.5-generation immigrants who were born abroad and raised in the United States (27% to 16%) or the second-generation children of immigrants (55% to 38%) than their peers. Given the immigrant composition of YO groups, YO alumni are less likely than the general population to be citizens.

The YO groups in this study are based in very low-income communities. Therefore, it may not be surprising that a very high proportion—88%—of YO alumni (compared to 38% of the general population) come from low-income backgrounds. We identify low-income students as those who were eligible for free and reduced lunch or whose parents relied on public assistance while they were in high school.

Notably, YO alumni are somewhat more likely than their peers (54% to 47%) to report that they received mostly A and B grades in high school. Differences in grades might reflect a selection bias—that a distinctive group of young people joins YO groups. But it is also possible that experience in YO groups promotes academic achievement. It is worth mentioning that 23% of respondents in the YO alumni sample and 13% of respondents in the general population were still in high school at the time of the survey or had recently graduated.

ACADEMIC OUTCOMES FOR YOUTH ORGANIZING ALUMNI AND COMPARABLE PEERS

To examine postsecondary educational enrollment we distinguish among those who never enrolled in college (but may have enrolled in a general educational development [GED] program, adult school, or vocational program); ever enrolled in a community college (but never enrolled in a four-year college); and ever enrolled in a four-year university. This analysis excludes respondents who were still in high school at the time of the survey or had recently graduated and had not had time to enroll in college by the time survey data collection had been completed in the summer of 2011.

Table 8.2 contains descriptive statistics showing the postsecondary enrollment of survey respondents from the YO alumni and general population.[3] Results indicate that 92% of YO alumni attended college, compared to 75% of the generation population. Although somewhat similar percentages of both groups enrolled in a community college, it is quite striking that 59% of YO alumni enrolled in a four-year institution, compared to 38% of the general population. These findings are impressive, given that YO alumni disproportionately come from lower socioeconomic backgrounds and generally attended under-resourced urban high schools.

In spite of the methodological concerns noted above, these survey results point to the possibility that YO groups facilitate the college enrollment of

Table 8.2. Postsecondary School Enrollment

	Youth Organizing Alumni	CA General Population
Did not enroll in college	8%	25%
Enrolled in a community college	33%	37%
Enrolled in a four-year institution	59%	38%

their members. For further evidence we turn to semistructured interview data. We contend that there are three ways in which YO groups orient their members toward college attendance, especially in four-year institutions. First, YO groups offer direct academic support and create opportunities for young people to acquire skills and develop intellectual interests in the context of campaigns. Second, YO groups provide members with holistic and culturally relevant college counseling and guidance. Third, YO groups encourage members to see college-going as connected to a broader political and community empowerment agenda.

Supporting Development of Academic Skills and Intellectual Interests

As the YO groups in our study work to advance social change, they also promote their members' academic success. This concern with academics is related to a more general interest in the welfare and development of youth members. Staff of YO groups noted that it would be "morally unjust" or a "contradiction" of core principles for their organization to involve young people in campaigns for social improvement without simultaneously helping these youth to grow as individuals. In addition, the commitment of some YO groups to redressing educational inequality has led them to emphasize school success. For example, adult staff at Californians for Justice tell youth members: "Hey, we're about educational justice and we can't have you dropping out because of challenges at school."

The organizing groups in our study provide youth members with tutoring and homework support during their after-school programs. Most groups establish a regular time and place when members can work on school assignments and access assistance (as needed) from staff, many of whom have college degrees. Several groups also developed personalized programs to help students with their schoolwork. For example, InnerCity Struggle creates an "individual empowerment plan" for each of its members that identifies academic challenges faced, outlines steps for improvement, and specifies how and when staff members will provide help.

In addition to assisting young people with their schoolwork, YO groups engage members in relevant and rigorous lessons about social change and inequality that foster a commitment to intellectual discussion and critical analysis. For example, Darryl, an AYPAL alumna, recalls:

We watch[ed] documentaries and then read articles about what's going on around the world. It's like receiving all this information that isn't given to us at school. There are so many injustices and AYPAL has educated us on what's happening around the world.

Darryl also adds that her experience allowed her to draw links between global and local issues. Meanwhile, Robbie, a member of YUCA, discussed how he learned the importance of data collection and analysis in campaigns. While working on an environmental justice campaign, Robbie claims that data collection and statistics proved critical in understanding how "toxic waste factories are affecting our community, and other low-income communities of color."

Alumni of YO groups also point to a variety of skills they developed in the context of organizing campaigns that contribute to their academic success. Mandy, a 22-year-old college student, notes that she learned to think creatively about difficult problems at the Community Coalition. The organizing staff encouraged members to "brainstorm different solutions," a strategy she still uses today when she approaches a research paper. Felipe, another alumnus from the Community Coalition, recalls that, in the course of the campaign to expand college access in Los Angeles, he had to plan actions, write op-eds, and speak publicly.

> It really kind of helped shape who I am as a person, my values and my work ethic, and developed a lot of leadership skills, my potential to think critically and to write, and to speak, and to articulate goals and solutions and problems.

Providing Culturally Relevant College Guidance and Mentoring

The YO groups in our study provided members with strong college guidance and support. These counseling services likely played a particularly important role for youth growing up in low-income families in California. Throughout the period of this study, California public schools offered few counseling services; California ranked last of all states in the number of students served by each counselor (Rogers, Bertrand, Freelon, & Fanelli, 2011). Yvonne, a Youth Together alumna, recalls that her high school counselors "were always busy and you always had to get an appointment." Similarly, Cliff, an alumnus of Californians for Justice (CFJ), notes that while his high school counselors "couldn't really afford the time," CFJ staff walked him through the college application process, reading his essay and providing timely feedback.

Alumni highlighted several types of college information that they accessed through their YO groups. Many alumni learned about the importance of college preparatory courses from their groups. Organizing staff helped youth to track the courses they needed to qualify for four-year colleges, and they encouraged young people to see these classes as part of a broader project of college access. Organizing groups also provided members with information on scholarships and financial aid, offering specific details to undocumented immigrant students who faced restrictions due to their citizenship status. "Wise Up!," one alumnus noted, "was really about inspiring us to go to college, even if we didn't have papers." In addition to talking with members about college, all of the groups in our study regularly led trips to college campuses. These trips often included meetings with current college students who previously had been members of these same organizing groups.

In addition to being conduits of information, YO staff served as mentors who had already navigated a path to college. Vanessa, an alumna from Wise Up!, remembers feeling a deep connection to one staff member who "had gotten out from that community that I came from and gone off to Berkeley." Patricia, from InnerCity Struggle, recounts:

> I had never been around people who were in college, who were going to UCLA, who were going to USC. . . . Being in those spaces kind of made you realize that maybe college was a possibility, and even though you had [a] 60 percent dropout rate at your high school, there was still kids making it out.

The organizing staff not only provided an inspiring image of a young adult role, but they also offered contextual information particularly relevant to the college experiences of a person of color from a working-class community. For Cynthia, an alumna from InnerCity Struggle, this meant that she entered college with confidence that she had the "inside scoop" of how a Latina could navigate a primarily white university.

The quality of relationships between youth and YO staff members created a unique context for guidance and support. Empathy and bonds of trust enabled organizing staff to "push" youth members in a manner that they experienced as encouraging rather than harsh. At times, this push came in the form of questions that prompted youth to think about their long-term plans. Eduardo from Youth Together explains:

> The organizers would always ask those questions that nobody would ask, like "What are you doing with your life? What are you planning to do after high school? What do you want to do?" Just having somebody ask those questions helped me out because I never really thought about anything like that. I was always, "OK, it's just high school," but I never thought about what would go on after high school. I probably wouldn't be in college now if it weren't for Youth Together.

Another type of "push" came in the form of organizing staff persuading youth that they could pursue a college pathway. Marco, a Wise Up! alumnus, recalls a common refrain among members: "Oh, I won't get accepted and I'm not competitive." But, he notes, the daily message of hope and possibility from one staff member "led me to believe that anyone can do it."

Connecting College-Going to a Broader Empowerment Agenda

In addition to providing academic supports and guidance, YO groups encourage young people to view learning as both a political and a personal project. An alumnus from Youth Together who later joined the staff reported:

> We have a whole set of curriculum that's around educational justice. Part of that curriculum is the understanding of the history of the education system and understanding the power of education. This curriculum is instilled [in] the students by everyone on staff.

A staff member at CFJ explains this process in more detail: "Constantly looking at . . . the systemic barriers to young people . . . not achieving an education" motivates members to "look at their own experience" in a new way. They realize, "It's not that I don't have a desire to go on to higher education. It's not that I don't value education. It's that there's a lot of systemic barriers."

We can see the relationship between participating in educational justice campaigns and personal academic commitments in the comments of Janessa, a recent alumna from Y-MAC. At weekly meetings preparing for an educational justice campaign, Janessa and her fellow members discussed explanations of the achievement gap. The discussions addressed "how some schools don't give you what you need . . . [and] . . . if you didn't get an education . . . how your life would be." These discussions led Janessa to understand that "sometimes you have to fight more for the things that you want in your school," *and* "you got to go to school, you got to be on time, you got to do [your] work and all that."

CIVIC ENGAGEMENT OUTCOMES FOR YOUTH ORGANIZING ALUMNI AND COMPARABLE PEERS

This section reports on the civic participation of YO alumni and other young adults in California. Before turning to our findings, it is important to note that many scholars have tracked a broad decline in civic participation over recent decades, particularly among young adults—with a drop in voting rates, participation in voluntary associations, and citizen knowledge of policy issues (Galston, 2001; Gibson & Levine, 2003; Putnam, 2000). Moreover, in our era of growing economic inequality, civic engagement has grown more and more unequal (American Political Science Association, 2004). This inequality plays out among young adults, with stark differences in civic knowledge and patterns of civic participation by social class and educational background (American Political Science Association, 2004; Levinson, 2012).

There is a growing body of work documenting the relationship between this broader civic inequality and the experience of young people. For example, Kahne and Middaugh (2008) have shown that African American and Latino students and students in low-track classes are less likely than their peers to participate in civic simulations, discuss current events, or meet civic role models. Kahne and Middaugh call this the civic learning opportunity gap. Other scholars have highlighted inequalities in civic learning opportunities beyond the school day (Hart & Atkins, 2002; Watts & Guessous, 2006).

Youth organizing represents a potential strategy for equalizing the opportunities for civic learning and energizing civic participation. This approach to youth development and leadership targets low-income urban neighborhoods and provides opportunities to practice politics. By galvanizing and directing civic energy, youth organizing aims to provide youth who otherwise have little formal power with the capacity to address immediate problems and challenge the status quo.

Do high school YO groups facilitate members' later civic participation in early adulthood? To begin answering this question we compare civic actions of YO alumni and the general population. We explore five indicators of civic engagement: (1) volunteering (whether or not the respondent reported volunteering in the past year); (2) community involvement (whether or not the respondent reported working with others to address a community issue within the last year); (3) online voice (whether or not the respondent reported sharing his or her perspective on a political/social issue online within the last year); (4) protesting or attending a public rally within the past year, and (5) registering to vote.

As shown in Table 8.3, YO alumni are much more likely than other young adults to have volunteered (71% to 46%), worked on an issue affecting their

Table 8.3. Civic Actions Completed within the Last Year

	Youth Organizing Alumni	CA General Population
Volunteered	71%	46%
Worked on issue affecting own community	65%	27%
Shared perspective online on social or political issue	56%	30%
Participated in a protest or rally	51%	13%
Registered to vote	75%	68%

community (65% to 27%), and shared perspectives on social and political issues online (56% to 30%). They also are almost four times as likely (51% to 13%) to have participated in a march or protest. YO alumni who are U.S. citizens are somewhat more likely to have registered to vote than citizens in the general population. These differences in civic activity are impressive given that YO alumni disproportionately come from families that experience socioeconomic or immigration-related challenges to civic and political participation (Terriquez, 2014; Terriquez & Kwon, 2015).

Interview Data Show a Distinctive Pattern of Civic Engagement

The above survey results demonstrate a correlation between high school membership in a youth organizing group and greater civic participation in young adulthood. In other words, results indicate that YO alumni are more civically engaged than their peers from the general population. To further understand differences in the civic engagement of YO alumni and their peers in the general population, we turn to in-depth interview data.

During in-person interviews, we asked YO alumni and other young adults: "Do you think that you or other people around your age can make a difference in the community? Or in politics? Why do you think that? Could you give examples of how you or people your age have made a difference?" In line with survey results, YO alumni were more likely to say that young people can make a difference. Yet, more striking is the discrepancy in answers to the follow-up question. Over a quarter of interviewees from the general population who believed young people can make a difference were unable to provide a concrete example of such action. Here is a typical response: "Like I don't know any examples. But I'm pretty sure somebody can make a big difference, even if they're young." By contrast, only 1% of YO alumni could not offer an example of young people making change; many provided extraordinarily detailed accounts from their own experience.

Alumni from YO groups also provided very different answers than other young adults to the question, "What does it mean to be politically engaged?" One key difference is that YO alumni were much more likely than other young adults to talk about political engagement as collective, as opposed to individualistic, action. More than 90% of interviewees with youth organizing experience defined political engagement in collective terms, meaning they spoke about young people coming together to solve a problem or exert collective force, whereas only half of other young adults did so. Further, when young adults in the random sample spoke of collective action, they often did so with little specificity or clarity. In contrast, the alumni of YO groups often offered rich descriptions of joint political action. Ann, a 25-year-old alumna, represents a case in point:

To be politically involved is to really understand our own individual agency and then our own agency as a collective. . . . To be involved, we need to feel the sense of connection with each other, and connection to, like, the fact that things don't need to be the way they are. Like if you're sick and tired of being sick and tired . . . the next step is not to sit there and think about that—I think the next step is to really get up and figure out how to change that. And who else is willing to change it with you?

We also see differences in the sorts of actions young adults associate with political engagement. YO alumni are more likely than the general population to talk about forms of engagement in elections that stretch beyond voting—participating in voter education and get out the vote activities. They also are more likely to discuss empowered deliberation—interacting with public officials, deliberating, or participating in decision making. And they are far more likely to speak of protests, rallies, marches, and organizing. Further, while many young adults talk about the importance of being informed, YO alumni are much more likely to note the importance of analyzing (rather than simply accepting) mainstream sources of information and gathering additional information themselves.

Youth Organizing as a Site of Robust Civic Development

Why do so many alumni of YO groups speak in similar terms about the power of collective action? Why do youth participants believe, in the words of one staff member, "that they're part of something greater"? And how do experiences in YO groups while in high school shape participants' beliefs and identities?

YO groups invite and enable new members to participate in what some theorists term "publics" or spaces where people come together and forge relationships of commonality, recognize and examine their shared concerns and hopes, and articulate their interests through joint action. The publics created by YO groups do this and more. They are shaped by a consciousness of the subordinate social position of their members and recognition of the need to challenge dominant social relations and prevailing understandings for the purpose of individual and political transformation.[4]

YO groups not only constitute a public, but they are also committed to developing new members as part of that public. At some level, all publics must concern themselves with integrating new members. But there is a distinctive focus on building the capacity of new members in YO groups. New member development is one of the core purposes of these groups. And this developmental focus centers on enabling young people to be vital members of the public. We can thus talk about YO groups as developmental publics.

In our interviews with YO alumni, many young adults articulate their trajectory from entry into organizing as moving from being a shy and inward-focused youth to being an active member who is outgoing and a vital partici-pant in collective action. The youth develop this identity in the course of participating in the work of organizing—recruiting other youth, conducting door-to-door campaigns in the community, speaking in public, and develop-ing social change campaigns. Each of these activities calls for a complex set of skills and ways of being that youth develop in the context of participat-ing. It is not easy for young people to take on these new roles, but they are propelled forward through intrinsic motivation and the support of older members and staff.

One activity that is important to this process of growth is recruitment of new members. The act of reaching out to potential new members prods young people to develop a public voice. Ignacia, a 20-year-old alumna, recounts:

> They would also make us—well, not make us but they would ask us if we wanted to phone bank. We would call other people reminding them about our weekly meetings. And then they would, I don't know—show us how to not get so nervous when we're talking in front of people. . . . they had made me a stronger person because before I would just—used to be in this shell.

Outreach also encourages youth to hear the interests of others and listen to them more empathically. Ryan, a 24-year-old alumnus, states:

> I learned . . . how to be an effective recruiter . . . not recruiting in the sense of just trying to get folks to just do things or come to meetings, but like, able to really, like, talk to somebody and be like, "Yo, this is what's going on. Like, what do you think about that?"

Similarly, conducting outreach in their neighborhoods places youth in novel and challenging situations that elicit agency and prompt the develop-ment of new social scripts. Tanya, an alumna from YUCA, notes: "I think if you can knock on somebody's door who's in their house minding their busi-ness, and think that you're probably selling 'em something, in the ghetto where you need to be safe not to open your doors, you kinda have to be con-fident. You really have to be confident . . . that they will accept you when they understand why you're going: 'Hi . . . [I'm] not here to sell you anything. Please don't slam the door.' . . . I think that gave me confidence, and I think I learned the ability to speak to a diverse public."

Tanya makes this process of forging a new identity sound easy. Other alumni acknowledge how difficult it is to take on new and challenging public roles. We hear this dynamic from Thuan, an alumnus from AYPAL: "I was really close-minded and kind of shy. But AYPAL made me more outgoing and a lot more understanding. AYPAL really just taught me to fight for what you want." Thuan, like others, found the courage to step out of his comfort zone and speak up at rallies, meetings, and other public events.

Responsibilities for public speaking also stretch members to think about what it means to communicate effectively, particularly in group settings. For some members, this reflection helps craft a more productive, public identity. Cassandra notes:

> I was able to learn how to control myself verbally. I got kicked out of, like, tons of classes, but after working with Y-MAC, I'm able to understand when is a good place to speak up and when isn't, and how to better utilize my opinion than to just be angry about everything. Like, you can't make any change if you're just angry about everything.

SUMMARY, IMPLICATIONS, AND EMERGING QUESTIONS

Our study finds that participation in YO groups while in high school is associated with a number of positive outcomes for low-income youth of color. Alumni of YO groups are more likely than their peers to move on to four-year colleges and universities and three and a half times more likely to enroll in the most selective higher education institutions. They also are more likely to volunteer, to participate in civic organizations, and to take a variety of political actions ranging from sharing information to marching in protests. Further, YO alumni are far more likely than their peers to believe in social change and understand what actions they can take to improve their local community and make the world a better place.

YO groups support these positive outcomes by providing members with an array of developmental opportunities. Groups establish engaging and culturally relevant contexts for members to acquire academic skills and access guidance and counseling. They also offer young people role models from their communities who use their strong relationships to provide additional encouragement and push that might not be so effective were it to come from teachers or other adults. In addition, YO groups foster a sense of intrinsic motivation for young people to participate in the group that, along with the supportive environment, propels members to engage in actions that stretch themselves and forge deep civic commitments.

The findings from this study suggest that the influence of YO groups extends beyond their capacity to project power and impact educational and social policy: these groups also can be important sites for learning and development. Other scholars have noted that some social movement organizations are developmental in the sense that they prefigure forms of political and social life that they seek to foster in the broader society (Maeckelbergh, 2011; Polletta, 2002). The YO groups in our study do that, but simultaneously they also promote valued academic and civic outcomes for their individual members. Since YO groups both target and appeal to low-income youth of color and immigrant youth, these outcomes advance equity and social inclusion.

We note above that YO groups *can be* powerful sites of learning and development because the eight organizing groups in our study do not represent the entire universe of youth organizing. Certainly there are differences across groups that likely shape their ability to promote educational and civic outcomes. It is important to note that all the YO groups in our study have been operating for at least 10 years. Their longevity is evidence of organizational capacity and likely has supported the development of expertise grounded in experience.

The developmental potential of YO groups means that organizations interested in supporting high school students' progress toward college and adult civic engagement—public schools, college access programs, and other youth development programs—would do well to study YO groups to inform their own practice. Certainly, not all of what YO groups do can or should be transposed into other settings. The point here is that YO groups present a unique approach to critical issues of engagement, motivation, and support; understanding this approach can enable other adults who work with youth to take a fresh look at their own practice. Much would be gained from structured opportunities for youth organizing staff to meet with educators and other adults to discuss different approaches to youth development.

While YO groups have great potential for shaping equity policy, supporting member development, and modeling powerful learning, they often have limited resources and hence limited capacity. The fact that YO groups promote college access and civic engagement among low-income youth of color makes them more compelling for governmental agencies and philanthropic organizations who fund youth programming. The findings of our study point to the value of further investment in established YO groups.

In addition, there is a need to support new or up-and-coming YO groups. Staff at the well-established YO groups represent an invaluable resource for this process. Indeed, the developmental focus of YO groups means that staff members in the established groups are reflective about the core ideas underlying their work and are skilled in communicating these ideas to broader audiences. We saw strong evidence of this capacity in the course of our interviews with staff members.

As we consider these and other possibilities, it seems only fitting to give the final word to Ann, a former member of Californians for Justice. Now

25 years old, Ann, sees her organizing experience as key to the development of her identity as a young adult.

> Not everyone is gonna be an organizer, right? . . . They wanna be a doctor or they wanna do something else or whatever and the only thing we can really give them . . . is really like a sense of the world and how it should be or could be and their place in it and that you can change that. And I think, like, that type of relationship building and that type of worldview is something they can stay with forever even if they never organize again.

NOTES

1. We use pseudonyms when referring to young adults in this chapter.
2. The phone survey was conducted by the Social Science Research Center at California State University, Fullerton.
3. Individuals who completed their intended degrees are counted among those who attended either community college or four-year universities.
4. For a broader discussion of "publics," see Dewey (1927); Habermas (1962/1991); Fraser (1990); and Warner (2002).

REFERENCES

American Political Science Association. (2004). *American democracy in an age of rising inequality*. Task Force on Inequality and American Democracy. Washington, DC: APSA.

Conner, J. (2011). Youth organizers as young adults: Their commitments and contributions. *Journal of Research on Adolescence, 21*(4), 923–942. http://dx.doi.org/10.1111/j.1532-7795.2011.00766.x

Dewey, J. (1927). *The public and its problems*. In J. A. Boydston (Ed.), *John Dewey: The later works, vol. 2 of the collected works* (pp. 235–372). Carbondale, IL: Southern Illinois University Press.

Endo, T. (2002). *Youth engagement in community-driven school reform*. Oakland, CA: Social Policy Research Associates.

Fraser, N. (1990). "Rethinking the public sphere: A contribution to the critique of actually existing democracy." *Social Text, 25/26,* 56–80.

Galston, W. (2001). Political knowledge, political engagement, and civic education. *Annual Review of Political Science, 4*(1), 217–234. http://dx.doi.org/10.1146/annurev.polisci.4.1.217

Gibson, C., & Levine, P. (2003). *The civic mission of schools*. New York, NY: Carnegie Corporation of New York.

Ginwright, S., & Cammarota, J. (2007). Youth activism in the urban community: Learning critical civic praxis within community organizations. *International Journal of Qualitative Studies in Education, 20,* 693–710. http://dx.doi.org/10.1080/09518390701630833

Ginwright, S., & James, T. (2002). From assets to agents of change: Social justice, organizing, and youth development. In B. Kirshner, J. O'Donoghue, & M. McLaughlin (Eds.), *Youth participation: Improving institutions and communities* (pp. 26–46). San Francisco, CA: Jossey-Bass.

Habermas, J. (1962/1991). *The structural transformation of the public sphere: An inquiry into a category on bourgeois society.* Boston: MIT Press.

Hart, D., & Atkins, R. (2002). Civic competence in urban youth. *Applied Developmental Science, 6*(4), 227–236. http://dx.doi.org/10.1207/S1532480XADS0604_10

Kahne, J., & Middaugh, E. (2008). *Democracy for some: The civic opportunity gap in high school* (CIRCLE Working Paper No. 59). Medford, MA: Center for Information & Research on Civic Learning and Engagement.

Kirshner, B. (2009). "Power in numbers": Youth organizing as a context for exploring civic identity. *Journal of Research on Adolescence, 19*(3), 414–440. http://dx.doi.org/10.1111/j.1532-7795.2009.00601.x

Larson, R., & Hansen, D. (2005). The development of strategic thinking: Learning to impact human systems in a youth activism program. *Human Development, 48*(6), 327–349. http://dx.doi.org/10.1159/000088251

Levinson, M. (2012). *No citizen left behind.* Cambridge, MA: Harvard University Press.

Maeckelbergh, M. (2011). Doing is believing: Prefiguration as strategic practice in the alterglobalization movement. *Social Movement Studies, 10*(1), 1–20. http://dx.doi.org/10.1080/14742837.2011.545223

Mediratta, K., Shah, S., & McAlister, S. (2009). *Community organizing for stronger schools: Strategies and successes.* Cambridge, MA: Harvard University Education Press.

Polletta, F. (2002). *Freedom is an endless meeting: Democracy in American social movements.* Chicago, IL: University of Chicago Press.

Putnam, R. (2000). *Bowling alone: The collapse and revival of American community.* New York, NY: Simon & Schuster.

Rogers, J., Bertrand, M., Freelon, R., & Fanelli, S. (2011). *Free fall: Educational opportunities in 2011.* Los Angeles, CA: UCLA Institute for Democracy, Education, and Access.

Rogers, J., Mediratta, K., & Shah, S. (2012). Building power, learning democracy: Youth organizing as a site of civic development. *Review of Research in Education, 36*(1), 43–66. http://dx.doi.org/10.3102/0091732X11422328

Rogers, J., & Morrell, E. (2010). "A force to be reckoned with": The campaign for college access in Los Angeles. In M. Orr & J. Rogers (Eds.), *Public engagement for public education: Joining forces to revitalize democracy and equalize schools* (pp. 227–249). Palo Alto, CA: Stanford University Press.

Shah, S. (2011). *Building transformative youth leadership: Data on the impacts of youth organizing.* Brooklyn, NY: Funders' Collaborative on Youth Organizing.

Sullivan, L., Edwards, D., Johnson, N. A., & McGillicuddy, K. (2003). *An emerging model for working with youth: Community development + youth development = youth organizing.* New York, NY: Funders' Collaborative on Youth Organizing.

Taines, C. (2012). Intervening in alienation: The outcomes for urban youth of participating in school activism. *American Educational Research Journal, 49*(1), 53–86. http://dx.doi.org/10.3102/0002831211411079

Terriquez, V. (2014). Training young activists: Grassroots organizing and youths' civic and political trajectories. *Sociological Perspectives, 58*(2), 223–242. http://dx.doi.org/10.1177/0731121414556473

Terriquez, V., & Kwon, H. (2015). Intergenerational family relations, civic organizations, and the political socialization of second-generation immigrant youth. *Journal of Ethnic and Migration Studies, 41*(3), 425–447. http://dx.doi.org/10.1080/1369183X.2014.921567

Torres-Fleming, A., Valdes, P., & Pillai, S. (2010). *Youth organizing field scan.* New York, NY: Funders' Collaborative on Youth Organizing.

Warner, M. (2002). "Publics and Counterpublics." *Public Culture, 14*(1), 49–90.

Warren, M., & Mapp, K. (2011). *A match on dry grass: Community organizing as a catalyst for school reform.* New York, NY: Oxford University Press.

Warren, M., Mira, M., & Nikundiwe, T. (2008). Youth organizing: From youth development to school reform. *New Directions for Youth Development, 117,* 27–42. http://dx.doi.org/10.1002/yd.245

Watkins, N., Larson, R., & Sullivan, P. (2007). Bridging intergroup difference in a community youth program. *American Behavioral Scientist, 51*(3), 380–402. http://dx.doi.org/10.1177/0002764207306066

Watts, R., & Guessous, O. (2006). Sociopolitical development: The missing link in research and policy on adolescents. In S. Ginwright, P. Noguera, & J. Cammarota (Eds.), *Beyond resistance: Youth activism and community change* (pp. 59–80). New York, NY: Routledge.

9

Studying Sociopolitical Development through Social Network Theory

Kira J. Baker-Doyle

This chapter presents a study of how relationships that youth developed with various allies through a Youth Participatory Action Research (YPAR) program influenced their sociopolitical development (or, the process of developing a critical consciousness to engage in social justice work) (Watts, Griffith, & Abdul-Adil, 1999; Watts & Guessous, 2006). The youth in the YPAR program were from low-income households and identified as Hispanic. Low-income minority youth in the United States have historically been marginalized in the civic arena (Kahne & Westheimer, 2003). In recent years, YPAR has emerged as a research practice employed by schools, community organizations, and youth organizing/activism groups to empower youth to address social and political issues in their communities (Berg, Coman, & Schensul, 2009; Ozer, Ritterman, & Wanis, 2010). In YPAR, youth identify issues of concern in their communities, conduct research on these issues, and take action to address the issues based on their findings. While YPAR is not exclusive to youth organizing groups, it has been described as "parallel and interchangeable" with youth organizing because a centerpiece of both is the work of researching social and political issues in order to develop collective strategic actions (Dolan, Christens, & Lin, 2015). Thus, by examining the work and interactions of YPAR youth, we can learn much about how young people organize for social change.

In order to study the ways in which youth developed relationships with a range of allies, including adults, other youth organizers, program peers, and undergraduate mentors, I used social network theory to frame my research design and analysis. My use of the social network theory framework allowed me to identify differences in the structural network patterns that existed between youth and allies, and the ways in which these patterns influenced their beliefs, actions, and social capital.

Social capital is a key concept in social network theory and has traditionally been defined as the resources and support that exist within a web of relationships (Lin, 2001). I take a critical perspective of social capital (Akom, Cammarota, & Ginwright, 2008), which contends that (1) social capital has been traditionally framed from a deficit perspective (measuring what is lacking according to a normative standard) regarding youth and marginalized communities, and (2) social networks operate within a broader system of social inequalities and oppression such as racism, sexism, class structures, and homophobia. As such, in my analysis of this research, I was interested in how social networking by participants shaped the development of their critical awareness, understandings, and engagement in work to address social inequalities and problems in their communities through YPAR.

I found that the different networks that youth developed played varied roles in the course of their sociopolitical development. This chapter describes the differences in networking practices and how they influenced students' sociopolitical development. The research offers a model of how to use social network theory as a lens to understand sociopolitical development and has specific implications for how youth organizers can foster sociopolitical development through collaboration and partnership-building with other youth groups. As such, throughout this chapter, I highlight the ways in which youth organizers can use these findings to be strategic in networking to foster liberatory sociopolitical thinking and development.

SOCIOPOLITICAL DEVELOPMENT AND YPAR

In YPAR, youth identify and research concerns in their communities and address these concerns through their work. Most YPAR programs share similar features. First, youth work to produce systemic change for social justice (Cammarota & Fine, 2008). Second, teachers, researchers, or adult facilitators commonly support youths' work. Third, YPAR typically occurs within the context of an organization or school. Fourth, most YPAR programs encourage collaboration with groups and institutions. Finally, the goals of many YPAR programs include the following: to support the sociopolitical and academic development of participating youth, for the group to form prosocial norms and social cohesion, and at the community level, to improve conditions for marginalized youth (Berg, Coman, & Schensul, 2009). While the emphasis with YPAR is on the research process and, to some extent, academic development, the practices, principles, and goals of fostering sociopolitical awakenings mirror those of youth organizing efforts.

In this study, we use the sociopolitical development framework designed by Watts and colleagues (1999) to examine the ways in which youth moved from minimal awareness of the underlying structures shaping social inequalities and their relationship to these structures to a critical consciousness and engaged actions for social justice. Watts and colleagues (1999) identify five stages of sociopolitical development: acritical, adaptive, precritical, critical, and liberation. In the *acritical* stage, youth are unaware of social inequalities or the social structures that reinforce social inequalities. In the *adaptive* stage, youth develop some acknowledgment of structural inequalities, yet see no role for themselves in changing or addressing them; they may instead develop adaptive, or work-around solutions such as avoiding news or media that describe injustices. In the *precritical* stage, youth develop a stronger awareness of inequality and begin to question whether adaptations are enough to solve problems. In the *critical* stage, youth are interested in learning more about inequalities and begin to understand their positionality and potential agency in relation to unjust social practices and structures. In the *liberatory* stage, youth move from awareness to action; youth engage in social justice work to change social inequalities.

Watts and Flanagan (2007) argue that this sociopolitical framework "pushes the envelope" (p. 779) in examining youth development because it moves beyond internalization to action. Watts and colleagues' framework has been applied to similar research on youth development, with promising findings for engagement, leadership, and future success of youth (Diemer & Blustein, 2006; Rosen, 2016).

SOCIAL NETWORK THEORY AS A LENS

Social network theory offers a framework for understanding how social capital (defined as the resources, information, and support within social networks [Lin, 2001]) operates within social networks (complex webs of relationships between people). For this study I aimed to uncover how various types of social networks and networking practices affected youths' sociopolitical development in YPAR. Therefore, I used social network theory as a lens in which to describe and analyze the youths' experiences and practices. While few studies have integrated social network theory to analyze data on YPAR (Langhout, Collins, & Ellison, 2014), the notion of social capital and social networks is not foreign to literature on youth development and YPAR work (Akom et al., 2008; Ozer & Wright, 2012; Rodríguez & Brown, 2009; Sánchez, 2009). Indeed, the study of youths' social interactions is often included in some form in most research on YPAR. Furthermore, young people's social networks are of particular importance because schooling tends to isolate youth from building networks with adults or community members, and thus youth are cut off from potential membership in outside social networks (Zeldin, Camino, & Calvert, 2007). Scholarship on social movement theory and community organizing often identifies the importance of developing power (social capital) through strategic alliances and networking in organizing work (Evans & Baker-Doyle, 2015). Therefore, understanding the ways in which networking influences youths' development is of critical concern to our understanding of the dynamics of youth organizing.

Scholars of social network theory have found several patterns or typical behaviors of social networks that reappear in many studies and have incorporated these patterns into the foundations of social network theory. In this study, I analyzed the data based on four of these known network behaviors or patterns: structural holes (and open networks) (Burt, 1992; Granovetter, 2003), closed networks (Lin, 1999), homophily (McPherson, Smith-Lovin, & Cook, 2001), and empowerment agents/social capital (Stanton-Salazar, 2001, 2011).

The first two network behaviors are closely tied to the concept of network density, or the degree to which people in a network are connected. Scholars have found that networks with low density and high diversity (known as "open networks") and networks with a high degree of structural holes (solo linkages between cliques) tend to foster social capital in the form of innovation (Burt, 1992; Granovetter, 2003). Conversely, when social networks are dense (highly interconnected) and homogeneous, the network fosters social capital in the form of trust (Lin, 2001).

Homophily is a network pattern in which people with similar backgrounds tend to develop networks with one another. McPherson and colleagues (2001) called it the "birds of a feather" phenomenon: people tend to seek others to whom they are similar. Yet, while homophily explains the status quo of networks, empowerment agents and empowerment social capital are examples of network diversity and change. Stanton-Salazar (2011) contends that because social capital is embedded in societal structures, it often helps to reproduce hierarchies and privileges for individuals in positions of power. However, it has the potential to disrupt the reproduction of such hierarchies if individuals with high levels of social capital provide marginalized persons with access to the resources and support in their networks via mentoring and facilitating their network development.

Stanton-Salazar's (2011) research on this topic has focused primarily on youth–adult relationships. He contends that when individuals in power help marginalized youth to make an upward move in institutional or societal structures, they are enacting what he has termed *empowerment social capital*. An adult who is willing to go "against the grain" in order to support marginalized youth toward greater access to educational opportunities is described as an *empowerment agent* (or, a person who enacts empowerment social capital). Stanton-Salazar's concepts of empowerment social capital and empowerment agents help to provide a critical lens on social capital, yet also offer an opening for critique regarding the question of youth-to-youth networking. Might youth also be able to be empowerment agents for each other? If so, what forms of social capital can youth build together? This will be a critical question that this study will explore and uncover.

STUDY DESCRIPTION

Context

The YPAR program we studied was part of the Penn State Educational Partnership Program (PEPP) program, a long-standing (22-year) educational partnership between Pennsylvania State University and the Reading, Pennsylvania, school district. Reading is a city of approximately 88,000 with a high Hispanic population (80%) and high poverty (incomes 12% below the national average) (U.S. Bureau of Economic Analysis, 2011). The YPAR program was called the PEPP Urban Teachers and Leaders Pipeline program (or PEPP-UTLP) and was an offshoot of the main PEPP program. The main PEPP program had traditionally focused on tutoring and helping students prepare for college applications. PEPP-UTLP was intentionally designed to have a different focus: to increase youth civic engagement and leadership in Reading from grade 7 through college.

PEPP 10th graders and Penn State undergraduate students (education majors) were the main participants in the PEPP-UTLP program. It was structured to include one intensive summer week, in which the youth researched and developed a YPAR plan, and weekly meetings during the school year to enact the plan. This chapter focuses primarily on the networking experiences of the first-year cohort during the summer of 2011, yet does include data from weekly meetings during September 2011 through December 2011. Ten high school youth participated in the program and three undergraduate students participated as "PEPP Learning Assistants" (PLAs) in the program. The PLAs were considered co-facilitators, occasionally participating in or facilitating activities. My colleague Guadelupe Kasper and I were the adult facilitators for the summer program. Ms. Kasper was the PEPP program facilitator during the school year and had prior relationships established with many of the youth.

The work of the intensive week was grounded in a set of objectives and goals that focused on youth empowerment and social change. (See Table 9.1.) As program designers, we believed that it was important to provide many opportunities for the participants to meet, connect, and collaborate with a range of individuals from adults to youth organizers. Thus, the week was formatted around a structure in which during the mornings the participants would work with guest visitors (or one another), and in the afternoons they would apply

Table 9.1. Summer Intensive Week Goals and Objectives, as Stated in Program Planning

Program Objectives

1. For participants to get to know each other and develop a supportive community cohort.
2. To help participants learn about ways to make positive, meaningful impacts on their communities, and see themselves as change-makers in their communities.
3. For participants to develop an awareness of social issues in their communities.

Goals for Participants

1. For participants to investigate and present knowledge about a social issue that is personally important to them and their communities.
2. For participants to work collaboratively with one another in an effective and engaging manner.
3. For participants to develop a five-year plan for their future.
4. For participants to develop strategies to positively impact their communities.
5. For students to make connections with people and organizations in the fields of civic leadership and education.

what they learned to their YPAR project. Guest visitors included adult community leaders (particularly Hispanic leaders), professors, youth organizing groups (two from Philadelphia, one local), and community-based media specialists and artists. In addition to this design consideration, we were also aware of the strong role we, as adults, played in the initial design of the program, and thus we organized the program to open itself to youth-led design over time. The final days of the summer program were designed in consultation with the high school youth, and the following school-year program was led in large part by the youth.

Data Collection and Analysis

Data were collected primarily through qualitative methods. During the summer, all formal activities were video-recorded, as well as captured in field notes by the study authors, who developed and facilitated the program, and the three undergraduates. High school and undergraduate participants were interviewed during the program and four months after the summer workshop in November. Video and audio recordings were subsequently transcribed for coding. All participants spent 20 minutes each day during the summer workshop writing reflections about their experiences in personal journals. Documentary evidence, such as individual and group notes, was collected from students and undergraduates. Daily feedback surveys and an end-of-week survey were distributed to high school students. In addition to the November interviews, field notes were recorded during the weekly meetings held throughout the school year. Youth outreach activities such as youth-led workshops and organizing work were also documented through the fall of 2011.

As a qualitative study, we employed social network theory as a theoretical framework to examine data. Rather than using sociometric surveys to quantitatively measure factors related to social capital, as is the approach to quantitative social network analysis, we used theoretical concepts of social network theory (specifically, density, homophily, and empowerment social capital) as a means of analyzing social grouping and interactions documented in the field. After this initial analysis of data, we applied Watts and colleagues' (1999) sociopolitical framework to examine the critical consciousness patterns that emerged through our first-stage analysis. Thus, social network theory guided our initial coding and Watts and colleagues' sociopolitical development framework was used to analyze the codes and themes that emerged from the third-round analysis.

YOUTH NETWORKING AND SOCIOPOLITICAL DEVELOPMENT

There are four key groups of individuals (allies) that program youth networked with in the PEPP-UTLP: adults, undergraduates, youth organizers, and program peers. In conducting this analysis, I was initially interested in the ways in which program youth networked with other youth (visiting organizers and program peers) and how this networking influenced program youths' sociopolitical development. However, in examining how these interactions contrasted youths' networking with other groups (adults and undergraduates), the unique role that youth organizers and program peers played as catalysts for emerging sociopolitical awakenings became even clearer. Therefore, I begin by describing the effects of networking with adults and undergraduates on program youths' sociopolitical development before describing the youths' networking with youth organizers and each other. For each group, I describe the following: (1) a picture and social network perspective-analysis of the networking activities and practices that PEPP-UTLP youth engaged in with the respective group, and (2) an analysis of how the networking influenced or shaped youths' sociopolitical development and strategy implications for youth organizers.

PEPP-UTLP YOUTH AND ADULTS

A Social Network Lens on Networking with Adults

Formal activities during the summer that involved adult mentoring and facilitation included the following: (1) a mentor-match day, in which high school students and mentors (civic leaders from Reading, many of whom had the same demographics as the students—low income, Hispanic—when growing up) engaged in a series of discussions that allowed mentors and mentees to share personal stories of leadership and challenge, (2) an education leadership panel, in which administrators and instructors from the college spoke with high school students about their educational experiences and how to overcome future challenges that might await them, (3) a presentation by a media entrepreneur and his family on how to "market your message," that is, get the word out about your work, and (4) a presentation by a program alumna on how the PEPP program helped her to apply for college and scholarship opportunities. In addition to these formal activities, the high school students developed relationships with the adult program facilitators.

In reflections after the events and in daily journals, the high school students noted that the formal activities had a significant impact on their views of themselves as future leaders and the need to be diligent students. Two themes that emerged repeatedly throughout adult-networking activities were the importance of speaking up and planning for the future. For example, in his journal, Jose reflected upon the ways in which adult mentorship re-shaped his sense of agency and possibilities for the future. After spending time with his adult mentor, he wrote, "Today made me think about my future & what I want to do with it. It made me think also about taking civil action when I feel something is wrong" (Jose's Journal, June 2011). Similarly, in an interview Marcos told how his interactions with the mentors helped him to prepare for the future:

> An important learning experience was hearing about the lifestyle of college and stuff and like all this stuff to build our character so we can be like good leaders and stuff. It was an important learning experience because like to be a leader you need all this knowledge and us getting it early is going to really help us in the future.

The participants' relationships with the adult program facilitators were also an important aspect of their adult networking. In whole-group discussions, we were described as parental types or adults who challenged them to think about their role in their community and society. After his summer interview with Baker-Doyle, Marcos wrote in his journal, "Today I had an interview with Kira and it made me think and realize how much this program opened my eyes. It opened my eyes to all the serious topics in society today." Yet, over the course of the year, the nature of our (Guadelupe and I) relationship changed with the youth; we became less central to their YPAR activities, acting more as resource-providers (such as being van drivers) and intermediaries between youth and other adults like school administrators or adult mentors. Thus, as with the other adults in the participants' networks, while our interactions and relationships did serve to empower youth, our roles were mainly peripheral. We supported participants' future planning and offered important resources and connections, yet we were neither the fuel nor the fire that sustained the participants' actions.

In terms of basic social network theory, adults offered the youths a link to a person outside of their typical network domain, building a bridge, or perhaps a structural hole, to resources outside of their own generally homologous network. Thus, in theory, such ties could provide social capital in the form of innovation and new, "outsider" information. Building on social network theory, Stanton-Salazar's research (2001, 2011) suggests that adult empowerment agents would provide a social capital that empowers youths to break out of societal structures that oppress marginalized youth and keep them in a cycle of academic and economic failure. Our research findings support both these theories. Through their interactions with adults, participants reported that they changed the way they thought about their futures, and they developed an increased awareness of the challenges and opportunities on the road to their academic and career goals. Also clear is the peripheral role of adults in these youths' networks. With the exception of the program facilitators, the adults were not close ties and offered support only when requested. Further, although the program facilitators developed closer ties to the participants, their primary roles were as linkages between groups or individuals. For example, during the school year, messages to and from youth and facilitators were often relayed through the participant network instead of directly to the facilitators. Although the adults had an important effect on the youth, shifting their thinking and offering outside resources, their impact on engagement and action was limited.

Sociopolitical Development and Networking with Adults

While the social network data showed that adults did act as empowerment agents (Stanton-Salazar, 2011), providing models for future leadership and engagement, their influence on the youths' sociopolitical development was somewhat limited. In modeling the ways in which they overcame challenges or through their suggestions of how to navigate social hierarchies, they brought a new level of awareness to the youths, yet these issues seemed to remain in the distant future for the youths. Their current situation did not seem like something on which they could have much influence, other than making tactical choices in their career paths. These perceptions reflect the adaptive stage of Watts and colleagues' sociopolitical framework. The youths became aware of social hierarchies and structures, yet they seemed immovable to them; their only option was to adapt.

These findings are supported by other research on adult-facilitated youth empowerment programs that has critiqued the central role of the adult in organizing the work, arguing that it constructs a false sense of youth leadership and agency (Hogan, 2002; O'Donoghue, Kirshner, & McLaughlin, 2002). For youth organizers and activists, one key takeaway from these findings is to consider the sociodevelopmental stages and needs of the members of the organization when designing opportunities to collaborate with adults. Adults can provide access to institutional resources and information (the type of empowerment social capital that Stanton-Salazar [2011] describes), but they may be less able to influence youths to see themselves as agents of change.

PEPP-UTLP YOUTH AND UNDERGRADUATE FACILITATORS

A Social Network Theory Lens on Networking with Undergraduates

Undergraduate facilitators assisted program coordinators by modeling engagement, helping to organize and facilitate activities, and researching the YPAR process. The high school students and undergraduates developed strong bonds through the program, spending social time together, communicating via phone and email, and collaborating online. In several instances, the undergraduate facilitators acted as advocates and translators for the participants. For example, adult facilitators wanted to do an activity that involved reflecting on lyrics from a current popular song or rap, but had some trouble identifying one that would resonate with the participants. The undergraduates suggested a rap by Common, which became an important and engaging element in the conversation around life choices, planning, and the future. Further, the undergraduates suggested an additional activity that they had experienced in their teacher education program about goal-setting that had a strong impact on their own actions. When they introduced the activity to the participants, the youth had a similarly strong reaction. Crista cited it as an activity that helped her to understand the purpose of the program. The youth continued to discuss the goals that they developed from the activity, and they implemented the activity during their workshops during their "Little Leaders" YPAR initiative (mentoring middle school youth).

The undergraduates bridged the network characteristics of adult empowerment agents and the peer networks. They were deeply embedded in the dense peer networks, but they also had greater access to institution-based social capital than youth organizers. The undergraduates offered high school students an avenue to communicate more easily about their program needs and interests. The undergraduates behaved as important boundary crossers (Kilpatrick, Cheers, Gilles, & Taylor, 2009) in the participants' networks—providing a connection to diverse networks and facilitating an exchange of ideas and understandings among them. Yet, in addition to their advocacy, they also provided models for the participants of leadership and boundary crossing. The participants implemented many of the same actions and behaviors as the undergraduates when they worked with younger middle school youth during the school year. Thus, in addition to facilitating resource and information exchange, the undergraduates fostered leadership and agency by modeling this behavior.

Sociopolitical Development and Networking with Undergraduates

In contrast to adults, undergraduates were important bridges between high school youth and adults, acting both as translators and models for the participants, which nurtured leadership and outreach by the participants to younger students and peers. Their translation work helped youth to have a deeper understanding of the social issues and inequalities in society. They also inspired some thinking about the youths' role in relationship to these issues. These beliefs and behaviors straddle the adaptive and precritical stages of youth development. Youth became less complacent about their roles in making change. They had models closer to their own age to demonstrate that they did not have to wait until they were older to make change.

These findings have implications for both the role of young adults (ages 18–25) in relationship to youth organizers, as well as the role of higher educational institutions in supporting youth organizers. Young adults who are themselves sociopolitically mature can serve as more realistic models of pathways for youth to develop their sociopolitical understandings and can help to translate and connect ideas and resources more readily to youth. One strategy for youth organizers to draw from this finding is to develop relationships with young adult activists to act as boundary crossers and brokers for youth members and adult allies.

PEPP-UTLP YOUTH AND YOUTH ORGANIZERS

A Social Network Lens on Networking with Youth Organizers

High school–aged youth community organizers from three different youth-led groups ran workshops for participants during the summer program. Youth from the Philadelphia Student Union, the Agaston Urban Nutrition Initiative (based in Philadelphia), and Project Peace (based in Reading) conducted the workshops. The Philadelphia Student Union is a youth-led organizing group that fights for educational equity among Philadelphia public schools. Youths from the group came to discuss youth stereotyping and oppression (Rosen, 2016). They shared their own experiences working to end youth stereotyping in the Philadelphia public schools. They described how they developed a counternarrative around peaceful youth-led flash mobs, which were being scorned by the media as dangerous and violent.

The Philadelphia student union members posited questions to the Reading youth about their own experiences in Reading High School. Initially, the participants were reluctant to share their perspectives. Evan, one of the participants, reflected afterward that his reluctance was partially due to surprise; he thought that they should just accept the ways that they were being treated because that was "how it was." Others also noted surprise that they could play a role in challenging injustices. Yet, toward the end of the day, participants became more passionate about how they were perceived and treated by adults. One youth, Alicia, who rarely spoke out loud during the week, wrote an impromptu poem in her journal: "Even though Reading has their problems / They are really intelligent / The youth care about their future/ they need to realize their voice matters / be outspoken." In the same vein, Carla wrote:

> I feel that youth should not be characterized as "bad" if they don't know that population as a whole. You can't let a few bad eggs ruin the bunch of good eggs. Not everyone is bad, they just make dumb decisions. . . . Find out who you are!

Thus, through these interactions, youths began to define their own stances toward social justice and the role of youth in communities.

The Agaston Urban Nutrition Initiative (AUNI) youth carried a similar empowerment message, yet their focus was primarily on food justice. They encouraged participants to reenact important "food justice events," such as Gandhi's Salt Satyagraha (Salt March), the Immokalee migrant farmworkers' union Taco Bell tomato boycott, and the Black Panther free food program in skits and retellings. The aim of this activity was to help participants develop an awareness of the impact of organizing for social justice. The AUNI group members modeled strong enthusiasm and participation during these exercises. They challenged participants to release their inhibitions about speaking out and standing up for what they believe in. Participants' journal entries reflected the impact of AUNI's modeling through a noted change in tense and action. Participants began to write in the present tense about what they needed to do, and what they—not others—should do to make a change. For example, Marcos noted the experience was eye-opening for him and that he wanted to participate more actively in the community:

> It opened my eyes to how big of a role I can play and how much of a leader I am. Now I'm trying and going to make a difference in my community and in society. I'm going to turn the whole view on Reading the other way. We are going to build a foundation for a brighter future.

Toward the end of the week, members of Project Peace came to speak with participants about their organizing work at Reading High School (the participants' high school). Project Peace is a school-based club that was initiated by students and has a faculty sponsor. The interactions with Project Peace students helped participants to focus on specific issues that occurred in their community. Similar to their initial reaction to the AUNI youth, several participants noted surprise that other youth were taking action on these issues, and stated that they planned to become involved in Project Peace during the school year.[1] Participants' journal entries and discussion points showed a great deal of personal reflection on injustices and inequity in their own communities, especially around drug violence. For example, during a group discussion the day after working with Project Peace, Marcos told the story of coming home 10 minutes later that afternoon than usual and learning that someone had been killed in gun crossfire in front of his house about 10 minutes earlier. He was visibly upset when telling the story and repeated, "It could have been me" several times. Later, in his journal, he wrote:

> I'm sick of seeing drugs and violence in my neighborhood. We do not want to have a reason to be afraid while walking home. Innocent people are being killed over unnecessary actions due to drugs and violence. Everyone deserves a life to live, especially us kids. We can make a difference.

Rather than take a stance only as a victim of violence, however, Marcos began to take on a sense of responsibility for speaking out about this community issue. As participants began to connect community issues with the youth in Project Peace and the other groups, they began to identify more personally with issues and consider their roles as change agents.

In addition to observing shifts in the youths' perspectives on issues, we also observed a stark contrast in social behavior and interaction between participants and youth organizers in comparison to their interactions with adults. During lunch hour, students chose to sit with the visitors to discuss the issues that each struggled with at their schools, and they exchanged contact information such as Facebook and email addresses in order to stay in touch. Before the groups left, students asked to take pictures together and parted with a round of hugs and high-fives. We noted how different these interactions were to students' interactions with visiting adults, of whom only one was asked by a participant to share his contact information for further contact.

Youth organizers did not have as much access to institution-based social capital as adult "empowerment agents," nor undergraduates. However, youth organizers had prior experiences that helped them to understand the structures of power in ways in which the adults could not. Thus, while they may not have been able to connect program youth with access to institutional resources (one form of social capital), they could help them understand and engage in a process to challenge hierarchies (a more critical form of social capital). Furthermore, the similarities in age and socioeconomic backgrounds of the participant and youth organizers' networks allowed them to connect on shared experiences and ideas, reinscribing their collective identities as youth. In social network terms, the "birds of a feather flock together" mechanism is known as homophily. In this case, the homophily of the program youth and organizers facilitated trust and thus an easier exchange of ideas and resources. For the participants, this helped them to personalize the issues and experiences they were studying. As a result of their interactions with the youth organizers, participants began discussing *changes* that they wanted to see occur in their community.

Sociopolitical Development and Networking with Youth Organizers

In addition to engaging in a more action-oriented stance, program youths' self-perceptions about leadership also changed through their work with youth organizers. With adults they talked of being future leaders, yet with youth organizers they talked of being leaders in the *present*. Consequently, their work with the youth organizers triggered an intense focus on problem solving in their community and communicating what they were doing to the public. For example, when working on their YPAR projects they began video-taping summaries of their research so as to share the information with others.

Hence, youth organizers were even more poignant models for youth than adults and undergraduates. Program participants' quick cultivation of relationships was facilitated through homophily and shared understandings of being marginalized in school. Since the youth quickly connected with youth organizers, they were more open to the ideas that the youth organizers shared. The youth organizers' modeling of youth voice and engagement helped participants to think of themselves as change-makers, ask critical questions about societal structures, and identify problems that were important to them, thus propelling their interest in the real-world problem-solving work of YPAR. They realized that they could make a change now, not just in the future. This shift represents a move into the critical stage of sociopolitical development. Youths were not only aware of inequalities, they also recognized that they could make a difference.

Several implications for practice can be drawn from these findings for youth organizers. First, these findings suggest that youth organizers can also be a type of empowerment agent for other youth. While Stanton-Salazar's concept of the adult empowerment agent centers on the agent's ability to provide access to institutional resources, the "youth empowerment agent" can provide the catalyst for critical sociopolitical development and key understandings of how structures of power operate within institutions. Second, youth organizers can play a key role in supporting nascent groups of youth organizers. Finally, youth organizers can draw upon the mechanism of homophily in building coalitions and relationships with other youth and youth organizers; shared experiences and backgrounds can facilitate the creation of trust and exchange of support more quickly and with greater intensity.

PROGRAM PEERS

A Social Network Lens on Networking with Peers

Throughout the summer intensive week, several activities were facilitated to enhance social cohesion and trust within the group. In addition to building a sense of group solidarity and shared norms, the activities established a sense of expectation held for group participation and ongoing involvement. One example of the way in which a socialization activity contributed to developing a sense of trust and expectation was the development of YPAR project presentations. Toward the end of the summer workshop, participants began to form smaller action groups. They knew that on the final day of the workshop they were expected to present their ideas for ongoing YPAR projects, based on the information they had gathered and experiences they had had during the week. Although the original program schedule set aside three hours of planning time for the group presentations, participants began to voice concern that it was not enough—they wanted more time to meet and plan. By the end of the week, participants spent an additional three to four hours of work on their presentations by choice. Inside these working groups, participants began to push each other to be leaders—to speak up and use their talents. They developed a shared respect for one another and a sense of caring. Participant Michelle described this emerging sense of trust and passion in terms of *la familia* in her journal, noting, "We are a *familia por la vida siempre*! (We are a family for the rest of our lives!)."

Peer pressure for involvement and leadership between participants occurred outside of the formal program as well. In one case during the summer, when Evan missed a day, the other participants contacted him by email and phone to encourage him to return. When he returned the following day, participants asked to make time to repeat an activity for him that he missed. During the school year, Marcos, Evan, Jose, and Tomas felt they did not have enough time to organize the leadership workshops for middle school students during the formal weekly meetings, so they facilitated planning over Facebook and also met over lunch at a pizza shop on weekends. Participants became extremely dedicated to their cohort projects and peers. For example, Evan took time off work to facilitate some leadership workshops, losing several afternoons' worth of pay that could have instead gone to pay for the car for which he was saving up.

The dense network developed by the participants created supports to facilitate their peers' engagement in the program. Alongside formal peer activities, participants continued communicating outside of the program, online and in person, about the YPAR research and their passions on the topics of their inquiry. Prior research on social networks strongly supports the relationship between dense networks (in which all network members have strong personal relationships with one another) and the development of trust and support (Lin, 2001). However, what is particularly interesting in this case is that not only did the dense networks facilitate the development of trust, but they also inspired action and engagement in their work and their "*familia.*" Other research on social networks has demonstrated how networks can serve as mediating forces in helping individuals make sense of their contexts and abilities (Coburn, 2005), yet this network went beyond acting as a mediating force to one that fostered commitment and dedication.

One concept in social network theory may help to explain the network's fostering of collective action (beyond mere collective understanding): expertise transparency (Baker-Doyle & Yoon, 2010). Expertise transparency describes the knowledge of the expertise held by others in the network, or how much people in a network know about one another's backgrounds and special skills. High expertise transparency in a network may lead to higher levels of advice-sharing and collaboration. The youth in the PEPP-UTLP program indicated a high level of expertise transparency through frequently identifying particular individuals as experts and assigning them tasks that fit their expertise. In previous research on educators (Baker-Doyle & Yoon, 2010), high expertise transparency has been shown to increase group participation. In the same vein, the high expertise transparency developed in the youths' network may relate to the higher levels of group participation and dedication to the group.

Sociopolitical Development and Program Peer Networking

The continuous collaboration of program peers developed a dense network that participants accessed for support, ideas, and feedback. This network, or "*familia*" (as one youth called it), supported the youths' transformation of ideas into actions through continuous, ongoing interactions and engagement. Youths who took action to change social inequalities embodied the liberatory stage of the sociopolitical framework. The youths were no longer critiquing inequalities; they were acting to change them.

There were several characteristics of this network that supported their agency and actions, which can be useful to youth organizers. First, the frequent, intense, and continuous meetings of the group supported the development of close relationships. Second, the intentional structuring of activities to help students discuss and inquire about their identities and expertise helped to foster a sense of expertise transparency in the group. Third, the ways in which the youth called on one another's expertise and held space and an expectation for one another's participation were important in helping develop a sense of commitment. Building intentional, frequent time to engage in identity work, recognizing one another's expertise, and calling on one another to step forward are all actions that would support this type of network development and move from collective understanding to collective action.

A FRAMEWORK FOR YOUTH NETWORKING AND SOCIOPOLITICAL DEVELOPMENT

The social network findings and analyses revealed a differentiation in the kinds of revelations and changes in the youths' critical consciousness and action in relation to types of networking experiences and relationships with particular groups. Table 9.2 illustrates the ways in which different kinds of networks and networking shaped youth sociopolitical development in the PEPP-UTLP program. There are clear differences in the ways in which youth networked with adults and how these relationships shaped their sociopolitical development. The adults and undergraduates served as distant models of possibility for youth, yet it was the youths' collaboration and engagement with youth organizers and one another that had the greatest impact on their sociopolitical development.

There is a limitation to this analysis, however: the problem of linearity in a developmental framework. Youths' social interactions and engagement in these networks did not progress in a linear fashion in alignment with a developmental progression from an acritical stage to a liberatory stage. Rather, these relationships developed over time, and participants' interactions with adults, undergraduates, and youth organizers occurred at various times

Table 9.2. Network Characteristics and YPAR Participation and Engagement Across Four Networking Groups

	Adults	Undergraduates	Youth Organizers	Program Peers
Network Characteristics	Empowerment agents	Bridging ties between adults and youth	Homophilic (similar) networks	Dense, strong ties
Features of Networking Outcomes	Models for future engagement and leadership in social change	Translating ideas and practices of adults to youth, and youth to adults	Models for current engagement and leadership in YPAR and youth voice	Solidarity, support, collaborative actions
Sociopolitical Development Stage Supported	Adaptive stage	Adaptive/precritical stage	Critical stage	Liberation stage
Examples of Youth Response to Networking Experiences	"It was an important learning experience because . . . to be a leader you need all this knowledge and us getting it early is going to really help us in the future."	"The PLA's activity really helped me understand what this program is about."	"It opened my eyes to how big of a role I can play and how much of a leader I am. Now I'm trying and going to make a difference in my community, and in society."	"We are a *familia por la vida siempre!*"

through the summer workshop and the school year. Yet, Watts and colleagues (1999) do suggest that sociopolitical development is not completely linear. In their description of the framework, they write, "it may prove more useful to think about these so-called states as statuses, to reflect the possibility that there is no common starting or end point" (p. 263). I contend that these network structures and interactions played varying roles in the course of the youths' sociopolitical development and that youth political development must be understood as a complex process, with movement back and forth between statuses. As such, the framework may serve as an example for future organizers, scholars, and advocates to draw upon when supporting youth in developing their sociopolitical stance.

CONCLUSION

As I write this now, it has been almost five years since the PEPP-UTLP program in this study took place. Several of the youths who were in the program are now working as the undergraduate PLAs for the upcoming summer program, and they continue to engage in PEPP volunteer work throughout the school year. The goals of the program, to empower youth to be change-makers and community leaders, were indeed met, in large part due to the influence of other youth organizers. In seeking to understand the relationship between social networks and youth sociopolitical development, this study revealed that youth had a more critical impact on the social capital and sociopolitical development of other youth than adults.

In this chapter, I described youth networking with four key groups: adults, undergraduates, youth organizers, and program peers. Using a social network lens I showed how each group had different networking structures and dynamics, which in turn influenced youth sociopolitical development in a different way. When youth networked with adult mentors, they rarely made close connections, and their life experiences were very different from those of many of the adults. The adults helped them to envision future possibilities and a sense of responsibility to the world, but did not push them beyond the adaptive stage of sociopolitical development. Likewise, while the youths had more in common with undergraduates, who often helped to broker understandings between youths and adults, youth sociopolitical development remained in the adaptive and precritical stages through their interactions with these groups. It was homophily and the dense network ties developed by the youth organizers and program peers that catalyzed youth in the program to move into the critical and liberatory statuses of the sociopolitical development spectrum.

Youth organizers can use these findings to think strategically about how to use networking and collaboration to support new and existing youth in their organization and community to develop their sociopolitical understandings. Start with assessing the needs of the youth in the community (at which stage of the sociopolitical development scale are they?), as well as the opportunities for collaboration and networking. Construct opportunities for collaborative work with intention, keeping in mind what was uncovered in this study. For example, if a youth organizing group needed access to institutional knowledge or support, working with adults would suit these needs (see also Kirshner, 2008, for examples of roles that adults can play in youth-led organizing). However, if their goal was to develop a more critical understanding of their role in society, seeking other active youth organizing groups for help and support may meet these needs better.

ACKNOWLEDGMENTS

With special acknowledgment to Guadalupe Kasper for her contributions to the research design and data collection.

NOTE

1. Two students did become leaders in Project Peace the next year.

REFERENCES

Akom, A. A., Cammarota, J., & Ginwright, S. (2008). Youthtopias: Towards a new paradigm of critical youth studies. *Youth Media Reporter, 2*(4), 1–30. Retrieved from http://www.youthmediareporter.org

Baker-Doyle, K. J., & Yoon, S. A. (2010). Making expertise transparent: Using technology to strengthen social networks in teacher professional development. In A. Daly (Ed.), *Social Network Theory and Educational Change* (pp. 115–127). Cambridge, MA: Harvard Education Press.

Berg, M., Coman, E., & Schensul, J. J. (2009). Youth Action Research for prevention: A multi-level intervention designed to increase efficacy and empowerment among urban youth. *American Journal of Community Psychology, 43*(3), 345–359. http://dx.doi.org/10.1007/s10464-009-9231-2

Burt, R. S. (1992). *Structural holes: The social structure of competition.* Cambridge, MA: Harvard University Press.

Cammarota, J., & Fine, M. (2008). *Revolutionizing education: Youth Participatory Action Research in motion.* New York, NY: Routledge.

Coburn, C. (2005). Shaping teacher sensemaking: School leaders and the enactment of reading policy. *Educational Policy, 19*(3), 476–509. http://dx.doi.org/10.1177/0895904805276143

Diemer, M. A., & Blustein, D. L. (2006). Critical consciousness and career development among urban youth. *Journal of Vocational Behavior, 68*(2), 220–232. http://dx.doi,org/10.1016/j.jvb.2005.07.001

Dolan, T., Christens, B. D., & Lin, C. (2015). Combining youth organizing and youth participatory action research to strengthen student voice in education reform. *Yearbook of the National Society for the Study of Education, 114*(1), 153–170.

Evans, M., & Baker-Doyle, K. J. (2015, April). *The dynamic nature of strategic alliances in education organizing.* Paper talk presented at American Educational Research Association Annual Conference, Chicago, IL.

Granovetter, M. (2003). The strength of weak ties. In R. Cross, A. Parker, & L. Sasson (Eds.), *Networks in the Knowledge Economy* (pp. 109–129). New York, NY: Oxford University Press.

Hogan, K. (2002). Pitfalls of community-based learning: How power dynamics limit adolescents' trajectories of growth and participation. *Teachers College Record, 104*(3), 586–624. Retrieved from http://eric.ed.gov/?id=EJ649787

Kahne, J., & Westheimer, J. (2003). Teaching democracy: What schools need to do. *Phi Delta Kappan, 85*(1), 34–66. Retrieved from http://www.jstor.org/stable/20440498

Kilpatrick, S., Cheers, B., Gilles, M., & Taylor, J. (2009). Boundary crossers, communities, and health: Exploring the role of rural health professionals. *Health & Place, 15*(1), 284–290. http://dx.doi.org/10.1016/j.healthplace.2008.05.008

Kirshner, B. (2008). Guided participation in three youth activism organizations: Facilitation, apprenticeship, and joint work. *Journal of the Learning Sciences, 17*(1), 60–101. http://dx.doi.org/10.1080/10508400701793190

Langhout, R. D., Collins, C., & Ellison, E. R. (2014). Examining relational empowerment for elementary school students in a YPAR program. *American Journal of Community Psychology, 53*(3), 369–381. http://dx.doi.org/10.1007/s10464-013-9617-z

Lin, N. (1999). Building a network theory of social capital. *Connections, 22*(1), 28–51. Retrieved from http://sociology.sunimc.net

Lin, N. (2001). Building a network theory of social capital. In N. Lin, K. Cook, & R. S. Burt (Eds.), *Social Capital: Theory and Research* (pp. 1–30). New York, NY: Aldine De Gruyter.

McPherson, M., Smith-Lovin, L., & Cook, J. M. (2001). Birds of a feather: Homophily in social networks. *Annual Review of Sociology, 27,* 415–444. http://dx.doi.org/10.1146/annurev.soc.27.1.415

O'Donoghue, J., Kirshner, B., & McLaughlin, M. W. (2002). Introduction: Moving youth participation forward. *New Directions for Youth Development: Theory, Practice, and Research, 2002*(96), 15–26. http://dx.doi.org/10.1002/yd.24

Ozer, E., Ritterman, M., & Wanis, M. (2010). Participatory action research (PAR) in middle school: Opportunities, constraints, and key processes. *American Journal of Community Psychology, 46*(1), 152–166. http://dx.doi.org/10.1007/s10464-010-9335-8

Ozer, E. J., & Wright, D. (2012). Beyond school spirit: The effects of youth-led Participatory Action Research in two urban high schools. *Journal of Research on Adolescence, 22*(2), 267–283. http://dx.doi.org/10.1111/j.1532-7795.2012.00780.x

Rodríguez, L. F., & Brown, T. M. (2009). From voice to agency: Guiding principles for participatory action research with youth [Special Issue]. *New Directions for Youth Development, 2009*(123), 19–53. http://dx.doi.org/10.1002/yd.312

Rosen, S. M. (2016). Identity performance and collectivist leadership in the Philadelphia Student Union. *International Journal of Leadership in Education, 19*(2):224–240. http://dx.doi.org/10.1080/13603124.2014.954628

Sánchez, P. (2009). Chicana feminist strategies in a participatory action research project with transnational Latina youth. *New Directions for Youth Development, 2009*(123), 83–97. http://dx.doi.org/10.1002/yd.316

Stanton-Salazar, R. D. (2001). *Manufacturing hope and despair: The school and kin support networks of U.S.-Mexican youth.* New York, NY: Teachers College Press.

Stanton-Salazar, R. D. (2011). A social capital framework for the study of institutional agents and their role in the empowerment of low-status students and youth. *Youth & Society, 43*(3), 1066–1109. http://dx.doi.org/10.1177/0044118X10382877

U.S. Bureau of Economic Analysis. (2011, August 9). Personal income for metropolitan areas, 2009. Retrieved from http://www.bea.gov

Watts, R. J., & Flanagan, C. (2007). Pushing the envelope on youth civic engagement: A developmental and liberation psychology perspective. *Journal of Community Psychology, 35*(6), 779–792. http://dx.doi.org/10.1002/jcop.20178

Watts, R. J., Griffith, D. M., & Abdul-Adil, J. (1999). Sociopolitical development as an antidote for oppression—theory and action. *American Journal of Community Psychology, 27*(2), 255–271. http://dx.doi.org/10.1023/A:1022839818873

Watts, R. J., & Guessous, O. (2006). Sociopolitical development: The missing link in research and policy on adolescents. In P. Noguera, J. Cammarota, & S. Ginwright (Eds.), *Beyond Resistance* (pp. 59–80). London: Routledge.

Zeldin, S., Camino, L., & Calvert, M. (2007). Toward an understanding of youth in community governance: Policy priorities and research directions. *Análise Psicológica, 25*(1), 77–95. http://dx.doi.org/10.14417/ap.431

10

Shifting Stereotypes and Storylines: The Personal and Political Impact of Youth Media

Barbara Ferman and Natalia Smirnov

Young people of color are forced to navigate a complex system of inequities in their schools, communities, and the larger society (see Warren & Kupscznk, this volume). Compounding these injustices, mainstream media often portray these individuals in extremely negative and demeaning ways, such as criminals and underachievers (Goodman & Greene, 2003). Under these conditions, media production can be one powerful tool to support youth as they negotiate the larger institutions and systems that shape their lives and opportunities. Youth-produced media include video, print, audio, and interactive work such as documentaries, journalism, radio storytelling, websites, and creative fiction made by young people. Cultural production is a critical site for challenging dominant narratives and articulating alternative identities and forms of social relations. As such, youth media can be a form of cultural activism, enabling youth to visibly "put forth critique and analysis of urban social inequality, as well as posit potential solutions to these problems" (Duncan-Andrade, 2007, p. 26).

Media making is also an important source of empowerment through skill building in collaboration, planning, technology, and argumentation, creating "pathways to the development of student agency against conditions of social inequality" (Duncan-Andrade, 2007, p. 26). While the legitimacy of youth-produced critiques can be easily dismissed by key stakeholders because of the age of the creators, style of delivery, and limited distribution (Hobbs & Moore, 2014; Levine, 2008), strategic production and circulation practices can effectively channel youth voice into larger public conversations and catalyze social change. The experience of POPPYN (*Presenting Our Perspective on Philly Youth News*) illustrates how youth media can be transformed from a tool for youth engagement and empowerment to a tool that also includes larger societal change.

POPPYN is a youth-produced TV news show of the University Community Collaborative, which we refer to as the Collaborative, for short. Housed at Temple University, the Collaborative "prepares and supports youth and young adults to become confident, effective leaders and creates cultures that value and integrate the contributions of youth, thereby building stronger communities" (University Community Collaborative, para. 1). The Collaborative carries out this mission through programming for high school students, and training and technical assistance for nonprofit, educational, and government organizations. (See www.UCCollab.org for more information.)

Started in 2010, POPPYN was born from the desire of youth participants at the Collaborative to shift stereotypes of Philadelphia teens and young adults in mainstream media. Frustrated by frequent representations of young people in local news as dropouts or dangerous miscreants in need of discipline, a group of youth media makers and adult allies developed youth-produced news as a storytelling strategy to challenge these portrayals. The key strategic components of POPPYN include a hybrid episode format that combines broadcast, documentary, and narrative genres, allowing multiple engaging ways of making meaning and grounding social problems; building infrastructures to connect and maintain relationships with diverse audiences (via a weekly spot on the local public access channel, community viewing parties, and social media distribution); and partnerships with other social justice and youth-serving organizations. Collectively, these components enable us to communicate important issues to youth audiences in engaging and culturally relevant ways, to insert the youth perspective into a variety of issue/policy areas and existing social movements, and to garner a larger and more diverse viewing audience. The impact of this project is both direct and distributed: the production process enables youth creators to build powerful skills and strategies such as critical thinking, media literacy and production, research, interviewing, teamwork, and networking, among others. The product in turn raises broader community awareness about issues impacting youth, how youth are addressing those issues, and the resources available to young people in Philadelphia. Undergirding all this are youth media educators who serve as colleagues and empowerment agents.

In this chapter, we examine these strategic components of youth-produced media and how they have contributed to the Collaborative's ability to shift negative mainstream stereotypes and storylines about youth. Drawing from specific episodes, we illustrate the loop between personal experience, media production, meaning-making, distribution strategies, and youth activism. The lessons drawn from the POPPYN experience will contribute to and expand our understanding of how youth-produced media can serve as a mediating tool for personal empowerment and as a contribution to larger civic discourse.

YOUTH MEDIA AS CIVIC MEANING-MAKING

The daily experiences of young people of color are highly complex and varied, characterized by a range of risks and supports that are unique to each person and community (Gutierrez & Rogoff, 2003; Lee, Spencer, & Harpalani, 2003; Swanson, Spencer, Harpalani, & Spencer, 2002). However, a disproportionate number of youth of color experience daily community violence, economic and food insecurity, persistent poverty, institutional marginalization, and the like (Milner, 2013). Collectively, minority youth must also navigate a world that circulates many stigmatizing narratives about people like themselves, including negative perspectives around academic achievement, criminal inclinations, and moral worth (boyd, 2014; Males, 1996, 1998; Watkins, 2004). Analyses of local and national news broadcasts find that adolescents are represented most often as "either the agents or victims of violent events, whether intentional or accidental" (Amundson, Lichter, & Lichter, 2005, p. 8). This negative tilt is more drastic for youth from historically stigmatized, culturally nondominant groups. More than 52% of stories about non-white youth focus on crime, compared to 35% for white youth (Amundson et al., 2005). As such, Black and poor youth in particular have attained "the dubious distinction of being a celebrity social problem" (Watkins, 2004, p. 562). These recurrent "crisis discourses" stigmatize adolescent Black bodies as dangerous, violent, and in need of containment, and lead to policies that reproduce segregation and social inequality (Massaro & Mullaney, 2011). How youth interpret, internalize, or resist these narratives has consequences for their self-esteem (Martins & Harrison, 2012; Wexler, DiFluvio, & Burke, 2009) and their collective possibility for enacting a more socially just world.

At the Collaborative, we have used a variety of pedagogical approaches to support marginalized youth in developing resilient strategies for dealing with the social and institutional conditions that affect their lives. These include power analysis, media literacy exercises, collaborative research, workshop development, and media production. In this chapter, we focus solely on the potential of collaborative youth media production for building the individual and collective power of youth.

Youth media production has been theorized by literacy scholars for the rich context it provides for learning critical media literacy (Buckingham & Sefton-Green, 1994; Goodman & Greene, 2003); mobilizing and remixing a variety of communicative modes such as text, visual, audio, and others (Burn & Parker, 2003; Hull & Nelson, 2005; Mills, 2010); as a tool for identity exploration (Halverson, 2010); and as a way for critically responding to limiting mainstream narratives (Curwood & Gibbons, 2010; Duncan-Andrade, 2007). Critical race scholars have considered media production's value for building economic and social capital[1] (Watkins, 2004). Elsewhere, we have written about youth media as a form of "social currency" that circulates valuable resources for different community stakeholders (Smirnov, Ferman, & Cabral, 2015). As media makers, youth are also cultural producers, thus contributing to a "sphere in which individuals, groups, and institutions engage in the art of translating the diverse and multiple relations that mediate between private life and public concerns" (Giroux, 2004, p. 63). Therefore, media production supports youth creators in developing skills in critical analysis, video and journalism conventions, filmmaking, and editing and serves as a form of public pedagogy for those who engage with it as audiences.

POPPYN provides a good example of youth media and its potential for political participation and public pedagogy. The project challenges mainstream stigmatizing narratives about youth by mobilizing the potential of media production and public distribution. The show does so by presenting the positive contributions Philadelphia youth make to their city and community, and the social challenges they face from their point of view. As such, the project aims to shift the dominant stereotype of urban teens from "youth as problems to be addressed" to "youth as partners in problem solving." In the show, curious and confident youth journalists report on ways that other young people and adults are addressing pressing social issues through service, organizing, poetry, art, entrepreneurship, and other activities. POPPYN thus creates the space for young people to challenge the debilitating effects of negative perceptions and actively cultivate their agency by imagining and enacting positive narratives and more promising futures for themselves and their peers. This shift is equally important for POPPYN crew members, many of whom have internalized these stereotypes. The POPPYN episode on disabilities, which is detailed below, illuminates this process.

Video production, which involves developing questions, interviewing, arranging multiple voices and sources of information through editing, creating voiceovers and transitions, and presenting the final product to others, engages young people in a process of mediated narrative meaning-making. In order to make sense of complex and contradictory lived realities, individuals actively seek to construct comprehensible and internally coherent interpretations of their experiences, using a variety of culturally available meaning-making resources. These include language, image, memory, authoritative interpretations (such as religious and ideological discourses), and personal narratives, among others (Bruner, 1991; Unsworth, 2006). Media-making involves using multimodal resources and genre forms to create representations that construct and communicate meaning to others (Hull & Nelson, 2005). Different genres afford different meaning-making potentials: narrative forms are particularly well suited for identity exploration and personal storytelling (Halverson, 2010), whereas documentary and journalistic genres are more effective for synthesizing multiple views of the same issue or phenomena (Lam, Smirnov, Chang, Easterday, & Rosario-Ramos, 2013; Montgomery, 2007).

POPPYN episodes focus on a single overarching theme (e.g., youth in the criminal justice system or homelessness) in order to interpret a complex issue through different media forms. In the course of a typical 30-minute episode, POPPYN operationalizes broadcast news tropes such as "person on the street" interviews and "on the scene" coverage of youth-led protests and events. Additionally, each episode incorporates a narrative skit that interprets a particular social challenge (such as peer pressure to have sex) through an exemplary personal fictionalized story. Finally, each episode features a segment called "breakin' it down" (resembling the late-night comedy talk show genre), which remixes popular news stories, images, statistics, and video clips about a particular phenomenon or issue using an entertaining scripted dialogue. Thus, in the course of an episode, POPPYN producers make meaning of social issues and personal lived realities by producing mediated representations that move from the concrete (e.g., interviews with random people on the street; their own personal experiences), to the collective (e.g., featured organizations and events, statistics), to the conceptual (e.g., "breakin' down" the "school-to-prison pipeline"), and back again. Meaning-making is accomplished by learning to see personal struggles as connected to larger political issues and by grounding larger issues in personal experiences, using a variety of multimodal resources and storytelling strategies.

Creating the links between personal experiences, storytelling, and meaning-making requires that youth feel safe, valued, respected, and supported by the other individuals within the shared space. Keeping the crew relatively small and using a layered mentoring approach, POPPYN has created what Deirdre Kelly (2006) terms "subaltern counterpublics" (p. 41), places where youth feel comfortable exploring their identities, formulating their perspectives, and preparing to articulate those to larger publics. The crew is never larger than 10 high school students and three former participants who are now in college. The college students are trained and paid to facilitate the process with the current high school students. Thus, the high school students are mentored by college students and, among the college students, the more senior ones mentor the more junior ones, with the entire crew being mentored by a full-time staff person. Within this layering, expertise, skills, and life experiences are shared in a supportive and trusting environment.

POPPYN's 2015 episode on disabilities illustrates how this process works. In response to requests from the participants, the POPPYN coordinator allowed each of the high school student crew members to produce his or her own video, capturing a personal story. Two major themes that emerged across the videos were disabilities and mental health. Realizing how prevalent these issues are for youth, the crew decided to devote the next episode to that topic. They interviewed an adjunct professor at Temple University and staff from three organizations—Eye to Eye,[2] a national mentoring organization for students with learning disabilities and ADHD that has a chapter on Temple

University's campus; La Puerta Abierta,[3] an organization that provides mental health services to youth and families in the Latino community, many of whom are undocumented; and Youth Health Empowerment Project (YHEP),[4] an organization that provides holistic health services and sexual health education to youth and young adults. The crew also created a skit that portrays the insensitive comments people often use when talking about individuals with mental health/disability issues. Through producing this episode, the youth developed a deeper understanding of the different forms that disability and mental health challenges take, how they shape people's identities and sense of self-worth, the impacts they have on people's lives, and some of the resources available for youth with mental health problems and disabilities. They also became more mindful of how they and others talk about these issues and the language they use to describe people. And, while not the focus of this episode, they became much more knowledgeable about and sensitive to the challenges faced by undocumented individuals as a result of interviews with staff and participants from La Puerta Abierta.

The episode also illustrates how the *process* of media-making flows into the process of meaning-making, allowing youth to create subaltern publics from where they generate new narratives about themselves. One of the crew members, Nasir, age 19, has been struggling with dyslexia for a long time, suffering educational setbacks along with ridicule and scorn from his peers. As part of the episode, he interviewed a 33-year-old college graduate who is an adjunct faculty member at Temple University and met several college volunteers with Eye to Eye. They talked about how their learning disabilities impacted them, where they found support, and some of their future plans. Through this episode, Nasir discovered communities of support, learned about resources available to students like him, and, perhaps most important, saw young people with learning disabilities who were not living in the shadows of degradation and shame, but, rather, were advocating for others in similar situations. Although we cannot predict the long-term impacts of this episode on Nasir, we do believe it has changed how he sees himself and his place in the world. Moreover, he is telling others to see him differently as well: "People will look at me like I'm a freak or I'm something not of nature or I'm different than other(s), but I'm not. I'm the same. I'm flesh, I bleed when you bleed, my nose runs when your nose run(s)" (POPPYN, 2015, 0:40).

INSERTING YOUTH VOICE INTO PUBLIC DIALOGUE

As a tool for leadership development, youth-produced media enables young people to develop many technical, analytical, research, and project development skills and to reflect on and share their personal stories, but it often fails to link these stories to larger social, political, and economic movements. At the Collaborative, staff struggled with those issues in the youth media work generated in the other programs. With the development of POPPYN, however, we became more strategic about the production and circulation of the media work, and we partnered with social justice and youth-serving organizations in the production process, both of which significantly broadened and deepened our distribution channels and provided access to other resources for POPPYN and the crew members. In essence, POPPYN represents a set of institutional practices that Ito and colleagues (2015) call "connected civics," which are activities that "support learning and consequential connections between spaces of youth cultural production, their agency, and their civic and political worlds" (p. 12). POPPYN's episode on the Black Lives Matter movement illustrates how these connections operate. While shooting the episode, POPPYN crew members observed and participated in several rallies and protests, activities that were new for the high school students. Subsequently, these students became very passionate about racial and economic justice issues, engaging in conversations with family members and friends and urging them to get involved in these larger movements. Several expressed a desire to join one of the youth organizing groups that was featured in the episode. Working on the episode enabled them to connect their personal experiences as young black individuals to larger political and social movements.

Building Infrastructures for Distribution

The production of alternative youth media narratives is necessary but not sufficient for impacting larger social perceptions. Shifting the pervasive stigmatizing portrayals of youth requires infrastructures for public distribution, reception, and action. Incorporating the lessons from our prior youth-produced media work, we were very intentional when we designed POPPYN about developing relationships with multiple distribution channels, including a weekly spot on a local public access channel[5] and creating our own outlets through YouTube, social media, community viewing parties, and targeted classroom screenings. These "cross-cutting infrastructures" leverage available media channels, affinity groups, social media platforms, and existing political movements to mobilize "young people's deeply felt interests and identities in the service of achieving the kind of civic voice and influence that is characteristic of participatory politics" (Ito et al., 2015, p. 11). These distribution strategies are necessary for incorporating youth voice into community dialogue.

For example, POPPYN has an institutional relationship with PhillyCam, the local public access channel, where the show is screened weekly at 4:30 p.m. on Thursdays. While we do not have precise audience metrics for POPPYN, PhillyCam has a viewership of 350,000 households in Philadelphia and its surrounding suburbs. The crew has often heard neighbors, friends, family, and classmates say "I saw you on TV!" suggesting that the show has a substantial organic reach (Smirnov et al., 2015, para. 8).

Additionally, POPPYN has a social media presence via YouTube, Facebook, Twitter, and Instagram. These channels are co-managed by the youth producers, connecting to their personal friends and followers. The networks include teen viewers from across the city, youth-led organizations that have been featured in the show, adult allies who are acquaintances of the Collaborative's staff, local journalists, and more. Since a new episode comes out only once every few months, social media are used to engage POPPYN fans and followers through hashtagged conversations related to the episode's theme and posted "behind the scenes" pictures of the production process. These more personal and dynamic communications help to cultivate and maintain audiences for the show.

We have also been intentional about hosting viewing parties at the wrap of each episode. These are typically attended by youth and adults from organizations featured in the episode, friends and family of the crew, and the community around the venue where the party is hosted (we vary the venues to foster more diverse relationship building and reach). Additionally, the crew travels to provide targeted screenings to college and high school classes, emphasizing the pedagogical potential of the POPPYN episodes. We have used our university location to screen films in graduate and undergraduate classes in African American studies, anthropology, criminal justice, education, political science, public health, and sociology. For faculty, POPPYN films introduce an element of "reality" that is missing from textbook analyses and typical classroom discussion, thereby making timely and pressing issues come alive in ways that are more relatable and digestable for the college students. A criminal justice professor who screened POPPYN in her classroom commented, "It allowed my students to reflect on the actual lives of those affected by the topics we discuss, in this case it is the targets of mass incarceration, young black men. It added a humanistic depth to class discussion that you can't get at through statistics or any amount of rational convincing that these issues are real and that they are politically actionable right now" (personal communication). Similar views have been expressed by high school teachers who also point out the "empowerment" aspect; youth-produced media show youth audiences the options available for becoming engaged, social change agents. In fact, at the end of POPPYN screenings, students routinely ask how they can get involved with the program.

We also seek community settings for POPPYN screenings including recreation centers, other youth programs, organizations that are featured in the episodes, and city parks. In July 2014, we participated in the Philadelphia International Action Center's Summer Film Series in Clark Park, a venue in

West Philadelphia that hosts progressive-oriented events.[6] There was an entire evening devoted to our films, resulting in requests from several teachers who were in the audience to do screenings and media literacy workshops in their high school classes.

Additionally, the Collaborative is one of the founding members of the Philly Youth Media Collaborative (PYMC), a network of youth media organizations whose mission is to "strengthen, connect, and promote organizations that engage youth in the creation, analysis, and distribution of media" (PYMC, para. 1). PYMC has screened POPPYN episodes in large festivals that showcase the creative work of Philadelphia's youth. Beyond the celebratory aspect, these festivals become a networking tool for youth, helping them to connect with their peers from across the city. PYMC also hosts the "Mashed Media Awards" event, an annual competition for youth-produced media in various categories including documentary, education, visionary, narrative, and music/audio. By emulating the award processes of professional associations (e.g., the Academy Awards) and recruiting local politicians and celebrities as judges and hosts, the event treats youth-produced media as a serious and legitimate form of cultural production.

These examples illustrate how through a combination of available broadcast, social media, and institutional and grassroots distribution channels, we have assembled and leveraged an infrastructure that enables us to increase the visibility and reach of youth media. These infrastructures consequently create stronger ties to the progressive political and issue-specific communities in Philadelphia, thereby building more consequential connections for youth civic action.

Partnerships with Other Social Justice and Youth-Serving Organizations

Paralleling the long-term infrastructure building process, we use each episode as an opportunity to deliberately build partnerships with other local activist and youth-serving organizations by featuring them in the show, and by involving them in screenings and discussions of the final episode. These partnerships are mutually beneficial, in that they encourage knowledge and resource sharing and network building across the Philadelphia social justice community. As noted, POPPYN episodes are developed around a central theme, such as sex, the criminal justice system, politics, education, or music. Each episode features organizations that are addressing the particular issue in some way. POPPYN creates short, high-quality, youth-friendly news packages about these organizations, which the programs in turn can share on their websites and social media, and which will be seen by POPPYN viewers on public access and YouTube. For example, POPPYN's episode on youth homelessness featured short segments on four organizations that work with homeless youth; the Salvation Army, the School District of Philadelphia, the Attic (one of the city's LGBTQ youth organizations), and the internationally known Mural Arts Program.

When the episode was completed, we assembled a panel of researchers and practitioners from across these organizations for the episode's first viewing party, which drew close to 200 attendees. Contacts made at that screening have resulted in additional screenings, participation in larger coalitions working to address youth homelessness in Philadelphia, and in a collaborative film production with the Juvenile Law Center, a long-standing and highly regarded youth policy advocacy organization.[7] The film, which is a partnership between youth from one of the Juvenile Law Center's programs who are now aging out of foster care and staff from the Collaborative, will be presented to the Department of Human Services, the major organization in Philadelphia responsible for foster care services. The film will accompany a report they produced on how to improve the foster care system and the aging-out process.

Staff members at the Collaborative have also been instrumental in the partnership-building process, leveraging their numerous networks to promote our media work. POPPYN's coordinator successfully leveraged her position as manager of the Black Star Film Festival to incorporate a youth programming component. This four-day film festival, which *Ebony* magazine nicknamed "the Black Sundance," showcases independent films "from emerging directors, producers and writers—all by and about people throughout the African diasporic experience."[8] POPPYN episodes have been screened at this festival since 2014. Heavily promoted by the city's office of tourism and official visitor information offices, the Black Star Film Festival significantly enhances the visibility and legitimacy of our youth-produced media work while also providing an opportunity for our youth to network with professionals in the media-making world.

Youth Media Educators: Colleagues and Empowerment Agents

Social change or policy change is always a long-term process, especially when those advocating for the change are under-resourced groups.[9] In our treatment of the political potential of youth-produced media, it is important to emphasize the long-term and often invisible labor that goes into making it a powerful tool for individual and social change. This work includes creating spaces that help youth develop the skills, confidence, and efficacy to question their current conditions and voice their perspectives; teaching youth technical and critical skills to produce media; supporting them to create narratives that make sense of challenging issues they face in their daily life; building infrastructures for distribution of youth media; and situating their projects within a larger network of cultural and educational institutions. The POP-PYN case illustrates one organization's set of strategies to accomplish each of these endeavors. However, it is adult allies acting from within institutions to leverage resources that make these outcomes happen.

Chávez and Soep (2005) have argued that in youth media spaces adults often act as colleagues who work alongside youth media-makers. In this "pedagogy of collegiality," adults and youth frame projects collectively, bridging youth-led inquiry and adult contributions, and share responsibility for the work, with adults providing assistance on aspects of the media production process that young people might not yet be able to complete on their own. While youth voice, leadership, and expertise are emphasized in this pedagogical approach, empowerment is not just pushing youth to the front lines. Adult facilitators and organizational leaders must recognize their institutional privilege and act as "empowerment agents" to advance opportunities for the mobility and success of less institutionally powerful youth. As defined by Stanton-Salazar (2011), empowerment agents are individuals who, by virtue of their position within the larger system of stratification, can access resources, services, and other supports that can empower the young person. They typically possess social capital that has high exchange value, which can be used to leverage resources on behalf of those who are on the margins of society (Stanton-Salazar, 2011). These individuals are well networked themselves, often in a bridging position between several communities. Additionally, they have a critical understanding of economic and political structures that affects the mobility and success of low-status youth, and they know the importance of brokering institutional support in advancing young people's opportunities.

Empowerment agents have been critical to POPPYN, helping young people of color develop connections, resources, competencies, and platforms necessary to exercise greater control over their lives and goals. The project coordinator, who herself is an award-winning filmmaker with many ties in the progressive and media fields, regularly uses her networks to facilitate coverage of local organizations and events and to secure screening opportunities in community venues. She also makes available institutional space and resources to youth who wish to pursue media-making beyond POPPYN, such as time in the editing lab, ability to borrow camera equipment, and use of university classrooms. The staff members at the Collaborative regularly write recommendation letters for students applying for college admission, scholarships, and jobs, using their positions to provide credibility and institutional backing. On several occasions, staff leveraged this credibility to intervene in academic and legal issues, staving off potentially dire consequences for some of the crew members. And they turned these situations into "teachable moments" for the individuals involved by taking time to discuss alternative approaches and courses of action in a challenging situation. In her role as university professor, the executive director (first author of this chapter) often facilitates introductions between the POPPYN crew and professors and local organizational leaders, which leads to opportunities to screen POPPYN in university classrooms or secure interviews with experts. Similarly, the executive director of Philly-Cam, the public access TV station in Philadelphia, has served as an empowerment agent, connecting the youth-produced media of many organizations in Philadelphia to adult audiences, to professionals in the film and music industries, and, in some cases, to philanthropic organizations. These activities build the "consequential connections" between the personal narratives and affinity networks of young people and larger and more powerful institutions and organizations (Ito et al., 2015). In short, they enable the entrance of youth-produced work into adult civic and political arenas.

We also support youth as they progress in the organization to become empowerment agents themselves through a system of layered mentoring. As noted above, the crew is comprised of high school and college students, with the latter occupying training positions (e.g., teaching them film and editing techniques). All of the college students were participants when they were in high school, which gives them a very nuanced understanding of current participants and enables them to also serve as mentors and role models. The fact that the college students are at different points in their POPPYN tenure and college experience creates a built-in mentoring system with more experienced college students helping newer ones both with film and academic issues. Finally, the high school students are from different grades and have different skill sets, allowing them to assume mentorship roles vis-à-vis their peers, which can be an empowering experience for them. Thus, each crew member is mentored and mentors someone else, creating an incrementally staged distribution of skills, expertise, and experience, which is empowering to all. As the more experienced POPPYN crew members embark on media work outside of POPPYN, they demonstrate a future path for newer members. In the process, they also generate contacts and opportunities that they could broker to their peers. Thus, over time youth in POPPYN become empowerment agents themselves.

CONCLUSION: LEARNING FROM POPPYN

POPPYN and other youth media programs strive to create spaces where young people feel valued and safe in exploring and sharing their identities, interrogating stereotypes (including their own), and dreaming of a better world. POPPYN has been instrumental in providing some of the "hope, healing, and care" that Shawn Ginwright (2011) so eloquently argued is a necessary foundation for civic engagement among African American youth. Ginwright suggests that community-based organizations that work with African American youth can provide pathways to critical consciousness, to action, and ultimately to well-being. In all of the Collaborative's programming, including POPPYN, we engage high school student participants in many activities designed to raise critical consciousness including conversations on race, oppression, power, and privilege; media literacy instruction; and examples of youth activism. By making and distributing media, youth take action on civic issues, while also imagining futures that value and include their voice. The entire process is designed to be a pathway to well-being, instilling participants with a sense of "purpose, optimism, hope, agency and direction" (Ginwright, 2011, p. 37).

While extremely important, these spaces are only a beginning. By nature, they are small since the kind of trust building that allows for intimate sharing is very difficult in large settings. Thus, it is imperative to create many such spaces and to strategically connect the dots. Our deliberate partnerships with institutions and citywide infrastructures such as the Philadelphia Youth Media Collaborative's events and festivals help to increase the visibility of this work by disseminating it to diverse audiences. Over time, these events and connections spiral up to create a stronger and more pervasive counternarrative of youth in Philadelphia. In sum, actualizing the power of youth media requires long-term strategizing and continual relationship building by empowerment agents within key institutions who understand their role as brokers in and members of a larger ecology of opportunities and supports. This has implications for youth activism in general and youth media in particular, and it raises questions for future research, items to which we now turn.

We have stressed the important role that empowerment agents play. However, they often negotiate a fine line, balancing the need to protect their own place within their institutions while supporting practices and products that challenge the power and privilege of those institutions and others like them. Institutions are about protecting the status quo while youth-produced media and youth activism constitute a direct challenge to that status quo. Operating "under the radar" is a necessary learned behavior for successful empowerment agents. Given the key role they play in the larger ecology of alliance building and opportunity formation, one question for researchers is: How do we identify, cultivate, and support empowerment agents?

Another consideration is scale. Youth activism, in all of its forms, is about challenge and change. Young people have identified issues and situations that they wish to change but, as noted above, the scale of this work is often overshadowed by the size of the problems. Funders and others talk about "scaling up," but such processes are fraught with many potential problems. Most important is the tension between scaling up and maintaining the integrity of the work. POPPYN's products, especially their authenticity, result from a process that rests on small groups of young people and caring adults working together. The early stages include building the kind of trust that enables honest and frank conversations on topics that have directly impacted them, usually in painful ways. Increasing the size of the group by any significant factor would undermine this key dynamic.

Moreover, almost all of the issues identified by our young people have their roots in the intersection of race and poverty. Poverty, and its debilitating effects on young people, must be shown in its rough and raw fashion. Scaling up, which requires additional resources, often involves dilution of content, thereby compromising the power of the message. Most funders shy away from controversial projects; those in the youth field typically fund "safe" areas such as youth development, violence prevention, or educational programs and stay clear of the less predictable and potentially more volatile area of youth organizing/activism. Thus, by definition, going to scale will require compromising on content. Despite the challenges involved in scaling up, these opportunities must be made available to more young people. Supporting youth in producing civic media in schools is one promising and scalable pathway for extending this work to more young people, but it presents additional challenges of adapting this work to the constraints and goals of the school environment. A related issue is the tension between attacking the status quo and gaining acceptance (and resources) from the very institutions that are being attacked. In many ways, this is parallel to the tension faced by empowerment agents. For researchers, these paradoxes raise the questions: How can youth document the role of mainstream society and institutions in their overall oppression while gaining legitimacy among enough people from that society? How can we harness resources for this work from institutions that are reproducing the very inequalities that youth media are challenging?

Finally, many funders and other adult stakeholders (e.g., policymakers, elected officials) have unrealistic time frames and expectations. They want to see immediate results, large numbers, and dramatic impacts. As we have stressed throughout, such expectations are totally out of sync with the nature, process, and overall reality of youth activism. This raises many questions including: How do we support youth activism? What are realistic expectations for this work? How do we measure and report on the work in ways that are meaningful and that can help to improve the quality and impact of the work? And how do we convince stakeholders of the merits of this work?

These questions defy simple responses. However, if our goal is to shift the stereotypes and storylines of young people of color, we need to tackle these questions with the same passion that our young people bring to their work. We owe it to them.

NOTES

1. Social capital is the value that an individual derives from his or her social networks and connections.

2. http://eyetoeyenational.org

3. http://icfamwell.org

4. https://www.fight.org/programs/y-hep

5. PhillyCam.

6. The Philadelphia organization is part of the International Action Center that was founded in 1982 by Ramsey Clark.

7. The Juvenile Law Center was the organization that investigated and brought to light the "kids for cash" scandal in Luzerne County, Pennsylvania.

8. http://www.visitphilly.com/events/philadelphia/blackstar-film-festival/

9. There is a voluminous literature on the difficulties that such groups face in challenging established practices. One of the classic works in political science was Michael Lipsky's (1968) "Protest as a Political Resource." For a recent examination of these challenges in the educational arena, see Ferman and Palazzolo (2015).

REFERENCES

Amundson, D. R., Lichter, L. S., & Lichter, S. R. (2005). What's the matter with kids today—Television coverage of adolescents in America. *Frameworks Institute*. Retrieved from http://frameworksinstitute.org/assets/files/PDF/Youth_Whats_the _Matter.pdf

boyd, d. (2014). *It's complicated: The social lives of networked teens*. New Haven, CT: Yale University Press.

Bruner, J. (1991). The narrative construction of reality. *Critical Inquiry, 18*(1), 1–21. Retrieved from http://www.jstor.org/stable/1343711

Buckingham, D., & Sefton-Green, J. (1994). *Cultural studies goes to school: Reading and teaching popular media*. London: Taylor & Francis.

Burn, A., & Parker, D. (2003). Tiger's big plan: Multimodality and the moving image. In C. Jewitt & G. Kress (Eds.), Multimodal literacy (pp. 56–72). New York: Peter Lang.

Chávez, V., & Soep, E. (2005). Youth radio and the pedagogy of collegiality. *Harvard Educational Review, 75*(4), 409–434.

Curwood, J. S., & Gibbons, D. (2009). "Just like I have felt": Multimodal counter-narratives in youth-produced digital media. *International Journal of Learning and Media, 1*(4), 59–77.

Duncan-Andrade, J. M. R. (2007). Urban youth and the counter-narration of inequality. *Transforming Anthropology, 15*(1), 26–37.

Ferman, B., & Palazzolo, N. (2015). *David and Goliath: Challenges, policy windows, and slingshots in the corporate education reform landscape*. Paper delivered at the Urban Affairs Association Annual Conference, April 8–11, 2015, Miami, FL.

Ginwright, S. (2011). Hope, healing, and care: Pushing the boundaries of civic engagement for African American youth. *Liberal Education, 97*(2), 34–39. Retrieved from http://eric.ed.gov/?id=EJ962005

Giroux, H. (2004). Cultural studies, public pedagogy, and the responsibility of intellectuals. *Communication and Critical/Cultural Studies, 1*(1), 59–79.

Goodman, S., & Greene, M. (2003). *Teaching youth media: A critical guide to literacy, video production and social change*. New York: Teachers College Press.

Gutierrez, K. D., & Rogoff, B. (2003). Cultural ways of learning: Individual traits or repertoires of practice. *Educational Researcher, 32*(5), 19–25. http://dx.doi.org/10.3 102/0013189X032005019

Halverson, E. R. (2010). Film as identity exploration: A multimodal analysis of youth-produced films. *Teachers College Record, 112*(9), 2352–2378. Retrieved from http://eric.ed.gov/?id=EJ902159

Hobbs, R., & Moore, D. C. (2014). Cinekyd: Exploring the origins of youth media production. *Journal of Media Literacy Education, 6*(2), 23–34. Retrieved from http://eric.ed.gov/?id=EJ1046508

Hull, G. A., & Nelson, M. E. (2005). Locating the semiotic power of multimodality. *Written Communication, 22*(2), 224–261.

Ito, M., Soep, E., Kligler-Vilenchik, N., Shresthova, S., Gamber-Thompson, L., & Zimmerman, A. (2015). Learning connected civics: Narratives, practices, infrastructures. *Curriculum Inquiry, 45*(1), 10–29.

Kelly, D. M. (2006). Frame work: Helping youth counter their misrepresentations in media. *Canadian Journal of Education, 29*(1), 27–48. http://dx.doi.org/10.2307 /20054145

Lam, W. S. E., Smirnov, N., Chang, A., Easterday, M., & Rosario-Ramos, E. (2013, May). *Multimodal voicing and scale making in youths' video documentaries on immigration*. Paper presented at the American Anthropology Association Annual Meeting, Chicago, IL.

Lee, C. D., Spencer, M. B., & Harpalani, V. (2003). "Every shut eye ain't sleep": Studying how people live culturally. *Educational Researcher, 32*(5), 6–13.

Levine, P. (2008). A public voice for youth: The audience problem in digital media and civic education. In W. L. Bennett (Ed.), *Civic life online: Learning how digital media can engage youth* (pp. 119–138). Cambridge, MA: MIT Press.

Males, M. A. (1996). *The scapegoat generation: America's war on adolescents*. Monroe, ME: Common Courage Press.

Males, M. A. (1998). *Framing youth: Ten myths about the next generation*. Monroe, ME: Common Courage Press.

Martins, N., & Harrison, K. (2012). Racial and gender differences in the relationship between children's television use and self-esteem: A longitudinal panel study. *Communication Research, 39*(3), 338–357.

Massaro, V. A., & Mullaney, E. G. (2011). The war on teenage terrorists: Philly's "flash mob riots" and the banality of post-9/11 securitization. *City, 15*(5), 591–604.

Mills, K. A. (2010). "Filming in progress": New spaces for multimodal designing. *Linguistics and Education, 21*(1), 14–28.

Milner, H. R. (2013). Analyzing poverty, learning, and teaching through a critical race theory lens. *Review of Research in Education, 37*(1), 1–53. http://dx.doi.org/10 .3102/0091732x12459720

Montgomery, M. (2007). *The discourse of broadcast news: A linguistic approach*. New York: Routledge.

Philly Youth Media Collaborative. (n.d.). Mission, vision, goals. Retrieved from http://www.phillyyouthmedia.org/mission-vision-goals/

Presenting Our Perspective on Philly Youth News. (Producer). (2015, September 6). Dyslexia chain: Nasir's story [YouTube series episode] from POPPYN. Retrieved from https://www.youtube.com/watch?v=DIUsM-iUWAg

Smirnov, N., Ferman, B., & Cabral, N. (2015). POPPYN: Presenting Our Perspective on Philly Youth News. *Civic Media Project*. Retrieved from http://civicmedia project.org/works/civic-media-project/poppyn

Stanton-Salazar, R. D. (2011). A social capital framework for the study of institutional agents and their role in the empowerment of low-status students and youth. *Youth and Society, 43*(3), 1066–1109.

Swanson, D. P., Spencer, M. B., Harpalani, V., & Spencer, T. R. (2002). Identity processes and the positive youth development of African Americans: An explanatory framework. *New Directions for Youth Development, 2002*(95), 73–100. Retrieved from http://www.ncbi.nlm.nih.gov/pubmed/12448287

University Community Collaborative (n.d.). About. *The Collaborative*. Retrieved from http://uccollab.org/about/

Unsworth, L. (2006). Towards a metalanguage for multiliteracies education: Describing the meaning-making resources of language-image interaction. *English Teaching: Practice and Critique, 5*(1), 55–76. Retrieved from http://eric.ed.gov/?id =EJ843820

Watkins, S. C. (2004). Black youth and the ironies of capitalism. In M. Forman and M. A. Neal (Eds.), *That's the joint! The hip-hop studies reader* (pp. 557–578). New York: Routledge.

Wexler, L. M., DiFluvio, G., & Burke, T. K. (2009). Resilience and marginalized youth: Making a case for personal and collective meaning-making as part of resilience research in public health. *Social Science & Medicine, 69*(4), 565–570.

11

Telling Our Stories, Claiming Our Space, and Becoming Change-Makers: Lessons for the Field from Black Girls and Women Organizers

Julia Daniel and Michelle Renée Valladares

To me, the effort to speak about issues of "space and location" evoked pain. The questions raised compelled difficult explorations of "Silences"— unaddressed places within my personal political and artistic evolution. Before I could consider answers, I had to face ways these issues were intimately connected to intense personal, emotional, upheaval regarding place, identity, desire.

—bell hooks

I think we don't talk about it enough. It's this change from victim to survivor but taking it a step further from victim to survivor to change-maker or societal transformer, to someone who can totally transform spaces in their community because of what we've survived.

—Tanisha Douglas

Led by young Black women, more than 300 community members and decision makers came together in Miami, Florida, on a Thursday evening in the spring of 2015 to share stories and critically examine the issues facing Black girls in their schools and communities. This Black Girls Matter Town Hall was collaboratively hosted by four local community organizations and two national civil rights organizations. Throughout the evening, participants shared experiences of discrimination, violence, and abuse and related them to systemic forms of oppression of Black women and LGBTQ people. By carving out specific spaces for themselves, these young organizers were able to assert their collective agency to build and transform the organizations they participate in and to challenge systems of oppression in the broader society.

The Town Hall was one public demonstration of this work—but was part of a long-term process of youth organizers and leadership from the convening organizations engaging with one another on these issues.

This chapter utilizes Black Feminist theory, feminist standpoint epistemology, Critical Race Theory, and social movement theory to synthesize lessons taught to us during our interviews with nine low-income Black young women and a Black gender-queer young person from four community organizations that hosted the Black Girls Matter Town Hall in Florida. By linking lessons from youth organizing to lessons from these theories, we hope to deepen understanding of both. Simply put, though theories from research can seem very esoteric, we demonstrate that they are very much alive in the lives and practice of these youth organizers.

While their work is often not as widely acknowledged as the work of their male and white counterparts, millennial Black women and girls are sharing their stories as counternarratives to the dominant stereotypes portrayed about them. In the process, these organizers are building cultures of sisterhood in which they can recognize common experiences and value themselves and one another. The consciousness-raising and leadership development work they engage in together builds their understanding of one another's lives such that they have a deep and collective analysis and commitment to work together to address all forms of oppression. This transformative work highlights new possibilities in the youth organizing field for using an intersectional lens to understand the processes of both youth organizing and leadership development.

THE CONTEXT OF YOUTH ORGANIZING IN MIAMI

We interviewed young women and gender-queer (not identifying as male or completely female) organizers that were part of four different community organizations that collectively organized the Miami Black Girls Matter Town Hall together with the African American Policy Forum and the Advancement Project. In this Town Hall, participants shared stories in front of more than 300 people. This was one part of the process of these four organizations' increasing collaboration in order to uplift the experiences and leadership of Black young women and gender-queer people in their community and in our nation.

As we listened to and observed the youth organizers in Florida examine their own identity formation, their activism, and the context surrounding their lives, it became immediately evident that their wisdom aligned with the knowledge found in social movement theory, feminist standpoint epistemology, Black Feminist theory, and Critical Race Theory. For example, the personal testimony some of our participants gave at the public Town Hall is similar to the idea of counter storytelling discussed by Critical Race theorists—the act of telling a story of oppression can bring forward the experiences and perspectives of people who are marginalized in society (Delgado, 1989; Solorzano & Yosso, 2001). By participating in public and private storytelling, the participants are creating what Ginwright (2015) calls healing circles, which "provide space for young people to both reflect on the wounds resulting from their personal struggles and be supported and guided to a political understanding of action" (p. 53). This helps to shape a form of Black women's culture that becomes a powerful challenge to both the logic and functioning of systems of domination and subjugation, highlighting the crucial need for the leadership of Black women.

Young Black women choosing to take collective action by publicly telling their own stories also very much aligns with feminist standpoint epistemology. The theoretical idea that the participants were enacting is that young Black women's experiences provide them with critical forms of knowledge that can deconstruct and contest what is traditionally accepted to be true (Collins, 2004; Harding, 2004; Harraway, 2004; Smith, 2004). By starting from young Black women's standpoints, we can better understand their experiences as well as broader patterns of inequality that uphold bourgeois, white supremacist, heteronormative patriarchal culture (Harding, 2004). Harraway (2004) argues that the standpoints of the subjugated are least likely to deny the critical and interpretative core of all knowledge (p. 88). Grounding our analysis in these standpoints is an attempt to keep the analysis honest about what their experiences demonstrate about the intersecting nature of systems of domination.

In this section, we continue to introduce the context of the youth organizations and organizers we studied by briefly reflecting on how their context connects to these diverse theories. Each of the four organizations our participants are active in builds the leadership of youth participants by healing trauma and developing the young people's critical thinking and social justice organizing skills. The oldest of the four organizations has a 15-year history of working in Miami, and the newest organization is three years old. All four organizations support the development of young people. Some do direct action organizing on a variety of issues, in addition to fully supporting their members with leadership development, consciousness-raising, and service provision. Below we explain each organization in more detail.

Yes Sister Friend!

This organization empowers and supports young transgender womyn, femme-identified nonbinary people, cisgender (meaning the gender that they identify with is the same as the gender they were assigned at birth), queer young womyn of color, and their allies. A few volunteer adults lead the organization, facilitating cohorts of young people in storytelling, healing, and leadership development. This work supports the youth as they organize on issues that matter to them. Youth participate in developing materials, outreach, leading facilitation, and creating the structure of the organization. For example, youth help design cohorts that work together to address the current needs and requests that organically arise from the participants.

Power U Center for Social Change

Power U is a youth-driven organization with a 15-year history of organizing in low-income Black communities in Miami. The organization has an all-youth membership and a staff comprised of both youth and adults. Power U was formed as an intergenerational organization working on environmental, educational, racial, and gender justice campaigns. In the past, it has organized campaigns to stop toxic dumping in a low-income Black community, ensure safe and affordable housing, end the school-to-prison pipeline through the implementation of restorative justice, and promote breastfeeding in local hospitals. Its current work is focused on school discipline and reproductive justice.

The Dream Defenders

The Dream Defenders formed after the death of Trayvon Martin to organize college students throughout Florida who were demanding justice for Martin. They have since organized many local actions, including a takeover of the Florida State Capitol building and local actions in cities around the state demanding justice for low-income youth of color. Their leadership includes mainly youth and young adults under 30, and they organize with college students and high school students throughout the state to transform local issues. They have successfully changed the narrative of racial justice politics in Florida by engaging young people and drawing public attention to various injustices. This has built a leadership pipeline for young people to challenge injustices statewide.

S.O.U.L. Sister Leadership Collective

S.O.U.L. Sister develops the leadership of young women of color to disrupt cycles of poverty and violence. It does this by empowering young women to heal, work for social justice, assume leadership, and participate in the arts. With organizations in both Miami and New York, S.O.U.L. Sister has adult women facilitate work with youth participants who have experienced the negative impacts of social inequality to become agents of social transformation.

Social Movement Theory

Social movement theorist Nancy Whittier (2002) outlines a theoretical approach to understanding social movements that includes four major components: meaning and structure are both important to understanding a social movement; meaning and structure are mutually constituted; internal dynamics constantly shape and are shaped by the external political context; and movements and the institutions social movements confront are shaped by structural inequality. These four components are fluid and interact as demonstrated below.

The structures of the social movement organizations in our study include the physical community in which these young women live, the organizations they lead or participate in, as well as state, local, and federal policies and politics. Miami Dade County, in which all the organizations work, is racially and ethnically diverse, being 66% Latino and 19% Black or African American according to 2014 Census estimates. The county is highly segregated, and these four organizations all focus their efforts in Black neighborhoods that are dealing with concentrated poverty, the lack of public infrastructure, struggling schools, and a dearth of available jobs.

The context the young people are organizing within is also important. This study took place in the spring and summer of 2015—a time in which Florida had just experienced life in the national spotlight because of the murder of Trayvon Martin and the acquittal of his murderer, as well as for the organizing that drew attention to the issue, as Black Lives Matter did nationally. The four local organizations in the study embarked on direct action organizing, leadership development, consciousness-raising, and service provision in this context. Touching on Whittier's third point, the internal dynamics of these organizations and the movements they are a part of constantly shape and are shaped by this changing external political context.

Returning to Whittier's (2002) framework, the "meaning" of this particular part of a larger social movement includes the cultural context and discourse surrounding the young organizers in their community. The participants live and organize in conditions largely shaped by different forms of structural violence (Ginwright, 2015). Collectively, our participants have experienced harsh school discipline and punishment policies, poverty, discrimination based on stereotypes of Black women, and sexual harassment or harassment based on their identity as LGBTQ. Black Feminist scholars explain that such experiences are not unique—Black girls in schools and communities are harmed by intersecting forms of oppression that devalue their academic work, subject them to harsh forms of discipline, and don't provide for their safety from interpersonal violence and sexual harassment (Crenshaw, Ocen, & Nanda, 2015; Morris, 2012). Indeed such violence is foundational to the history of the United States and its institutions (Crenshaw, 1995; Roberts, 2011; Wun, 2014) and works to maintain systems of dominance through punishing and controlling the bodies of Black women (Roberts, 1999).

Black Feminist and Critical Race Theory

Like other Black women around the nation, the young organizers in this study are engaged in collective action to challenge such structural forms of violence and build the critical leadership of more Black women. These four organizations see the importance of healing work to support and build young people's capacity to do other organizing work. S.O.U.L. Sister and Yes Sister Friend! focus on developing the leadership of young women by helping them to heal from trauma and build critical consciousness skills. The Dream Defenders and Power U Center focus on leadership development through social justice organizing for policy changes to end the criminalization of people of color. The young women and gender-queer people build power and consciousness through this combination of leadership development and real-world organizing.

Our participants explain their experiences and particular approach to collective action through the lens best described as intersectionality (Crenshaw, 1989)—that Black women are oppressed by intersecting and layered forms of violence from the state, from institutions, and within communities (Richie, 2012). The literature in this field explains that analyses of oppression need to account for how power operates in interlocking systems of oppression in order to fully understand social, political, and cultural realities of both the group at the center of the analysis and the rest of society (Collins, 2000). Community organizations that use intersectional approaches tend to be grassroots, small, and comprised of people who are marginalized by society, including women of color, youth, and low-income people (Collins, 2014).

Particularly relevant, Love, Booysen, and Essed (2015) found that Black women of the millennial generation who are engaged in social justice work more readily acknowledge the intersectionality of their multiple identities than women of previous generations. Our participants—all of whom are part of the millennial generation—described themselves as Black women and gender-queer activists who navigate and challenge oppressive tropes while collectively creating liberatory models of Black womanhood. We examine how this group of Black women experience and resist forms of stigmatization and the regulation of their bodies that seeks to maintain systems of domination (Su, 2007; Yosso, 2005).

All four organizations we observed collaborate by sharing resources such as space and access to transportation, exchanging ideas, and encouraging their members to participate in other organizations. They host events together, organize actions, and support one another's work. The power of this collaboration provides a clear example of Whitter's (2002) point that meaning and structure are mutually constituted—by supporting their participation in different programs at the different organizations, young people are able to build deeper understandings of the systemic oppression around them at the same time that they grow the structure of the organizations by sharing resources and knowledge that they learn from each program or action. This point is similar to claims made by Ginwright and James (2002), who explain that social movement organizing increases young people's ability to act as agents of social change in addition to creating real changes in society.

Finally, all of these theories challenge us to acknowledge how our positions as white women engaged in racial justice organizing work shape our understanding of our research. Julia has participated with Power U Center for Social Change in Miami, one of the groups in this study, for 12 years, and she has helped develop some of the work featured in this study. She also organizes white people to do racial justice work and feels that such organizing must be deeply informed and driven by an understanding of how people of color experience racism, especially in intersectional ways. Michelle engages in racial justice work across education sectors. She translates education research from the language of the academy into empirically grounded tools that community organizers, school leaders, teachers, and others can use to transform the inequity of education systems. As queer white women researchers engaged in the battle for racial justice, we acknowledge our multiple forms of privilege and our tremendous responsibility to acknowledge and challenge racism, classism, sexism, and homophobia in our work. We recognize that our position as white women means that we have sizable blind spots in understanding the experiences of people of color and that our attempt to use Black Feminist thought and Critical Race Theory can be problematic. We also feel that these theories are the most appropriate lens for analyzing and understanding the lessons these Black women and gender-queer organizers taught us. We hope that our research brings attention to some important organizing work that is often overlooked because of the marginal position of participants, and we attempt to foreground their words and ideas in this chapter.

METHODOLOGY

The research question guiding this study is: What can the broader field of education organizing learn from youth organizers engaged in the emerging Black Girls Matter movement in Miami? We used a combination of Critical Race Theory, Black Feminist theory, and social movement theory to develop our study design and interview protocols. We conducted participatory observations and dialogic interviews (Naples, 2003) of nine Black self-identified women and one gender-neutral participant from the four organizations that work with Black youth in Miami, Florida, during the spring and summer of 2015. We selected participants to represent a range in organizational affiliation, age, and position in the organization. Seven of the interviewees are between 25 and 35 years old and are paid or volunteer organizers at the organization they represent. The other three interviewees are between ages 18 and 24 and are members of the organizations with considerable leadership roles.

All interviews were transcribed. To add additional context to the interview data, we conducted participatory observations and a brief review of organizational materials and media (social media sites, press coverage, flyers, etc.). We then used inductive and deductive coding to look for themes in the discourse (Miles, Huberman, & Saldana, 2013). We identified major themes that led to our findings. As we analyzed our data and identified the alignment with several theories, we conducted a more extensive interdisciplinary review of the literature to create the grounded theoretical framework guiding this chapter.

The participants of our study chose to include their own names and organizational affiliations with the exception of a few particular quotes. We honor their choices out of respect and as an example of how the theoretical underpinnings of this chapter seek to center the experiences and leadership of young Black women in social justice organizing work.

DISCUSSION OF FINDINGS

The young organizers in our study created spaces specifically for Black women and gender-queer people to tell stories about their experiences. In the process, they built strong sisterhood bonds through which they understood their individual experiences as partially shaped by forms of structural violence. Because of this, many of them were moved to action, working with other organizations for social change, sharing their stories in public spaces to challenge unjust policies and practices, and shaping the direction of their own organizations to provide space for and address issues facing young Black women and LGBTQ people. While the activists acknowledge that there is still much work to be done, they explain that their personal transformations from feelings of isolation to having communities of support based on shared experiences provide hope for larger shifts in social justice movement work.

An Issue: Lack of Space for and Investment in Young Black Women

When we think of systemic oppression and think intersectionally about race, class and gender, it means that people who are directly impacted

and hurt the most are often not talked about, and they aren't given
enough space. So if we can centralize our work to address those ele-
ments that affect them at the grassroots level, we can start to address
everyone's issues. It's not to exclude anyone but to uplift everyone,
which happens when we centralize Black women and queer people.
                    —Ruth Jeannoel, Power U Center for Social Change

All of the organizers in our study noted a lack of separate formal and informal spaces for young Black women, including peer mentoring programs,
organizations, and simply physical space on a school campus or in the community. They explained that in mixed spaces their voices and issues were
often dismissed, and so they rarely had spaces in which they could truly be
themselves. Many of the activists shared sophisticated critiques, identifying
the absence of space as reflective of issues of patriarchy, racism, and hetero-
sexism within dominant institutions, philanthropic groups, and social justice
organizations. As Yeshimabeit of Power U Center pointed out:

There's this idea of the strong Black woman that can be resilient
through anything, but Black women are human beings, and the focus
on Black men is a lack of acknowledgment of Black women's experiences because of patriarchy. There's no evidence to understand how the
girls are doing because all the research and energy is put to black men
and boys.

Such disparities are very evident in schools and outside school programs
alike. Schanetta, a youth member of Yes Sister Friend! (YSF), shared that her
high school had mentorship programs for young men, but the only space specifically for the young women focused on teaching them etiquette and how to
act like a lady. In interracial spaces for young women outside of schools,
young Black women have a hard time being themselves because they might
be judged or stereotyped by others, according to Schanetta. Likewise, Qual-
isa, a young leader of Yes Sister Friend! who participated as a youth member
and then a leader, experienced her voice being silenced in coed spaces at
other community organizations, while men's ideas were uplifted.

According to Alina, the adult founder of YSF, other organizations that
serve youth do not adequately affirm young Black and Brown people that
identify as lesbian, bisexual, queer, questioning, and trans female. In order to
address this, YSF creates a separate space for those who are normally left out
by other organizations. For example, they make sure to include trans women
in the women's group. As Alina shares, "At YSF, one thing that's been very
magical is that, specifically for trans female young women, there's a validation
that I am a woman too. I'm calling you she, I'm calling you my sister friend. I

see you as a woman." For the young queer and gender nonconforming people, this was a critical space in which, as Logan, a gender-queer youth member, says, "We are able to create a sense of unity."

The organizers further explained that creation of these spaces counters the dominant approach in schools that sees certain girls as disposable. Yeshimabeit, a youth organizer at Power U, pointed out that school counselors would refer the girls they didn't know what to do with to Alina from YSF, knowing that she could work with them using an entirely different approach. Alina relates to the younger women she works with, saying, "When I see someone who the system has given up on, I see an agitator, I see an advocate, I see me. I've had a lot to fight through." Creating spaces for young Black women and gender-queer people to come together is essential to validating their experiences.

Many of the organizers identified lack of funding as part of the reason that there is a lack of space for young people facing intersectional oppression. They report that funders have rejected their organizations because they do not focus on the experiences of Black men and boys and/or because their focus on working with young women of color was deemed too narrow. This reflects a lack of awareness in the philanthropic community about the importance of building the leadership of Black women in spaces of their own. Notably, these organizations did a lot of their work with little to no funding, as members of the community and the organizers themselves volunteered time, money, space, transportation, and energy.

One Solution: Storytelling as Transformative Counternarrative

It isn't like you're the only person going through this, having this struggle. You don't know that until you get with other people like you and talk. There are so many barriers to getting to that. YSF was a safe space because they made sure to include trans girls so I knew I could have that be my space.

—Logan Meza, Yes Sister Friend!

The power of telling stories that serve as counternarratives emerged as a second theme in this study. During our interviews, young activists shared stories of being unfairly disciplined in school for behavior, of being sexually harassed by security guards at school, and of teachers criticizing and outing them to their parents for being lesbian. These experiences are all isolating forms of trauma enacted by adults. The experiences and the lack of a collective space to process them often led to feelings of isolation and frustration.

All four organizations in this study work to create safe spaces for their members to share these stories, recognizing similarities between their own stories and others' stories. Jonel from the Dream Defenders shared that "the more that you have these conversations with other people who are able to connect with your stories, it changes from a singular story—you're not the only person involved." Storytelling was validating and empowering for the participants, increasing their sense of connection to the other participants.

Having one's experiences validated and affirmed is an important part of what Armah (as cited in Paul, 2015) has termed emotional justice. She argues that, due to cycles of violence, Black people have a legacy of intergenerational trauma that needs to be addressed:

> Emotionality matters. . . . It is too often set aside or overlooked in battles for a justice that looks like a courtroom, a verdict or policy passage. Emotionality requires process and practice to navigate it. We need tools to deal effectively with this violence, born of a toxic masculinity that makes girls and women responsible for the traumatized emotionality of men. (Armah, as cited in Paul, 2015)

Armah argues that having tools to acknowledge and explore trauma and create counternarratives and the time to use these tools and to challenge systems that create violence and trauma are essential for creating emotional justice.

Tanisha, the adult leader of S.O.U.L. Sister, shared how storytelling not just about oneself but about what is happening in the community is emotional justice work:

> A lot is happening in our communities that's triggering for our young people that they don't get asked about. We talk about what they're seeing in their communities that's notable. A lot of times we talk about young people they see and hear in their communities who have been killed, teachers who have been fired that they love, statements that people like Nikki Minaj are making—for the girls there is so much in it. That to me is emotional justice work too. For them to have an opportunity to take what they're seeing on their phone and bring it into real life and analyze it is tremendously important for their healing work.

When participants recognized the collective nature of their experiences, they were able to explore the historical and systemic nature of their experiences with oppression. Ruth, an adult staff member at Power U, shares,

> I've found that once you give somebody the language like "racism" or "capitalism," we can help them understand that they're not the one that caused an issue and that there's a system that exists that created

what trauma they've gone through. We invite the young women from other organizations to Power U to do political education and then they also want to bring Power U to their spaces.

Through storytelling, the young women are identifying their experiences as part of systems of oppression that they choose to challenge in ways that call attention to the root causes rather than blaming individuals. Sherika of the Dream Defenders points out how Black women of the millennial generation challenge stereotypes in new ways that also challenge politics of respectability:

Challenging the stereotype isn't saying, "No, we're not on welfare. I have a job that pays six figures." It's shifting the narrative so we can say, "Yeah, I'm on welfare, and it's because of the system being unjust."

In this way, storytelling as counternarrative is a process that begins with an individual naming her experience, then understanding how her story is shared by others. Together people collectively transform their understanding of their experiences into a shared critique of systemic inequality. From this shared critique, members then begin to take collective action, like organizing the Black Girls Matter Town Hall or speaking out at a rally of a different organization. This process is iterative and constant; it is part of the daily cycle of organizing for these four organizations. The young activists in this study credit much of their power to this intensely personal method of community organizing.

Impacts of the Work

Collective healing, justice, sisterhood, and resistance.
Doing this work has given me opportunities to take up space. I've developed awesome leadership skills, but I constantly forget that I'm only 18. I've been on TV, talking to commissioners, my name is going places but in the back of my head there's a fear that I might out myself by doing this work. I have no idea how to cross that bridge when I get to it. I know I have to do this work because it's necessary and we have to power through.

—Logan Meza

As they shared stories, the youth saw connections between their own and others' experiences with oppressive forces. Seeing these connections allowed for both personal and community healing. Such experiences also moved many of them to take other forms of political action. For example, working with the Power U Center, Schanetta of YSF spoke publicly at a hearing about police misconduct.

Organizations created different but similar models of providing healing spaces for young women to share their stories and build sisterhood. At S.O.U.L. Sister, Tanisha explains the importance of this work:

> We conceptualize it as everyone has the right to heal. The dominant belief is that there are some people in our society who are not seen as hurting. They are seen as villains. . . . It's important to acknowledge the reality of the impact of conditions, of poor Black women's conditions on our hearts, minds and spirits. We can acknowledge that there's an emotional impact of these conditions and then in community—for one another, by one another—walk through that and do the healing work.

While the women understood that there is trauma in their communities stemming from structural violence that they want to address, they also acknowledged a long history of their community having what Tanisha called "ancient tricks to move through a lot of pain." One of those "ancient tricks" is not to individualize or pathologize people or cultures for that trauma.

Rather, moving through trauma collectively (an "ancient trick") is combined with a strategy that the millennials bring to the table—articulating intersectional understandings of their world. Alina explains YSF's ideas about healing justice:

> I resist those that just talk about the ugly, but the truth is we do go through too much. I know that by the time we get to 15 or 16 years old, we have big stories. Let's start peeling back some of the onion to that story. Let's see if we can heal some of that, let's see if we can clear some of that. That's the first part. The second part is creating the sisterhood. That's the reason this is called Yes Sister Friend.

The inclusive nature of these spaces allowed young Black women to express themselves in new ways and create not only bonds of sisterhood but also increased political awareness. Logan, from YSF, shared how this happened:

> Police, people in privileged statuses, white men, white women profile us a lot. We have to be very wary of police and it's so hard to explain that to someone who doesn't understand. But being in a group we can help each other to advocate not only for ourselves but also for each other. Usually we start off telling a story and then it's like popcorn: "I relate."

"I relate." "Yeah, I understand because I go through this too." It's building community.

Through such experiences with YSF, Logan has learned not only leadership
skills, but also how to be more compassionate and listen better to others and
take on leadership roles in multiple organizations. Logan, who identifies as
gender-queer, shared, "It helped me feel more rooted in my identity and think
about what kind of space would be really for people like me—challenging
organizations to have spaces for people like me." This led Logan to create a
mobile safe space that is inclusive for youth of color across the gender spectrum at S.O.U.L. Sister. Tanisha, also from S.O.U.L. Sister, reflects on the
importance of Logan's leadership and work:

> The safe space then is taken advantage of by people from all walks of
> life, so it isn't just Black women organizing for Black women. Black
> women organize and the world gets better! We have these experiences
> and organize, and it creates space for everyone to access their authentic
> humanity, heal from their pain. That's the power of Black women's
> organizing.

The importance of Black women supporting one another and organizing
together was salient. As Sherika of the Dream Defenders shared,

> As women, the only way that we're going to be able to address
> patriarchy or capitalism is if we do it together. That's why elevating
> the experiences of young Black women, making their experiences
> be heard and addressed, is what's going to create new leaders that we
> need.

Participants explained that their existence and work is threatening to the
status quo. The intersectional perspective and leadership that they bring
challenge systemic oppression.

Organizational transformation and the leadership of Black women.

> *As Black women, we hold not only our own struggles in dealing with*
> *oppression in terms of sexism, racism, heterosexism, transphobia, but*
> *also we as Black women are often the holders of community. That's our*
> *role. Aunties, and grandmas, little sisters taking care of little brothers,*
> *big sister, this is the type of thing that happens in our community—this*
> *is how it's always been. We're staying and we're holding it down while,*
> *unfortunately, our Black men are leaving because of their own "choice"*
> *in quotation marks, or being taken, but we're staying so we carry pain*

and oppression differently. I think because of that we're able to really
see what needs to be happening, spaces that need to be created.
                                                            —*Tanisha Douglas*

The organizations in this study had different focuses and constituencies. Participants pointed to blind spots that existed previous to their collaboration on the Town Hall that they are now working to address collectively. For example, Alina from YSF shared that she has talked with leaders at another organization about creating and supporting LBQT women by making sure to address homophobic or transphobic comments that come up in the organization's spaces. Because the collaborative storytelling spaces have increased awareness of issues and solidarity between organizations, Black women are leading the change within their organizations to address issues as they come up.

This is reflective of shifts happening in organizing work nationally as well, as Black women and transgender people are increasingly bringing intersectional analyses to social movement work (Love et al., 2015). As Ruth, an adult leader from Power U, says, "We're in an interesting time now where organizations are understanding intersectionality and people live it everyday and know it, like 'because I'm Black, because I'm low-income, because I'm a woman I get treated differently.'" This interplay between each organization's internal dynamics and the larger social movement is one of the key components of a social movement discussed by Whittier (2002). Our participants report that organizing at the national and local levels is growing together in a way that mutually strengthens their intersectional framing of issues and highlights the leadership of Black women.

Transformational work for organizing groups also includes addressing oppression within their organizations and making sure their social change work reflects an intersectional approach to change. One leader explains that her organization is thinking about how they organizationally tackle issues of patriarchy, centering it in their work. Understanding and then acting on the connections between multiple forms of oppression, especially when they exist within a movement, suggests that this generation of organizers has an increasingly intersectional approach to organizing.

One example of how this work has led to political activism by young people is the anticriminalization work of both the Dream Defenders and Power U Center for Social Change. Both organizations focus on systemic change through organizing, and the intersectional lens has sharpened their analysis of the issues. Ruth explains how Power U has reflected on this:

From the Town Hall and the organizing with our partners we see the need for healing and storytelling for young Black people. Imagine the possibilities of using restorative justice as a space not only for this in schools, but also as a space of holding each other and administrators accountable to create systemic change in the schools.

The experiences of collectively organizing the town hall and building the leadership of Black young women led organizations to focus their energy on addressing intersectional oppressions and collaborating more with one another. What began as a series of organizations working on individual transformations like storytelling and healing has led to relationships that strengthen and challenge organizations and the broader social movements to grow.

CONCLUSION

Engagement in healing justice work (Ginwright, 2015) that seeks to connect individual traumatic experiences to larger forms of structural violence is an important part of the consciousness-raising process. When the young Black women and gender-queer people in our study shared their stories with one another, they created powerful counternarratives that challenge the dominant tropes that blame individual Black women for their experiences. As Collins (2004) points out, "many of the attributes extant in Black female stereotypes are actually distorted renderings of those aspects of Black female behavior seen as most threatening to white patriarchy" (p. 107). In challenging how they are portrayed, they are defining themselves in ways that interrogate the nature of oppression.

As neoliberal trade policies decrease the number of jobs available to Black people, the portrayal of Black men as criminal and unwilling to work becomes increasingly important to justify both the proliferation of the prison industrial complex and the persistence of Black poverty and unemployment. Black women's strength and independence, on the other hand, are praised when in service to white capital (Collins, 2005), while they are otherwise stigmatized and blamed for their poverty. Black women who are able to have "financial independence (albeit in poverty) [are] seen as usurping a masculine prerogative . . . becom[ing] labeled as 'bitches,' 'bad mothers,' 'matriarchs,' and 'welfare mothers,' terms that blame them for taking responsibility" (Collins, 2005, p. 203). By defining and valuing themselves in ways that acknowledge the root causes of inequities, they are not only challenging dominant narratives about Black women, but also pointing to the systemic nature of the issues.

These self-definitions and self-valuations (Collins, 2004) are forms of resistance in which Black women use qualities that are often exaggerated to negatively stereotype them as a way to challenge racist and sexist ideologies. Sherika's example of acknowledging that people, including Black women, are on welfare because of systemic inequality demonstrates how they challenge the underlying logic of the stereotypes.

> When Black females choose to value those aspects of Afro-American womanhood that are stereotyped, ridiculed, and maligned in academic scholarship and the popular media, they are actually questioning some of the basic ideas used to control dominated groups in general. (Collins, 2004, p. 107)

The unique ways that these participants collectively shared stories, built consciousness, and challenged one another and their organizations to address multiple forms of oppression is informative for the broader movement for social justice.

The processes of storytelling, healing, and political action certainly parallel the multiple theories we laid out in the introduction of this article. While academics like ourselves have the privilege of analyzing and writing about the connections between social movement theory, Critical Race Theory, Black Feminist theory, and feminist epistemology, the young women organizers and the organizations at the center of this study are living and creating these blended connections. They live through the policies and acts of terror that result from marginalization, including the school-to-prison pipeline (Fernández, Kirshner, & Lewis, this volume), under-resourced and largely unsupportive schools, and lived experiences of harassment based on their race, class, gender, and sexual orientation (Stoudt et al., this volume). Still, they come together to collectively heal, become leaders, and transform the systems that marginalize them.

Young Black people centering the leadership of Black women and gender-queer people are not only carving out new spaces for thought that challenges dominant discourses, but also providing models of leadership for the larger movement. As social movements work to understand and fight systems of oppression, the leadership and experiences of millennial Black women and gender-queer people provide new insights and forms of fighting that challenge and support new possibilities. The individuals and organizations in this study are engaged in a transformative process to both internally and externally challenge multiple manifestations of oppression. This powerful work helps liberate us all.

REFERENCES

Collins, P. H. (2000). Gender, black feminism, and black political economy. *Annals of the American Academy of Political and Social Science, 568*(1), 41–53. http://dx.doi .org/10.1177/000271620056800105

Collins, P. H. (2004). Learning from the outsider within: The sociological significance of black feminist thought. In S. Harding (Ed.), *The feminist standpoint theory
reader* (pp. 103–126). New York, NY: Routledge.

Collins, P. H. (2005). *Black sexual politics: African Americans, gender, and the new racism*. Great Britain: Routledge.

Collins, P. H. (2014). Intersectionality's definitional dilemma. *Annual Review of Sociology, 41*(1), 1–20. http://dx.doi.org/10.1146/annurev-soc-073014-112142

Crenshaw, K. (1989). Demarginalizing the intersection of race and sex: A black feminist critique of antidiscrimination doctrine, feminist theory and antiracist politics.
University of Chicago Legal Forum, 1989(1), 57–80. Retrieved from http://chica
gounbound.uchicago.edu/

Crenshaw, K. W. (1995). Mapping the margins: Intersectionality, identity politics,
and violence against women of color. In K. Crenshaw, N. Gotanda, G. Peller, &
K. Thomas (Eds.), *Critical race theory: The key writings that formed the movement*
(pp. 357–383). New York, NY: New Press.

Crenshaw, K. W., Ocen, P., & Nanda, J. (2015). *Black girls matter: Pushed out, overpoliced and underprotected*. New York, NY: Center for Intersectionality & Social
Policy Studies.

Delgado, R. (1989). Storytelling for oppositionists and others: A plea for narrative.
Michigan Law Review, 87(8), 2411–2441. http://dx.doi.org/10.2307/1289308

Ginwright, S. (2015). *Hope and healing in urban education: How urban activists and
teachers are reclaiming matters of the heart*. New York, NY: Routledge.

Ginwright, S., & James, T. (2002). From assets for agents of change: Social justice,
organizing and youth development [Special issue]. *New Directions for Youth Development, 2002*(96), 27–46. http://dx.doi.org/10.1002/yd.25

Harding, S. (Ed.). (2004). *The feminist standpoint theory reader: Intellectual and political
controversies*. New York, NY: Routledge.

Harraway, D. (2004). Situated knowledges: The science question in feminism and the
privilege of partial perspective. In S. Harding (Ed.), *The feminist standpoint theory
reader* (pp. 81–102). New York, NY: Routledge.

Love, C. D., Booysen, L. A. E., & Essed, P. (2015). An exploration of the intersection
of race, gender and generation in African American women doing social justice
work. *Gender, Work & Organization*. Advance online publication. http://dx.doi
.org/10.1111/gwao.12095

Miles, M. B., Huberman, A. M., & Saldaña, J. (2013). *Qualitative data analysis: A
methods sourcebook* (3rd ed.). Los Angeles, CA: Sage Publications.

Morris, M. W. (2012). *Race, gender and "the school to prison pipeline": Expanding
our discussion to include black girls*. Los Angeles, CA: African American Policy
Forum.

Naples, N. A. (2003). *Feminism and method: Ethnography, discourse analysis, and activist research*. New York, NY: Routledge.

Paul, D. (2015, December 3). Emotional justice: What Black women want and need.
The Guardian. Retrieved from http://www.theguardian.com

Richie, B. E. (2012). *Arrested justice: Black women, violence, and America's prison nation*. New York, NY: New York University Press.

Roberts, D. (1999). *Killing the black body: Race, reproduction and the meaning of liberty.* New York, NY: Vintage Books.

Roberts, D. (2011). Prison, foster care, and the systematic punishment of black mothers. *UCLA Law Review, 59*(6), 1474–1500. Retrieved from heinonline.org.

Smith, D. (2004). Women's perspective as a radical critique of sociology. In S. Harding (Ed.), *The feminist standpoint theory reader* (pp. 21–34). New York, NY: Routledge.

Solorzano, D. G., & Yosso, T. J. (2001). Critical race and LatCrit theory and method: Counter-storytelling. *International Journal of Qualitative Studies in Education, 14*(4), 471–495. http://dx.doi.org/10.1080/09518390110063365

Su, C. (2007). Cracking silent codes: Critical race theory and education organizing. *Discourse: Studies in the Cultural Politics of Education, 28*(4), 531–548. http://dx.doi.org/10.1080/01596300701625297

Whittier, N. (2002). Meaning and structure in social movements. In D. S. Meyer, N. Whittier, & B. Robnett (Eds.), *Social movements: Identity, culture, and the state* (pp. 24–48). New York, NY: Oxford University Press.

Wun, C. (2014). Unaccounted foundations: Black girls, anti-black racism, and punishment in schools. *Critical Sociology.* Advance online publication. http://dx.doi.org/10.1177/0896920514560444

Yosso, T. J. (2005). Whose culture has capital? A critical race theory discussion of community cultural wealth. *Race, Ethnicity and Education, 8*(1), 69–91. http://dx.doi.org/10.1080/1361332052000341006

12

The Implications of Youth Activism for Health and Well-Being

Parissa J. Ballard and Emily J. Ozer

Youth are often thought of as "recipients" of social policy and political life. However, youth are also stakeholders and active participants in their own lives and the lives of their communities and society (Ginwright & Cammarota, 2002). Across the United States, youth are involved in many types of civic activities (Center for Information and Research on Civic Learning and Engagement, 2011), and examples of youth exerting an impact on their communities are plentiful. When young people take a collective and public stand on social issues that affect them, they also shape their own developmental pathways. For example, activism can influence adolescents' academic, psychosocial, and sociopolitical development (Christens & Kirshner, 2011; Strobel, Osberg, & McLaughlin, 2006; Watts & Guessous, 2006). In this chapter, we discuss the implications of youth activism for health and well-being. We first define what we mean by activism, adolescence, and adolescent health and discuss why it is important to study this topic. Next, we propose mechanisms linking activism and health, and we review relevant theory and evidence considering both how activism might promote health as well as how it might be problematic for health. Finally, we provide suggestions for future research on the topic as well as practical suggestions for youth practitioners.

WHY STUDY THE LINKS BETWEEN ACTIVISM AND ADOLESCENT HEALTH?

Youth activism—the organized efforts of groups of young people to address the root causes of problems in their local, national, and global communities—is one way that youth interact with civic life. Activism comes in many forms (including in person or virtual, grassroots or joining an established organization or cause, one-time participation or long-term commitment). In this review, we define activism broadly and do not review how various forms, or the quality of activist experiences, likely operate differently in youth development. Youth civic development broadly and activism in particular have the potential to impact youth and community development: When youth develop the knowledge, skills, and inclination to address social issues in their communities, they can experience personal benefits at the same time as benefiting others around them. This potential makes youth activism an important developmental process for psychologists to understand.

Adolescence, considered here as the period between the ages of 12 and 21, is an especially important life stage for the development of both civic (Hart, Donnelly, Youniss, & Atkins, 2007; Watts & Flanagan, 2007) and health (Viner et al., 2015) trajectories. This phase of life is marked by converging changes in biology and social roles that create unique windows of opportunity for development (Dahl, 2004). A major developmental task of adolescence is identity formation, which includes defining one's role in relation to society (Erikson, 1968; Yates & Youniss, 1998). Multiple developmental frameworks suggest that youth engagement within their communities can play an important part in development. For example, Positive Youth Developmental (PYD) theory highlights the central role of community engagement in healthy youth development. One particular PYD approach often used to frame youth civic engagement research argues that when youth exhibit the "5 Cs"—competence, confidence, connection, caring, and character—they are then prepared to experience the sixth C, contribution (Lerner et al., 2005). In this approach, positive developmental contexts (families, schools, communities) support thriving youth; in turn, thriving youth take action to contribute to the world around them (Hershberg, Johnson, DeSouza, Hunter, & Zaff, 2015).

In general, PYD theories focus primarily on domains and indicators of civic participation that occur in relation to mainstream institutions for middle-class youth living in economically stable and well-resourced communities, such as formal volunteerism or political campaigning. The standard PYD framework does not explicitly consider that many U.S. youth grow up in communities that are less connected to mainstream political and economic institutions, and must further negotiate major structural barriers of oppression and disadvantage (Watts & Flanagan, 2007). The Sociopolitical Development (SPD) framework provides additional insight about developmental processes in the context of oppression and disadvantage. SPD is defined as "the evolving critical understanding of the political, economic, cultural, and other systemic forces that shape society and one's status within it, and the associated process of growth in relevant knowledge, analytical skills, and emotional faculties" (Watts & Guessous, 2006, p. 59). According to this approach, connection with mainstream institutions and the related behavioral indicators of civic engagement are not always an appropriate fit for marginalized youth of color, for whom youth activism and resistance are important means of engaging with social and political systems and promoting healthy development (Ginwright & Cammarota, 2002; Ginwright & James, 2002; Watts, Diemer, & Voight, 2011; Watts, Williams, & Jagers, 2003). Thus, developmental theory suggests that how youth engage with civic life, especially in forms of activism among marginalized youth, plays a role in healthy development.

Youth Activism and Adolescent Health

Adolescent health is multidimensional. For our purpose of linking youth activism with health and well-being, we are concerned with three aspects of adolescent health: mental health and psychological well-being, physical health, and health behaviors. As described further below, activism has been linked with indicators of mental health such as self-esteem, empowerment, and self-confidence. Volunteerism has been linked to physical health among adolescents, bringing up the intriguing possibility that certain types of engagement with communities can promote physical health, although there is not yet evidence linking activism and physical health. Finally, activism aims to provide youth with a sense of purpose and a chance to make meaningful community contributions, which can have implications for positive health behaviors. For these reasons, the review below includes studies that focus on these three types of health and well-being outcomes.

There are troubling disparities in both adolescent health and levels of youth civic engagement across socioeconomic and racial/ethnic lines. On average, youth of color and adolescents from lower socioeconomic backgrounds have poorer health status, measured by markers such as disease (e.g., HIV/AIDS), some indicators of behavioral health (homicide, dating violence, unintended pregnancies), as well as access to health services (National Association of Social Workers, 2001; Newacheck, Hung, Park, Brindis, & Irwin, 2003). At the same time, youth of color and adolescents from lower socioeconomic backgrounds are presented with fewer opportunities for high-quality civic engagement (Kahne & Middaugh, 2008; Levinson, 2010). We submit that these are not unrelated phenomena, but rather, that the structural realities of socioeconomic hardship and the related opportunity gaps in the United States underlie both health and civic disparities. Youth activism can provide a path for young people to lobby for necessary structural changes that might improve community health, while potentially experiencing health benefits of empowerment during the process. Thus, youth activism has the dual potential to affect youth and community health positively (Ballard & Syme, 2015).

Given the theoretical importance of civic engagement for healthy adolescent development and the disparities in youth civic participation, there has been surprisingly little systematic research on the role of activism for youth health and well-being. Although most youth researchers and practitioners share an assumption that youth activism is beneficial for youth, it is important to provide evidence supporting or challenging this assumption. At a time when youth activism is on the rise as new technologies enable new forms of activism (Kahne, Middaugh, & Allen, 2014), we ask: What does activism mean for healthy youth development?

WHAT DO WE KNOW ABOUT THE LINKS BETWEEN ACTIVISM AND HEALTH?

In this section, we focus on how activism can affect adolescent health and well-being. We consider how activism can potentially exert promotive effects on health as well as how activism might serve to undermine health. We review theory and evidence for each possibility below before concluding with suggestions for a research agenda on this topic as well as suggestions for practitioners working with youth activists to increase the likelihood that activism will promote adolescent health and well-being. Most literature reviewed draws on U.S.-based youth samples, but we review studies outside the United States where relevant as well.

How Might Activism Affect Health?

There are multiple pathways by which youth activism can potentially support health and well-being. Key concepts and psychosocial processes for understanding these potential pathways are considered below, including coping with stress, generating psychological and political empowerment, developing a sense of purpose and identity, forming connections with others and building social capital, and effecting systemic change. (See Figure 12.1.) However, it is too optimistic to expect uniformly positive effects of youth activism on adolescent health and well-being. At the same time as these pathways may promote health and well-being, participating in collective community efforts is not easy, takes time and effort, and often involves setbacks. From the perspective of sociopolitical development, it is reasonable to expect that the effects of youth activism on health and well-being will be mixed. Thus, we will also consider the ways that activism might undermine health and well-being.

Stress and coping.   A key theoretical framework for understanding the potential links between activism and health is the transactional stress model that emphasizes the roles of coping and appraisal in determining the effects of environmental stressors on mental and physical health (Lazarus & Folkman, 1984). Decades of research in health psychology have demonstrated the

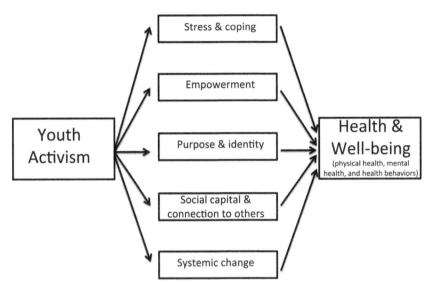

Figure 12.1. Conceptual Model of Potential Pathways Linking Youth Activism with Adolescent Health and Well-being.

importance of perceived control as a buffer in the stress response process (Zimmerman & Rappaport, 1988). These theoretical frames are highly relevant for considering the relationship between activism and health in that activism may provide one way for young people to engage in active, instrumental coping approaches to alleviating problems that are causing them stress rather than feeling powerless in the face of stress, as well as helping to promote a sense of perceived control over the stressors themselves (e.g., Israel, Checkoway, Schulz, & Zimmerman, 1994).

Understanding activism as a coping response is especially salient in light of evidence showing that feeling angry or frustrated with the status quo and being concerned about specific issues are common motivations for youth civic action (Ballard, 2014; Ballard, Malin, Porter, Colby, & Damon, 2015). For example, activism has been proposed as a potential coping response to specific stressors such as experiencing discrimination (Jensen, 2010; Padilla, 2008), and perceived discrimination is cross-sectionally associated with more involvement in activism (Hope & Jagers, 2014). When young people turn to activism out of anger, such involvement can provide a prosocial channel for self-expression.

Recent research on youths' online participation raises interesting questions related to anger and activism. For example, a study in China found that anger is a common and contagious emotion expressed on social media (Fan, Zhao, Chen, & Xu, 2014); anger was often triggered by social and political issues such as government bribery or incidents such as the 2010 U.S. and South Korean military drills in the Yellow Sea. Online expressions of anger may be therapeutic and empowering, allowing people to express their rage or concern about issues that feel out of their control and in this way serving as a kind of coping mechanism. This mechanism is especially relevant for young people, who more often feel disempowered and left out of in-person political processes because of their age (Zeldin, Larson, Camino, & O'Connor, 2005).

Some evidence suggests that people who turn to activism as a way to cope with social and political stressors might experience health benefits. In a longitudinal German study, Boehnke & Wong (2011) showed that among youth who appraised nuclear war as a salient threat in the 1980s, becoming an activist predicted better mental health trajectories across adulthood (to age 35) compared to those who appraised nuclear war as a salient threat but *did not* become involved in activism. These authors interpreted activism as a productive and active coping response to "macroworries," that is, worry about entities external to the self—the wider society, world, or universe.

Potential stressors associated with activism. The transactional stress framework is also helpful for understanding the potential negative effects of activism on health. Activism makes demands on time, resources, and emotions, potentially creating stressors instead of reducing stress. A relevant framework for understanding activism as a stress-producing coping response to life circumstances comes from the social epidemiologist Sherman James who outlined a phenomenon he named "John Henryism," defined as "a strong behavioral predisposition to cope actively with psychosocial environmental stressors" (James, 1994). In his work, James has documented negative effects of exerting effort to better one's conditions in contexts where conditions are difficult or impossible to change. For example, he has shown that African American men from low socioeconomic backgrounds who were high in "John Henryism" show worse stress-related health outcomes (such as hypertension) across the life course. In recent work, scholars have examined how high effort (in this case through measured self-regulatory abilities or "self-control") relates to many outcomes among African American young adults (Miller, Yu, Chen, & Brody, 2015). They found that, among low-socioeconomic status (SES) young adults, self-control predicted better mental health outcomes (less depression) and health behaviors (e.g., less substance use and aggression) but poorer physical health (indexed by more rapid immune cell aging).

Applied to youth activism, the same principle might suggest that encouraging youth to expend high amounts of effort actively engaging in changing structural conditions might have negative physical health consequences. A related argument, that changing individuals' perceptions of efficacy without changing the systems youth are embedded in, has long been a criticism of focusing on individual youth civic development rather than systems change (Kahne & Westheimer, 2006). In other words, a focus on coping should be accompanied by training youth in critical analysis of the situations affecting them and a serious effort to change those systems. If we consider youth activism to be an "active coping" strategy for marginalized young people, through pathways laid out by James (1994) and others, this strategy might entail health costs as well as benefits.

It is important to note that devoting oneself to the service of others can also be emotionally stressful. In recent research that investigated family roles, Fuligni and colleagues (2009) found that the amount of time youth spent helping their families (e.g., cooking, cleaning, and sibling care) was associated with long-term elevations in levels of inflammation (a marker of disease vulnerability). Activism reflects a different type of service to others that may entail self-interest as well, but may similarly burden youths' immune systems by placing demands on youth time and creating emotional stress.

Empowerment. Community psychologists define psychological empowerment as the psychological aspects of processes through which people gain greater control over their lives, take a proactive approach in their communities, and develop critical understandings of their sociopolitical environments (Zimmerman, 1995). Programs encouraging youth activism aim to empower young people (Christens & Kirshner, 2011; Watts et al., 2003), and youth empowerment is proposed to lead to better health (Cowen, 1994; Wallerstein, 1992). Youth empowerment is a desirable outcome for many reasons but among them is that psychological empowerment is argued to be central in attempts to promote and sustain well-being (e.g., Christens, 2012). The argument is that people are happier, and perhaps healthier, when their lives feel under their control.

There is some empirical evidence supporting the link between empowerment and health. For example, perceived control is associated with health behaviors such as lower substance use (Wills, 1994) and subjective well-being (Chen & Feeley, 2012; Itzhaky & York, 2000). Psychological empowerment is also positively related to indicators of psychological functioning such as self-esteem and social connectedness with peers and adults at school (Ozer & Schotland, 2011). Studies also document a moderating or mediating role of empowerment on health. For example, in a study of African American young men, perceived sociopolitical control decreased the link between feelings of helplessness and mental health, suggesting a protective role of perceived control for mental health (Zimmerman, Ramirez-Valles, & Maton, 1999). In another study connecting empowerment to health, Christens and Peterson (2012) tested the role of empowerment as a mediator between ecological assets and health outcomes. They found that empowerment (operationalized as sociopolitical control) explained associations between family cohesion and self-esteem; further, self-esteem predicted fewer psychological symptoms.

In work being conducted by the first author, the links between a civic empowerment program and self-reported civic and health outcomes are being evaluated. The program, Generation Citizen, is a school-based semester-long intervention. In it, middle and high school students participate in an action civics course (Gingold, 2013) where students go into their communities to assess community needs, collectively choose a civic issue to address, and take action toward addressing it. This approach to civic education is very different from the traditional way that teens learn civics, and the program is built around the idea of empowering young people to understand the root causes of social issues and their role in addressing the social issues (Pope, Stolte, & Cohen, 2011). Preliminary analyses investigating outcomes of physical and mental health reveal a small overall gain in self-reported health from pre- to post-participation in Generation Citizen (Ballard, 2015a), especially among those who increase in civic self-efficacy over the course of program participation.

Potential negative effects on empowerment. Although activism can be empowering, it also involves young people in dealing with a range of challenges. Without adequate scaffolding and support, youth could feel overwhelmed by these challenges, undermining their sense of control and empowerment. For example, activism approaches such as youth organizing and youth-led participatory action research engage youth in reflecting on inequalities in power and resources. While many young people have firsthand experience living with the realities of inequalities, active reflection on these issues can be painful as well as illuminating. It is critical that activism approaches that occur as part of youth development efforts are mindful of the need for "small wins" (Foster-Fishman et al., 2006) and for reflecting on lessons learned in order to guard against unintended consequences of actually promoting youths' sense of powerlessness or hopelessness.

Further, activism can place youth in public situations where they might experience backlash for expressing their views. This is evident in news coverage of the 2014–2015 protests against police brutality from Ferguson to Baltimore. These displays of activism made civic actors vulnerable to criticism and further exposed them to discrimination; some of the backlash and commentary against the protests might disempower young people and damage their mental health and well-being. Research is needed to assess these potential effects.

In support of the possibility that activism can lead to some degree of disillusionment and perhaps negatively affect health, one study found that self-reported well-being was significantly higher among less experienced community activists in Israel compared to more experienced activists, which the researchers interpreted as a result of disillusionment among those who had been involved in activism for longer (Itzhaky & York, 2000). In one longitudinal study of the links between perceived discrimination and civic activism (i.e., protesting and expressing political opinions), Ballard (2015b) found that activism in high school predicted increased perceptions of discrimination over time, suggesting that activism can place people at risk for exposure to more actual or perceived discrimination. Returning to the example of anger expression on social media, we speculate that anger may represent active coping as discussed above, but it may also lead to perseverating on negative events, consolidating negative opinions, or "catching" secondhand anger from others (Fan et al., 2014). These findings suggest that activism is part of a complex developmental process where action is not always empowering and can have negative consequences as well.

Purpose and identity.   Positive engagement with communities can provide youth with the opportunity to develop a meaningful social role. Especially at a time when most youth feel left out of civic and political processes (Ballard, 2014; Zeldin, Camino, & Mook, 2005), well-implemented youth activism projects can invite youth to make a meaningful contribution to those around them. Activism is one route to finding purpose and consolidating a positive social identity (Malin, Ballard, & Damon, 2015). An explicit goal of many youth activism programs is to help young people find ways to contribute to their communities, create social change, and promote a sense that they matter.

Several constructs such as purpose, identity formation, feeling that one matters, finding meaning in life experiences, and role fulfillment are posited as routes to well-being (Flanagan & Bundick, 2011; Roepke, Jayawickreme, & Riffle, 2014). For example, in the study mentioned earlier that found that providing assistance to one's family (for example, helping clean the apartment or house, taking care of siblings, running an errand for the family) placed a burden on teenagers' immune systems, a key finding was that this effect was buffered for young people who found more fulfillment in the family helping role (Fuligni et al., 2009). This suggests that the psychological appraisal of role responsibilities, namely finding meaning and role fulfillment in potentially costly social roles, can buffer the stress of such roles. Further, Fuligni and Telzer (2013) found through an fMRI study that assisting family via giving money, at a cost to themselves, engaged the reward circuitry in the brain of Latino but not European American youth. This provides intriguing evidence for the rewarding nature of having a responsibility role toward families perhaps moderated by the cultural or familial meaning assigned to such a role. Although providing assistance is very different from activism, in a similar way, enacting responsibilities toward nonfamilial others, an experience provided by some types of youth activism, might be a rewarding and thus health-promoting endeavor.

Sense of purpose.   Purpose broadly indicates that one feels he or she has an important social role to play. Purpose has been linked with various health benefits among older adults including physical and mental health and longevity (Boyle, Barnes, Buchman, & Bennett, 2009; Krause, 2009). For example, Hill and Turiano (2014) analyzed data from a longitudinal study of health and well-being in the United States and found that having a purpose in life buffered against mortality risk among young, middle-aged, and older adults. Researchers have used innovative methods to specify that one potential mechanism of this link is stress-buffering (Burrow & Hill, 2013). In these studies, purpose was broadly conceptualized as having a clear set of goals; however, other conceptions of purpose include an explicit "beyond-the-self" component (Damon, 2008; Malin, Reilly, Quinn, & Moran, 2014), and more recently a specific form of purpose, called civic purpose, has been specified to capture the special meaning of having a purpose in the civic domain (Malin et al., 2015). These civic types of purpose might amplify associations between purpose and health and longevity.

Risks in linking the self with activism.   While activism might be a way of finding or enacting one's identity and purpose, it is also possible that the more closely tied activism is with the "self," the stronger the risk of activism undermining health. Revisiting Boehnke and Wong's (2011) distinction between "microworries" (self-relevant worries) and "macroworries" (worries about things external to the self—the wider society), we can see how youth activism blends the micro and macro. Whereas some forms of civic engagement might be exclusively about causes external to the self (e.g., volunteering to help others with whom you have little in common), youth activism tends to center around personally relevant issues (Ballard, 2014; Ginwright & James, 2002) and thus may be particularly stressful if positive outcomes are not achieved.

Social capital and connection to others.   Social capital theory is also relevant for understanding the potential linkages between activism and health (Putnam, 2000). Social capital can be defined as "resources that are accessed by individuals as a result of their membership in a network or group" (Kawachi & Berkman, 2014, p. 291). Such resources can be both structural (e.g., physical, place-based, contextual) and social (people-based, relational). Youth activism aims to increase the social capacity of youth in their communities while at the same time providing them a chance to improve structural conditions in their communities. Activism can provide youth with the opportunity to connect with others, perhaps fulfilling what some consider to be a basic human need for connectedness and thus promoting well-being (Ryan & Deci, 2000). Youth activism provides opportunities for both peer-to-peer connections and youth–adult connections (Baker-Doyle, this volume); in high-quality programs, such connections can be described as youth–adult partnerships (Zeldin, Larson, et al., 2005).

In terms of relational forms of social capital, it is well documented that psychological social connectedness promotes good health, and social isolation is deleterious for health at the individual level (Hawkley, Masi, Berry, & Cacioppo, 2006; Kawachi & Berkman, 2001). Social connectedness is robustly linked with well-being, more so than many other well-known influences on well-being including economic predictors (e.g., Stiglitz, Sen, & Fitoussi, 2009). In a recent meta-analysis of 148 empirical studies, Holt-Lunstad and colleagues (2010) documented a very strong link between social relationships and mortality risk among adults and noted that the effect is strongest when social relationships are measured through social integration (e.g., social network size and participation). This suggests an added boost of *community* social connectedness above social connectedness to family and friends. In one study, self-reported sense of community modestly predicted self-reported general and mental health after accounting for neighborhood participation and perceived neighborhood control (Parker et al., 2001), again suggesting the powerful nature of social connectedness for health. Feelings of community membership are also proposed to be associated with lower problematic health-related behaviors like participation in violence (Zeldin, 2004).

At the community level, living in geographic areas that are rich in social capital (e.g., where social networks are strong and social trust is high) is associated with better health (Kawachi & Berkman, 2014; Kawachi, Kennedy, & Glass, 1999). For example, in states characterized by higher social capital, measured through higher levels of social trust, individuals report better overall health after controlling for many individual-level determinants of health (Kawachi et al., 1999). In most versions of social capital theory, civic engagement (which typically includes forms of activism) is included in the definition of social capital. Although evidence of social capital and social connectedness promoting health is relevant, social capital theory tends to treat social capital as something one "has" or can acquire; it is important for future work to treat civic activism as an active process that might influence health trajectories (Ballard & Syme, 2015).

Risks of social capital for health. Although experiencing a strong sense of community connection is generally positive for youth development, it is also crucial to understand *which communities* youth are connecting to. Links between social connectedness and mental health are well established

(Kawachi & Berkman, 2001); however, links between social ties and physical health and health behaviors should also depend on the nature of social ties. Peer groups influence health behaviors (Prinstein, Boergers, & Spirito, 2001), so becoming connected to communities or peer groups engaged in negative health behaviors would likely undermine rather than promote health.

Systemic change.   Youth activism brings young people together around community causes, ideally to improve conditions in their communities (Ginwright & James, 2002). This process can strengthen community social capital while also contributing to structural change in local policies or the distribution of resources within communities. Such changes can provide a feedback loop to improve conditions that support the health of youth and families. As a special case, activist projects sometimes focus on health issues. For example, youth activists often choose issues centered on physical health (obesity, healthy food choices, exercise), mental health (e.g., stress and well-being), or behavioral health (sexual education, AIDS, suicide). Even when not directly focused on health issues, youth activists often take on projects that can promote healthy development in a broader sense given the interconnected nature of youth issues in the domains of health, education, safety, transportation, and human rights.

As one example, youth from the San Francisco Youth Commission (California) engaged in a multiphase process to identify teen transportation needs and to lobby for policy changes. After three years, the Youth Commission succeeded in convincing the San Francisco Municipal Transportation Agency (MUNI) board to approve a "Free MUNI for Youth" program with an expansion to include 18-year-olds from low- to moderate-income families among those eligible for free MUNI passes (SF Youth Commission). In this example, engaged youth formed peer partnerships across districts as well as partnerships with local political leaders. Although transportation access is not directly a health issue, such policy change can improve the well-being of San Francisco teen residents and families by providing transportation access for some of the city's most vulnerable and isolated young people. Indirectly, this access should feed back to support adolescent health and the broader health of communities. For example, this program is critical in allowing young people access to school, health care appointments, and healthy food options, and more broadly the program might promote feelings of connection with their city of residence.

Risks of social change for health.   Trying to change structural conditions might undermine adolescent health and well-being when things don't change. In the course of trying to make changes in their schools and communities via activism, youth have to deal with the slow pace of change as well as setbacks and losses. If not part of an intentional framing about the process of activism, such setbacks could lead young people to question whether social problems are too entrenched to change. Most people experience feelings of burnout when putting effort toward a personally meaningful issue and seeing little or no signs of progress. An additional barrier for youth in a political context is the reality that youth power is limited in our current society (Sarason, 1996; Zeldin, Camino, et al., 2005). While all social change efforts are slow, youth may experience extra barriers in their activism efforts by virtue of the U.S. political system not being well set up to include their voices on political and social issues. Even in youth institutions, power tends to be centralized at the top, although recent efforts in many contexts to include youth in decision-making and to create authentic youth–adult partnerships are promising (Mitra, 2008, 2009; Ozer & Wright, 2012; Sarason, 1996; Zeldin, Camino, et al., 2005; Zeldin, Larson, et al., 2005).

SUGGESTIONS FOR RESEARCHERS AND FOR YOUTH PRACTITIONERS

Based on the promising early evidence cited thus far, we believe that understanding the complex links between youth activism and health is a key topic for future research on youth activism and on youth development more broadly. Future work on the topic should attend to the nuances of linking activism and health and well-being. We highlight four particularly important sources of complexity. First, what are the short- and long-term effects of activism on adolescent health? According to theory and preliminary evidence, it might be reasonable to expect short-term dips in mental health and well-being or physical health, offset by long-term gains under certain conditions, for example, when activism is properly scaffolded and is empowering.

A second critical question is *for whom* activism affects health. Activism might benefit some youth more than others. Politically marginalized young people—who tend to be lower SES, ethnic minority, and immigrant—potentially stand to gain the most from opportunities for empowerment and gaining a political voice. Youth who are marginalized are often the ones most attracted to activism because activism is centered on organizing efforts that often arise as a response to a group of people feeling that their needs are not being met by the political and social status quo (Ballard, 2014; Ballard et al., 2015; Watts & Flanagan, 2007). Such youth might also stand to gain the most from the processes laid out above, such as empowerment, connecting with others, and coping with stress (e.g., Zimmerman, Ramirez-Valles & Maton, 1999).

Third, of course, any benefits of activism depend on the participation being high quality and empowering rather than futile or overly burdensome. It is beyond the scope of this chapter to address important aspects of program quality and implementation, for example, differences in the quality, quantity, or characteristics of experiences provided by various youth activism programs or experiences. We refer the reader to prior work that focuses on specific programs and aspects of activism that promote youth development (Christens & Kirshner, 2011; Kirshner, 2007; Ozer & Douglas, 2015).

Finally, it is important to distinguish among aspects of adolescent health, including mental health, physical health, and health behaviors. For example, activism might promote psychological well-being while undermining physical health. Given reasons to expect complex links between activism and health and well-being, it is important to investigate how activism is linked with various aspects of health and well-being over the course of youth development.

Although many questions remain unanswered about how youth activism affects health, evidence from research and practice in youth activism points to several areas that practitioners can focus on in order for activism to promote health. Here, we offer practical suggestions for youth practitioners. First, as much youth activism work points out, youth should be taken seriously; having a voice can be empowering. Second, practitioners can help youth find meaning in their activism work. Adults can connect youth with activities that will be personally meaningful and can help them continue to find meaning when activism work gets challenging to mitigate the stress and burden associated with taking on a social role that consumes time and energy. Even in contexts where youth have limited power (e.g., schools), skilled adults can find ways to offer youth autonomy and control, or what Ozer and colleagues call "micropower compensation" (Ozer, Newlan, Douglas, & Hubbard, 2013).

Third, practitioners can help youth form realistic expectations and goals for their activism to frame some of the inevitable frustration of challenging work. At the same time, it is important to allow youth to be frustrated and help channel the frustration constructively. Larson and Walker (2010) provide an in-depth analysis of how skilled youth development practitioners can turn dilemmas that arise in youth development practice into opportunities for further youth development; for example, by including youth in crafting solutions to the dilemmas and serving as advocates for youth. Finally, practitioners can help youth see "small wins" en route to big change (Foster-Fishman et al., 2006). Change is slow, but there are many types of success in youth activism work (public presentations, gaining an audience with someone in power, a good conversation about an important issues), and youth should be encouraged to celebrate their successes, while not giving up on longer-term goals. In high-quality youth activism programs, ideally adults scaffold this process by helping young people understand social realities and their roles in society.

We want to end by noting that activism is important for social justice and youth development regardless of its link with health. We have outlined theory and preliminary evidence suggesting that youth activism is linked with health and well-being, potentially in both promotive and problematic ways. We believe that these links are important to understand descriptively, so we know the full range of implications of youth activism for development, as well as prescriptively, so we can design youth activism opportunities that are as constructive as possible for both youth and their communities.

REFERENCES

Ballard, P. J. (2014). What motivates youth civic involvement? *Journal of Adolescent Research, 29*(4), 439–463. http://dx.doi.org/10.1177/0743558413520224

Ballard, P. J. (2015a, May). Engaging youth in communities: A process to promote individual and community health. Robert Wood Johnson Foundation Health and Society Scholars Annual Meeting, Chapel Hill, NC.

Ballard, P. J. (2015b). Longitudinal links between discrimination and civic development among Latino and Asian adolescents. *Journal of Research on Adolescence.* Advance online publication. http://dx.doi.org/10.1111/jora.12221

Ballard, P. J., Malin, H., Porter, T. J., Colby, A., & Damon, W. (2015). Motivations for civic participation among diverse youth: More similarities than differences. *Research in Human Development, 12*(1–2), 63–83. http://dx.doi.org/10.1080/15427609.2015.1010348

Ballard, P. J., & Syme, S. L. (2015). Engaging youth in communities: A framework for promoting adolescent and community health. *Journal of Epidemiology and Community Health.* Advance online publication. http://dx.doi.org/10.1136/jech-2015-206110

Boehnke, K., & Wong, B. (2011). Adolescent political activism and long-term happiness: A 21-year longitudinal study on the development of micro- and macrosocial worries. *Personality and Social Psychology Bulletin, 37*(3), 435–447. http://dx.doi.org/10.1177/0146167210397553

Boyle, P. A., Barnes, L. L., Buchman, A. S., & Bennett, D. A. (2009). Purpose in life is associated with mortality among community-dwelling older persons. *Psychosomatic medicine, 71*(5), 574–579. http://dx.doi:.org/10.1097/PSY.0b013e3181a5a7c0

Burrow, A. L., & Hill, P. L. (2013). Derailed by diversity? Purpose buffers the relationship between ethnic composition on trains and passenger negative mood. *Personality and Social Psychology Bulletin, 39*(12), 1610–1619. http://dx.doi.org/10.1177/0146167213499377

Center for Information and Research on Civic Learning and Engagement. (2011, November). Understanding a diverse generation: Youth civic engagement in the United States. Retrieved from http://www.civicyouth.org/wp-content/uploads/2011/11/CIRCLE_cluster_report2010.pdf

Chen, Y., & Feeley, T. H. (2012). Enacted support and well-being: A test of the mediating role of perceived control. *Communication Studies, 63*(5), 608–625. http://dx.doi.org/10.1080/10510974.2012.674619

Christens, B. D. (2012). Targeting empowerment in community development: A community psychology approach to enhancing local power and well-being. *Community Development Journal, 47*(4), 538–554. http://dx.doi.org/10.1093/cdj/bss031

Christens, B. D., & Kirshner, B. (2011). Taking stock of youth organizing: An interdisciplinary perspective. *New Directions for Child and Adolescent Development, 134*, 27–41. http://dx.doi.org/10.1002/cd.309

Christens, B. D., & Peterson, N. A. (2012). The role of empowerment in youth development: A study of sociopolitical control as mediator of ecological systems' influence on developmental outcomes. *Journal of Youth and Adolescence, 41*(5), 623–635. http://dx.doi.org/10.1007/s10964-011-9724-9

Cowen, E. L. (1994). The enhancement of psychological wellness: Challenges and opportunities. *American Journal of Community Psychology, 22*(2), 149–179. http://dx.doi.org/10.1007/BF02506861

Dahl, R. E. (2004). Adolescent brain development: A period of vulnerabilities and opportunities. Keynote address. *Annals of the New York Academy of Sciences, 1021*(1), 1–22. http://dx.doi.org/10.1196/annals.1308.001

Damon, W. (2008). *The path to purpose: Helping our children find their calling in life*. New York, NY: Simon and Schuster.

Erikson, E. H. (1968). *Identity: Youth and crisis*. New York, NY: W. W. Norton.

Fan, R., Zhao, J., Chen, Y., & Xu, K. (2014). Anger is more influential than joy: Sentiment correlation in Weibo. *PLoS ONE 9*(10), e110184. http://dx.doi.org/10.1371/journal.pone.0110184

Flanagan, C., & Bundick, M. (2011). Civic engagment and psychosocial well-being in college students. *Liberal Education, 97*(2). Retrieved from http://www.aacu.org/publications-research/periodicals/civic-engagement-and-psychosocial-well-being-college-students

Foster-Fishman, P. G., Fitzgerald, K., Brandell, C., Nowell, B., Chavis, D., & Van Egeren, L. A. (2006). Mobilizing residents for action: The role of small wins and strategic supports. *American Journal of Community Psychology, 38*(3–4), 143–152. http://dx.doi.org/10.1007/s10464-006-9081-0

Fuligni, A. J., & Telzer, E. H. (2013). Another way family can get in the head and under the skin: The neurobiology of helping the family. *Child Development Perspectives, 7*(3), 138–142. http://dx.doi.org/10.1111/cdep.12029

Fuligni, A. J., Telzer, E. H., Bower, J., Irwin, M. R., Kiang, L., & Cole, S. W. (2009). Daily family assistance and inflammation among adolescents from Latin American and European backgrounds. *Brain, Behavior, and Immunity, 23*(6), 803–809. http://dx.doi.org/10.1016/j.bbi.2009.02.021

Gingold, J. G. (2013, August). CIRCLE Working Paper 78. Building an evidence-based practice of action civics: The current state of assessments and recommendations for the future. *CIRCLE*. Retrieved from http://www.civicyouth.org/wp-content/uploads/2013/08/WP_78_Gingold.pdf

Ginwright, S., & Cammarota, J. (2002). New terrain in youth development: The promise of a social justice approach. *Social Justice, 29*(4), 82–95. Retrieved from http://www.jstor.org/stable/29768150

Ginwright, S., & James, T. (2002). From assets to agents of change: Social justice, organizing, and youth development. *New Directions for Youth Development, 2002*(96), 27–46. http://dx.doi.org/10.1002/yd.25

Hart, D., Donnelly, T. M., Youniss, J., & Atkins, R. (2007). High school community service as a predictor of adult voting and volunteering. *American Educational Research Journal, 44*(1), 197–219. http://dx.doi.org/10.3102/0002831206298173

Hawkley, L. C., Masi, C. M., Berry, J. D., & Cacioppo, J. T. (2006). Loneliness is a unique predictor of age-related differences in systolic blood pressure. *Psychology and Aging, 21*(1), 152–164. http://dx.doi.org/10.1037/0882-7974.21.1.152

Hershberg, R. M., Johnson, S. K., DeSouza, L. M., Hunter, C. J., & Zaff, J. (2015). Promoting contribution among youth: Implications from positive youth development research for youth development programs. In E. Bowers, J. G. Geldof, S. K. Johnson, L. J. Hilliard, R. M. Hershberg, J. V. Lerner, & R. M. Lerner (Eds.), *Promoting positive youth development: Lessons from the 4-H Study* (pp. 211–228). New York, NY: Springer.

Hill, P. L., & Turiano, N. A. (2014). Purpose in life as a predictor of mortality across adulthood. *Psychological Science, 25*(7), 1482–1486. http://dx.doi.org/10.1177/0956 797614531799

Holt-Lunstad, J., Smith, T. B., & Layton, J. B. (2010). Social relationships and mortality risk: A meta-analytic review. *PLoS Medicine, 7*(7), 1–20. http://dx.doi.org /10.1371/journal.pmed.1000316

Hope, E. C., & Jagers, R. J. (2014). The role of sociopolitical attitudes and civic education in the civic engagement of black youth. *Journal of Research on Adolescence, 24*(3), 460–470. http://dx.doi.org/10.1111/jora.12117

Israel, B. A., Checkoway, B., Schulz, A., & Zimmerman, M. (1994). Health education and community empowerment: Conceptualizing and measuring perceptions of individual, organizational, and community control. *Health Education & Behavior, 21*(2), 149–170. http://dx.doi.org/10.1177/109019819402100203

Itzhaky, H., & York, A. S. (2000). Sociopolitical control and empowerment: An extended replication. *Journal of Community Psychology, 28*(4), 407–415. http:// dx.doi.org/10.1002/1520-6629(200007)28:4<407::AID-JCOP3>3.0.CO;2-R

James, S. A. (1994). John Henryism and the health of African-Americans. *Culture, Medicine and Psychiatry, 18*(2), 163–182. http://dx.doi.org/10.1007/BF01379448

Jensen, L. A. (2010). Immigrant youth in the United States: Coming of age among diverse civic cultures. In L. Sherrod, J. Torney-Purta, & C. A. Flanagan (Eds.), *Handbook of research on civic engagement in youth* (pp. 425–443). Hoboken, NJ: Wiley.

Kahne, J., & Middaugh, E. (2008). High quality civic education: What is it and who gets it? *Social Education, 72*(1), 34–39. Retrieved from http://eric.ed.gov/?id=EJ784395

Kahne, J., Middaugh, E., & Allen, D. (2014, March 19). Youth, new media, and the rise of participatory politics. YPP Research Network Working Paper #1. *Youth Participatory Politics Research Network.* Retrieved from http://dmlcentral.net/sites /dmlcentral/files/resource_files/ypp_workinpapers_paper01_1.pdf

Kahne, J., & Westheimer, J. (2006). The limits of political efficacy: Educating citizens for a democratic society. *PS: Political Science & Politics, 39*(2), 289–296. http:// dx.doi.org/10.1017/S1049096506060471

Kawachi, I., & Berkman, L. F. (2001). Social ties and mental health. *Journal of Urban Health, 78*(3), 458–467. http://dx.doi.org/10.1093/jurban/78.3.458

Kawachi, I., & Berkman, L. F. (2014). Social capital, social cohesion, and health. In L. F. Berkman, I. Kawachi, & M. M. Glymour (Eds.), *Social epidemiology* (2nd ed., pp. 290–319). New York, NY: Oxford University Press.

Kawachi, I., Kennedy, B. P., & Glass, R. (1999). Social capital and self-rated health: A contextual analysis. *American Journal of Public Health, 89*(8), 1187–1193. http://dx.doi.org/10.2105/AJPH.89.8.1187

Kirshner, B. (2007). Introduction: Youth activism as a context for learning and development. *American Behavioral Scientist, 51*(3), 367–379. http://dx.doi.org/0.1177/0002764207306065

Krause, N. (2009). Meaning in life and mortality. *Journals of Gerontology Series B: Psychological Sciences and Social Sciences, 64*(4), 517–527. http://dx.doi.org/10.1093/geronb/gbp047

Larson, R. W., & Walker, K. C. (2010). Dilemmas of practice: Challenges to program quality encontered by youth program leaders. *American Journal of Community Psychology, 45*(3), 338–349. http://dx.doi.org/10.1007/s10464-010-9307-z

Lazarus, R. S., & Folkman, S. (1984). *Stress, appraisal, and coping.* New York, NY: Springer.

Lerner, R. M., Lerner, J. V., Almerigi, J. B., Theokas, C., Phelps, E., Gestsdottir, S., . . . Simpson, I. (2005). Positive youth development, participation in community youth development programs, and community contributions of fifth-grade adolescents: Findings from the first wave of the 4-H Study of Positive Youth Development. *Journal of Early Adolescence, 25*(1), 17–71. http://dx.doi.org/10.1177/0272431604272461

Levinson, M. (Ed.). (2010). *The civic empowerment gap: Defining the problem and locating solutions.* Hoboken, NJ: John Wiley and Sons.

Malin, H., Ballard, P. J., & Damon, W. (2015). Civic purpose: An integrated construct for understanding civic development in adolescence. *Human Development, 58*(2), 103–130. http://dx.doi.org/10.1159/000381655

Malin, H., Reilly, T. S., Quinn, B., & Moran, S. (2014). Adolescent purpose development: Exploring empathy, discovering roles, shifting priorities, and creating pathways. *Journal of Research on Adolescence, 24*(1), 186–199. http://dx.doi.org/10.1111/jora.12051

Miller, G. E., Yu, T., Chen, E., & Brody, G. H. (2015). Self-control forecasts better psychosocial outcomes but faster epigenetic aging in low-SES youth. *Proceedings of the National Academy of Sciences, 112*(33), 10325–10330. http://dx.doi.org/10.1073/pnas.1505063112

Mitra, D. L. (2008). Balancing power in communities of practice: An examination of increasing student voice through school-based youth–adult partnerships. *Journal of Educational Change, 9*(3), 221–242. http://dx.doi.org/10.1007/s10833-007-9061-7

Mitra, D. L. (2009). Collaborating with students: Building youth–adult partnerships in schools. *American Journal of Education, 115*(3), 407–436. http://dx.doi.org/10.1086/597488

National Association of Social Workers (2001, November). Adolescent health and youths of color. *Adolescent Health, 2*(1). Retrieved from http://www.naswdc.org/practice/adolescent_health/ah0203.asp

Newacheck, P. W., Hung, Y. Y., Park, M. J., Brindis, C. D., & Irwin, C. E. (2003). Disparities in adolescent health and health care: Does socioeconomic status matter? *Health Services Research, 38*(5), 1235–1252. http://dx.doi.org/10.1111/1475-6773.00174

Ozer, E. J., & Douglas, L. (2015). Assessing the key processes of youth-led participatory research psychometric analysis and application of an observational rating scale. *Youth & Society, 47*(1), 29–50. http://dx.doi.org/10.1177/0044118X12468011

Ozer, E. J., Newlan, S., Douglas, L., & Hubbard, E. (2013). "Bounded" empowerment: Analyzing tensions in the practice of youth-led participatory research in urban public schools. *American Journal of Community Psychology, 52*(1–2), 13–26. http://dx.doi.org/10.1007/s10464-013-9573-7

Ozer, E. J., & Schotland, M. (2011). Psychological empowerment among urban youth: Measure development and relationship to psychosocial functioning. *Health Education & Behavior, 38*(4), 348–356. http://dx.doi.org/10.1177/1090198110373734

Ozer, E. J., & Wright, D. (2012). Beyond school spirit: The effects of youth–led participatory action research in two urban high schools. *Journal of Research on Adolescence, 22*(2), 267–283. http://dx.doi.org/10.1111/j.1532-7795.2012.00780.x

Padilla, A. M. (2008). Social cognition, ethnic identity, and ethnic specific strategies for coping with threat due to prejudice and discrimination. In C. Willis-Esqueda (Ed.), *Motivational aspects of prejudice and racism* (pp. 7–42). New York: Springer.

Parker, E. A., Lichtenstein, R. L., Schulz, A. J., Israel, B. A., Schork, M. A., Steinman, K. J., & James, S. A. (2001). Disentangling measures of individual perceptions of community social dynamics: Results of a community survey. *Health Education & Behavior, 28*(4), 462–486. http://dx.doi.org/10.1177/109019810102800407

Pope, A., Stolte, L., & Cohen, A. K. (2011). Closing the civic engagement gap: The potential of action civics. *Social Education, 75*(5), 265–268. Retrieved from http://eric.ed.gov/?id=EJ944291

Prinstein, M. J., Boergers, J., & Spirito, A. (2001). Adolescents' and their friends' health-risk behavior: Factors that alter or add to peer influence. *Journal of Pediatric Psychology, 26*(5), 287–298. http://dx.doi.org/10.1093/jpepsy/26.5.287

Putnam, R. (2000). *Bowling alone: The collapse and revival of civic America.* New York, NY: Simon & Schuster.

Roepke, A. M., Jayawickreme, E., & Riffle, O. M. (2014). Meaning and health: A systematic review. *Applied Research in Quality of Life, 9*(4), 1055–1079. http://dx.doi.org/10.1007/s11482-013-9288-9

Ryan, R. M., & Deci, E. L. (2000). Self-determination theory and the facilitation of intrinsic motivation, social development, and well-being. *American Psychologist, 55*(1), 68. http://dx.doi.org/10.1037/0003-066X.55.1.68

Sarason, S. B. (1996). *Revisiting "The culture of the school and the problem of change."* New York, NY: Teachers College Press.

Stiglitz, J. E., Sen, A., & Fitoussi, J. P. (2009). *Report by the Commission on the Measurement of Economic Performance and Social Progress.* Retrieved from http://www .stiglitz-sen-fitoussi.fr/en/index.htm

Strobel, K., Osberg, J., & McLaughlin, M. (2006). Participation in social change: Shifting adolescents' developmental pathways. In P. Noguera, J. Cammarota, & S. Ginwright (Eds.), *Beyond resistance: Youth activism and community change* (pp. 197–214). New York, NY: Routledge.

Viner, R. M., Ross, D., Hardy, R., Kuh, D., Power, C., Johnson, A., . . . Batty, G. D. (2015). Life course epidemiology: Recognising the importance of adolescence. *Journal of Epidemiology and Community Health.* Advance online publication. http:// dx.doi.org/10.1136/jech-2015-205607

Wallerstein, N. (1992). Powerlessness, empowerment, and health: Implications for health promotion programs. *American Journal of Health Promotion,* 6(3), 197–205. http://dx.doi.org/10.4278/0890-1171-6.3.197

Watts, R. J., Diemer, M. A., & Voight, A. M. (2011). Critical consciousness: Current status and future directions. *New Directions for Child and Adolescent Development,* 2011(134), 43–57. http://dx.doi.org/10.1002/cd.310

Watts, R. J., & Flanagan, C. (2007). Pushing the envelope on youth civic engagement: A developmental and liberation psychology perspective. *Journal of Community Psychology,* 35(6), 779–792. http://dx.doi.org/10.1002/jcop.20178

Watts, R., & Guessous, O. (2006). Sociopolitical development: The missing link in research and policy on adolescents. In S. Ginwright, P. Noguera, & J. Cammarota (Eds.), *Beyond resistance: Youth activism and community change* (pp. xiii–xxii). New York, NY: Routledge.

Watts, R. J., Williams, N. C., & Jagers, R. J. (2003). Sociopolitical development. *American Journal of Community Psychology,* 31(1), 185–194. http://dx.doi.org /10.1023/A:1023091024140

Wills, T. A. (1994). Self-esteem and perceived control in adolescent substance use: Comparative tests in concurrent and prospective analyses. *Psychology of Addictive Behaviors,* 8(4), 223–234. http://dx.doi.org/10.1037/0893-164X.8.4.223

Yates, M., & Youniss, J. (1998). Community service and political identity development in adolescence. *Journal of Social Issues,* 54(3), 495–512. http://dx.doi.org /10.1111/j.1540-4560.1998.tb01232.x

Zeldin, S. (2004). Preventing youth violence through the promotion of community engagement and membership. *Journal of Community Psychology,* 32(5), 623–641. http://dx.doi.org/10.1002/jcop.20023

Zeldin, S., Camino, L., & Mook, C. (2005). The adoption of innovation in youth organizations: Creating the conditions for youth–adult partnerships. *Journal of Community Psychology,* 33(1), 121–135. http://dx.doi.org/10.1002/jcop.20023

Zeldin, S., Larson, R., Camino, L., & O'Connor, C. (2005). Intergenerational relationships and partnerships in community programs: Purpose, practice, and directions for research. *Journal of Community Psychology,* 33(1), 1–10. http://dx.doi.org /10.1002/jcop.20042

Zimmerman, M. A. (1995). Psychological empowerment: Issues and illustrations. *American Journal of Community Psychology,* 23(5), 581–599. http://dx.doi.org /10.1007/BF02506983

Zimmerman, M. A., Ramirez-Valles, J., & Maton, K. I. (1999). Resilience among urban African American male adolescents: A study of the protective effects of sociopolitical control on their mental health. *American Journal of Community Psychology, 27*(6), 733–751. http://dx.doi.org/10.1023/A:1022205008237

Zimmerman, M. A., & Rappaport, J. (1988). Citizen participation, perceived control, and psychological empowerment. *American Journal of Community Psychology, 16*(5), 725–750. http://dx.doi.org/10.1007/BF00930023

13

Working for Change, Learning from Work: Student Empowerment and Challenges in the Movement to End Campus Gender Violence

Alexandra Brodsky

"Are you ready for your life to change?" Hannah asked me. When I had picked up her call, I had assumed Hannah had a question about an article for *Broad Recognition*, the campus feminist magazine that we worked on together. But when she asked that question, I knew she wasn't calling about a deadline or new interview: the Department of Education's Office for Civil Rights (OCR) had agreed to open an investigation into Yale, our school, based on a Title IX complaint we had submitted along with 14 other classmates. The federal government would soon arrive on campus to determine whether Yale did, as we claimed, mistreat student survivors of gender-based violence in violation of civil rights law that forbids discrimination on the basis of sex.

Hannah was right. Her call changed my life in ways that even now I cannot fully grasp. In the nearly five years since that call, I have proudly worked with students across the country to build a national youth movement to end gender-based violence, including rape and sexual assault, on college campuses. As part of that work, my dear friend Dana Bolger and I started an organization called Know Your IX, which supports students across the country in their efforts to end gender violence. Now, with my law school graduation looming, I have taken a step back from my work, anticipating a life after student organizing as a new generation takes the reins. With the time to reflect, I can start to recognize how lucky I have been to be part of this youth uprising.

One thing I have learned from the last few years of organizing is that there are a million entry points like mine, a million life-changing telephone calls, and no single linear narrative for a movement. Our organizing has been heavily watched. Our demands have been featured in every major newspaper and on every national television station; I know of at least two books coming out about this wave of student action; Dana and I met in person for the first time in New York's Penn Station with a camera crew following us around. Often, media accounts homogenize. In their search for a compelling story, they simplify a diverse, decentralized movement into the actions of a central character or two, as though thousands of young people had followed in lockstep with a compelling—usually white, usually cis female, usually straight-performing, usually pretty—young activist.

Those narratives make me hesitant to tell my own story. How many different students receiving life-changing calls came together to build this movement! So my disclaimer is that this is my story of student organizing, not a comprehensive or representative history. I hope, and think, it can provide insight into a larger movement and demonstrate the great education that is youth organizing. But it is no metonymy.

THE COMPLAINT

The harassment arrived like clockwork, an annual Yale tradition like the Halloween concert or football game against Harvard. Each year, starting in the mid-2000s, a fraternity or sports team had engaged in very public, very misogynistic harassment. In 2005, the Yale Women's Center hung shirts decorated with testimonies of sexual violence on a central quad; the next morning, many of the shirts had reportedly been stolen by fraternity members (Buttrick, 2010; Gordon, 2011). Three years later, in 2008, members of the fraternity Zeta Psi held up a sign declaring "We Love Yale Sluts" outside of the Women's Center, a small office in the basement of a freshman dorm (Abrahamson, 2008). The year 2009 saw the "Preseason Scouting Report," an email circulated through sports teams ranking incoming freshman women based on how many beers a male would need to consume before agreeing to sleep with each (Rosenthal & Yee, 2009). In the fall of 2010, the new members of Delta Kappa Epsilon (DKE) marched through the campus chanting "No means yes, yes means anal" and "Fucking sluts, fucking sluts" (Zeavin, 2010). Faced with this explicitly antiwoman—and in the case of DKE, definitively violent—rhetoric, the Yale administration did little. The college delayed significantly before publicly acknowledging the Zeta Psi incident (Schwartz, 2008), and when Yale finally agreed to hear a complaint against the brothers, they were found not responsible. There are no public records detailing the reasons, and those involved in the hearing were prohibited from speaking publicly about their experiences (Abrahamson, 2008). The administration similarly delayed action in the case of the email, and the only student against whom action was taken was merely "reprimanded" by the Executive Committee, a response to guilt with no practical repercussions (Yale College Executive

Committee, 2011). The administration, then, sent a clear message to its students: we will tolerate your harassment.

That same message was coming through clearly, if less publicly, to individual students reported by their classmates for committing gender-based violence. Students rarely spoke openly about sexual assaults, but news of the school's responses to reported violence spread through whispered paths, and the punch line was bleak: Yale doesn't care about victims of gender violence. In the wake of DKE's chants, a reporter for the *Yale Herald* wrote about two of her friends who had turned to the university for help after they had been raped. One transferred schools after the school denied her the opportunity to introduce her rape kit as evidence and found her assailant not responsible; the other was told "not to discuss her experience because the man who forced himself inside of her filed a counter-complaint for 'defamation of character'" (Achs, 2010).

The only thing I found surprising about these stories was just how similar they were to my own. As a freshman, I had reported an attempted rape to the school: I shared a small American literature seminar with my assailant, a friend (and sometimes more) I had met my first week of school, and I could not bear to discuss *Beloved* with him in a wood-paneled room.

Thankfully, under Title IX of the 1972 Education Amendments, unbeknown to me, Yale had to respond to my report. Thanks to innovative feminist lawyering in the 1970s, Title IX's prohibition on sex discrimination extends to a responsibility for federally funded schools to provide accommodations and support for survivors of gender violence. Yale moved my assailant out of our class. Yet the school failed on many other points: administrators discouraged me from filing a formal disciplinary charge that could lead to repercussions for my classmate and also advised I not tell friends or family for fear that "word might get out" and harm my reputation. When I presented my principal evidence—text messages from my former friend admitting to wrongdoing—a dean told me they were proof that my assailant loved me (Brodsky, 2012).

Students like me observed commonalities between Yale's response to public instances of sexual harassment and to our own private reports. In both contexts, Yale seemed more concerned with keeping things quiet and amiable rather than holding student perpetrators accountable in order to end gender violence.

This was not a new problem on campus. In the 1970s, shortly after the passage of Title IX, students had filed a lawsuit, known as *Alexander v. Yale*, based on Yale's failure to set up a grievance board to hear and respond to reports of gender violence (Brodsky & Deutsch, 2014). And in the years leading up to my enrollment, passionate student organizers had called on the university repeatedly to change its ways. They protested. They held meetings. The year before I arrived on campus, after Zeta Psi professed its love for "Yale sluts" in front of the Women's Center, the center's board blasted students with a mass email. "This time we sue," they wrote. One of the center's organizers that year was the daughter of Ann Olivarius, one of the original *Alexander* plaintiffs and now an accomplished attorney.

Each time students rose up, the school promised: *we'll do better next time.* Yale would create a new committee on gender violence. Administrators would commission a report. Nothing changed.

In retrospect, I think a significant part of the problem was that we did not know our legal rights. When I had reported violence to Yale, I knew that its response was unethical, but I did not realize it was illegal. As far as I knew, Title IX had something to do with women's sports. Many of my classmates were in the same boat. Had we known our rights, we could have stood up for ourselves when we reported violence and, as activists, used the law as a threatening tool to force the school to take our demands seriously. In the fall of my junior year, I took a seminar on sexual rights at Yale's law school and learned for the first time that Title IX requires schools to respond responsibly to gender violence—and prohibits it from behaviors like discouraging victims from filing reports or threatening retaliation, as Yale had done.

After the DKE incident, during my time in that sexual rights seminar, something in me settled into certainty: what felt wrong *was* wrong. When Hannah Zeavin and Presca Ahn, the editor-in-chief and founder of our campus feminist magazine, approached me to sign a Title IX complaint to the Department of Education's Office for Civil Rights (OCR) alleging that Yale failed to adequately respond to sexual harassment and violence on campus, I did not hesitate.

For the next few months, we worked with a small group of lawyers and law students to draft a complaint to OCR, which is responsible for enforcing Title IX. Together, we built a coalition of 16 students and young alumni—survivors, friends, and partners; men and women—to sign their names to the complaint. Knowing the professional and social risks involved, these students worked with the attorneys to shape powerful testimony illustrating how Yale's policies held back individual students from flourishing on campus. We also included a timeline of the inevitably yearly frat "incident," which sprung up each year as though on cue. During spring break, we sent in the document, fingers crossed that OCR would find our stories compelling enough to open an investigation.

On March 31, 2011, Hannah gave me that call. My life was about to change: based on our complaint, OCR would open an investigation into Yale's Title IX compliance.

A DISAPPOINTING INVESTIGATION

The first week of April 2011, walking home from my friend Marina's big, bohemian house on Lynwood, a frat boy in pajama pants yelled out to me from a keg on his front lawn. "Yo," he called out. I walked faster. "I agree," he shouted after me.

When OCR opened the investigation against Yale, it invited a community referendum on the state of gender violence on campus. In part, our task as advocates was to convince our classmates we had a problem. Before the current national wave of attention, many simply did not believe rape and abuse could happen at elite colleges, as though our admissions office could weed out rapists based on high SAT scores. Terms like "rape culture" that are now part of the media's common vocabulary were strange then: one student wrote an op-ed in the *Yale Daily News* claiming that if Yale had a rape culture, we would all talk about our favorite kinds of rape over breakfast (Fisher, 2011). "Obviously, the existence of a rape culture is a farcical idea," she wrote dismissively. "These things just don't happen at Yale."

Obviously, though, they do. They did. And just as some of our classmates dismissed the Title IX complaint out of hand, many others came forward in support, like the unexpectedly friendly frat bro on Lynwood. Many survivors reached out to tell us, in the women's restroom or over email, that they knew too well that rape happened here. Our inboxes flooded with notes from alumni saying that the problem we faced was nothing new. Some Yalies explained that we were the first people they had ever told about their victimizations. I was both grateful and overwhelmed by the outpouring: glad to know we were right to pursue the complaint, heartbroken to hear just how needed it was, and unsure, as a 21-year-old with no training in mental health care, how to respond to an inbox full of survivors who needed more and better support than I knew how to provide.

During these times, the investigators from the Office for Civil Rights were a source of great hope. They did not need to be convinced that Yale had a gender violence problem because they had heard from far too many mistreated survivors to doubt our claims for a moment. In our meetings, they were up front: from conversations with students and administrators it was entirely clear that Yale was violating Title IX. Each time a classmate brushed off the complaint as a frivolous overreaction to an imagined problem, I took comfort in the finding of noncompliance I was sure OCR was about to make.

After a year-long investigation, while I was busy preparing for my graduation from Yale, OCR officials gave us a call: they had the information they needed. Yet, shockingly, they weren't planning on doing much with it. OCR knew Yale had broken the law but, they explained, they wouldn't officially find the university out of compliance. Instead, they would enter into what is called a "voluntary resolution agreement" (VRA), by which Yale would agree to make policy changes in order to avoid an embarrassing public announcement that the school hadn't followed Title IX. When we pressed for explanation, the investigators shrugged off our questions. *That's just how we do things,* they told us. Like survivors who are asked to give their abusers second chances, we were expected to trust that the Yale administration had made some well-meaning mistakes and deserved another opportunity to get it right.

We were devastated.

The policy changes were real and important. During the course of the investigation, Yale overhauled its reporting system and appointed a Title IX coordinator; in the VRA, the school promised to make sure survivors knew about their options and to protect students from retaliation, rather than threatening adverse consequences for reporting (Voluntary Resolution Agreement, 2012). That matters. Back on campus now as a law student, I have seen the ways these and other changes instigated by the complaint and VRA have made life better for students.

Yet without the finding of noncompliance, Yale was able to spin the investigation as good press. The president of the university, Richard Levin, sent out an email announcing that OCR has announced "no findings of noncompliance." Unsurprisingly, the school paper reported this brilliant manipulation of the VRA as "Yale found in compliance with Title IX" (Brodsky, 2012). We had turned to the government not only for policy change, which we had achieved, but also for public validation that the status quo was unethical as well as illegal. On that account, we had failed. OCR provided ammunition to our opponent classmates, who were convinced, as that columnist had written, that rape doesn't happen at fancy schools like Yale.

TAKING IT NATIONAL

A year or two ago, another activist privately criticized my Yale co-complainants and me for not talking about violence at other schools back in 2011. Now that we have a national student movement against campus gender violence, the fact of widespread sexual abuse and institutional mistreatment is the starting point for any organizer calling out Title IX violations on their campus. *Us too!* But back in my undergraduate days, we felt very much alone.

That was all to change very quickly. In the few years after the Yale investigation, which was announced just before OCR published new guidance clarifying schools' responsibilities to address gender violence, thousands of students across the country came together. We called out gender violence on hundreds of campuses, as well as the widespread apathy by college administrations and the federal government that allowed rape and harassment to continue unfettered. The movement was never planned. There was never a central strategy. But there was a silent problem, and once we found one another—through friends of friends, over social media—we built something bigger than we ever could have anticipated.

In the spring of 2012, as I prepared for graduation, a friend from high school sent me an email. A classmate of his at Amherst College, Dana Bolger, was dealing with some issues like those we had protested at Yale. Would I be up for talking with her? A few months after Dana and I first talked over the phone, she and a handful of Amherst classmates launched a startling campaign, *It Happens Here*. The effort exposed what is now old news but was then shocking: students were regularly raped, abused, harassed, stalked, and assaulted, and the school responded not with care but instead with remarkable cruelty. In a magazine and poster exhibit, survivors recounted stories not only of interpersonal violence but also of institutional betrayal—like when a dean recommended Dana leave campus, get a job at Starbucks, and return to campus when her assailant had graduated (Choi, 2012).

The campaign took off in earnest in October 2012 when Amherst student Angie Epifano published a long, detailed account of Amherst's response to her rape report, which included forcibly institutionalizing her. The article, titled "An Account of Sexual Assault at Amherst College," went viral, sparking national conversation not only about Amherst's practices but also about campus gender violence more broadly. I will admit, with embarrassment, the mix of excitement and frustration I felt. Without a doubt, I was thrilled that a survivor had so courageously sparked tremendous concern, but I couldn't help wondering why the Yale classmates who had shrugged off the complaint against our school were now so quick to share the link to Angie's story on social media. In retrospect, the reason is clear: Angie wrote her full, awful story without shame, attaching her name where so many—including myself—had spoken as advocates but never survivors, seeking refuge in anonymity when we did speak about our experiences. Angie provided a face to a problem that we at Yale had spoken about in abstract terms while we secretly felt the harms intimately, personally.

I hate that it took survivors coming forward with their names and faces for the nation to take notice. "Sharing your story," as survivor activists call it, comes with a terrible cost and an immovable Google history. But it worked, and Angie started us off.

After Angie's story, dozens of students reached out to Dana, who was busy organizing behind the scenes at Amherst. Some who were interested in filing Title IX complaints reached out to me over Twitter and Facebook. After those survivors went public, marrying the legal strategies we had used at Yale with the narrative-driven advocacy at Amherst, many more reached out to them. Often, we heard about one another through news articles. Soon we had an organic, rapidly growing community of student and young alumni organizers determined to change their campuses and support one another in those efforts. We never established a formal strategy, movement blueprint, or organizational structure. Instead, we coalesced on email chains and Facebook groups to share tips and ask for advice. As student actions emerged at campuses across the country, the national trend was impossible to ignore.

LAUNCHING KNOW YOUR IX

Student organizing is messy. The organization I co-founded and co-directed for nearly three years, Know Your IX, is a marriage of different organic, disparate efforts students initiated to address the urgent problems we saw.

In the spring of 2013, after conversations with survivors across the country, Dana and I grew convinced that student legal literacy was necessary to combat campus sexual violence. After all, the Title IX complaint had pushed Yale to change its ways, but I wished I had been able to stand up for my rights when I reported—and I had heard the same story from many of the other students in our growing network. Dana, a couple of our activist friends, and I decided to create an educational website and short-term social media campaign to condense accessible legal information for survivors and get the word out. We predicted we would be done by August 2013, when I was scheduled to start law school. We decided to call the campaign Know Your IX.

So we asked student survivors and activists a question: What do you wish you had known when you reported violence? And what strategies do you wish you had been exposed to before you started organizing? We built a website, knowyourIX.org, collecting these student-written guides, edited by attorneys where necessary. They covered topics from "Nine things to know about Title IX" to power-mapping university decision-making processes to dealing with administrative and intramovement racism. We published a couple of activist case studies so students could learn from the successes and missteps of organizers on other campuses.

While we were busy creating the website, Dana and I also started thinking about the Department of Education's failure to enforce Title IX. My disappointment with OCR's impact on Yale's campus still stung, and the agency's historical inaction had been one of the reasons Dana decided not to file a complaint against Amherst. As we connected with more students, we heard too many stories like mine: OCR came to campus, uncovered massive legal violations, and then left, satisfied by a school's promise to change. Yet, despite OCR's inaction, the growing media coverage of campus gender violence stylized the agency as the great hero that would take down the evil schools—even though we knew OCR was very much part of the problem.

Changing the agency's ways would be hard, particularly given a lack of information about its enforcement efforts. Almost no information—what schools were investigated, for how long, and to what end—was publicly available. To make our case, we had to piece together stories we heard from students across the country. The survivor who had filed a Title IX complaint only to learn her school had already been under investigation for four years. The students, Wagatwe Wanjuki and John Kelly, who had, five years apart, filed complaints based on the actions of the same dean. By the time we were done putting together our cases, no one was surprised that the dean had been allowed to continue his mistreatment of survivors with impunity after OCR refused to push the school to change its ways after the first complaint (Bolger & Brodsky, 2014).

So we decided to use our voice the best way we knew how as student organizers: we would protest outside the Department of Education. Wagatwe, an experienced antiviolence organizer, hatched a plan to circulate a petition for better Title IX enforcement and then use the protest to deliver the signatures. Suzanna Bobadilla, another activist plugged into the network, called us ED ACT NOW, a name that perfectly encapsulated our demands.

Working remotely with a small core of activists from across the country, we spent a frantic few weeks trying to collect all the information we could and levy our social networks to rally support. With just a few days to go, we were in desperate straits—scrambling for information shielded by an opaque agency, hoping to break 1,000 signatures—when the tides changed. Change .org organizer Shelby Knox, a former student activist, now on Know Your IX's board, found our petition and helped us promote it over email lists, eventually bringing in more than 175,000 signatures. As the word spread, student stories rolled in, and activists from across the country booked their tickets to make their way to DC.

To our shock, the Obama administration got nervous. The weekend before the event, both Vice President Biden's staff and the Department of Education invited us to meet after our planned rally. We had not been able to catch a meeting with our school presidents—and now we were headed to the White House.

I do not think I have ever been as anxious as I was the night before the rally. After hours of rehearsing speeches with organizers from Arizona, New Jersey, and New Hampshire, refining our presentations for the administration, and mapping out all the logistical obstacles for the next day, I made my way to crash on my friend's couch along with a new friend and co-organizer, Kate Sim, whom I had just met in person for the first time that day. I was exhausted but couldn't sleep. I woke up sick three times.

What a day that was. For the first time, survivors from across the country—most of us who had never met in person before but felt like old friends from the online connections we had already made—gathered to demand that the Department of Education protect our civil rights (Lipka, 2013). Walking from the offices of the American Association of University Women (AAUW), which provided us with meeting space and a much-needed morale boost, we carried boxes of signatures to the Department of Education. In the square outside the imposing gray building, survivors from across the country, sporting T-shirts with their schools' names, demanded accountability from an agency that had forgotten us. Many of us had exchanged emails and Facebook messages before, but few had ever met in person.

In our meetings that afternoon with policymakers, Wagatwe, John, Dana, Suzanna, Kate, long-time activist Laura Dunn, and I presented a set of concrete demands: *Find schools publicly noncompliant with the law. Fine them for their abuses. Make sure undocumented student survivors can file civil rights complaints without risking deportation. Engage schools to serve queer students and students of color, who are particularly vulnerable to violence but so often left out of policy discussions.* No sweeping policy changes emerged from these meetings. Yet the Obama administration took notice.

So did the media. Survivors had already powerfully utilized public attention to put pressure on their schools to change, but I was proud of the way the protest shaped national dialogue, exposing OCR's complicity in schools' abuses. In the years since, OCR, under the leadership of Assistant Secretary Catharine Lhamon, has radically changed its ways. Change doesn't happen because of one protest, of course. We spent the months after the rally hearing "no" from OCR many times before it started saying "yes," and these successes came only through partnerships with allies, like the AAUW and National Women's Law Center, that had worked on these issues for years before we had even arrived on our campuses. But I do think that the group of survivors who gathered in front of the Department of Education in July 2013 sent us down a much-needed path toward institutional accountability.

After the rally, as we waited to hear the department's response to our demands, we sprinted to finish the Know Your IX website. When it went live in August 2013, Dana and I thought our work was basically done: we had worked with smart, savvy survivors to make an informational website for students to use as they want. I was about to return to Yale for law school and Dana still had another semester left at Amherst. We were tired.

But the response to Know Your IX quickly showed us we were far from done. Students thanked us but also asked for, and offered, more. They had more questions to ask, and more support to provide to allies on campuses across the country.

KNOW YOUR IX TODAY

Nearly three years later, Know Your IX is now a nonprofit with a three-person full-time staff—including Dana—part-time student team, and national network of activists on campuses across the country. What I thought would be a summer project before law school ended up turning into an organization that would consume me for the first two years of my JD. A few months ago, I stepped down as co-director but remain chair of the board, dedicated to building a sustainable organization to last until student organizers have finally ended campus gender violence.

Since our early days, Know Your IX's mission and structure have evolved. We see our work as twofold: providing students with the support they need to make change on their campuses and bringing those voices to policymakers to make sure the law and its enforcers are responsive to the reality on the ground.

For the first prong, we continue to build the website and our educational social media campaigns, but now we also offer more direct support to student activists, including one-on-one mentoring and weekend-long regional trainings where organizers share strategies and learn from one another. Our efforts were bolstered by our merger with Carry That Weight, a national student network that grew out of Emma Sulkowicz's powerful performance art piece at Columbia University, where she carried around a mattress as a physical manifestation of the burden of attending school with the man she says raped her. Know Your IX's online resources now explain the law in greater depth and provide more robust guides for activists building campus movements.

Policy work keeps the team busy, too. In 2014 the campaign merged with ED ACT NOW and expanded our policy work outside of OCR enforcement. That shift came in large part because OCR has been responsive to our demands: the agency now publicly finds schools out of compliance with Title IX. Some of our policy work now focuses on pushing OCR's enforcement to be more responsive to overlooked forms of harm, like the financial impact of violence, and Know Your IX has collaborated across movements to push shared policy goals, like a recent effort with United We Dream to increase protections for undocumented survivors. However, much of Know Your IX's time is spent on the defensive: both state and federal lawmakers are pushing bills that would require survivors to report to the police if they want help from their schools. Yet we know from surveying survivors that this measure would radically depress reporting rates, denying students the services they desperately need in the wake of violence.

Know Your IX has been shaped, and will continue to be shaped, by the movement in which it is embedded. No single nonprofit makes up a social movement. Instead, change is happening across the country thanks to thousands of student activists tackling rape culture and institutional apathy on their campuses. Sometimes, media exaggerates how centralized the movement is, claiming that Know Your IX or another nonprofit coordinates each student group from afar. In reality, the movement is heterogeneous and constantly in flux. Know Your IX goes where we are needed, providing the support most helpful to young people best positioned to understand and transform their local university communities.

FEMINIST BOOT CAMP

For most of my time with Know Your IX, I have been a law student, but the greatest education of my life so far has been organizing with student survivors. I sometimes refer to the past few years as a feminist boot camp. By the time this chapter goes to print, I will have moved to DC to work as a civil rights attorney at a feminist law nonprofit, representing girls facing discriminatory disciplinary actions in local public schools. Without a doubt, I will draw as much from my student organizing as my formal legal training.

In about the same time it takes to get a law degree, I learned how to draft policy proposals and force high-level lawmakers to grapple with these demands. I learned how a bill becomes a law and how to help move a proposal forward or stop it in its tracks. I learned how to build coalitions with like-minded allies, navigate factitious relationships with nominally progressive opportunists, and responsibly find commonalities with strange bedfellows. I learned how to appeal to a public audience's best nature and how to resist their well-meaning but destructive impulses, like calling on schools to turn over all reports of sexual violence to the police. I learned to churn out a ghost op-ed on my own in half an hour and draft a petition with 12 other writers overnight.

What an education. What an opportunity for a whole generation, too. Going forward, I am committed to support student activists because today's campus protester is tomorrow's civil rights attorney, legislator, or union leader. A whole cohort of student organizers, mostly women, developed robust experience and expertise through organizing around gender violence on campus. Many will stick with this issue, but others will carry these skills with them to the other feminist and progressive struggles they join over the rest of their lives. I have met many remarkable students through this work who, I am confident, will continue to create grassroots change.

Organizing also provided fertile ground for relationships with older, more experienced feminists, even as some tensions arose between generations of activists. I hesitate to fuel the age-old story of feminist intergenerational conflict, so often wielded by our enemies. Yet at times I have been disappointed by groups of established feminists and nonprofits who seemed more interested in hosting conferences about our lives and fundraising with our stories than actually supporting us. It is equally true, though, that many experienced organizers, professors, lawyers, and policymakers reached out to Know Your IX and our allies provide invaluable guidance. I learned a lot from them about the law. Just as importantly, though, I learned about movement history and what it means to live a life of social justice. Many of these women have been remarkable mentors for me over the past few years, taking long-distance calls to help me brainstorm options for life after student organizing, and I am sure I will continue to rely on their wisdom as a practicing attorney.

THE CHALLENGES

To say we have learned a huge amount is not to say we figured everything out. I know I made a lot of mistakes, and there are plenty of puzzles I still have not solved.

One unexpected challenge was our rapid success. Student activists are used to shouting from the outside and to being ignored. The day of the rally, we barely had time to change out of the T-shirts we had worn for the protest before our meeting with Education Secretary Arne Duncan. I do not want to trivialize how truly awful it is to be ignored by decision makers, isolated from the centers of power that determine how and whether we can live in safety with dignity. Yet I have found that it takes time to adjust to the light inside, too. Know Your IX has been lucky to find audiences with congresspeople, senators, and key officials within the Obama administration. Yet we sometimes struggled to navigate these relationships of power and privilege, particularly as survivors so accustomed to being let down by adults who claim to have our best interests at heart. When do you trust a government official? When do you play nice to maintain a relationship, and when do you storm the gates? We were good at being outsiders; I'm not sure I ever found my rhythm as a (relative) insider.

The process of building an organization, too, exposed to me how hard it can be to structure and manage groups of people in a manner consistent with our political commitments. In particular, organizing with survivors of trauma poses unique challenges. Not everyone is always able to do the work, but the work still needs to get done—which often results in terribly heavy burdens on those who remain. Too often, under-resourced collectives like Know Your IX end up in vicious cycles where some activists, in attempts to support others in their ranks, take on more than they can bear, until they, too, are too exhausted to live up to their responsibilities and offload their work onto others. To exclude all those who struggle would violate our commitments to centering survivors, but mutual accountability is essential to maintain the work and individuals' well-being. I stepped down as co-director in large part to pass off leadership to a younger generation of activists but also because I was thoroughly burned out. No sustainable movement can use up organizers in that way.

Student activism cannot run on passion alone. We need funding. In her book *Do What You Love and Other Lies about Success and Happiness*, Miya Tokumitsu (2015) writes about how the exhortation to "do what you love" is often used to demean the value and toll of work we care about. Care workers in particular find their labor trivialized and deemed unworthy of financial compensation, because we assume that the very gendered work of raising children, aiding the elderly, or nurturing the needy is its own reward.

Women's labor, we are told, is instinctual and emotionally, if not economically, rewarding.

A similar pattern plays out in youth organizing, its own form of collective care work. The work is, of course, personally rewarding, and many of us entered the movement to end the abuse and violence we knew too intimately. Yet, despite widespread acclaim for students' successes, funding is scarce. The image of scrappy student organizers excuses our collective unwillingness to invest in young people's work, which results in understaffed, unsustainable organizations wearing themselves thin. Certainly, almost all nonprofits struggle to find funding, but student organizers face an additional barrier because few donors recognize that young people, just like established nonprofit workers, still need salaries and office supplies. Printing those protest signs costs money. So does a bus ticket to protest in DC.

A sustainable future for student organizing will require a general acknowledgment that youth activism is hard work. It is hard, and it is work. And this work, like any other, should be compensated.

The lack of financial support is a real shame for many reasons, including the fact that the un- and underfunded structure of student organizing can present barriers to leadership by marginalized students. Many young people simply cannot afford to spend a few hours each week working an underpaid job. Similar to unpaid internships, unpaid activism is most accessible to the wealthiest—who are disproportionately white.

By highlighting an obstacle for marginalized students, I do not want to suggest that the movement is uniformly driven by students with great privilege. Many powerful activists inside Know Your IX and among our allies are students of color, trans students, low-income students, queer students, or students from publicly funded institutions. The country is indebted to their organizing.

Yet so many forces work to silence marginalized students' voices even as they drive the conversation forward that we simply cannot tolerate the fact that a lack of funding poses yet another obstacle. Once, on our way to a meeting with powerful national policymakers, two students of color—who were both from immigrant families and had ethnicity-marking names—were held up by security for over an hour. That moment has remained a terribly literal reminder of a much broader problem. The diversity of the movement has been distorted by the whitewashing prism of a media insistent on celebrating only white, cis, straight women from elite schools who were raped at frat parties and protest wearing T-shirts emblazoned with the names of famous schools. Too often, survivors and activists who do not fit that mold were told by reporters that their stories were too complicated, too unusual, too niche. A reporter told one queer survivor of intimate partner violence that the experience was "alternative rape."

We joked about it for months afterward—*is your rape alternative? hip? emo?*—but those dismissals hurt individuals and the national student body. The country may be up in arms over campus gender violence, but public empathy has been restricted for a certain kind of survivor who, let me be clear, looks like me. That matters. Selective media coverage deprives marginalized students of sanitizing light. As Princess Harmony Rodriguez (2015) wrote in *Black Girl Dangerous*, little makes a school change its ways like some bad headlines, but those headlines are only available for a select few (Rodriguez, 2015).

For those who do find access to media, the "survivor" label has been a double-edged sword, wielded by us and against us. The personal stories of student victims have been essential to push schools and the government to change their ways. I know firsthand, though, how hard it is to *stop* talking about your own experiences once you have started. Too many reporters have asked my co-organizers and me to "tell our stories"—by which they always mean our rape stories, not our activist stories—when we thought we were speaking as advocates. When the Department of Education released the list of schools under investigation in response to a long public campaign led by Know Your IX, I was invited to speak on a radio program. On a preparatory call, I explained to the producer that I planned to speak about the policy change I had championed, not my personal backstory. Shortly thereafter, I was disinvited. "We already have an expert, so we need a survivor," the producer explained, as though one could not be both at the same time.

That's frustrating and hurtful—and also a great shame for progressive causes. If coming out as a survivor relegates activists to a singular identity for the rest of their lives, our country will miss out on a cohort of remarkable advocates. We need to listen to survivors, but then we need to allow them to be more than that one identity, too.

LOOKING FORWARD

More than five years after Hannah's call, my life is still propelled by the news she delivered. I probably will not spend my whole life working on Title IX issues, and I imagine many of the young people with whom I have organized will devote themselves to a range of social justice issues. As is the nature of student organizing, all of us will grow out of our roles; at the time of this writing, I only have a few more months to call myself a student activist. Yet I know that I will keep returning to this moment for energy, for education, in gratitude. My years of student organizing will give me strength and expertise but also, I hope, give me pause. There is much to learn from students. I will stop to listen.

REFERENCES

Abrahamson, Z. (2008, April 28). ExComm found rushes "not guilty." *Yale Daily News*. Retrieved from http://yaledailynews.com/blog/2008/04/28/excomm-found -rushes-not-guilty/

Achs, R. (2010, October 22). Justice denied: It's the time for reform. *Yale Herald*. Retrieved from http://yaleherald.com/op-eds/justice-denied-it%E2%80%99s-the-time -for-reform/

Bolger, D., & Brodsky, A. (2014, July 8). Want colleges to take action to protect students from sexual assault? Take action to give Title IX teeth. *The Nation*. Retrieved from http://www.thenation.com/article/want-colleges-protect-students -sexual-violence-take-action-give-title-ix-teeth/

Brodsky, A. (2012, June 18). Was Yale really cleared on sexual harassment? *Slate*. Retrieved from http://www.slate.com/blogs/xx_factor/2012/06/18/was_yale_really _cleared_on_sexual_harrassment_.html

Brodsky, A., & Deutsch, E. (2014, December 3). No, we can't just leave college sexual assault to the police. *POLITICO Magazine*. Retrieved from http://www.politico .com/magazine/story/2014/12/uva-sexual-assault-campus-113294

Buttrick, A. (2010, October 22). A culture of silence. *Yale Herald*. Retrieved from http://yaleherald.com/homepage-lead-image/cover-stories/a-culture-of-silence/

Choi, V. (2012, October 25). Amherst severely mishandles rape charge. Amherst's female students are not surprised. *Slate*. Retrived from http://www.slate.com/blogs /xx_factor/2012/10/25/after_angie_epifano_amherst_rape_victims_speak_out_no _wonder_college_students.html

Fisher, J. (2011, September 22). Not a rape culture, just a PC one. *Yale Daily News*. Retrieved from http://yaledailynews.com/blog/2011/09/22/fisher-not-a-rape-culture -just-a-pc-one/

Gordon, C. (2011, April 1). Title IX complaint against Yale has a case. *Huffington Post*. Retrieved from http://www.huffingtonpost.com/claire-gordon/yale-sexual -harassment-title-ix_b_843273.html

Lipka, S. (2013, July 16). Protesters call for stricter sanctions on colleges that mishandle sexual assault. *Chronicle of Higher Education*. Retrieved from http://chronicle .com/article/Protesters-Call-for-Stricter/140375/

Rodriguez, P. H. (2015, February 12). How the myth of the "ideal" survivor hurts campus anti-violence movements. *Black Girl Dangerous*. Retrieved from http:// www.blackgirldangerous.org/2015/02/myth-ideal-survivor-hurts-campus-anti-violence -movements/

Rosenthal, L., & Yee, V. (2009, September 3). Vulgar e-mail targets freshmen. *Yale Daily News*. Retrieved from http://yaledailynews.com/blog/2009/09/03/vulgar-e-mail -targets-freshmen/

Schwartz, A. (2008, January 30). Days later, officials still ignoring "sluts" incident. *Yale Daily News*. Retrieved from http://yaledailynews.com/blog/2008/01/30/days -later-officials-still-ignoring-sluts-incident/

Tokumitsu, M. (2015). *Do what you love and other lies about success and happiness*. New York: Regan Arts.

Voluntary Resolution Agreement Yale University Complaint No. 01-11-202 (2012, June 11). Retrieved from https://www2.ed.gov/about/offices/list/ocr/docs /investigations/01112027-b.pdf

Yale College Executive Committee. (2011). *Executive Committee chair's report, 2009–2010*. New Haven, CT: Yale College.

Zeavin, H. (2010, October 14). The last straw: DKE sponsors hate speech on Yale's old campus. *Broad Recognition*. Retrieved from http://broadrecognition.com /opinion/the-straw-that-broke-the-camel%E2%80%99s-back-dke-sponsors -verbal-assault-on-yale%E2%80%99s-old-campus/

Part III

How Youth Activism Strengthens Society

Introduction

Contemporary youth activists work within and outside of existing legal and political structures to produce systemic change. In a market-based neoliberal state, the power and responsibility to govern shift away from a government that is beholden to the public and toward powerful private-sector actors that are primarily driven by profit motives. As a result, the public has little control over significant decisions that impact public space and constrain the lives of those at the economic and social margins of society. The work of youth activists pushes back against neoliberal constructions of private-sector actors as having the right to govern by reclaiming public space and asserting an inclusive definition of what is our collective "public." In effect, youth activists are changing both legal conceptions about and popular discourse around the notion of the "public," transforming existing systems of governance and sometimes even expanding government institutions to include voices that traditionally have been excluded.

The final chapters of this book highlight the unique contributions youth activists make to strengthen society by making tangible changes to practice, policy, power structures, and paradigms. The section begins with two examples of immigrant youth who sought to change policy. In one case, they did not fully succeed in changing the law but were able to alter the broader discourse on immigration and the public's view of immigrants. In the other, the campaign resulted in important districtwide policy changes and the setting of legal precedent. Other chapters highlight how youth activism can institutionalize young people's role in local and regional policymaking and reenvision who has the right to participate in public governance. We end with an examination of how youth have changed the environmental justice movement and helped the movement become part of the public imagination. Together, these examples demonstrate the potential of youth activists to establish public spaces that are inclusive and democratic even in the face of social and economic structures that privilege the participation of powerful elites.

Opening Youth Essay

Janelle Astorga-Ramos

My palms were sweaty and I could feel my heart beating out of my chest; there was so much I wanted to ask and so much I wanted to learn. Hearing these women speak so eloquently and so passionately about their work made everything so much more interesting. So I kept going back. Meeting after meeting, I was there: the fire in my eyes was only sparks to the feelings I felt in my heart. Every time we discussed new campaigns, I knew that was where I wanted to be. The environment. The people. Everyone wanted the same thing—Justice.

That was my first time at a meeting with Young Women United (YWU), a nonprofit organization that focuses on reproductive justice. I first started in their group for young women ages 12–19 called Circle of Strength, and with them I helped write and pass a memorial through the senate that stated every August 25 would be Recognition of Young Parents Day. This meant so much to me not only because it introduced me to the organizing field but because my mother also had me very young, and helping other young parents feel empowered and happy was the greatest first experience ever. I've been volunteering with YWU for about five years now, and other than the Recognition of Young Parents Day, we have been working around Albuquerque informing and educating young women about our bodies, gender, and sexuality, and offering sexed 101s. We also have a campaign about access to health care and have done projects about clinics and what support they offer for young women (mostly of color), and we experimented with different stores to educate ourselves about the barriers young people have when buying contraceptives. I learned so much through that organization not only about myself and how to protect and sustain my reproductive health, but also about the gender identity spectrum and how all of this falls into politics. As I keep developing my skills in this area I will continue to share my knowledge with others and help young women of color become more empowered when discussing their reproductive systems.

About two years ago I was introduced to the SouthWest Organizing Project (SWOP) and found my true passion for organizing in the area of education. I was first a summer intern with SWOP when they educated me about the school-to-prison pipeline and I was completely invested in working toward creating a more equitable education system. We have a campaign whose tag line is "Youth are the solution, not the problem," and we used that to encourage people to stand with young people and help stop the trend of marginalizing, tokenizing, and criminalizing youth. We focus a lot on youth rights and informing students about their rights in and out of the education system. We do "Know Your Rights" workshops, and we also have a youth group that meets every Thursday to help us work on youth-related campaigns.

A big campaign that I actually led myself as a senior at Albuquerque High School was a walkout that actually ran statewide. Recently, the state of New Mexico added a new high-stakes standardized test named PARCC, which is a college and career readiness exam for grades 3–12. Many students, including myself, felt that the PARCC test was very unfair because it incorporated many more consequences than normal standardized tests, such as teacher evaluations, determining graduation for a student, and most importantly the privatization of our education system. The effects that privatization would bring to our schools are less funding, more standards-based assessments, and eventually big out-of-state companies coming in and buying out all of our schools. After hearing about the upcoming test and all it would bring, students got together and decided that we should fight this and prove to our governor that students do care about our education and we are not for profit. We first started doing petitions and writing letters to our governor expressing how PARCC is harmful to our education system. We got more than 1,000 signatures. After a month had passed and there was no response from our governor, we students decided that it was time to do a direct action in order to gain the attention of New Mexico decision makers. At first we didn't really know what to do, but then we started to talk about the walkout that happened in Los Angeles for Chicanos in the 1960s, and that's when we came to the conclusion of doing a walkout in Albuquerque. We were very strategic in our planning and even made information sheets for students who chose to walk out, but it wasn't easy. I was personally threatened by the administration and the principal at my school about not being able to graduate and having the police department shut down our walkout. Luckily, two other students and I were very prepared and knew the rights we had as students, and we also researched PARCC and knew all that was needed when talking to authority figures. We announced that we knew the consequences of walking out of class, and we were still going to go through with the walkout. We were all a little scared inside but we knew that standing up for the betterment of our education was worth it all. There was three days of walkouts and in those three days hundreds of students walked out, not just in Albuquerque. It became a statewide event. Although the walkouts were in some ways successful, there were incidents of civil rights being violated that weren't reported. Students were physically stopped from going back to class, pepper sprayed, and caged in like animals. We were fortunate enough to have many people and even lawyers who were on our side. The walkouts got national coverage and encouraged students in other states such as Mississippi to walk out too. After the walkouts, the successes were small but important: we managed to get the test shortened and found out new information about students being able to do an Alternative Demonstration of Competency (ADC). In January 2016, we got news that our secretary of education, Hanna Skandera, recently became the chair of Pearson's board. Pearson is the company that manufactures the PARCC test. This just means our fight is not over, but as students, we will not give up. This isn't just for us. It's also for our brothers, sisters, and cousins, all whom deserve a high-quality education. As long as PARCC is still around, students will keep standing up.

Activism for me is more than just helping people or changing the norms; it's about creating change not only in the present but for generations to come. I intend to use my activism and community organizing to really inform and educate community members in order to create a generational effect, which will eventually change society.

14

Unlawful Entry: Civil Disobedience and the Undocumented Youth Movement

Genevieve Negrón-Gonzales

In 2008, I stood in a crowded hallway outside of Congresswoman Nancy Pelosi's San Francisco office. At the time, Pelosi was Speaker of the U.S. House of Representatives. Undocumented students activists chose to target her office for a protest because despite her verbal support of the DREAM Act,[1] she had taken no real steps to make it a legislative priority. The activists were young people, mostly college students, who had caravanned to San Francisco from around the state of California to demand a meeting with Congresswoman Pelosi. I participated as a scholar-activist and participant observer, learning from the movement that, in my estimation, had the potential to meaningfully change the political terrain of the state. When Pelosi's office staff realized what was happening, they quickly shut the interior doors to the office just in time to be able to nudge the group of protesters into the hallway. A young, fresh-faced congressional aide came out and said calmly to the group, "I would be happy to speak with you all but not in this manner. If you all vacate the building and assemble on the front steps outside, I'll come down to meet with you." The students agreed, in part because a sizable portion of their contingent remained outside, unable to enter the federal building because they lacked the appropriate identification. Once the group had reassembled outside (and away from the entrance, as the aide was clear to instruct), a handful of students read prepared statements, sharing their testimonies as undocumented students; a collection of stories of family migration, family separation, financial strains, unfulfilled college acceptances, college degrees that they could not use, interrupted dreams thwarted by an unforgiving system that had no regard for their potential contributions to society. The aide—a young white man in a crisply pressed suit—listened earnestly until the students finished. He promised he would "share with Representative Pelosi" everything they had shared, thanked them, and exited back into the building, where stern-faced armed guards stood at the entrance eyeing the students, silently ensuring that they would not gain access again.

Sitting on the lawn in front of San Francisco City Hall for a postaction debrief, a young woman named Alma[2] questioned how successful the action had been. Some felt positively; they had read their statements to someone from Pelosi's office, which is what they had come to do. Others struggled with the feeling that nothing had actually been accomplished. Alma was visibly working through conflicting feelings, and finally spoke up.

> It's like, we come here, and it's important. But I mean really, once we leave, it's back to their normal lives and they can just put us in the backs of their minds again. Then we come back, they tell us, "Oh yeah, we are working on it." And I mean, it's starting to feel like a big cycle where nothing ever gets done. I am tired of waiting. I don't have time to wait. We need to step it up, so they can't just keep ignoring us.

Alma and other young people in that circle were grappling with an unsettling reality that had begun to emerge for the young leaders of this movement. As the campaign to pass the DREAM Act stretched toward the 10-year mark since it was first introduced as the Student Adjustment Act in 2001, it was clear that they were no closer to getting it passed. Perhaps even more unsettling was the reality that the DREAM Act had bipartisan support in name, but no politicians were actually advancing it as a legislative agenda item, buckling under the weight of the largely anti-immigrant national context. Some of the young activists in that circle had been involved since the beginning. They had made this fight a priority in their lives, sinking countless hours of work into building this campaign, and they were increasingly coming to terms with the unsettling reality that there were two likely outcomes: the DREAM Act would never pass or if it did, they would likely be too old to benefit from it when that happened.[3]

In the months and years that followed, the character, nature, strategy, and tactics of the undocumented youth movement began to change. I often thought back to Alma and her words that day, her grappling with what to me was clearly a realization of the limits of nonconfrontational protest; her growing sense that if they truly wanted to be heard, they would need to "speak" in a different way. When I began researching undocumented students a decade ago, I was a young woman myself—a graduate student who saw my academic work as a part of my political work, drawn to this study because immigration politics are a part of who I am, how I grew up, and where my passion lies. I grew up in a Chicano family on the U.S.-Mexico border in south San Diego County. I became engaged in political activism as a teenager fighting Proposition 187, a state proposition that sought to deny access to public services such as K–12 education and emergency room care to undocumented Californians, and Operation Gatekeeper, a Clinton-era measure that embodied the trends toward further militarization of the border. At age 17, I landed on a college campus embroiled in a fight around affirmative action, which then became a fight around the preservation of Ethnic Studies. I was mentored as a young activist by a group of slightly older and much more experienced women of color who introduced me to the world of movement history and critical theory. It was through the combination of this study and the experiences of these fights on the ground—facing a police line, being arrested as a part of a protest action, actively confronting authority figures, and bearing witness to their unrelenting policies—that I began to understand the limits of the system and the legacies of civil disobedience and direct action of which oppressed people in this country are a part. And so on that sunny spring day, when I saw Alma grappling with the limits of letter-writing campaigns and permitted marches and polite protest, I understood what she was trying to make sense of.

Over the past 10 years, the daring activism of undocumented young people has changed the landscape around immigration policy in this country. Part researcher-reflection and part qualitative analysis, this chapter draws on my experience researching and supporting the undocumented student movement since 2007 to examine the way civil disobedience has been utilized as a strategy by these young activists. Through an examination of three key acts of civil disobedience staged by undocumented students—at the office of a U.S. senator in a state implementing a draconian immigration policy, in the U.S. Capitol building during a congressional session, and at the U.S.-Mexico border—I posit that civil disobedience has enabled undocumented young people to confront the state about the hypocrisy of the broken immigration system and challenge the politics of deservingness, which have dominated the debate about immigration reform. As such, these acts of civil disobedience and the movement of which they are a part have shaped not only policy but also the national conversation on "illegality" and belonging. I begin by framing the undocumented youth movement in terms of its broader political and legislative context, then briefly discuss the tradition of civil disobedience as it relates to the undocumented student movement, and finally examine each of these three moments in order to draw out broader themes and lessons.

LEGISLATING "ILLEGALITY" AND BELONGING

Of the estimated 12 million undocumented people living in the United States, 1 million are believed to be children under the age of 18 (Passel & Cohn, 2011). Despite growing up in this country, undocumented children are repeatedly faced with the constraints of their "tolerated illegality" (Oboler,

2006, p. 15). Undocumented young people who grow up in the United States are often caught between a context in which they navigate institutional spaces in similar ways as their documented peers, thereby having to "learn to be illegal" (Gonzales, 2011, p. 603) and grappling in an ongoing, continuous way with the reality of life in an undocumented family; threats of detention and deportation, fearfulness as a default mode because of the risk of exposure, and the mental consequences of harboring a shame that comes along with this stigmatized status are elements of this experience (Negrón-Gonzales, 2013). In the educational realm, despite having the protection of the 1982 Supreme Court ruling *Plyler v. Doe*, which secured the right of undocumented students to primary public education, undocumented young people face significant barriers. As low-income, racialized immigrants in a school system that is de facto segregated by race and class (Orfield, Bachmeier, James, & Eitle, 1997), the promise of *Plyler v. Doe* frequently falls short of ensuring access to an equitable education (Gonzales, Heredia, & Negrón-Gonzales, 2015). As López and López (2010) articulate, undocumented children are caught in the intersection of two broken systems—the education system and the immigration system. Barriers to higher education are significant as undocumented students are not allowed to apply for federal financial aid, which is the way most low-income students are able to access postsecondary education. Further dynamics shaping postsecondary access vary by state. Georgia, for example, bars undocumented students from attending its highest-ranking state universities. Those who are unable or choose not to pursue postsecondary education enter the context of work as undocumented migrant laborers, one of the most vulnerable and exploitable locations one can occupy in the labor market. Given the United States' indisputable dependence on immigrant labor, many scholars have noted the ways in which restrictive immigration policy and border enforcement do not principally aim to keep out poor migrants, but rather seek to include them conditionally (Bacon, 2008; Chacón, Davis, & Cardona, 2006; Oboler, 2006). Undocumented young people face an uncertain future in a nation that is unsure of what to do with them, reinforcing the conditionality embedded in their tenuous status.

Nearly a decade and a half ago, undocumented youth who stood on the edge of this uncertain future began a movement for a legislative solution to their situation. The Student Adjustment Act, the precursor to the DREAM Act, was first introduced in 2001 as a piece of federal legislation that offered a path to citizenship for undocumented students. That same year, Texas passed HB 1403 (Rincón, 2008) and California passed AB 540 (Seif, 2004), legislation that enables eligible undocumented students to apply for a designation that categorizes them as in-state residents for tuition purposes at state colleges and universities. This movement sought to revive the promise in *Plyler v. Doe* by extending this right to higher education and full legal citizenship. Led in the early years by student- and campus-based organizations, the DREAMer movement at its inception was largely characterized by legal, sanctioned forms of protest—letter-writing campaigns, lobbying visits, press conferences, and educational events.

Over the past five years, undocumented youth activism has taken on a different character. Undocumented youth around the country have engaged in daring acts of civil disobedience and direct action, employing a set of political tactics that had previously been considered far too dangerous for a movement comprised of people with vulnerable legal status. In addition to escalating to more confrontational tactics, we have also seen a broadening of leadership and engagement of undocumented young people in a broad cross-section of social, political, and economic issues. Undocumented young people have built solidarities and joined multisector campaigns to demand the rights of undocumented workers, fight against draconian immigration laws and policing procedures, challenge deportation and detention policies, and draw clear connections to other marginalized identities and communities.

The undocumented youth movement, along with allies in the broader immigrant rights movement, has put pressure on local, state, and federal politicians, securing some surprising wins—particularly in the state of California where my research is principally located—which have resulted in a qualitatively different political terrain for undocumented young people. The last few years have seen the development of local, statewide, and federal policies and programs that 10 years ago were unimaginable, particularly around the question of undocumented students and educational access. In California, we have seen the state university system emerge as a national model of undocumented student support—DREAM Resource Centers on every University of California campus, research programs opened up to undocumented students, and a growing awareness of this unique student population. On a statewide level, the California DREAM Act was implemented—a combination of state senate bills that make undocumented students eligible for some forms of college financial aid. On a federal level, President Obama utilized his executive authority to establish Deferred Action for Childhood Arrivals, which allows undocumented young people who meet a stringent set of criteria to be eligible for a two-year-renewable protection from deportation and a work permit. Though there is much more work to be done and these policies and practices are limited, the political terrain has shifted significantly in a short period. These significant shifts, I contend, are the result of this grassroots action by undocumented young people, immigrant communities, and their allies.

The time period I reflect on in this chapter is that intermediate moment—the moment between a nascent and emergent undocumented student movement and a movement so powerful it secured several meaningful victories. I contend that civil disobedience was a critical component of the bridge that got us here from there. Fifteen years ago, the idea that this vulnerable population with so much to lose could emerge as a potent political force with whom politicians would have to contend was nearly unimaginable. Undocumented young people risking deportation because of engaging in civil disobedience as a political strategy was unthinkable 15 years ago; today it is a cornerstone of this movement. Even in the face of profound risk, undocumented student activists have been resolute in their response, proclaiming a clear message: We are undocumented, unafraid, and unapologetic. In this proclamation, they have raised critical questions about the possibilities for political mobilization within a climate of fear, repression, and criminalization. My intention in this chapter is not to give a chronology of the undocumented student movement as it relates to civil disobedience but rather to reflect as a researcher on what it is we can learn from this movement through an examination of three key moments in its evolution.

UNDOCUMENTED STUDENT MOVEMENT AND THE CIVIL DISOBEDIENCE TRADITION

While the tactical shifts toward the inclusion of civil disobedience as a cornerstone of the undocumented youth movement was unanticipated by many because of the vulnerability of the movement leaders as a result of citizenship status, civil disobedience has long occupied a critical and central place in social movements rooted in oppressed and marginalized communities for generations, both domestically and internationally (Bromley et al., 1999; McAdam, 2010; Meyer, 2007; Muñoz, 1989). History has demonstrated the myriad ways in which marginalized people who have few material resources and low levels of formal political power can mobilize and exert collective action. Political protest as a practice of democracy is critical in this articulation because, as Piven and Cloward (1980) argue, despite democracy's promises of populism and inclusion, access to democratic process and practice is repeatedly denied to the dispossessed. Thus, this claim to the practice of democracy comes to be situated as a central feature of social movements led by marginalized and oppressed communities, and civil disobedience is one of the key ways in which that claim is staked (Polletta, 2012). Civil disobedience has long been a central political tactic in protest history in the United States and around the world.

Over the last few years, activists, scholars, and students have theorized the place of direct action and civil disobedience in the undocumented youth movement. Building on this emergent body of work concerned with the political activism of undocumented young people (de la Torre & Germano, 2014; Gonzales, 2008; Seif, Ullman, & Núñez-Mchiri, 2014; Swerts, 2015; Terriquez, 2015), the place of civil disobedience in particular highlights some important nuances of the movement as they relate to questions of political agency, confrontation to the state, and political messaging. The undocumented student movement, as many have noted, has not only initiated policy change but is also inextricably engaged in the project of remaking the meaning of citizenship and "illegality" (Glenn, 2011). In earlier work (Negrón-Gonzales, 2014), I examined the meaning-making practices of undocumented youth activists and argued that the tension between their juridical identities as undocumented migrants and their subjective identities as U.S.-raised children have served as a catalyst to political action. In other work (Negrón-Gonzales, 2015), I analyzed the ways in which their civil disobedience and *testimonio* act as counterspectacle and shift conceptions of citizenship in a country entrenched in a debate around who has the right to belong. Several scholars have examined the role of *testimonio* and counterstories (Galindo, 2012; Huber, 2010) in shaping the political mobilizations of undocumented young people, at times connected to civil disobedience (Carrasco & Seif, 2014). Heredia (2016), in her analysis of one of the acts of civil disobedience I discuss later in this chapter, argues that one of the axes of these acts is the ways in which civil disobedience by undocumented young people who occupy the space of "extralegality" by virtue of citizenship status calls into question the politics of respectability as they are applied to migrants in this country. The role of civil disobedience in the undocumented student movement has come to claim a central role not only in the tactics of the movement but also in the overall strategy, messaging, and tenor of the movement as it grew in infancy from a movement that pushed for a set of policy prescriptions around educational access to a multisector, multi-issue movement that pushes back against nativist conceptions of belonging, illegality, and civil rights for immigrants more broadly.

UNLAWFULLY ENTERING: THREE MOMENTS OF CIVIL DISOBEDIENCE AND THE MAKING OF A MOVEMENT

The DREAM Act 5

Nearly a decade after its inception, the DREAM Act movement took a sharp turn in 2010. The national political terrain around immigration, shaped by the global economic recession, which peaked during this period, was marked by a flare-up of the anti-immigrant sentiments that had characterized previous moments of national financial instability. Federal inaction on comprehensive immigration reform since the 1980s passage of the Immigration Reform and Control Act resulted in a situation in which many states took up the policing of "illegality," and these local terrains became the site of contention around national immigration politics. Arizona came to be seen as ground-zero for this debate, as the passage of State Bill (SB) 1070 came to embody this sort of model of draconian immigration enforcement (Santos, Menjivar, & Godfrey, 2013). SB 1070, regarded by opponents as state-sanctioned racial profiling, allowed law enforcement officials to demand documentation of lawful residency from anyone they suspected was in the country "illegally." This policy created a hostile political climate in the state and tangible fear on the ground, as it was being enacted within the context of record numbers of deportations overseen by the Obama administration (Lopez, Gonzalez-Barrera, & Motel, 2011). It was this racially charged climate in which immigrants were being openly targeted that a small group of young activists chose as the site for the first act of civil disobedience by undocumented students, as undocumented students.

On May 17, 2010, a group of young people who came to be known as the DREAM Act 5, four of them undocumented, staged a sit-in at Senator John McCain's Tucson office, calling for an end to the criminalization of immigrants and for passage of the DREAM Act (Preston, 2010). The undocumented young people—Tania Unzeta, Lizbeth Mateo, Yahaira Carillo, and Mohammad Abdollahi—entered Senator McCain's office demanding that he act on moving forward the DREAM Act. When ordered to leave, the students, who were dressed in caps and gowns to represent the broken dreams of undocumented students who have no path to citizenship, sat down in the office and refused to leave. In a private interview with me months later, Lizbeth Mateo, one of the protesters, explained,

> We wanted to take ownership of our lives and our future. We decided to do it inside his office, because outside—they would close the office, lock us out. We need to be in their space; it's a direct thing. That's the purpose of direct action. You need to be completely unafraid and face your biggest fear. Putting ourselves in front of a huge obstacle. Doing it face to face. Going to his office.

Allies, like me, were nervous. It was, so far as is known, the first-ever act of civil disobedience by undocumented students in the nation. We had no idea what would happen with these students. Would they be sent out on a plane, expedited for deportation by the next morning? Would they languish for months on end in detention centers, like so many other members of their community? The government later dropped charges against the protesters who had been arrested and placed in removal proceedings (Lal & Unzueta, 2013) and they returned to their normal lives in the United States, though the broader impacts of this daring action stretched on for the weeks, months, and years that followed. This tactic, connected to the shared histories of struggle of marginalized and oppressed people around the world, was once considered off-limits for this movement because its leaders, by virtue of being both young and undocumented, were considered too vulnerable to take such risks. While citizens who engage in civil disobedience in this country may face misdemeanor criminal charges, undocumented activists also face potential deportation. This daring act of civil disobedience provided the impetus for many other acts of civil disobedience around the country in the following months and years.

The significance of this act was multilayered. As was previously stated, it was significant because undocumented young people engaging in civil disobedience risk deportation along with arrest. It was also significant because of geography; it was an act of civil disobedience carried out in the office of a U.S. senator in a state that was embroiled in a national battle about belonging and illegality. In a moment and in a statewide context in which activists were pushing against a legalized racial profiling, which would put undocumented residents in the precarious position of having to produce legal paperwork to prove their right to live their lives, these young people went to a government building and publicly identified themselves as undocumented. As René Galindo (2012), writing about the DREAM Act 5, states, "This first act of civil disobedience . . . both introduced a new political strategy in the struggle of undocumented immigrant students and contributed a new chapter to civil disobedience in this country" (p. 590). This action not only opened up the tactic of civil disobedience as a strategic possibility for the undocumented student movement and served to catalyze action in that regard, it was also important in that it targeted a purported ally of the movement. Their choice of McCain as a target was not confusing, as some detractors argued; it was intentional. Dressed in caps and gowns, the protestors called on McCain to act on what was the failed promise brought on by the lack of federal action on the DREAM Act as well as the failed promise of the educational system they had successfully navigated. The act of civil disobedience garnered national attention and cracked open tactical space in the undocumented student movement and discursive space in the national conversation around immigration in challenging conceptions of what undocumented immigrants look like, who they are, and the mistreatment they will (not) tolerate because of their vulnerable status.

Sit-in at the Capitol Building

A few months after the protest at McCain's office, in July 2010, undocumented students on the other side of the country engaged in another highly publicized act of civil disobedience. Twenty-one undocumented young people, who were members of DREAM Act organizations around the country, dressed in caps and gowns and staged an act of civil disobedience in the U.S.

Capitol building. Donning signs that said "What now?", undocumented student activists were handcuffed, arrested, and led away. Their demand was the same—federal action on the DREAM Act. Capitol police wasted little time in escalating to arrests; the striking visual of young people in graduation gear being led away by police became an iconic symbol of the movement for years to come. The image not only came to represent the unfulfilled dreams of promising undocumented young people but also made visible the confrontation between undocumented youth and agents of the state—that they would rather arrest these young people rather than meet their demand for societal inclusion—in a way that the McCain office arrests had not because those arrests were carried out behind closed doors.

Building on the action at McCain's office only a couple months before, the student activists expanded their message and their tactics. While the previous action attempted to encourage action on the part of one political leader by going to his office, this action went to the center of power in Washington, D.C., symbolic on multiple levels. In confronting this center of power and multiple politicians, their action called for federal action on the DREAM Act and called out the hypocrisy of the system—a point underscored by the visual representation of granting a deserving student a diploma and then arresting her for unlawfully entering. This action was a challenge to the state and its power.

What was perhaps most significant about this action was the response. Almost immediately, Dick Durbin, a Democrat from Illinois and one of the initial drafters of the DREAM Act, came out publicly to denounce the action in a public statement released by his office:

> Today's demonstrations by some DREAM Act supporters . . . crossed the line from passionate advocacy to inappropriate behavior. The tide of public opinion has long been on the side of the DREAM Act—it has broad bipartisan support in Congress, and poll after poll shows that people of all political persuasion believe in its goals. Sen. Durbin believes that we will win this fight on the merits, not through public demonstrations or publicity stunts. (Wilkie, 2010, para. 5)

Just as the sit-in at McCain's office was a critical moment in cracking open the tactic of civil disobedience for the DREAMer movement, the moment at the Capitol building was significant because it signified a struggle over the question of who these students were. Until this point, the movement had been largely dominated by nonconfrontational sanctioned action—permitted marches, letter-writing campaigns, lobbying visits, student testimonials. This action was significant not only in its own right but also because it signified a struggle between undocumented students and their more institutionally rooted allies who, for the most part, had hinged their support of these students and their movement by arguing the politics of respectability, that these were good kids who played by the rules.[4] This action contested that narrative and positioned undocumented students not simply as waiting patiently for politicians to act but as young people who would risk their safety and take whatever action necessary in order to fight for reform legislation. Durbin's reaction, while a public admonishment to the students involved in these protests, was also an attempt to win back the frame of undocumented youth that had prevailed for nearly 10 years: that of the innocent child who obeys, the undocumented student who will act nicely and not demand.

This was a moment of reckoning for the undocumented student movement—a pivotal moment in which they were forced to contend with the constraints of their institutionally entrenched allies who upheld accommodation rather than confrontation as a campaign tactic. The students not only refused to retreat, they escalated. This pattern of escalation, I contend, is what made statewide policies like the California DREAM Act and federal action such as Deferred Action for Childhood Arrivals politically possible. It was in this moment and through these actions that the undocumented youth movement came to be seen as a viable political force that politicians would need to take seriously. As it became clear that the undocumented youth movement was not going to fizzle out and disappear, and also that it was building important connections to allies in other sectors and movements, the issue of legislative relief for undocumented young people came to be constituted as a salient political issue particularly in relation to Latino voters that politicians needed to attend to.

What is critically important about this civil disobedience action at the Capitol building in the summer of 2010 and the legislative victories that were secured in its wake is that it was not the big, well-funded, D.C.-based immigration groups that secured this victory. In fact, by denouncing nonviolent direct actions such as this one, in many cases they were working against it. Institutionally entrenched allies were unwilling to take the only kind of action that would result in these policy changes. It was the young people who did this. It was the young people who took these risks. Though their political power paled in comparison to the political power of the politicians who claimed to speak on their behalf, they fought back; it was precisely that vulnerability, that precariousness that came to be the central strength of the movement.

Bring Them Home Campaign[5]

In the summer of 2013, undocumented youth activists planned one of the most confrontational direct actions to date, directly confronting the disciplinary technologies deployed against migrants at the U.S.-Mexico border. Called the "Bring Them Home" campaign, it was spearheaded by two national organizations that have been a leading force in the undocumented youth movement: the National Immigrant Youth Alliance and DreamActivist.org, organizations grounded in the leadership of undocumented young people. Three undocumented young people left the United States and returned to Mexico, their country of origin. After a couple of weeks, the youth activists, wearing graduation robes, attempted to recross the border into the United States, together with six other undocumented long-term U.S. residents who had been previously deported. This group of undocumented young men and women, who had been raised in the United States, presented themselves at the U.S.-Mexico border as undocumented young people who had grown up in the United States and requested entrance to this country, their home. They were accompanied by a camera crew, allowing the entire action to be live-streamed over the Internet.

As expected, the ICE officials denied them entry. The activists refused to be turned away and were taken into custody. Once in custody, the young activists began gathering information by talking to other detainees, confirming what immigrant rights activists and allies have long suspected: despite President Obama's verbal assurances that his administration is not deporting "low-priority" detainees with clean records, ICE detention centers are in fact teeming with these supposedly low-priority cases. This action was groundbreaking in several respects. It was a blatant confrontation with state power that took place at the border, a site of both geographic and symbolic importance where immigrants directly interface with border patrol personnel, where disciplinary technologies are enacted upon migrant bodies, and where border crossers are made "illegal."

Significantly, this initial event was never intended to be the end of the actions. There were two more rounds of the Bring Them Home campaign. The third round, rather than focusing only on youth, involved a large, multigenerational group of undocumented people. But this time, they were not DREAMer students. They were families. Mothers who had been separated from their children. Children who had been forcibly removed from their parents. Brothers and sisters. Fiancés. They were not honor students, not valedictorians, not college graduates, not "professionals-in-waiting." They were immigrant workers. Housecleaners. Janitors. Farmworkers. Construction workers. One was the well-known activist Elvira Arellano, who became a symbol of the broken immigration system when she took refuge in a Chicago church with her U.S.-citizen son for more than a year before she was finally deported in 2007. In these subsequent actions, protesters explicitly challenged the prioritization of DREAMers over other undocumented groups by arguing for humanitarian visas or asylum for migrants who were not raised in the United States, did not attend school here, and could not easily pass as "Americans." Their message was clear: these migrants also deserve to be treated with respect, dignity, and due process. In this sense, this action built on the previous two actions by confronting state power and calling attention to the broken immigration system; it also challenged the politics of deservingness by expanding the campaign to include deported undocumented migrants who do not have the convenience of a student status through which to leverage a claim to belonging.

Undocumented youth activists redefined the parameters of the debate and used their position as relative "insiders" not simply to make a claim for themselves, but to push the door open more widely. Their message is clear—you may be willing to tolerate us because we fit into your standards of success or "Americanness," but our struggle is wrapped up in a much bigger fight, and we are unwilling to leave our families and our communities behind to ensure our own acceptance. This message, symbolically embedded in this action, has emerged loudly from the undocumented youth movement over the course of the past few years, pushing directly back against the politics of respectability that have insisted on a demarcation among immigrants along the axis of "deservingness."

THE POLITICS OF HOPE: REFLECTIONS FROM AN ALLY, A RESEARCHER, AND A STUDENT OF THE UNDOCUMENTED YOUTH MOVEMENT

A little more than a decade ago, I was in a room full of educators who worked with undocumented students; it was a meeting that was held at a nearby university and convened by educators and community workers who were concerned about what to do with this student population who was, at the time, newly gaining visibility to them. AB 540 had passed in California and the first generation of students were being admitted to California universities under this groundbreaking in-state tuition bill, but there was still not a collective awareness or a set of best practices for supporting these students in their academic and personal goals—particularly within the context of what was still a national climate that was hostile toward undocumented students. A chorus emerged in that room, suggesting that what we should do was help these students get through "under the radar" and that when enough of these students were out in the world doing amazing things, the argument for citizenship would make itself. This argument bears a similar resonance to the conversations we hear today about the emergent Latino majority in California, which falsely draws a connection between numerical majorities and political power, assuming that one is constitutive of the other. However, what the undocumented youth movement story—and specifically their escalated embracing of the tactic of nonviolent civil disobedience—demonstrates is that political possibilities are created when the powers-that-be are forced to act because inaction becomes more politically costly than conceding to the demands. The national terrain around not only educational access for undocumented students, but also immigration policy as a whole, is changing.

In 2014, President Obama announced Deferred Action for Parental Accountability (DAPA)—the first hints at deportation relief and protected status for undocumented migrants who do not have the protection of student or youth status. Though the policy has been tied up in the courts by Republican opponents who dominate what has become an obstructionist Congress and is unlikely to actually make it into policy before Obama leaves office, the fact that the space exists for this argument to be made is not only politically significant, but is also historically unprecedented and completely inconceivable just a few short years ago; DAPA marks more than 20 years of complete federal inaction on immigration reform. While we cannot make a causal argument about the activism of undocumented young people leading to the DAPA executive order—because, quite simply, politics does not work that way— what is clear is that this generation of undocumented young people demanded a seat at the table. Undocumented youth activists called out not only federal inaction but also the hypocrisy of immigration reform, the inhumanity of the state, and the politics of deservingness that began to emerge through holding up undocumented children as not to be blamed for the crimes of their parents. This created the sort of space for the kinds of reforms we are seeing now. As I have seen this movement take shape over the course of the last 15 years, I have seen these young activists and organizers develop an understanding that the political system was not set up to protect them, defend them, or look out for them, and come to the decision that they would need to force it to see them as human. In this sense, I also saw well-meaning people tell them to stay quiet, to play by the rules, to be patient. And I saw how in refusing to do so, the undocumented young people at the helm of this movement changed the course of history in this country. They have demanded a sort of hope that does not accept, but that resists. Drawing on Duncan-Andrade's (2009) work on hope, I look to the work that undocumented youth have done and think about the ways in which this is a lesson that holds resonance far beyond simply the undocumented student movement. Duncan-Andrade differentiates between various kinds of hope, saying,

> Hokey hope would have us believe this change will not cost us anything. This kind of false hope is mendacious; it never acknowledges pain. Audacious hope stares down the painful path; and despite the overwhelming odds against us making it down that path to change, we make the journey again and again. There is no other choice. (Duncan-Andrade, 2009, p. 191)

Undocumented young people have marched on, emboldened with that vision, armed with those tactics, and have gained concessions from a political system that never intended to regard them as serious players.

ACKNOWLEDGMENTS

I would like to acknowledge the undocumented young people who shared their stories with me and whose fight has served as an inspiration to so many. I would also like to thank my two graduate assistants, Lindsey Greene and Megan Sykes, who provided editorial and research support for this chapter.

NOTES

1. The DREAM Act is a failed piece of federal legislation that would have created a path to citizenship for undocumented young people who meet a specific set of stringent criteria.

2. A pseudonym. Real names used are those associated with actions that are a part of public record.

3. Though specifics of the DREAM Act change each time it is introduced, most versions of the DREAM Act have an upper-age cutoff of approximately 30 years old.

4. Roberto Gonzales, PhD, Luisa Heredia, PhD, and I presented this idea first at the International Symposium on Youth, Illegality and Belonging Symposium held at Harvard University, Cambridge, Massachusetts, in October 2013, in a talk titled "On School Grounds: Schools as 'Safe Spaces' & Sites for the Policing of 'Illegality.'"

5. This section draws and builds upon previous work published on this research, namely my article "Undocumented Youth Activism as Counter-Spectacle: Civil Disobedience and Testimonio in the Battle around Immigration Reform," published in *Aztlan: A Journal of Chicano Studies* (2015).

REFERENCES

Bacon, D. (2008). *Illegal people: How globalization creates migration and criminalizes immigrants*. Boston, MA: Beacon Press.

Bromley, D. G., Cutchin, D. G., Gerlach, L. P., Green, J. C., Halcli, A., Hirsch, E. L., . . . Whittier, N. E. (1999). *Waves of protest: Social movements since the sixties*. J. Freeman & V. Johnson (Eds.). Lanham, MD: Rowman & Littlefield.

Carrasco, T. A. U., & Seif, H. (2014). Disrupting the dream: Undocumented youth reframe citizenship and deportability through anti-deportation activism. *Latino Studies, 12*(2), 279–299. http://dx.doi.org/10.1057/lst.2014.21

Chacón, J. A., Davis, M., & Cardona, J. (2006). *No one is illegal: Fighting violence and state repression on the U.S.-Mexico border*. Chicago, IL: Haymarket Books.

de la Torre, P., & Germano, R. (2014). Out of the shadows: DREAMer identity in the immigrant youth movement. *Latino Studies, 12*(3), 449–467. http://dx.doi.org/10.1057/lst.2014.45

Duncan-Andrade, J. (2009). Note to educators: Hope required when growing roses in concrete. *Harvard Educational Review, 79*(2), 181–194. http://dx.doi.org/10.17763 /haer.79.2.nu3436017730384w

Galindo, R. (2012). Undocumented & unafraid: The DREAM Act 5 and the public disclosure of undocumented status as a political act. *Urban Review, 44*(5), 589–611. http://dx.doi.org/10.1007/s11256-012-0219-0

Glenn, E. N. (2011). Constructing citizenship exclusion, subordination, and resistance. *American Sociological Review, 76*(1), 1–24. http://dx.doi.org/10.1177/0003 122411398443

Gonzales, R. G. (2008). Left out but not shut down: Political activism and the undocumented student movement. *Northwestern Journal of Law & Social Policy, 3*(2), 219–239. Retrieved from http://scholarlycommons.law.northwestern.edu/njlsp /vol3/iss2/4

Gonzales, R. G. (2011). Learning to be illegal: Undocumented youth and shifting legal contexts in the transition to adulthood. *American Sociological Review, 76*(4), 602–619. http://dx.doi.org/10.1177/0003122411411901

Gonzales, R. G., Heredia, L. L., & Negrón-Gonzales, G. (2015). Untangling Plyler's legacy: Undocumented students, schools, and citizenship. *Harvard Educational Review, 85*(3), 318–341. http://dx.doi.org/10.17763/0017-8055.85.3.318

Heredia, L. L. (2016). Of radicals and DREAMers: Harnessing exceptionality to challenge immigration control. *Association of Mexican American Educators Journal, 9*(3).

Huber, L. P. (2010). Using Latina/o Critical Race Theory (LatCrit) and racist nativism to explore intersectionality in the educational experiences of undocumented Chicana college students. *Educational Foundations, 24,* 77–96. Retrieved from http://eric.ed.gov/?id=EJ885982

Lal, P., & Unzueta, T. (2013, March 28). How queer undocumented youth built the immigrant rights movement. *HuffPost Gay Voices.* Retrieved from http://www .huffingtonpost.com/prerna-lal/how-queer-undocumented_b_2973670.html

Lopez, M. H., Gonzalez-Barrera, A., & Motel, S. (2011, December 28). As deportations rise to record levels, most Latinos oppose Obama's policy. *Pew Hispanic Center.* Washington, DC: Author. Retrieved from http://www.pewhispanic.org

López, M. P., & López, G. R. (2010). *Persistent inequality: Contemporary realities in the education of undocumented Latina/o students.* R. Delgado & J. Stefancic (Eds.). New York, NY: Routledge.

McAdam, D. (2010). *Political process and the development of black insurgency, 1930–1970* (2nd ed.). Chicago, IL: University of Chicago Press.

Meyer, D. S. (2007). *The politics of protest: Social movements in America.* New York, NY: Oxford University Press.

Muñoz, C. (1989). *Youth, identity, power: The Chicano movement.* London: Verso.

Negrón-Gonzales, G. (2013). Navigating "illegality": Undocumented youth & oppositional consciousness. *Children and Youth Services Review, 35*(8), 1284–1290.

Negrón-Gonzales, G. (2014). Undocumented, unafraid and unapologetic: Re-articulatory practices and migrant youth "illegality." *Latino Studies, 12*(2), 259–278. http://dx.doi.org/10.1057/lst.2014.20

Negrón-Gonzales, G. (2015). Undocumented youth activism as counter-spectacle: Civil disobedience and testimonio in the battle around immigration reform. *Aztlan: A Journal of Chicano Studies, 40*(1), 87–112. Retrieved from http://www.ingentaconnect.com

Oboler, S. (Ed.). (2006). *Latinos and citizenship: The dilemma of belonging.* New York, NY: Palgrave Macmillan.

Orfield, G., Bachmeier, M. D., James, D. R., & Eitle, T. (1997). Deepening segregation in American public schools: A special report from the Harvard Project on School Desegregation. *Equity and Excellence in Education, 30*(2), 5–24. http://dx.doi.org/10.1080/1066568970300202

Passel, J. S., & Cohn, D. (2011). *Unauthorized immigration population: National and state trends, 2010.* Washington, DC: Pew Research Center.

Piven, F. F., & Cloward, R. A. (1980). *Poor people's movements: Why they succeed, how they fail.* New York, NY: Vintage Books.

Polletta, F. (2012). *Freedom is an endless meeting: Democracy in American social movements.* Chicago, IL: University of Chicago Press.

Preston, J. (2010, May 17). Illegal immigrant students protest at McCain office. *New York Times.* Retrieved from http://www.nytimes.com/2010/05/18/us/18dream.html?_r=0

Rincón, A. (2008). *Undocumented immigrants and higher education: Sí se puede!* New York, NY: LFB Scholarly Publishing.

Santos, C., Menjívar, C., & Godfrey, E. (2013). Effects of SB 1070 on children. In L. Magaña & E. Lee (Eds.), *Latino politics and Arizona's immigration law SB 1070* (pp. 79–92). New York, NY: Springer.

Seif, H. (2004). "Wise up!": Undocumented Latino youth, Mexican-American legislators, and the struggle for higher education access. *Latino Studies, 2*(2), 210–230. http://dx.doi.org/10.1057/palgrave.lst.8600080

Seif, H., Ullman, C., & Núñez-Mchiri, G. G. (2014). Mexican (im)migrant students and education: Constructions of and resistance to "illegality." *Latino Studies, 12*(2), 172–193. http://dx.doi.org/10.1057/lst.2014.32

Swerts, T. (2015, July). Spaces of (non-citizen) citizenship: The liminal politics of undocumented activism. In *Diversity & Equality Working Group and the Center for Political Science and Comparative Politics.* Paper presented at the 22nd International Conference of Europeanists, Paris, France.

Terriquez, V. (2015). Intersectional mobilization, social movement spillover, and queer youth leadership in the immigrant rights movement. *Social Problems, 62*(3), 343–362. http://dx.doi.org/10.1093/socpro/spv010

Wilkie, C. (2010, July 20). Durbin's office chastises some DREAM Act backers. *The Hill.* Retrieved from http://thehill.com/blogs

15

"We Have the Power to Make Change": The Struggle of Asian Immigrant Youth against School Violence

Mary Yee

On December 3, 2010, Wei Chen, Duong Nghe Ly, and other first-generation Asian immigrant[1] students led a group of multiracial, multiethnic high school students in cheers and chants in front of South Philadelphia High School (SPHS) in Philadelphia. They were there to commemorate the one-year anniversary of a severe racial assault on Asian immigrant students a year earlier. More significantly, they were there to celebrate a victory over the School District of Philadelphia (SDP). The Asian immigrant youth along with their community advocates had just received word of a favorable ruling from the U.S. Department of Justice (DOJ) on a civil rights complaint, alleging blatant racial discrimination on the part of the SDP. In the words of the Settlement Agreement, the SDP was found to be "deliberately indifferent to known instances of severe and pervasive student-on-student harassment of Asian students based on their race, color, and/or national origin at South Philadelphia High School" (*U.S. v. School District of Philadelphia & School Reform Commission*, 2010, December 15, p. 1). This was tremendous news, given the years of racial intimidation and bullying that Asian English language learner (ELL) students at SPHS had endured, the outright denial by the SDP superintendent that Asian immigrant students had been targeted, and the intensive organizing and media campaign that the youth activists and their community advocates had led to expose the district's callous disregard for their plight. It was a triumph for the group of youth, who had become activists through this struggle. It was especially so because these first-generation immigrant students had limited English proficiency, limited cultural knowledge of how to negotiate urban high schools, little or no previous experience of racism, and a cultural disposition to avoid conflict. Moreover, they had united across language and ethnic boundaries. Within the group were native Vietnamese speakers and native Mandarin or Fujianese speakers at differing levels of English proficiency. Ironically, when no interpretation was available, the students often had to use English as the common language. At this rally, in English, Duong Nghe Ly led the chant: "Leaders, we are; thinkers, we are; artists, we are: innovators, we are; organizers, we are; youth, we are a youth movement." By taking on the agentive identity of youth leaders and organizers, they had begun to counter stereotypes of Asian immigrant youth as silent, passive, and deferential to authority, thus doing the political work of "refashion[ing] the ideological landscape through which particular racialized representations of youth are constructed and naturalized" (Hosang, 2006, p. 5).

This chapter is about the struggle of the Vietnamese and Chinese youth activists against school violence and how they prevailed in the face of tremendous odds through a multipronged approach, enlisting various strategies. The central research question was as follows: What were the approaches and strategies that first-generation Asian immigrant youth brought to bear in the South Philadelphia High School struggle, and how did their efforts bring about institutional change in the school district?

BACKGROUND AND CONTEXT

School Violence and Immigrant Communities

This story is set in the context of endemic school violence in poor urban neighborhoods and comprehensive high schools. The issue of school violence in urban schools is an ongoing theme in the dominant discourse about education in America. This discourse fosters the image of schools as prisonlike institutions with security cameras, police, and strict punitive and disciplinary policies. We hear continually about student on student assaults in Philadelphia, Chicago, Los Angeles, New York, Boston, and other cities (Crouch & Williams, 1995; Goode, 2013; Shah, 2013; Taylor, 2015). In *Learning a New Land*, a mixed-method longitudinal study spanning three U.S. cities, the authors talk about the experience of first-generation immigrant students and the inimical school climates they endure (Suárez-Orozco, Suárez-Orozco, & Torodova, 2008). However, overall the most vulnerable populations are special education students and ELLs, especially recent immigrant students (Olsen, 2000). Research shows Asian immigrant students are more likely to be bullied or harassed than other immigrant students (Koo, Peguero, & Shekarkhar, 2012).

Community Struggles

The victory of the Asian immigrant youth was not an isolated event but part of the history of struggle in the Philadelphia Asian American community, including its struggle for educational equity. In *Y.S. v. School District of Philadelphia* (1985), a civil rights class action suit, the plaintiffs represented recently arrived Southeast Asian refugee students with limited English proficiency who were denied equal access to educational opportunities. The case resulted, among other things, in a restructuring of ESOL (English for speakers of other languages) instruction, provisions for the hiring of bilingual staff, and access to support services; however, no school board policy regarding the education of ELLs resulted from this case. The Philadelphia Asian American community had also waged struggles against numerous government-sponsored projects such as the Vine Street Expressway, a baseball stadium, a federal prison, and a casino as well as organized campaigns against anti-Asian violence, police profiling of youth, and library closings[2] (Somekawa, 1995). Consequently, there was a history of political action, the lessons of which still resided in the staff and members of community-based organizations, such as Asian Americans United (Gammage, 2010). As discussed later, these veteran community activists afforded the "bridging social capital" (Gittell & Vidal, 1998, p. 10) that allowed the transmission of political analysis, strategy and tactics, contacts, and resources to the youth leaders.

South Philadelphia High School

South Philadelphia High School (SPHS) has been the high school for successive waves of immigrant families, most recently South and Southeast Asians and Latinos. While interracial fighting between Asians and African Americans in the 1990s and early 2000s was curtailed, changes in district superintendents, coupled with high principal turnover (five principals in six years) beginning in 2004, resulted in a highly unstable instructional and disciplinary environment.

For the 2010–2011 academic year, the racial breakdown of the student population at SPHS, numbering about 1,000, was approximately 65% African American, 22% Asian, 6% Latino, 6% white, and 1% other. The school, once a world language magnet, had had an ESOL program for more than 20 years; the student body averaged 20% ELL. From 1999 to 2010, SPHS had a bilingual Chinese program. From 2006 to 2010 student attendance averaged about 75–80%, though the graduation rate was about 48%. The 2010 results of the state standardized assessment, the Grade 11 PSSA, showed 12–15% of students scored proficient or advanced in math or reading compared to 36–38% for the district overall. In 2011, about 84% of students were deemed "economically disadvantaged." The school had been on the "persistently dangerous" list (according to No Child Left Behind criteria) for the last three years.[3]

Since the large influx of Southeast Asian refugees in the early 1980s, many myths about their circumstances, not to mention racial stereotypes, circulated in the overwhelmingly African American neighborhoods in which they were resettled. Among these were that families were getting government assistance far beyond what African Americans who were citizens or veterans were receiving after centuries of oppression. At SPHS, controversies arose as immigrant and refugee ELL students continually took the highest honors at graduation; some faculty and non-Asian students argued that the ELL curriculum was easier than the mainstream curriculum. Furthermore, African American parents believed that funds for ESOL and related programs were reducing funds for the general school population. Unmitigated resentment from these circumstances lay just below the surface at the school and in the neighborhood.

The December 3, 2009, Incident

On December 3, 2009, South Philadelphia High School was the scene of a violent assault on 30 Asian immigrant students, all ELLs, by a crowd of predominantly African American students. Over the previous year, the Asian students and community organizers had tried to meet several times with the principal about ongoing issues of racial intimidation and bullying inside and outside the school. However, the community's request for added preventive measures and warnings of impending violence went unheeded. The buildup to the physical assault on December 3 started inside the school with freely roaming students breaking into ESOL classrooms looking for victims, then escalated to fighting in the lunchroom, where some adults egged on the attackers. The Chinese students, some of whom were already beaten up and bleeding, managed to stay inside the school with the help of a community organizer, who rushed to the school after a cell phone call from Wei Chen. Wei had participated in the meetings with the administration and had kept a meticulous record in Chinese of the assaults and school responses. Knowing from experience that hostile students would try to attack them upon dismissal, in another part of the school the Vietnamese ELL students asked the principal if they could remain in the building. She refused, escorted them to the sidewalk, and immediately disappeared back into the building. A mob on four corners attacked; that day 17 students required hospital care.

In protest, close to 50 Chinese and Vietnamese ELL students boycotted the school for nine days. Contrary to the promise of the regional administrator, the district had the school inform their parents by phone that the students were illegally absent and threaten disciplinary action. The district did not acknowledge the trauma of continual racial intimidation and victimization of the students; no counseling help was ever offered.

The December 2009 SPHS assault instigated a citywide dialogue on school violence. After a yearlong series of town meetings, the Philadelphia Commission on Human Relations (2012) issued a report featuring testimony from parents, students, teachers, and community members alike. In spring 2011, the *Philadelphia Inquirer* printed a seven-part report on the newest principal (Gammage, 2011). National and other local media (e.g., CNN, *New York Times*, *Washington Post*, *Philadelphia Magazine*, and *City Paper*) also featured stories about the SPHS struggle.

METHODOLOGY

This is a qualitative study employing ethnographic methods, namely, interviews, focus groups, and archival document review. Four student leaders emerged from this struggle: Wei Chen, who was a senior; Duong Ly, who was a junior; and Trang Dang and Bach Tong, who were sophomores, in 2009–2010. Data were gathered over nearly three years from the four youth activists, who went on to establish the Asian Student Association of Philadelphia (ASAP); from community advocates who participated in the SPHS Asian Student Advocates (SASA)[4] coalition and other allies; from school district personnel; and from digital and print media. I examined audiofiles, interview transcriptions, and archival documents, marking them initially with predetermined codes (such as youth demands, strategies, ally support, and legal actions) and then later with codes that emerged emically from the data (such as youth leadership, broadening horizons, and media). During data analysis, certain codes merged into themes. I present these themes in the findings section. In the discussion section, I use the theoretical frameworks from the following section to illuminate the human agency and social processes that led to institutional change. In the conclusion of this chapter, I discuss the significance and implications of young people's activism on institutional policy, the Asian American social justice movement, and educational reform.

THEORETICAL FRAMEWORKS

To explain the dynamics of youth activism in relation to institutional change, I have relied primarily on Freirean social theory and critical organizational analysis. These frames provide ways to understand the youths' acquisition of political or "critical consciousness"; the power dynamics between the district on one hand, and youth and community on the other; and the processes instigated by contradictions between different institutions in the fields of power (namely, education and government).

As have many researchers of youth activism, I embraced the concepts of "critical consciousness," "praxis," "reading the world; reading the word" to explain the trajectory of youth activists (Freire, 2000; Ginwright & Cammarota, 2002; Morrell, 2008). Freire (2005) defined "critical consciousness" as acquiring a historical and sociopolitical understanding of the world in which we live, its emancipatory aspect as seeing ourselves as self-determining beings. "Praxis" is social action informed and motivated by critical consciousness (Freire, 2000). Freire (1985) learned from his own experience that educationally marginalized people acquired political consciousness and literacy skills when literacy practices are relevant to their lives and to their everyday struggles. Thus, he used people's life knowledge (their "reading the world") to develop school literacy ("reading the word"). Furthermore, the Freirean notions of intergenerational equity between teachers and students and the democratic notion of teacher as facilitator rather than authority figure play a significant role in current discussions of activist youth leadership development (Cammarota & Fine, 2008; Ginwright & Cammarota, 2002).

Critical organizational theorists have explained institutional change and human agency in ways that recognize contradictions within and between institutions and between institutions and social actors (Seo & Creed, 2002). Seo and Creed offered a model that explained how these contradictions lead to increased tensions and conflicts both inside and outside institutions and, consequently, to actors' increased consciousness of the power dynamics of the situation. Furthermore, institutions, products of their sociohistorical context, are interrelated and operate on multiple levels (e.g., in this case, the school district is accountable to the local community, as well as the state and federal governments). When conflicts arise, they propel social actors to gain political awareness and engage in activities to change social patterns, such as policies and practices—here exemplified by the actions of the Asian immigrant youth and their allies. These patterns (e.g., district policies and procedures regarding harassment and bullying) in turn become institutionalized and affect the institutions that instigated their creation in the first place, as a result of internal and external contradictions. In this way, the process of institutional change is considered dialectical or in continuous movement between opposing states of contradiction and resolution of conflict in which people play an agentive role. (See Figure 15.1.)

Approaches and Strategies for Moving the Struggle Forward: A Multipronged Effort

The Asian immigrant youth implemented a multipronged effort in their struggle to find justice after the December 3 incident. Overall, they focused on three main approaches: organizing, legal action, and communications, under

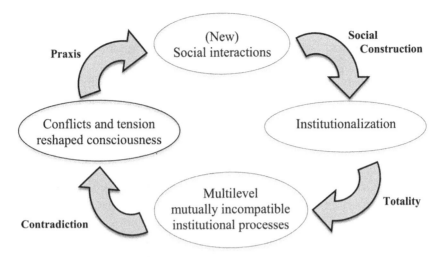

Figure 15.1. Institutionalization and Institutional Change: Process from a Dialectical Perspective (Seo & Creed, 2002, p. 25).

which they practiced various strategies. While the approaches are discussed under discrete headings, they often merged or overlapped in any particular action. The strategies assumed many forms, as is demonstrated by a short chronology of the first month of the struggle. The crisis set a frenetic pace as youth and advocates immediately held a press conference on December 4; over the weekend, they prepared testimony for the School Reform Commission meeting on December 9. Beginning on December 7, they took decisive action by boycotting SPHS until December 15. On December 14, they had a confrontational meeting with Superintendent Arlene Ackerman, and on January 2 they testified before the Philadelphia Commission on Human Relations. At the same time, youth were reaching out to the local and national Asian community for support. This intense activity continued as youth leaders organized more youth and community supporters, engaged in legal action, and got their stories out into the world.

Organizing

Building toward and taking collective action.   For the purposes of this chapter, in the definition of organizing I have included outreach to potential allies, forming networks of support, consciousness-raising, and the formation of an immigrant high school student organization. As a former AAU director stated, "Organizing was key." A coalition of advocacy organizations formed spontaneously to support the youth; this included AAU, Boat People

SOS (BPSOS), Cambodian Association of Greater Philadelphia (CAGP), and Victim Witness Services of South Philadelphia (VWSSP). The youth activists connected with local community-based organizations and local chapters of national Asian American organizations, such as SEAMAAC, PCDC, Mayor's Commission on Asian American Affairs, Organization of Chinese in America (OCA), and Japanese American Citizens League (JACL). These organizations issued press releases and other public statements on behalf of the SPHS youth, invited them to speak, and fundraised. Individual local Asian businesses also contributed food and money. In addition, the youth built recognition and support from student organizations such as the Philadelphia Student Union (PSU), Northeast Union of Vietnamese Student Associations (NEUVSA), Dreamactivists Pennsylvania, and National Immigrant Youth Alliance by attending and presenting at trainings and conferences. They also met with national figures such as Grace Lee Boggs, Helen Zia—well-known Asian American community activists—and members of the Congressional Asian Pacific American Caucus. In this way, the youth activists created a broad-based network.

On the grassroots level, supported by adult advocates and allies, the youth worked hard to organize mass actions, such as the march to the SDP headquarters on December 9 and packing the various SRC, PHRC, and PCHR hearings. Recognizing common cause with Martin Luther King Jr. Day organizers and immigrant rights groups, they organized contingents for rallies and marches. On the district level, the ASAP youth leaders reached out to high schools beyond SPHS, recruiting new students from magnet and vocational technical schools.

Working with adult advocates and allies.   Veteran organizers at AAU and BPSOS were essential in helping the students understand power relations and the necessity of organizing widespread support for their cause. The youth developed close relationships with the veteran community organizers and advocates, in particular, building strong working relationships and friendships with the SASA members. Six years later, core members of the youth leadership still maintain frequent contact with their mentors. Wei Chen and Duong Ly became youth organizers for AAU and BPSOS, respectively. The crucible of intense struggle formed the tight and lasting emotional bonds that sharing the experience of crisis, trauma, and joint work brings to personal relationships. As both youth and advocates have noted, these relationships in struggle, fortified by common political beliefs, were nothing less than "transformative." Bach Tong reflected on this time:

This was the most transformative experience of my life. What I really learned is that change has to be grassroots. It needs to come from the bottom up, from those who really suffer from the struggles and demand change. . . . Change doesn't come in one click, you have to gradually lift experiences of oppression, day by day, little by little. Creating change is the life you live. (Asian Americans United, Finkel, & Shimizu, 2013)

The historical lessons of the Asian American struggle in Philadelphia, embodied in the longtime community activists, were crucial in educating the youth, raising their political consciousness, providing a strong sense of self-determination and agency, and connecting them to networks of support. Although many youth initially were skeptical about their ability to change the SDP bureaucracy or lacked confidence to speak out, adult advocates and allies taught them about the community victories against government-sponsored projects like the Vine Street Expressway and a baseball stadium and how these were won with community organizing, mass actions, and disrupting the dominant narratives and stereotypes about the Asian community. In meetings and workshops I attended, the adult advocates and allies modeled and taught collaborative, inclusive democratic processes and introduced the language of political analysis and activism.

While the adult advocates presented the youth with different frameworks to help them analyze and comprehend the forces and events around them, the youth were asked to brainstorm ideas and solutions, consider the pros and cons of various strategic decisions, and develop public statements. The youth came to decisions collectively as the advocates refrained from being involved in the actual decisions. The adult community organizers guided them but always let their presence and words be primary. As one veteran organizer said, "It was really important for each student to be able to tell an authentic story and be clear about history and responsibility to the community. We [adults] needed to be clear about how to help young people speak with extreme clarity and voice." As Ginwright and Cammarota (2006) have suggested, youth should have the "right to civic representation and decision-making," to be at the table when laws and policies are created (p. xx). The development of a strong and confident youth voice was a result of the fact that the SASA organizations were committed to a participatory youth-centered decision-making process.

Legal Actions

Given the history of Y.S. v. School District of Philadelphia, the Lafayette HS[5] case in New York City, and the Asian American Legal Defense and Education Fund's (AALDEF) ongoing Philadelphia presence dealing with attacks on immigrant students at other schools, it was natural to consider legal action. However, the youth and their advocates saw the legal struggle as one aspect of an overall community organizing movement (Chen & Leong, 2012). AALDEF attorney Cecilia Chen, a daily presence throughout the boycott and afterward, discussed the legal alternatives with the youth: private lawsuits by individual students or administrative complaints to the Office of Civil Rights, which might culminate in a federal lawsuit against the SDP (Chen & Leong, 2012). Past community experience, for example, in the Y.S. v. SDP lawsuit, showed that positive change occurred and was sustained only when there was continual public pressure from the community. After deliberations about the length of time to go through the courts and the participants' ability to sustain the struggle, the youth and advocates felt that an administrative complaint would be the most effective leverage for pressuring the SDP and garnering media attention.

Consistent with the collaborative democratic process used in the youth meetings and the advocates' belief in youth self-determination, AALDEF practiced the concept of "community lawyering," which Chen and Leong (2012) describe as "lawyering through a democratic consensus community building model" (p. 16) with a "social justice and transformative goal" (p. 46). This meant that the community clients, not expert attorneys, led the process and made the major decisions. This was crucial in developing youth leadership and modeling respectful adult process.

On January 19, 2010, AALDEF filed an administrative civil rights complaint with the U.S. Department of Justice (DOJ) against the School District of Philadelphia on behalf of the Asian immigrant students. Following an investigation, the DOJ alleged that the district's "actual knowledge of and a clearly unreasonable response to severe and pervasive harassment, which bar[red] students from enjoying the educational benefits afforded to them based on race, color, and/or national origin, constitutes discrimination" (*U.S. v. SDP*, 2010, Complaint, p. 3). By August the DOJ announced that it had found merit in the allegation (Gammage & Graham, 2010). By December, the DOJ concluded that the civil rights of the Asian immigrant students had been egregiously violated (*U.S. v. SDP and SRC*, 2010, p. 2). On December 15, 2010, the two parties signed a remediation agreement, which included provisions for the SPHS Action Plan and policies and procedures directed at SPHS regarding harassment, training, incident reporting, and monitoring (*U.S. v. SDP*, 2010, Settlement Agreement). Simultaneously, community complainants reached a similar agreement with the PHRC (*Asian Americans United v. SDP*, 2010). While the severely violent incidents at South Philadelphia High School stopped, the struggle for a safe school was not over.

In the chronology of events, there are not many discrete entries for legal action because discussions and decision making were continually integrated into the meetings of youth and advocates. Cecilia Chen explained legal documents and concepts in plain language; these were then interpreted into Vietnamese and Mandarin so the students could comprehend and offer their opinions. At each step of the way, the youth were involved in the decision making on what legal strategy to undertake. The process, which was inclusive of all language groups and transparent about the legal actions, paved the way for youth to learn how the legal system worked, to analyze the pros and cons of legal action, and to emerge armed with more knowledge, confidence, and critical consciousness—while understanding the limitations of what could be accomplished.

Communications

Under "communications" I include general public relations, such as press releases and public statements; more formal testimony to government or public agencies; and the counternarratives and power analysis of school violence that youth presented at workshops, conferences, and award ceremonies. Additionally, the young people were asked to participate in numerous newspaper interviews, newscasts, and a documentary, titled *We Didn't Come Here to Fight* (Lee, Li, Palomino, & Redai, 2011). The youth were also the subject of a yearlong photography exhibit, *We Cannot Keep Silent* (Asian Americans United et al., 2013) at the Philadelphia Folklore Project. All these communications served to disrupt the SDP's victim-blaming narrative and denial of the racialized nature of school violence on the part of adults and peer students. Furthermore, they helped gain support from the Asian American community, student and professional organizations, activist student organizations, and other allies, and they helped to broadly raise awareness about school violence and power relations between immigrant communities and the public education bureaucracy. Duong Ly spoke about the importance of youth speaking out:

> I realized that I can't remain silent when something outrageous or bad happens to me or my friends. I have to be outspoken and to constantly educate myself about all the social issues, about social oppression, so that I can have the power to stand up for myself, for others or with others to fight against those issues. (Asian Americans United et al., 2013)

Many of these communications activities served the tasks of community organizing and advancing public knowledge and support for the legal struggle. For example, the December 3 incident is widely remembered among Philadelphians, and many Asian former district staff came forward to speak to DOJ investigators about the their experiences at SPHS.

CHANGES IN INSTITUTIONAL POLICY AND PRACTICE

Youth Demands and the DOJ Settlement

During the boycott, the youth drafted a list of demands. While adult advocates and allies from the coalition provided guidance, they did so without intruding. They asked the youth what they wanted to happen at SPHS to improve the climate and make it safe for their return. Youth brainstormed the list and collectively agreed on the final demands. These 29 final demands, divided into two categories, 12 "Security Concerns" (e.g., "retraining of all security personnel," "quick and effective responses to fights, not waiting till it is over," "bilingual security and safety staff") and 17 "Climate Concerns" (e.g., "school to accept responsibility for violence," "multi-cultural/global education," "Asian representation in school administration"), addressed the immediate problems of physical and psychological safety as well as broader issues of cultural sensitivity training and ethnic studies.

In the negotiations to end the student boycott, Superintendent Ackerman committed to having security cameras installed and more security personnel assigned to SPHS, two of the students' demands. The majority of the youths' concerns, however, were not addressed until the DOJ Settlement Agreement, and even then, not all were resolved. Creating this list of demands represented the beginning of youth activists' involvement in the policy formation process. At this point, the legal strategy was inchoate, not to mention any ideas about how to fashion lasting resolutions or solutions. Nonetheless, engaging youth in this respect was significant because it provided young people with "a substantive outlet for civic participation" and increased "the likelihood that adopted policies will succeed in ameliorating social problems by drawing upon the knowledge, insights and experiences of young people who are most familiar with the problems being addressed" (Noguera & Cannella, 2006, p. 341).

Taken to the table by AALDEF, the demands formed the basis for the DOJ Settlement Agreement, which included these major stipulations for the SDP:

- Retain an expert consultant in the area of harassment and discrimination based on race, color and/or national origin to review the district's policies and procedures concerning harassment
- Develops and implements a comprehensive plan for preventing and addressing student-on-student harassment at the high school
- Conducts training of faculty, staff and students on discrimination and harassment based on race, color and/or national origin and to increase cultural awareness
- Maintains records of investigations and responses to allegations of harassment

- Provides annual compliance reports to the department and the PHRC as well as makes harassment data publicly available. (United States Department of Justice, 2010)

I mapped the 29 student demands onto the provisions of the Settlement Agreement and found the stipulations and provisions in the agreement fulfilled 24 of the students' demands, including issues of language access for parents and students and the establishment of a student committee; but five of the demands for bilingual or Asian representation among faculty, administrators, or security staff or the desire for bilingual programs or a multicultural curriculum, including immigration history, were not met. In early 2010, the superintendent brought in various partners to conduct extracurricular activities to promote positive cross-cultural relationships. For a variety of reasons, these were not successful and were replaced by others under Principal Otis Hackney, who later established an Asian American Studies course. In summary, the youths' demands were largely addressed by these institutional actions: Superintendent Ackerman's actions immediately after the boycott, the DOJ's Settlement Agreement about a year later, and Principal Hackney's school-based decisions during his first year at SPHS.

Incorporated into the settlement agreements were the September 2010 School Reform Commission–approved Policy 248, Unlawful Harassment, which provided for a district-level compliance officer to which students could report incidents and Policy 249, Bullying/Cyberbullying. If it had not been for the incisive and critical feedback of SASA and ASAP over the summer, the SDP policies would not have satisfied the fundamental demands of the campaign or been included in the SDP's Code of Student Conduct for all students. In the following section, I discuss one of the remaining student demands, that "the school accept responsibility for the violence." This demand became a priority, almost a *sine qua non*, for the youth activists and community advocates in order to accept the legal agreements.

The Legal Agreements: DOJ Settlement Agreement and PHRC Conciliation Agreement

Over the course of 2010, ASAP and the community advocates continually presented the case for identifying the assaults against the Asian immigrant students as "bias or racial harassment," not simply bullying or a consequence of gang affiliation. Without this fundamental acknowledgment, they believed real progress in changing the school climate would be impossible. This was a difficult struggle, as it became a media battle without an arbiter. It was not until the DOJ announcement that it had found merit in the students' allegations that the activists felt vindicated. Consequently, one of the main points that

the youth activists and community organizers wanted included in the Settlement Agreement was the district's acknowledgment that the attacks at
SPHS had been racially motivated and targeted against immigrant students.
The youth and advocates had no say at the DOJ table, although they were
able to forward input through their AALDEF attorney. The DOJ did not agree
to this point. Furthermore, the standard process of arriving at a Settlement Agreement to avoid long and costly litigation allowed for denial of
misconduct and no admission of liability or fault on the part of the SDP.
Consequently, the recitals in the Settlement Agreement contain both the
finding that the district had violated the Asian immigrant students' civil rights
and the district's denial that it deprived the students of equal protection of
the law (U.S. v. School District of Philadelphia, 15 December 2010, Settlement
Agreement, p. 2).

In contrast, the PHRC process provided for the complainants to be nego-
tiators of the settlement terms. Thus, after intensive advocacy, the preamble
of the PHRC Conciliation Agreement stated without qualifiers that the respondent (School District of Philadelphia)

> acknowledges that on December 3, 2009, numerous Asian immigrant
> students were assaulted by their peers, due in part to their race and na-
> tional origin, throughout the day inside and outside of South Philadel-
> phia High School, and acknowledges that the assaults on December 3,
> 2009 are an example of the harassment of Asian immigrant students at
> South Philadelphia High School based in part, on their race and na-
> tional origin and may reflect an anti-Asian/immigrant bias by some stu-
> dents. (PHRC, Conciliation Agreement, 2015, p. 3)

This important admission represented a win on the state front but not on
the federal. In both situations, SPHS and the SDP avoided any requirement
to implement ethnic studies, a multicultural curriculum, and a Vietnamese
bilingual program. Nevertheless, across the district African American History remained a mandated course for graduation; some magnet schools had
these course offerings; SPHS had a Chinese bilingual program; and SDP Policy 102, Multi-Racial Multi-Cultural-Gender Education, mandated a multicultural curriculum (School District of Philadelphia, 2004).

Post Legal Agreements

After the legal settlements and administrative changes in policies and
procedures were enacted in 2010, there were significant improvements to
the school climate at SPHS. Hackney, the new principal, was able to
establish good rapport with school staff and students as well as the Asian

youth and their community advocates. The Safe Schools Collaborative, a foundation-funded initiative involving SASA members and the Philadelphia Student Union (PSU), conducted cross-cultural, cross-linguistic youth leadership development at the school and informally monitored the Settlement Agreement. However, after a couple years, the formal monitoring reports from the SDP to DOJ ceased as did the foundation grant. Moreover, the SDP's budget crises, another school's merger with SPHS, and changes within the SDP leadership all hampered the school's ability to develop more interethnic understanding and collaboration. As a result, hope for widespread implementation of the remedial measures to extend throughout the entire SDP diminished. On the community side, the community-based organizations, which were continually stretched financially, could not sustain long-term involvement at SPHS.

DISCUSSION

In what follows, I use theory to illuminate the processes by which the youth activists effected change both in their individual trajectories and in their institutions. I discuss how they created new spaces for youth to exercise their voice and power, the conditions for the development of critical consciousness and agency, and the dynamics at play that forced the school and the district to adopt new policies and practices.

Space for Youth Voice and Power

Trang Dang, one of the student leaders, talked about how her experience with the SPHS boycott and the Asian Student Association of Philadelphia (ASAP) affected her: "My mind's more open. . . . I changed the most. There is nothing we cannot change. As long as you have people with you, you can change" (Asian Americans United et al., 2013). Understanding the power of organization, in September 2010, led by Wei Chen, the students decided to form ASAP, an autonomous youth organization, youth-run and youth-led. Nine months after the SPHS incident, the core of young people, including Wei Chen, Duong Ly, Bach Tong, and Trang Dang, had gained considerable exposure to people, places, and events, including veteran civil rights activists and other immigrant youth activists; various college campuses and cities; award ceremonies at the Kennedy Center in D.C., and the national Immigration Reform March in D.C. Over this time, they also attained a high level of skill in agenda setting, facilitation, prioritization, and division of labor, not to mention public speaking and workshop planning. As I observed many ASAP meetings and several workshops, I found the process sophisticated in providing for language access, participant interaction, and a safe space for all voices to be heard. (As an adult ally, I was welcome to observe and sometimes offer an opinion or advice, but proscribed from participation in decision making.) Access and exposure to forums both inside and outside the Asian community and the freedom to direct their own organization were crucial in developing youth vision and leadership. Thus, as noted in Ginwright and James's Social Justice Youth Development model (2002), the space to be heard, explore, learn, and grow was a necessary condition for the young people—as was the nurturing by their mentors and allies—to gain new knowledge and skills, develop their critical consciousness, and exercise their collective strength.

Critical Consciousness and Youth Agency

In the case of SPHS, the youth who were victims of racial harassment began to "read the world" (Freiere, 1985), to understand the power relations and racialized terrain of their situation vis-à-vis the SDP hierarchy and their student peers. With the guidance of veteran activists, they were able individually to attain varying levels of "critical consciousness" about the powers that constrained or facilitated the array of possible actions. With this knowledge and the goal of achieving a safe school environment for all SPHS students, they engaged in "praxis"— social justice action animated by critical consciousness. For English language learners, "reading the word" also involved literacy. While "reading the world," many of the youth accelerated their mastery of English speaking and writing at a surprising pace; many also improved their first-language proficiency in Vietnamese and Chinese because of the frequent need to interpret or translate for peers. As Freire posited, marginalized literacy learners are motivated to learn about issues that are directly relevant to their lives and then can use that literacy to take action toward social justice goals. This was the situation with the youth activists, who began to learn about and gain the vocabulary and language structures to talk about their experiences of racialization and minoritization, school violence, alienation, and isolation, as well as community organizing, legal maneuvers, and other strategies for resistance and attaining social justice. Regarding violence, Bach Tong explained, "There are three levels—interpersonal, intergroup, and institutional—which are all interrelated." With growing critical consciousness, space for voicing their concerns without adult interruption, and participation in democratic decision making, several of the youth who participated in the boycott matured into the youth leadership of ASAP.

Critical Organizational Theory

Seo and Creed (2002) offer a way to understand how the exposure of internal contradictions within the SDP, that is, between district administrators and the SPHS Asian immigrant students and between its purported nondiscriminatory policies and its racialized practices, laid bare the external contradictions between SDP policies and federal and state law. District officials gave lip service to complying with Title VI of the Civil Rights Act (1964), the Pennsylvania Fair Educational Opportunities Act (1992), and its own Policy 102, Multiracial-Multicultural-Gender Education (2004), thus coming into contradiction with other institutions (namely, DOJ and PHRC) at different bureaucratic levels.

While the complete exposition of Seo and Creed's (2002) dialectical perspective deals with more nuanced aspects of the dynamics of agency and change, suffice it to say here that the SDP existed in an environment where its practices were "incompatible" internally with its own mission and the well-being of the Asian immigrant youth and externally with the legal mandates, the enforcement of which was the responsibility of other institutions at the federal (DOJ) and state (PHRC) levels. In the dialectical schema, praxis is seen as the core mediating mechanism of institutional change; it is undergirded by the key concepts of the "partially autonomous social actor in a contradictory social world and the active exploiter of social contradictions" (Seo & Creed, 2002, p. 230). Thus, when the contradictions internally precipitated the crisis of December 9, 2009, the praxis of the Asian immigrant youth activists manifested as a boycott, an unsanctioned act of resistance, and a civil rights complaint against the district, an act that exploited the contradictions between institutions. The "reshaped consciousness" of the activist immigrant students instigated forced negotiations or "new social interactions" at SPHS and the SDP, which resulted in new policies and procedures formalized in the DOJ and PHRC agreements.

Starting the cycle with the bottom oval, I have adapted Figure 15.1 (see p. 295) to show the SPHS struggle as an example of the dialectical process of institutional change. (See Figure 15.2.)

CONCLUSION: SIGNIFICANCE AND IMPLICATIONS

Making meaning of this story of how immigrant youth activism forced institutional change was a process of recognizing new models or paradigms, reaffirming the power of collective action, and corroborating well-recognized tenets of youth activism such as the development of critical consciousness and praxis, the importance of counternarratives, and activism's transformative power. In the SPHS case, Asian immigrant youth were the capable leaders challenging the callous disregard of the SDP. Youth activism forced an institution to take notice and act. Over three and a half years, ASAP with SASA were able by way of federal and state juridical agreements to get new SDP policies and procedures formulated, approved, implemented, and

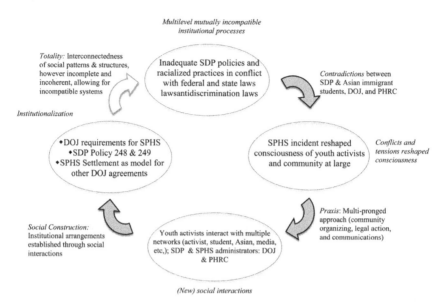

Figure 15.2. Institutionalization and Institutional Change: Process from a Dialectical Perspective Adapted Model.

monitored—important measures in diminishing the fear and physical harm previously suffered by Asian immigrant students at SPHS. The experience of school violence and school quality deeply affect the academic outcomes of first-generation immigrant students (Suárez-Orozco et al., 2008, p. 3). While the passing of policies and procedures by the school district is typically regarded as institutionalizing certain beliefs, definitions, and practices, the longevity of these changes—or at least their bona fide enforcement—is often uncertain in the face of budget crises and changing central office administrations. Regardless, youth were the driving force in compelling important institutional change. In advocate Helen Gym's words, this struggle "renewed faith that communities can create solutions to intractable situations" and instilled this belief in the young people. She added, "It was a platform for youth to go on to understand broader social issues." As such, the struggle marked a singular chapter for the development of activist youth leadership in the Asian American movement.

The legal struggle, chosen as an approach by the SPHS youth activists, had reverberations beyond Philadelphia. As community advocates pointed out, the DOJ Settlement Agreement was a model for other situations where districts neglected to address instances of school violence. Specifically, the DOJ's 2012 Anoka-Hennepin (MN) Settlement Agreement regarding LGBTQ harassment demonstrably built on the SPHS agreement by increasing demands on the district: required prolonged monitoring for five years; widespread dissemination to parents and students of the antiharassment policies in many languages; the creation of a task force representative of all stakeholders; and the extension of the order to encompass the entire school district (*Jane Doe v. Anoka-Hennepin School District No. 11*, 2012).

Significantly, multilingual activist youth formations and their intergenerational collaboration with the community advocates were models for social justice work in immigrant communities. Youth-serving organizations can adapt practices to develop the critical consciousness of first-generation immigrant youth of color and recognize the importance of providing language access. Moreover, we need to acknowledge the invaluable role of veteran activists in transmitting social and cultural capital, as advocates and allies, and often as mentors.

On the theoretical level, those of us working with activist youth have found it necessary to push the definitions of youth civic engagement beyond the traditional ideas of community service and participation in partisan politics. The SPHS struggle is an example, among many, of sustained youth engagement that was built on the development of "critical consciousness" and "praxis." The experiences of gaining a political analysis and taking action to change the world are likely to embed a deep sense of social responsibility in youth activists to their communities and to the world at large—that is an enormous contribution to society as a whole. Locally, the organizing around SPHS raised the level of discourse about school violence and broadened it within Philadelphia and among various Asian American community-based, student, and professional organizations. Moreover, it brought into the spotlight the counternarrative to widely held stereotyping discourses about Asian immigrant youth. It further highlighted the largely unrecognized capabilities of recent immigrant students to challenge unjust treatment; to understand the racialized landscape of power in schools and neighborhoods; and to have the courage to challenge a monolithic institution on legal and moral grounds. Through accumulating cultural and social capital as a result of their social justice work, the youth changed themselves in the process of changing the world. Their increased self-confidence in their abilities and a broadened perspective on life and their possible trajectories have meant that they know the possibilities of both personal and collective agency. The youth leaders in this particular struggle continue to contribute to their own racialized and marginalized communities by continuing to do youth leadership development and community organizing, branching out into environmental justice issues, and bringing back knowledge of other marginalized peoples and their struggles as they travel. They inspire others to be like them and to challenge hegemonic practices. As Wei Chen, the founder of ASAP, expressed, "We have the power to make change; we can do something. It is not only the adults who can do something; we can do something. I trust this."

NOTES

1. In this chapter, "first-generation immigrant" denotes a person born abroad arriving in adolescence or later.

2. Also see AAU and PCDC websites.

3. Statistics from School District of Philadelphia webpage: https://webapps.philasd.org/school_profile/view/2000, and 2011 High School Directory, http://www.philasd.org/students/HSDirectory2011_web.pdf.

4. AAU, BPSOS, VWSSP, AALDEF, and former staff of CAGP.

5. This case litigated by AALDEF also involved school district negligence in the face of racial intimidation of Asian ELL students.

REFERENCES

Asian American Legal Defense and Education Fund (AALDEF). Education equity. Retrieved from http://aaldef.org/programs/educational-equity2.html

Asian Americans United et al. v. School District of Philadelphia. (2010, December 15). Pennsylvania Human Relations Commission (PHRC) conciliation agreement regarding South Philadelphia High School.

Asian Americans United, Finkel, H., & Shimizu, K. (2013). *We cannot keep silent* [Photography exhibition]. Philadelphia, PA: Philadelphia Folklore Project.

Cammarota, J., & Fine, M. (Eds.). (2008). *Revolutionizing education: Youth participatory action research in motion.* New York, NY: Routledge.

Chen, C., & Leong, A. (2012). We have the power to make change: The role of community lawyering in challenging anti-Asian harassment at South Philadelphia High School. *Asian American Law Journal, 19,* 1–50.

Crouch, E., & Williams, D. (1995). What cities are doing to protect kids. *Educational Leadership, 52*(5), 60–62. Retrieved from http://eric.ed.gov/?id=EJ497540

Freire, P. (1985). Reading the world and reading the word: An interview with Paulo. *Language Arts, 62*(1), 15–21.

Freire, P. (2000). *Pedagogy of the oppressed.* Revised 30th Anniversary Edition. New York, NY: Continuum.

Freire, P. (2005). *Education for critical consciousness.* New York, NY: Continuum.

Gammage, J. (2010, February 1). Asian American group fights against injustice. *Philadelphia Inquirer.* Retrieved from http://articles.philly.com/

Gammage, J. (2011, April 3). Healing the wounds of S. Phila. High. *Philadelphia Inquirer.* Retrieved from http://articles.philly.com/

Gammage, J., & Graham, K. A. (2010, August 28). Feds find merit in Asian students' claims against Philly school. *Philadelphia Inquirer.* Retrieved from http://articles.philly.com/

Ginwright, S., & Cammarota, J. (2002). New terrain in youth development: The promise of a social justice approach. *Social Justice, 29*(4), 82–95. Retrieved from http://eric.ed.gov/?id=EJ667326

Ginwright, S., & Cammarota, J. (2006). Introduction. In S. Ginwright, P. Noguera, & J. Cammarota (Eds.), *Beyond resistance!: Youth activism and community change* (pp. xiii–xx). New York, NY: Routledge.

Ginwright, S., & James, T. (2002). From assets to agents of change: Social justice, organizing and youth development. *New Directions for Youth Development, 2002*(96), 27–46. http://dx.doi.org/10.1002/yd.25

Gittell, R., & Vidal, A. (1998). *Community organizing: Building social capital as a development strategy.* Thousand Oaks, CA: Sage Publications.

Goode, E. (2013, March 14). Focusing on violence before it happens. *The New York Times.* Retrieved from http://www.nytimes.com

Hosang, D. (2006). Beyond policy: Ideology, race and the reimagining of youth. In S. Ginwright, P. Noguera, & J. Cammarota (Eds.), *Beyond resistance!: Youth activism and community change* (pp. 3–20). New York, NY: Routledge.

Jane Doe v. Anoka-Hennepin School District, No. 1. No. 11-cv-01999-JNE-SER (D. MN 2012). Consent decree between DOJ and plaintiffs and school district regarding sex-based harassment.

Koo, D. J., Peguero, A. A., & Shekarkhar, Z. (2012). The "model minority" victim: Immigration, gender, and Asian American vulnerabilities to violence at school. *Journal of Ethnicity in Criminal Justice, 10*(2), 129–147. http://dx.doi.org/10.1080/15377938.2011.609405

Lee, R., Li, J. Z., Palamino, J., & Redai, A. (2011). *We didn't come here to fight: The struggle for a safe education.* University of Pennsylvania Law School student documentary video about South Philadelphia High School. Retrieved from https://www.law.upenn.edu/institutes/documentaries/studentvideos/

Morrell, E. (2008). *Critical literacy and urban youth: Pedagogies of access, dissent, and liberation.* New York, NY: Taylor and Francis.

Noguera, P., & Cannella, C. M. (2006). Youth agency, resistance, and civic activism: The public commitment to social justice. In S. Ginwright, P. Noguera, & J. Cammarota (Eds.), *Beyond resistance!: Youth activism and community change* (pp. 333–347). New York, NY: Routledge.

Olsen, L. (2002). Learning English and learning America: Immigrants in the center of a storm [Special issue]. *Theory into Practice, 39*(4), 196–202. http://dx.doi.org/10.1207/s15430421tip3904_2

Philadelphia Commission on Human Relations. (2012). *Widening the circle of our concern: Public perceptions of the School District of Philadelphia's responses to intergroup conflicts.* Report from a year of public hearings on school violence. Retrieved from http://www.wideningthecircle.org/

School District of Philadelphia. (2004). *Multiracial-Multicultural-Gender Education, Section 102.* Retrieved from http://www.phila.k12.pa.us/offices/administration/policies/102.html

Seo, M. S., & Creed, W. E. D. (2002). Institutional contradictions, praxis, and institutional change: A dialectical perspective. *Academy of Management Review, 27*(2), 222–247. http://dx.doi.org/10.5465/AMR.2002.6588004

Shah, N. (2013, February 15). Armed educators a reality in some schools, debated in others. *Education Week.* Retrieved from www.edweek.org

Somekawa, E. (1995). On the edge: Southeast Asians in Philadelphia and the struggle for space. In W. L. Ng, S. Chin, J. S. Moy, & G. Okihiro (Eds.), *ReViewing Asian America: Locating diversity* (pp. 33–47). Pullman, WA: Washington State Press.

Suárez-Orozco, M., Suárez-Orozco, C., & Todorova, I. (2008). *Learning a new land: Immigrant students in American society.* Cambridge, MA: Harvard University Press.

Taylor, K. (2015, April 29). New York city underreported school violence to state, audit shows. *The New York Times.* Retrieved from www.nytimes.com

United States Department of Justice (DOJ). Office of Public Affairs. (2010, December 15). Justice department reaches agreement with Philadelphia school district to resolve harassment allegations. Press release. Retrieved from http://www.justice.gov

U.S. v. City of New York, Case No. 04-Cv-2248 (E.D. N.Y. June 1, 2004). Consent decree regarding Lafayette High School.

U.S. v. School District of Philadelphia (SDP) No. 2:10-CV-07301-SD (E.D. Pa. Jan. 19, 2010). Asian American Legal Defense and Education Fund (AALDEF) complaint regarding South Philadelphia High School filed with the U.S. Department of Justice, Civil Rights Division.

U.S. v. School District of Philadelphia (SDP), No. 2:10-CV-07301-SD (E.D. Pa. Dec. 15, 2010). Settlement Agreement regarding South Philadelphia High School.

Y.S. v. School District of Philadelphia (SDP), C.A. 85-6924 (E.D. Pa. 1985).

16

Youth Taking the Lead in Education Policy

Rachel Gunther

Young people have been making history for hundreds of years in the United States—from demanding child labor laws in the early 1900s, to being front and center during the civil rights movement, the Berkeley Free Speech Movement, and the Student Nonviolent Coordinating Committee (SNCC). During the Vietnam War, young people brought to light how they were impacted by national policies, and in 2015, thousands of young people, using social media and community-based activism, were organizing around numerous social and economic justice campaigns, including education equity, high-stakes testing, juvenile justice and the school-to-prison pipeline, student feedback to teachers, and immigration reform.

Young people bring a level of innovation and creativity in their responses to social issues that is often missing from adult leaders. After years of being in the trenches, adult decision makers can feel hopeless and lose their energy, vision, and creativity. However, young people often come to the decision-making table like a breath of fresh air, full of enthusiasm and optimism.

In addition to bringing their creativity and energy, young people are able to provide a perspective only they can as the people who are living with the issues and policies every day. As much as many adults would like to say we can remember what it is like to be young, we cannot experience what young people are going through today in every program, school, and classroom. By listening to young people and purposefully giving them a voice at the decision-making table, we open ourselves and our programming to a vast range of new possibilities of what is important, relevant, and achievable.

When young people are fully engaged—when their voices are heard, their opinions matter, and their unique perspectives are respected—they commit themselves to making their schools, their communities, and their own lives better. Knowing this, adults tap into young people's incredible positive energy, skills, and enthusiasm by engaging them in the institutions that affect them most. Engaging young people as partners in efforts to improve schools, youth organizations, and neighborhoods benefits both young leaders and entire communities.

Right now young people are changing the landscape of their own education, starting with their own classrooms, schools, and districts. Administrators and teachers are listening to young people's ideas with a growing level of respect, and Youth on Board is excited to be part of, and witness to, these changes within the city of Boston and in districts across the country. This chapter will shed light on how Youth on Board (YOB) and the Boston Student Advisory Council (BSAC) function programmatically, discuss the ways that we purposefully and strategically engage and train adults and young people for the work, and highlight successes and lessons learned during the past 20 years.

INTRODUCTION TO YOUTH ON BOARD

Youth on Board was founded in 1994 and is proud to be part of the ongoing movement working to ensure that young people between the ages of 13 and 21 have a voice in the decisions that affect them. When we began, youth governance and youth in decision making were in their infancy. The movement was fledgling, but the country seemed ready to listen to young people in a genuine way about what they believed, wanted, and could do. This coincided with an economic upturn, and many youth-serving organizations had the space and finances to look at how their programmatic decisions were being made. Many made an investment, both financially and programmatically, by incorporating youth voice in their decision-making process.

During this period, there was increased activism in the Campus Outreach Opportunity League (COOL) and other youth in decision-making organizing groups, and the Bill Clinton administration started Americorps. The Kellogg Foundation believed that Youth on Board co-founders, Karen Young and Jenny Sazama, could be part of this change movement and gave YOB a seed grant to begin our work to improve youth/adult partnerships in an effort to increase youth voice in organizations that serve young people. YouthBuild USA's founder and president, Dorothy Stoneman, agreed to house our project, and we began to develop materials and trainings utilizing our shared vision that all young people have the capacity and right to have a seat at the decision-making table. We began to provide consultations and trainings to organizations, churches, foundations, and schools that were interested in working with young people as engaged and informed citizens, leaders, and real decision makers.

From the beginning, we envisioned a world where young people are fully respected and treated as valued and active members of their families, communities, and society. To reach that end, we work to change attitudes and strengthen relationships among young people and between young people and adults; support young people to be an active force for change in all aspects of their lives; and ensure that policies, practices, and laws reflect young people's role as full and valued members of their communities.

Using this vision statement as our guiding principle, for the next several years we provided hundreds of trainings to thousands of young people and adults across the country on how to build positive intergenerational relationships; openly discussed the problems associated with adultism (systematic disrespect and mistreatment of young people), sexism, and racism; provided tips on how to be a good listener and communicator; and taught hands-on organizing skills. Based on our years of training and curriculum development, YOB published a book called *15 Points—Successfully Involving Youth in Decision Making* that has sold thousands of copies around the globe (Young & Sazama, 2006).

In 2000, YOB was selected by the Pew Charitable Trusts to help them develop a training curriculum for Project 540, an initiative that engaged more than 100,000 students across the country in decision making in their schools. The experience deepened our understanding of the intersection between youth governance and public education. As a result of this success, we were called in by the Boston Public Schools to help them design four small schools using the relationship-based multigenerational approach for which we were known.

We didn't know at the time that this work would lead us toward one of our most important projects, co-administering the Boston Student Advisory Council (BSAC). Through our work with BSAC, we deepened our understanding of district, state, and federal education policy change, became national leaders in student voice in decision making, and became providers of technical assistances to districts interested in replicating our work in Boston. Currently, we have staff that work directly with the BSAC program and other employees that focus on our role as a resource to organizations on youth voice and governance. These pieces are mutually supportive and one enhances the success of the other.

OUR INSIDE/OUTSIDE PARTNERSHIP—BSAC

There are various ways to organize in communities, each of which has benefits and drawbacks. An outside organization can have complete autonomy and flexibility in what it does, what policies it supports, and with whom it has relationships. This allows organizers significant latitude in what campaigns they take on, but they may end up with limited access to key decision makers. Some organizing takes place from within the policymaking system.

This type of inside work has incredible benefits due to access to decision makers, but often organizers are constrained in what policies they can push due to
political concerns.

YOB integrated these two options to create a unique inside/outside partnership model that is fundamental to our success. BSAC has the power to
push for initiatives that may not be on the radar of our district partners *and*
we have unique access to key decision makers at the district level. This position allows us to bypass some institutional barriers that get in the way of other
outside organizing groups. There are times when this partnership can be limiting if a policy seems too out front politically for the district, but because of
our longtime and trusted relationship, there are very few issues that our students bring up that are not appropriate to move forward with the district. If
there are campaigns that arise that have the potential to cause controversy,
we move them forward through our work with the several coalitions of which
we are part.

Our relationship with BSAC began in 2000, when we were contracted by
the Boston Public Schools to "revamp" the district's program. In 1971, Student Advisory Councils were mandated in a Commonwealth of Massachusetts law that stated, "School committees of cities, towns and regional school
districts shall meet at least once every other month, during the months in
which school is in session, with a student advisory committee to consist of
five members to be composed of students elected by the student body of the
high school or high schools in each city, town or regional school district"
(Mass. Gen. Laws ch. 71, § 38M). However, many districts' SACs do not
function as spelled out in the law. This was the case in Boston when we were
called in to help. Shortly after our consultation, we began doing private
fundraising so we would have the capacity to co-administer the BSAC
with staff from the Boston Public Schools (BPS) Office of Engagement.
This began what is now a 15-year partnership with BPS. Now BSAC is a
powerful citywide body of student leaders that represent most high schools
in the district and consists almost entirely of low-income students of color,
with demographics that closely mirror those of the district. BSAC members
identify and organize around pertinent student-identified issues and put
these key stakeholders at the center of the decisions that affect them
the most.

According to district policy, BSAC has three main roles: (1) to serve as
the only systemwide voice of young people on the School Committee; (2) to
inform the student body at each school of BSAC policy changes, campaigns,
and other issues that affect BPS students; and (3) to organize campaigns and
projects around issues affecting young people.

When we first began working with BSAC, we spent significant time setting
up programmatic structures, roles, and responsibilities for staff and students

and developed a year-long training curriculum to prepare and support their organizing work. Another critical component of BSAC is peer support sessions that will be described in detail later in the chapter. BSAC builds the power of the students of BPS by providing them with a thorough understanding of school issues, a way to express their concerns, and multiple avenues for engaging in advocacy and activism.

We work directly with young people as they develop an understanding of the ways economic and political power is distributed in our society, and they learn how to change structures and policies that reinforce inequity. BSAC students have led organizing efforts, forged relationships with district and city leaders, created and changed school policies, lobbied for increased student representation on the School Committee and other decision-making bodies, and advanced the voice and status of young people throughout Boston. Our projects often operate on multiple levels, addressing district-level systems change, as well as systemic change on the state level, while developing workable models of student-led campaign development and movement-building for replication across the country.

The majority of BPS high schools have one or two BSAC representatives who serve on either the BSAC Working Group or the BSAC Steering Committee. The 12-member Working Group meets for three to four hours every week and is paid for this work. The 50-person Steering Committee meets with the Working Group once every other week to support and contribute to the more intense planning and organizing of the Working Group. During these meetings, members learn about citywide policies under consideration, work on and research student-developed campaigns, meet with city and district officials, and receive training in relevant skills. They also strategize about how to advocate for their positions with the School Committee, superintendent's office, and other district officials. Each year, BSAC members are appointed through elections and nominations by their peers. Once selected through a peer-interview process, members sign a commitment letter and participate in an orientation and training led by YOB and the BSAC coordinator who sits in the BPS Office of Engagement.

SOCIAL-EMOTIONAL LEARNING (SEL) IN BSAC

While BSAC is best known for our education organizing work, what sets BSAC apart from other youth organizing and leadership development groups is our focus on social-emotional learning (SEL) and its role in our members' long-term success in future endeavors, including and extending beyond their school experiences. We call our two-pronged approach *action and support*. We believe that supporting young people in their emotional and personal lives as they navigate this important organizing work is fundamental to our success as a program. The philosophy that guides our work is that caring, empathic, and respectful relationships are at the center of emotional *and* social change. Engaging young people as partners in community change in BSAC, as well as the supports and trainings we provide, gives our young people a greater feeling of safety and belonging, a heightened sense of confidence and self-efficacy, and a deep understanding of and connection to their peers and the broader community.

The vast majority of BSAC students experience a variety of structural barriers to their growth and success, such as poverty, racism, homelessness, and community and interpersonal violence—factors that often contribute to students being labeled "high risk" for dropping out of school and other problems. These factors also mean that many are less likely to encounter practices in their daily lives that promote healthy social-emotional learning. Rather than stigmatizing students for their "risk factors," our model compels students to identify the unique value they contribute to social-change efforts. We have found that young people facing these challenges are able to engage effectively in community change efforts, and that joining BSAC propels their social and emotional growth and development. The lynchpin of our work is meaningful relationship building, which underlies everything that BSAC students do, from meeting with district and school officials to creating a cohesive support system among themselves. BSAC's ultimate strength lies in its ability to balance young people's civic engagement with their personal development.

We have witnessed the transformative power that being part of BSAC can have on young people. It is very common for members to come to their first meeting feeling frustrated, isolated, and dejected and on the verge of being pushed out or dropping out of school. However, as a result of our program, most of them become engaged leaders and powerful members of their school community.

Teena, our lead youth organizer on staff, began with us as a 15-year-old student contemplating dropping out of school. When Teena first came to BSAC she was skipping school and getting very poor grades. A staff person in her high school saw that she needed direction and support and suggested Teena attend a BSAC meeting—that meeting changed the trajectory of her life. Teena now talks about how transformative her experience with BSAC has been to her life. She has learned to understand how racism and adultism affected her life and education, and she became a persuasive advocate for public education and stopping the school-to-prison pipeline and skilled in sharing her deep understanding of the importance of relationship building in all aspects of her life. Teena is just one example of the dozens of young people who come through the program each year whose lives are changed not only by organizing around important social and educational issues but also by the experience of the respectful, loving relationships we build as part of doing the work.

In BSAC, we implement SEL in a variety of ways, including twice monthly peer-support groups where students are able to discuss their personal struggles and successes, and where they collectively wrestle with the realities facing their lives, communities, families, and schools. These adult-moderated spaces give young people an opportunity to understand how their personal lives and their organizing work are interconnected in their daily experiences. Students are supported to develop skills and habits, such as the art of listening, empathy, and effective ways to express their appreciation for one another. These skills transfer to the ongoing organizing meetings, where they discuss current campaigns, meet with officials, present findings to district administrators, and learn about policies and their implications. Members also participate in sessions on professionalism and meeting etiquette, leadership 101, meeting facilitation, public speaking, public funding and budgeting, and how to build successful youth/adult partnerships, to name a few. As a result of our successful implementation of SEL in our program, we were one of eight programs selected by the Susan Crown Exchange to study best practices in order to develop a comprehensive framework that can be shared with other youth projects. We are pleased to finally have the opportunity to highlight the importance of SEL in the youth organizing world, something that many programs like ours have been doing for a long time.

Our program's success is evident when adults see our young people testifying to the school committee, sitting on a panel in D.C., or being interviewed on television. We are asked, "How is this possible? Where do you find these young people?" And our response is always the same: If you support, listen to, train, and love the young people in your program and lives, they are capable of incredible strength, resilience, power, and leadership. In order to achieve this goal together, the commitment to supporting young people must be there by the adults in their lives.

POLICY SPOTLIGHT: CONSTRUCTIVE FEEDBACK AND STUDENT INPUT IN TEACHER EVALUATION

During the past 15 years, BSAC pushed forward more than 15 policies, including school lockout, cell phone use, homework assignment quality, dress code, school start time, climate justice, and others. (For a full list, please visit http://media.wix.com/ugd/c8aa42_4cea35bc17bb43acaa1df54981c0f42b .pdf.) We conduct yearly outreach through our school-based campaigns to ensure students understand and are aware of their rights and responsibilities, as well as the district's policies. This year, we decided to bring information to the palm of students' hands, where they can most easily use it. We developed and launched a smartphone application called "Boston Student Rights" (www.bostonstudentrights.org), which provides students with their rights and responsibilities and informs them of the proper procedures for suspension and expulsion. This project is part of our campaign to end the school-to-prison pipeline by decreasing harsh discipline policies and increasing consistent use of the new and improved code of conduct that we helped develop. Students have shared that by having easy access to this information, they feel safer, more empowered, and in control of their educational experience. In addition to working on numerous student-led campaigns, which are developed by the young people themselves, BSAC provides feedback to the district on surveys and policy decisions, participates in hiring processes (BSAC members helped interview the incoming superintendent and mayor), and takes part in numerous citywide and national coalitions on issues members find important.

Some campaigns succeed in only a few months, such as the campaign to address the lockout policy, and others require protracted efforts. For more than nine years, we have been working on policies concerning constructive feedback and student input in teacher evaluation. In 2006, BSAC members started to discuss the problems they experienced with the quality of their homework assignments. After sharing their concerns and experiences within the group, they conducted a literature review, interviewed almost 800 high school students, and decided to wage a campaign to improve the quality of homework assignments in the district through the adoption of a new homework policy. Students knew they would need to work with teachers, the superintendent, the administration, and the teachers' union to ensure a successful campaign. They were determined to push for a new policy that would ensure that homework assigned was more than busywork and actually supported and built on the work they did during the day. BSAC members then asked the question: Why were teachers assigning low-quality homework tasks? After going through teachers' contracts and manuals, they found that teachers were not being held accountable for the quality of homework assigned to students—it was not something administrators looked at and was not part of a teacher's evaluation. In fact, they discovered that many teachers were not evaluated in any meaningful way at all. If administrators were conducting teacher evaluations, it was only for an hour or so out of the entire year. BSAC members realized that *students*, in fact, were with teachers more than anyone, and could provide a much richer and broader evaluation of their teachers than administrators could. This revelation brought BSAC to the decision to work on both the quality of homework assignments and supporting student input in teacher evaluations through constructive feedback, with a focus on the high school level.

For Youth on Board, this campaign fit perfectly into our mission of creating positive relationships between adults and young people. Constructive feedback had the power to build positive relationships between students and teachers, improve teaching and learning, and shift school climate and culture to one in which students felt heard, understood, and seen as a partner in their own education. We knew that we needed to work in collaboration with teachers and use this campaign as a way to find common goals, not only improving teaching and learning and relationships, but also moving away from evaluation based on punishment, testing, and one-time classroom visits by administrators. What could have become an adversarial campaign became one of unity with teachers across the district.

When the teacher evaluation campaign began in Boston, it was revolutionary—very few organizing groups or districts were even thinking about the issue. Initially, the Boston Teachers Union opposed the proposal, but we had always worked well together and they had been supportive of student voice in general. Our ongoing positive relationship with the union presented an "in" to move forward. In 2007 we met with then superintendent Dr. Carol Johnson, and she suggested working on a more modest form of student input that would not carry any weight in the formal evaluation process, but would provide teachers and students with a feedback loop. At first, the conversation with the superintendent felt like a setback, but part of our learning process in this project was recognizing that sometimes campaigns are won with incremental steps as opposed to one giant leap. If we had not taken this interim step, it is unlikely we would be where we are today.

We decided to move forward with Dr. Johnson's idea and called the new process "constructive feedback." Between 2008 and 2010, BSAC met with teachers, school committee members, and the superintendent to garner support for our newly revised constructive feedback campaign. In May 2010, BSAC members presented their argument for student feedback to the Boston School Committee persuasively, emotionally, and prepared with data. That night BSAC's constructive feedback policy was unanimously approved.

As we began to develop a sample survey, we met with students, teachers, administrators, and Pennsylvania State University professor Dr. Dana Mitra to develop a tool that students could use to give teachers constructive feedback on homework, teaching styles, and engagement, while also providing an opportunity for teachers to learn about how each student learns best. Ensuring there was space for students' own self-reflection was critical to our project and consonant with our ongoing belief that this campaign was not about penalizing teachers but about improving the classroom for students and teachers alike. Students told us they wanted to be more involved in their learning, and this tool provided a way for them to take responsibility for their role in the student/teacher relationship. Questions such as "Do you pay attention in class? Do you get to class in time? Do you learn by reading or by listening?" are examples of how students provide information to their teacher. Students answer these questions before they provide feedback to their teachers. Students

worked very hard to make sure the questions about the teachers were supportive, useful, and constructive so that the answers would be useful to improve
teaching techniques. When BSAC received permission to pilot the tool with
a small group of students and teachers, members felt that they were making
great progress and were excited.

With the support for the use of the feedback form from the BTU membership, BPS administrators, and the superintendent, BSAC officially administered the survey in BPS high schools in 2010. We created an implementation
guide for teachers to use with the survey, and the union promoted it in its
newsletter and meetings. Students felt empowered and teachers felt more
knowledgeable about their students. It seemed to be a win-win situation. In a
teacher survey that was conducted by the district, more than 65% of teachers
reported finding the constructive feedback tool useful. More than 40% of
teachers said they would implement changes in the classroom based on student feedback.

In order to continue to build support for the survey, BSAC requested
permission by the Boston Teachers Union to make a presentation during one
of its membership meetings. In February 2011 students shared their experiences in the classroom, presented the research they conducted, and made
such a persuasive case that 70% of teachers in attendance supported constructive feedback on the spot. In fact, one BSAC member who spoke was in
tears as she discussed the meaning and impact this policy would have on her
life as well as her siblings' lives. BSAC's presentation was such a success and
so well received that the BTU president has continued to invite our students
back for annual presentations of our work. It is this type of relationship and
first-person communication that has led to our program's success and provides
our young people a reputation of respect and integrity.

Although the first year brought strong positive results, it also made us realize the challenges associated with administering a paper survey to thousands
of students in a district. While we received more positive feedback than negative, we knew that we could not be responsible for administering this survey
in the future; the district had to take on this responsibility. Fortunately, a
study from the Measures of Effective Teaching (MET) Project on teacher
evaluation and student perception data supported our belief that students
provide the most reliable way to measure teacher effectiveness (Measures of
Effective Teaching, 2010).

With support now from the Boston superintendent, the BTU, and the
Boston School Committee, we decided to approach the Massachusetts Board
of Secondary Education (MA BESE) and charge them with incorporating
student input as they developed a new statewide educator evaluation regulation. The timing was right because the state needed to update its evaluation
system in order to receive federal Race to the Top funds, and the student

member of BESE was supportive of our campaign. BSAC rallied hundreds of people in front of Boston's City Hall in May 2011 to bring awareness to the upcoming state education board vote, and developed the slogan "We are the ones in the classroom, Ask Us!" (Youth on Board, n.d.). Michael D'Ortenzio, the student representative on the state BESE, suggested BSAC testify before the board, and many members gladly did. In June 2011, MA BESE unanimously agreed to adopt new regulations requiring all districts in Massachusetts to include student feedback in grades 3 through 12 as a form of evidence in educator evaluations by the 2013–2014 school year.

The passage of the policy at the state level was a resounding victory and marked a transition to a phase of our work focused on the nitty-gritty of implementation. Issues related to capacity, funding, timing, and staffing changes made this campaign move more slowly than we anticipated. Both the state and Boston completed pilot projects during the 2014–2015 school year, and we expected full implementation in the 2015–2016 school year.

We pushed to create a student feedback working group, with a BSAC student member, that pulls together district officials, teachers, and young people to discuss the complicated implementation plans, issues, and concerns in Boston. The creation of intergenerational multistakeholder working groups has become a key part of our process with all of our campaigns. We have found that it leads to successful relationships among all the participants. Having young people at the table with adults who can hear the innovation and ideas that young people bring improves outcomes and processes for all. As a result of our campaign successes in Boston, we were asked to provide feedback to the state when it issued guidance to districts in the Commonwealth.

Although the district has incorporated youth voice into the constructive feedback policy, one of the biggest obstacles we continue to come up against is that of funding. A policy is only as good as the implementation, but implementation can only be successful if there is adequate financial support behind it. This campaign has taught us so many things, most importantly flexibility and patience. One of the biggest lessons learned during these years, both for staff and our young people, is understanding the importance of ensuring there are funds associated with policy requests. This is not always simple to do, we realize, but it is helpful to be thinking about the "how" and "with what staffing and funds" as we move ahead with this campaign and others.

An interesting subplot developed because of limited resources in the district to implement the policy. We were informed that every student was not going to be able to provide feedback to every teacher, and we believed this element was critical to building successful student/teacher relationships. This change was removing the relationship piece and making the process based on feedback alone, which is important but also a change from our original vision. As a result, we have come full circle and are working with the district and the union to ensure there are pathways where students can provide constructive feedback directly to every teacher they have, even if it is not included in the teacher's evaluation. In the end, we realized that it is improving the teaching and learning and building relationships that were crucial to our process and belief system. Under current district evaluation policies, student feedback goes directly to the evaluator, bypassing the eyes of the educator. This means that in order for teachers to see what type of feedback and encouragement their students have for them, they will need to continue implementing the constructive feedback survey separately. In Boston, we are continuing to work with BPS to change the procedures so teachers will be able to see the results in the evaluation from their students, so there is no need to conduct two separate surveys, one for constructive feedback and one for teacher evaluation.

As this chapter goes to print, we are pleased to share that we have recently learned that our advocacy has paid off, and BPS is currently selecting a vendor to customize a survey that will reflect all elements of the BSAC-designed constructive feedback tool. Plans are now set for surveys to be administered in every third- through 12th-grade classroom in the district in May 2016. Both teachers and administrators will be able to see the results of the surveys. As we had hoped, survey results will not penalize any teacher, but instead will be used to set goals for the coming year.

This campaign has been a tremendous opportunity for learning patience and persistence, both for young people who inherited the campaign from previous BSAC members and for YOB staff. Fortunately, we have alumni who continue to charge forward and provide some continuity on the campaign and students who continue to see the clear benefits of the process for their own education.

TAKING IT NATIONAL

Developing a national campaign around constructive feedback was a way to connect young people and their allies around a unifying message and build momentum, not just for this specific issue, but also for youth voice in education policy in general. We developed messaging and outreach materials that would enable young people to see how constructive feedback is related to many other issues they were concerned about: high-stakes testing, school pushout, and school climate. By making these connections across the country, young people felt unified and supported in their shared efforts.

After our local and statewide win, we developed a video that documented the first phase of our campaign and has been viewed by thousands of people across the country. We hope it inspired other organizing groups and districts to push for student feedback in the classroom. As word got out nationwide about our local success, students and districts came to us asking for help as they undertook their own campaigns. As a result of these inquiries, we sought support from the Kellogg Foundation and eventually received a three-year grant to develop a manual, website, social-media campaign, and training materials that would help other districts make this campaign their own. Knowing that this is not a one-size-fits-all type of project, with support from the Novo Foundation, we were able to bring together 70 leaders from across the country to talk about what was and wasn't working in their districts. We have provided trainings and support to Providence Student Union, A Better Greenville (Mississippi), New York City, Sanford (Maine), Kentucky, YouthBuild USA, Free Minds Free People, and many other groups that were interested in promoting student voice in the classroom. We developed a social-media campaign on Facebook and a website called www.studentvoicematters.org.

In 2014 YOB/BSAC developed another video that interviews teachers and students about how constructive feedback benefits them in the classroom. Teachers gave specific examples about how student feedback changed and improved their teaching; students discussed how the process made them feel listened to and improved their classroom experience. It is very powerful when students hear the hope and optimism in the voices of other young people who share a common experience and vision for their own education. This video has been viewed by almost 5,000 people. It is critical to remember that this campaign all started when a small group of low-income students of color sat around a table in an underfunded public school in Boston, questioned the status quo, believed things could be improved, developed a clear idea of how to change the education of thousands of their peers, and then acted to make their vision reality.

When we first started to think about having a national campaign, we conducted an extensive Internet search and interviewed numerous organizations and districts across the country. We learned that some districts were using student input into teacher evaluations to punish teachers or push them out of their jobs, instead of using it to improve teaching and learning. In these instances, the policy most often came from the administration instead of from grassroots organizing and the students themselves. We aimed to work with groups at the grassroots level to ensure that relationships and policies are built on trust and mutual respect. We see student feedback to teachers as a crucial indicator of what is going on inside a classroom—more relevant and immediate than standardized test scores or a quick visit by a principal. Student feedback, coupled with administrator assessments, provides a 360-degree view of a teacher. We look forward to working with other schools or districts that are interested in implementing constructive feedback. Feedback can take many forms and still be beneficial: it can be a formal two-page document such as the survey we developed, a suggestion box at the front of the classroom, or a simple weekly or monthly check-in process between teachers and students. Any way to improve communication between teachers and students benefits the relationship and the learning environment. The key element is that students need to be engaged in the process.

THE FUTURE

We feel optimistic about the role of student voice and student engagement in education policy and in other social justice campaigns. Since the economy has improved during the past few years, we are seeing an uptick in the number of organizations interested in putting in the time, resources, and effort it takes to change their organizational structures to ensure young people are partners in decision making. We have been promoting and supporting student voice for a long time, and we understand that there needs to be adequate support and infrastructure to make it work well. Staff and organizations need to be committed, and staff members need to be given the support they need to ensure ongoing success for the young people involved. During the past six months, we have been contacted by at least a half dozen organizations that are ready to move forward in developing new youth policy councils in their schools or organizations, and we are invigorated by this growth in interest. We are doing trainings and consultations in Idaho, New Hampshire, New York City, and other places across the country—we have momentum.

On the national level, there is growing interest in creating a Presidential Youth Council (PYC). YouthBuild USA has been very active in pushing this forward. PYC and more than 40 members of Congress are currently on board. There is also an increased level of organizing around concerns regarding high-stakes testing, education equity, harsh discipline practices, and school push-out. College students across the country are speaking out about racism and violence. Students in Chicago are taking to the streets fighting school closings and police brutality. Organizers are banding together to fight and make real changes on the local and national levels. Coalitions of youth organizers and intragenerational multistakeholder groups are growing, as we are realizing these models are the most successful way to function. New relationships are being made, young people are being inspired, and change is happening all around us. We can feel it in the air in Massachusetts and with our colleagues across the country. Young people are leading this movement. We can't wait to see what's next!

ACKNOWLEDGMENTS

Thank you to Caroline Lau and Debasri Ghosh for their contributions to this piece and to all of the BSAC members for their amazing work through the years.

REFERENCES

Mass. Gen. Laws ch. 71, § 38M, 1971.

Measures of Effective Teaching. (2010). *Learning about teaching: Initial findings from the Measures of Effective Teaching project* [Policy Brief]. Seattle, WA: Bill & Melinda Gates Foundation.

Young, K. S., & Sazama, J. (2006). *15 points: Successfully involving youth in decision-making*. Somerville, MA: Youth on Board.

Youth on Board. (n.d.). We are the ones in the classroom—Ask us! *Student Voice Matters*. Retrieved from http://www.studentvoicematters.org/

17

Participatory Action Research as Youth Activism

Brett G. Stoudt, Caitlin Cahill, Darian X, Kimberly Belmonte, Selma Djokovic, Jose Lopez, Amanda Matles, Adilka Pimentel, and María Elena Torre

> *I was coming home with some friends and the cops had stopped us, and they jumped out the car—and they were, like, told us to put our hands against the wall. And we were like, "What did we do?" and they were just like, "Shut up!" They started patting us down, and I don't really know my rights that well so I didn't know what to say. So I just did what they told me to do basically. And they checked us down and then I'm like, "Oh are you finished and stuff? Can we go?" And they were like "Give me your ID," but at that time I didn't have an ID, so then, he's like, "You know you could go to jail for not having an ID" and I was, like, "We didn't do nothing wrong, we were just walking." So then he's, like oh, "Just be quiet." So, I just shut up. And that's when he ran our names, and that's when he saw we had no warrants, and that's when he was like, "Alright, y'all free to go." And then as we were walking away he said "I better not catch you guys over here again."*
>
> —Stephfon, 17, Brooklyn

The police stopped Stephfon with his friends on their way home from the movies on a Saturday afternoon. His story is not unique. More than a million young people have been stopped by the New York Police Department (NYPD) since 2010, mostly Black and Latin@[1] young men, like Stephfon and his friends. Encounters with the police are part of everyday experiences of securitization for young people growing up in New York City (NYC) (Stoudt, Fine, & Fox, 2011). As Stephfon's testimonial suggests, this experience is fraught and raises critical questions regarding criminalization and the right to have rights that are at the heart of today's social movements demanding an end to the aggressive policing of communities of color. Drawing upon our work with the Researchers for Fair Policing project, we discuss the relationship between participatory action research (PAR) and youth activism, offering insights for practice.

Young people are on the front lines of social movements across the country, challenging state-sanctioned violence, extrajudicial killings, and the surveillance of communities of color. Researchers for Fair Policing was inspired by the same impulse, to do something, to mobilize research as a method of resistance to the carceral state. We began our project with a desire to understand the experiences and attitudes of young people growing up policed in order that we might intervene and help put a stop to the injustice. Our research is informed by the ongoing struggles of young people negotiating discriminatory policing. This is how, in fact, we began our project, with the stories of young people's police encounters, like Stephfon, a member of our research team. Many young people of color in NYC wake up, and the police are in their hallways and their courtyards. They walk to school, and the police are in cars and standing on street corners. They enter school, and the police greet them with metal detectors and are involved all day in school discipline. After school, especially after school, police presence and surveillance are pervasive in their neighborhoods from the moment they leave to the moment they get home. When the officers told Stephfon "I better not catch you around here again," they effectively produced the neighborhood as a criminalized space, what Rashad Shabazz (2015) identifies as the "prisonized landscape" of carceral geographies (p. 43). It is within this context that we began our participatory research focusing on the human costs of Broken Windows policing. In this chapter, we discuss the development of the Researchers for Fair Policing project, with a particular focus upon our survey development and findings. Along the way, we share the principles of PAR, one of the less commonly discussed forms of youth activism.

BACKGROUND

Researchers for Fair Policing is an intergenerational PAR collective from Make the Road New York (see maketheroad.org) and the Public Science Project at the City University of New York (see publicscienceproject.org). We were motivated to examine the impact of current policing practices *on* NYC youth *with* NYC youth *for* NYC youth. Our intergenerational research collective includes community organizers, young people, university professors, and students—all committed to studying what it means to grow up heavily policed in NYC (Stoudt et al., 2011; Stoudt et al., forthcoming). We sought to provide an avenue for young people to be involved in the production of their own knowledge about the policing policies that disproportionally impact their lives. Informed by what Appadurai (2006) identifies as "the right to research," our work is guided by the principle that young people of color can and should ask the questions that frame the research. Appadurai insists that within this political economic context of globalization, which for many is a state of ongoing crisis, research is a right to "systematically increase the stock of knowledge which they consider most vital to their survival as human beings and to their claims as citizens" (p. 168). This is the focus of our work in the face of state-sanctioned violence. We claim the right to research as part of our activism, as another front in our struggle against the carceral state, and as essential to our "right to the city" (Cahill et al., forthcoming; Lefebvre, 1996).

We engaged with PAR not as participation appended to a set of techniques or methodologies (Arnstein, 1969; Cooke & Kothari, 2001), but as a political and epistemological commitment. In the tradition of critical PAR, we set out to document the uneven structural distribution of opportunities and injustice, shifting what we define as "problems" off the backs of individuals and onto systems, structures, and policies (Torre, Fine, Stoudt, & Fox, 2012), here focusing on the geopolitical structures of state-sanctioned surveillances and violence. Our work was guided by the commitment that those most intimately impacted should take the lead in shaping research questions, framing interpretations, and designing meaningful products and actions. Starting with the concerns and questions of youth organizers focused on their everyday experiences with the police, young people of color at Make the Road New York were involved from the beginning in conceptualizing the research and throughout the progression of the project. PAR, as a form of activism, involves ongoing dialogue and critical reflection that moves from personal experiences toward social theorizing through inquiry and analysis. For us, this project was a process of collaborative knowledge production that built upon the capacity of young people and all involved to analyze and transform their own lives and communities (Freire, 1997; Hall, 1992). Reflecting contemporary conceptualizations of youth (Cahill, 2007; Cammarota & Fine, 2008; Torre & Fine, 2006), our partnership understood young people as "agents of change" (Ginwright & James, 2002).

Researchers for Fair Policing developed out of a series of conversations between organizers and researchers in late 2011, the year that the NYPD's aggressive use of "stop-and-frisk" reached its peak at nearly 700,000 people. We were all alarmed not only with the pervasive use of stop-and-frisk but also its guiding theory of public safety known as "Broken Windows" that prevailed for more than 20 years in NYC (Wilson & Kelling, 1982). Broken Windows policing aggressively cracks down on minor offenses such as jumping the turnstile, selling loose cigarettes, holding open containers of alcohol, and biking on the sidewalk, with the intent to maintain order and civility as well as lower or deter serious crime. It is defined by a reliance upon the frequent use of surveillance practices such as stop-and-frisk, asking for IDs, and preventing people from assembling publicly by asking them to "move along." Extensive research has thoroughly critiqued the assumptions and effectiveness of Broken Windows policing (Harcourt, 2001; also see policeandcommunity.org).

We started the project officially in 2012 with these concerns in mind and in the context of Make the Road New York's five-week Summer Youth Action Project. Over the course of the first summer with 15 interested young people of color, two organizers, two professors, and a graduate student, we educated ourselves about the issues by watching videos, collecting newspaper articles, and exploring what was officially being debated and what realities were being portrayed about policing. We shared personal experiences and began to think critically about policing. This is how our project started, but, as the first summer unfolded into four years and the borders of our collective were intentionally designed for inclusivity and flexibility, we grew to include another professor, two additional students, and two more organizers. Some youth researchers moved on and many others joined. We met regularly: sometimes three times a week, other times once a week, other times once a month. Over our many meetings, this project benefited from the energy, knowledge, and skills of numerous young people of color, mostly in high school, as well as adult organizers and university researchers.

Our project started right at the beginning of the current police reform movement in NYC (see changethenypd.org) and a few years before social movements like Black Lives Matter (see blacklivesmatter.com) captivated national attention and reframed the conversation on state-sanctioned violence. Our research should be understood in this light and as part of this burgeoning citywide and now countrywide movement. Young people at Make the Road New York are first and foremost organizers; they are activists. This identity informs our commitment to be accountable to and in dialogue with social justice movements and struggles. Many of the people involved in this project—young people and adults—were and continue to be on the front lines of protests and informing policy at local, state, and national levels.

Our name, Researchers for Fair Policing, reflects the contradictions we engaged at the very foundation of our project: the desire for justice, a motivation to act, and extensive experiential knowledge to inform our inquiry—we wanted to think through just what "fair policing" might look like in the neighborhoods of NYC—particularly in communities of color. With a sense of what Cornel West (2008) calls "critical hope," we held in tension possibilities for community safety that resisted a singular reliance on the omnipresence of police, while analyzing side by side the NYPD data on stop-and-frisk that reflected the clear racial disparity of aggressively proactive policing in communities of color. The paradox of "fair policing" and whether indeed there is even such a thing as "fair policing" within our current racialized political economy and a political culture that uncritically champions order-maintenance (Harcourt, 2001; Wacquant, 2009) marks where the team began, with a desire and many questions.

Beginning with "the understanding that people—especially those who have experienced historic oppression . . . hold deep knowledge about their lives and experiences, and should help shape the questions, [and] frame the interpretations [of research]" (Torre & Fine, 2006, p. 458), our project, over much critical discussion, started with the questions generated with/by youth organizers:

- What are the human costs of Broken Windows policing for young people?
- What experiences do young people have with police and how does that contact look/feel from the perspective of young people?
- In what ways do young people negotiate their environment of constant police surveillance?
- In what ways would young people like to speak back to the NYPD?

Grounded in the experiences of the youth researchers, these questions reflected our desire to enter the larger city policy debate and conversation while, in good faith, wanting to imagine effective solutions or alternatives to Broken Windows policing. Young people of color have long been subjected to criminalization *under* various policing policies and practices, though they are seldom part of the public debate *about* policing policies and practices. This was deeply felt by the young people who participated in our research and was what inspired the project from the outset.

OUR PROCESS: BIG DATA AND OUR DATA

Our research was conceived as a project of "contestation" that "interrogates the gap between dominant ideologies and human lives, using deeply participatory methodologies accountable to the goals of social justice" (Torre et al., 2012, p. 171). Over the course of several years our project developed to encompass qualitative methodologies including focus groups and an archive of more than 30 video testimonials of young people's experiences with the police. With a commitment to creative public scholarship as both a research process and a way of engaging with diverse publics, especially other young people of color, we also employed creative methodologies that included the participatory documentary short *Who's Impacted by Stop & Frisk?*, comic strips, and spoken word performances. In addition, we helped organize a pop-up exhibition, "More than a Quota" (2014), where we displayed our findings and video research. All of the work is featured on our interactive website, ensuring that the results of this research remain in the public sphere (see researchersforfairpolicing.org). However, our research began with a quantitative analysis of the NYPD's own data, and this in turn inspired the development of our Researchers for Fair Policing survey.

Official NYPD data are presented to New Yorkers as "facts," an objective window into policing practices, productivity, and impact. The public generally does not possess the statistical knowledge and access to software needed to (re)explore the raw data sets. In our project, we wanted to analyze and interrogate these "big data" ourselves, to question their validity as "truth," and provide an avenue for young people to actively produce their own knowledge by reframing the public narrative. This is what we call "stats-n-action," where we engage and interrogate data—publicly available and homegrown—in a participatory way with community members (Stoudt, 2016; Stoudt & Torre, 2014). Over the course of the project, we collectively examined the major indicators of Broken Windows policing—including misdemeanors and summonses—but analysis of recorded police stops was an obvious place for our research to start.

At the time our project began, the NYPD's extensive use of stop-and-frisk was the focus of substantial public debate and the raw data had only recently been made publicly accessible. By analyzing and mapping these data across the nine available years (2003–2011), we confirmed that the NYPD's widespread use of stop-and-frisk was, in many ways, a policy focused on youth of color. We learned, for example, that young people were involved in 53% of all the police stops (n = 2,251,296) and of all those millions of incidents 83% were Black and/or Latin@. What this revealed was that Broken Windows policing, as practiced through stop-and-frisk, targeted young people of color and needed to be understood as a racialized youth discriminating policy. We also learned that nearly all of the recorded stops on young people failed to uncover guns (99.81% of the time) and failed to result in a summons and/or an arrest (89%). And, as part of our analyses of the NYPD data, we mapped the geography of stop-and-frisk, demonstrating the geopolitics of policing that targeted whole communities of color. While this may have felt obvious for organizers, activists, and youth of color—we heard many stories of feeling targeted because of race and because of where they live, having done "nothing wrong"—the empirical data represented a powerful validation of their experiences.

Our exploration of the NYPD data also revealed unexpected findings. Youth researchers were surprised to see that the most commonly reported justifications for recorded police stops of young people (2003–2011), according to data produced from the official UF-250 forms that police officers fill out, were "furtive movements" (45%) and contextual factors (64%) like "area has high incidence of reported offense of type under investigation" that had nothing to do with them personally. We also found that 19% of the stops involved young people who "fit relevant description." Markeys, one of the youth researchers, described what this was like:

> When me and my friends were walking in the neighborhood, these two cop cars stopped in front of us and grabbed us and like, they started frisking us, they slammed my friend on the floor. They told us they stopped us because we fit the description; dark skinned, Latino with their pants sagging. They were like, oh that we were sagging. They described our sneakers, they described our hair.

Indeed, the youth researchers were surprised by how discretionary and potentially biased these reasons were and continued to be surprised when looking closer at the justification of frisks, something experienced by many in the group including Markeys and his friends. The most common reason police provided to escalate a stop-and-question into a frisk, again, involved "furtive movements" (65%), an obviously broad and highly subjective category. Another notable discretionary reason involved "inappropriate attire—possibly concealing weapon" (14%). Youth researchers like Markeys noted that the linking of clothing (e.g., hoodie or saggy pants) and other "suspicious" demeanors with criminal behavior is often steeped in racist assumptions, as in you "fit the relevant description [of a Black or Latin@ criminal]." The young people rightly asked, how could the police be continuously so wrong in their discretionary judgment? And, what then was the underlying purpose of this policy?

NYPD data, generally the center of hotly contested public debate, represent police activity from the perspective of police. Collaborative analysis of the NYPD data sets allowed the research team to take control of, explore, map, and interpret NYPD data from the perspective of youth. This allowed us to use the "master's tools" (Lorde, 2003) to begin to dismantle the master's house, and tell a "counterstory" to "refuse dominant constructions of social realities, reveal the fractures in structures, discourses and practices of domination, and indeed, change the subject" (Harris, Carney, & Fine, 2001, p. 6). Our critical engagement with big data, in turn, informed how we developed our own survey, as we wanted to make sure that it could be accurately compared to the NYPD stop-and-frisk data. In this way, we hoped our youth-produced data might stand next to and push back on police data. As Darian, one of the youth researchers on our team and a co-author of this chapter, explained:

We also worked on public NYPD data—we didn't want to just go and reinvent the wheel—as if this data set wasn't available or wasn't around. We actually wanted to take the information that the state was saying was accurate and challenge that with our own youth data, you know, the people who are actually experiencing policing firsthand and on the streets.

Deeply involving those who were most affected by discriminatory policing in the research process created an opportunity to choose the questions young people of color were most interested in asking, reanalyze (or analyze for the first time) "official" data from a youth-oriented standpoint, and then make comparisons between the youth survey and the police data. Our comparative analyses suggest important avenues for advocacy and police reform, as we shall describe.

DEVELOPING OUR SURVEY

We came together as a research collective with a shared commitment to addressing aggressive policing as activists and scholars. All of us had a stake in the project in terms of the integrity of the research, the personal and political implications involved in representation, the production of knowledge, and the potential impacts (Chávez & Soep, 2005). At the same time, we were dedicated to creating diverse democratic spaces of inquiry, what María Elena Torre (2005) identifies as a "participatory contact zone," a messy social space where differently situated people "meet, clash, and grapple with each other" across their varying relationships to power (Pratt, 1992, p. 4). Conceptualizing our work along these lines allowed for textured analysis that took into account differences. This involved paying attention to how we were situated not only in terms of intersectional identifications including race, ethnicity, gender, sexual orientation, and age, but also our different positionalities in terms of our relationship to the police. Our process for developing the survey within a participatory contact zone illustrates our commitment to do work across differences.

Members of our team reconvened to review our meeting notes from when we constructed the survey in the summer/fall of 2012. The notes revealed the rich and complicated discussions we had at the beginning of the process. Adilka, an organizer and co-author of this chapter, described our group's dynamics: "We didn't avoid having the uncomfortable and difficult conversations." Some of the research team members felt, for example, ambivalent about the police, sometimes feeling safer when the police were around and other times feeling targeted by the police or desiring to be treated with dignity and respect but still seeing the need for aggressive policing in their neighborhood. Others wanted the police to stay away and wanted a radical restructuring of the criminal justice system. Another critical debate occurred across gender lines. Some of the young women on our team placed emphasis upon young people's knowledge of their rights when dealing with the police, whereas some young men countered, from experience, that rights do not matter if police disregard your rights, or if you are too afraid to open your mouth in their presence. Encouraging and embracing disagreements as a bright indicator of potential knowledge production, we incorporated these tensions into our survey. Debates like these informed the questions we asked and, later, our analyses. In this way the process of developing our survey was itself a space for developing and testing our theories. For example, concerned with how stereotypes effectively ontologized young people of color as criminal (Cacho, 2012), we created a line of inquiry, based on examples from our discussions, to document and explore how young people negotiate, experience, and resist this characterization.

Adopting what feminist scholar Sandra Harding (1993) calls "strong objectivity," which honors the rigor of situated knowledge, we were committed to exploring competing perspectives in our process of survey development. In this way, our work reflects new ways of thinking about validity, revising metrics of expertise that expand our understandings of research and its relationship to activism and everyday life (Torre et al., 2012). We engaged with *expert validity*, reflecting our commitment to deep participation and contesting and opening up traditional views of expertise that foreground the wisdom of young people who have much experience negotiating structural systems. At the same time, keeping in mind the ways that policies such as Broken Windows policing are rooted in a historical context of urban disinvestment, we also paid attention to critical questions of *ecological validity* that theorizes the way a "problem" can be understood at multiple scales and levels of analysis, from the intimate to the global, or the micro to the macro. This was especially significant for our research as we designed our survey in a way that would contextualize our understandings of the structural, social, and spatial relations of policing (Torre et al., 2012).

Some of the most important openings in our survey development reflected intersectional identifications along race, gender, sexual orientation, and geography. For example, we piloted drafts of the survey with other young people. We asked them for feedback about which questions they thought could be cut since our survey was too long initially. We found that some differences of opinion fell along gender lines. Young women wanted to cut the open-ended qualitative questions, while young men, who had experienced being stopped by the police more often, felt it was very important to hold spaces for richer responses about these experiences, especially items that deepened our understanding, such as how/if young people's feelings about the police had changed over time. On the other hand, it was young women of color and young people who identified as LGBTQ (particularly trans identified) who encouraged us to develop questions focused on sexual identity and unwanted sexual attention. These issues were seldom discussed and raised important questions to pursue as a way to resist simply collecting data that reproduced the dominant narratives of the heavily policed Black male. We found that questions like these, emerging from diverse participatory contact zones, were important in helping us redefine and broadly document young people's relationships with police.

Taking seriously the agreements and the disagreements in our ongoing discussions, these consistencies and inconsistencies provided confirmation for the importance of survey questions, provided validity checks in the construction of the survey, and suggested types of analyses we should run that focused on critical questions of intersectionality that are obfuscated in the NYPD data. Excavating our differences, working in participatory contact zones, and taking seriously participatory conceptualizations of validity informed how we produced knowledge and, in turn, what we learned. After many drafts and discussions, we designed a nine-page survey with five sections. The first section involved experiences with stops, questioning, frisks, searches, and the criminal justice system. The second section asked about both encounters with the police and the socioemotional experience of these interactions. The third section asked about specific experiences with police in their neighborhood, including witnessing police activity, calling the police for help, and attitudes toward police. The fourth section asked about school discipline and experiences with school safety agents, school police, and security guards. And the fifth section asked demographic questions such as gender, race/ethnicity, and sexual orientation. We ended the survey with several open-ended questions to allow space for young people to describe their experiences, questions, and concerns in their own words and on their own terms.

Once the survey was finalized, we distributed them to young people in NYC between the ages of 14 and 25 using a series of online and hardcopy strategies that combined education and organizing with data collection. For example, we recruited principals from public schools who allowed us to distribute the surveys in classrooms. Youth researchers designed a classroom presentation/workshop beginning with a brief introductory activity and then concluding with a debriefing discussion about taking the survey, policing, as well as civic engagement. In this way, they made the survey data collection a peer-to-peer educational event. We reached young people not currently associated with school (e.g., pushed/dropped out, graduated) online through a large network of organizations across NYC. We also "tabled" at neighborhood events organized by Make the Road New York and other youth-oriented organizations; gave surveys to family, friends, and acquaintances; and canvased neighborhood sidewalks, distributing surveys to young people passing by. This allowed youth researchers, once the survey was completed, to hold discussions or circulate information related to police reform and other campaigns (e.g., voter registration, know-your-rights education). Additionally, all respondents received as incentive a glow-in-the-dark wristband (a popular item with youth) designed by youth researchers that said, "Stand up, Speak Back" and "Researchers for Fair Policing" to carry forward the message of the collective even after the survey experience was over. These strategies helped us capture a range of attitudes and experiences from 1,084 young New Yorkers, nearly all of color, while also providing opportunities for youth activism.

WHAT WE LEARNED

The collaborative development of our methods and subsequent participatory analyses provide an illustration of how young people's expertise informed the validity of our research. Here we focus on what we learned from our survey of young people living throughout NYC and how this work reflects a process of theory building that is relevant to youth activism and policymaking. Young people of color ages 14–25 years were among the most directly impacted by Broken Windows policing. We chose to focus entirely on them in our survey analysis and throughout the larger study (for more discussion of the video testimonials and other methods see Cahill et al., forthcoming; Stoudt et al., forthcoming).

We structured our survey in such a way that we could explore individual incidents rather than individual people. This allowed our results to be comparable with the NYPD data and served as a platform to gain richer information unobtainable from the NYPD data. For example, a startling finding was the large difference in how the NYPD recorded searches on young people of color and how the young people of color who took our survey perceived their searches. The NYPD data showed that for young people of color ages 14–25 years between 2010 and 2013, 9% of all the recorded stops by police ultimately involved a search. Our survey data of the same age group and over the same years revealed something very different. We found that nearly half (46%) of all the stops reported in our survey resulted in a search and of those, nearly all (86%) were *without* consent. What this demonstrates is that from the perspectives of many young people of color who took our survey, they felt as though they were searched even if the police actions did not technically constitute a search. Or, significantly, we wondered if perhaps the NYPD was not recording all their searches. And, of equal significance, we wondered if perhaps the NYPD was frequently not seeking consent, as is the person's right under most circumstances.

These findings and subsequent questions/concerns about the experiences of police searches are obviously quite important for youth activism and organizing. Many of the young people involved in our project also did trainings with other youth about their rights during police encounters. Our findings highlighted the continued need for more trainings, so that all young New Yorkers know how they can assert their rights during a stop, know under what circumstances police can lawfully search, and especially, know that they are not required to consent. Additionally, our findings reinforced the need for a critical policy reform measure, the Right to Know Act (see changethenypd .org), intended to help lower the rates of unconstitutional searches by requiring police to explain to people they have the right to refuse searches and obtain proof when people consent to a search. We used these data to testify in support of this bill at a city council hearing.

We also structured our survey in such a way that we could extend *beyond* the individual incidents found in the NYPD data to explore the experiences of individual people. By doing this, we gained greater insight into how experiences of police contact accumulated in the same Black and Brown bodies over a relatively short few years—this was information unavailable from the NYPD data. For example, many youth researchers told stories of police stopping them frequently—sometimes even hundreds of times since they were preteens. Our survey revealed that many youth of color held similar narratives. We learned that of the young people of color we surveyed, more than half (53%) were stopped at least once between 2010 and 2013. Of those who were stopped, 76% were stopped more than once and 31% were stopped five or more times. Later, in our video testimonials and focus groups, it was not uncommon for young people to indicate they were stopped countless times in their young lives.

Our survey indicated that nearly every young person of color (89%) had contact with police at least once between 2010 and 2013. Additionally, we were able to learn about the types and quality of that police contact from a youth perspective, something obviously not present in the NYPD data. Our youth researchers shared story after story about how the police were omnipresent in their everyday lives. They were frequently asked to move in various public and private activities and spaces and constantly surveilled in their homes, on the streets, and in the schools. Collectively, we mapped these stories as part of our process of understanding the uneven geography of policing and how young people respond to the unceasing presence of the carceral state. Because the youth researchers prioritized these experiences as important to ask their peers about, we included questions on our survey about places and activities where young people might encounter police. We constructed multiple questions that focused on each of these separate spaces (e.g., were you "asked to show ID in or just outside your apartment building"; were you "taken into a private room to be searched by school safety agents, school police or security guards"; were you "told to move while standing on the street corner"?) as well as many questions about negotiating surveillance. As a result of this process, we learned that most young people of color (57%) who took our survey have been asked to move by police at least once since 2010. We learned that 51% had direct contact with police surveillance practices in the street, 44% in or around their homes, and 51% with School Safety Agents (or school police). We learned that 75% of the young people of color who took our survey reported that they regularly felt and thought about police surveillance, while 41% reported using coping strategies to negotiate the police surveillance. Documenting this type of spatially organized data was important so that we could establish a stronger understanding of the relationship between policing, the privatization of public space, and the gentrification of our communities (Cahill et al., forthcoming).

Meaningful differences also emerged along lines of gender. We found that many youth researchers, and in particular young men of color, told stories of negative contact with police such as being spoken to with disrespect and, at times, experiencing extreme force. Young women of color, meanwhile, explained that while police might not stop them as frequently as young men, they experienced other types of negative police contact. For example, young women told stories of sexualized street harassment perpetrated by police. We developed our survey to help us understand the breadth and depth of what police contact specifically looked and felt like, and so we included questions about verbal and physical violence as well as sexual violence. As a result, we learned that of those who had contact with police, more than half (57%) of the young people of color had experienced at least one negative encounter—at least one unhelpful, discourteous, unprofessional, disrespectful, aggressive, and/or violent encounter with police. Nearly a quarter of the young people of color reported physical abuse (23%). This involved police force ranging from being pushed, kicked, or punched to being hit with a baton, tased, or having a gun pulled. And, as suspected, young men were more than twice as likely to report physical abuse as compared to young women (32% to 13%). Equally troubling, though not as often discussed as physical violence, our survey revealed that a fifth (20%) of the young people experienced verbal violence during their police encounters. This involved experiences with police that ranged from violent threats to racist or homophobic slurs (no substantial gender differences emerged). Outrageously, 7% of the young people of color reported experiencing sexual attention (e.g., "whistles," "catcalls" "sexualizing stares," "asked for my phone number"), including being asked for sexual favors from police. As the youth researchers predicted, young women were six times as likely to report sexual attention as compared to young men (12% to 2%). These are data not collected by the NYPD (not surprisingly), and they highlight the importance of youth–oriented/generated surveys to shed grounded light on what many young people of color are experiencing all too frequently.

REFRAMING THE PUBLIC NARRATIVE THROUGH PAR

While all research asks questions of purpose, PAR explicitly engages the intertwined questions of purpose and publics throughout the process. In our case, we came together as a team with the shared commitment to produce research addressing the policing crisis in NYC and the urgent concerns of young people of color. However, there have been many social, political, and economic shifts over the past several years. Since we started our project in 2012, NYC has elected a new mayor, Bill de Blasio, who ran on a platform of ending stop-and-frisk policies. Yet, despite a federal court decision determining that stop-and-frisk as practiced by the NYPD was illegally conducted and racially biased, violating the Fourth and Fourteenth Amendments (*Floyd, et al. v. City of New York*), Mayor de Blasio (re)appointed Police Commissioner William Bratton, who had previously served as NYC commissioner in 1994 under Mayor Rudy Giuliani and was credited as the father of Broken Windows policing (Giuliani & Bratton, 1994). Most significantly, we did not anticipate the powerful social movements that have captured national attention in the wake of Michael Brown's killing in Ferguson and, closer to home, the police killings of Eric Garner and Akai Gurley. There is a dramatic shift in public consciousness that has changed the nature of how we understand the significance of our research and our potential contributions to reframing the public narrative about policing from the perspective of young people of color.

Collectively, we have grappled with how we might strategically position our research to be "of use" (Fine & Barreras, 2004), knowing that the relationship between scholarship and social change is not straightforward. If social inequities such as the related violence of patriarchy, racism, and poverty that are at the heart of our focus on aggressive policing are not cognitive problems (in other words, not a matter of the public needing more information), how might we contribute to change? Fine and Barreras (2004) argue that social change "is a long haul that demands the engagement of multiple players, relying upon multiple discourses, working on multiple levels and constantly (re)forming allies" (p. 179). With this in mind we discuss our theoretical findings; how we mobilized our research for multiple publics, and our contributions to reframing the public debate about policing.

Staeheli and Mitchell (2005) suggest that how we frame our research matters and that it is crucial to frame our findings in a way that allows people to understand how the results might actually affect day-to-day practice. With these insights in mind, we developed analytic frameworks to contest the underlying logic and assumptions of Broken Windows policing and to offer a "counterstory," a new narrative for understanding young people's experiences with police. First, we argue that Broken Windows policing itself produces "disorder" by severing community relationships and creating a hostile environment in the public and private spaces of young people's everyday lives. Our analysis is based on findings from our survey, video testimonials, and focus groups, all of which offer a fine-grained and nuanced picture of how Broken Windows policing functions as a racialized method of spatial and social control for young people of color. As Markeys explained, "It makes me feel like I shouldn't even come outside anymore if I'm just gonna get harassed by a policeman that's supposed to be protecting me." Further, our historical and contextual research demonstrates that the "disorder" that Broken Windows policing seeks to "contain" is a deeply rooted structural issue (re)produced in policies over many years that we think would be best addressed within and by communities, using an assets-based approach to strengthening communities and building capacity.

This leads us to our second critical frame: that young people's experiences of overpolicing are intimately connected with other forms of dispossession. At the same time that young Black and Brown people are being policed on an everyday basis in NYC, rents are going up, and families are being displaced from their neighborhoods. School discipline and suspension rates are often too high, graduation rates too low, and few living-wage jobs are available. This intense policing and heavy surveillance contributes to an overall feeling of dispossession and the sense that people do not feel as if they have rights to, or ownership of, their communities. Policing is not experienced in a vacuum. Along these lines, our research points to the necessity of rethinking police reform and reframing the public debate about policing, in terms of community investment.

Finally, another important frame in our research is that the everyday experience of policing impacts the whole community. While the police may be most focused on young men of color, Broken Windows policing is experienced collectively as a community under siege. Our research demonstrates the aggressive police presence in the everyday spaces of people's lives, most importantly in the home, school, and neighborhood public spaces—key sites of social reproduction. Our testimonials make clear the implications of aggressive policing upon family members, mothers who worry about their sons, little brothers and sisters watching their big brother being handcuffed, and grandmothers who are tired of opening the door to the police. For each of these analytical frames we have data that offer insights into particular questions and policies, but our overall project suggests how we might change the public conversation.

Committed to making a meaningful contribution to social change beyond an "armchair revolution" (Freire, 1997), we want to reach publics beyond the academy. Taking seriously the political nature of knowledge production and the question of impact, as well as the form in which we present our research, we grappled with the following questions: How might our analysis inform a sense of responsibility and incite the possibility for change? What is our research asking audiences to do? And, finally, how might our research effectively provoke actions that feed organizing campaigns, theoretically reframe the issues, nudge those in power, and/or motivate audiences to shift how they think and act in the world (Cahill & Torre, 2007)? With this in mind, we have developed multiple products including our website (researchersforfair policing.org), videos, exhibitions, and spoken word performances by and for young people.

A critical front of our work as activist scholars was to find avenues through our research for youth to engage meaningfully in the public debates and important policy decisions that directly affect their lives. The rigor of our systematically collected data combined with youth-oriented findings have proven highly valuable in our efforts to insert our data into the political process at the city and national levels. At the city level, we have had multiple opportunities to testify to the New York City Council in various committee hearings. For example, Darian presented our findings at the Public Safety hearing, "Examining Community Policing in NYC." Establishing his authority and expertise as more than a young man of color who has been stopped relentlessly by the police, Darian also presented himself as a researcher. This changed the nature of the conversation, as he was able to use a set of persuasive rhetorical strategies that combined the collective weight of survey statistics, "Our survey discovered that 66% of young people believe that the police discriminate," with the intimacy of direct interview quotes and his own personal experiences. Backed by data, he convincingly explained to city council members, "Throughout the research process we have learned there is a beckoning call for true systemic change" and then described important reforms drawing upon our analytic research frameworks described above. In the ensuing question and answer period, Darian held a command of data (ours and others') to support his points, define his own narrative, and even push back on how policymakers framed the issues. For example, he addressed a question about the efficacy of Broken Windows policing, saying, "As a driving theory, it is flawed and there have been no data or statistical proof that it works in any form or capacity."

When some policymakers sought potential alternatives to Broken Windows policing, Darian rejected this as too myopic a premise, drawing upon our analytic frames to rethink police reform as community development:

> It is about total reinvestment in our communities of color. . . . Crime is caused by lack of housing, lack of job opportunities, lack of sound

educational systems and institutions, lack of extracurricular things for our young people to get involved in after school. After school, young people are going back to homes where their parents have to work until 9, 10 o'clock at night to support them, so there is no one home when they get back there. There is nothing but the community that has been criminalized, that has been broken down systemically, so what we need to do is really uphold, support, and reinvest in young people in communities of color.

Where city council members wanted to focus on a particular policy reform, Darian, as an activist and researcher, resisted and called for a complete reorganization of the state's relationship to communities of color. Darian's standpoint of comprehensive reform and his experience thinking about research, measurement, and outcomes allowed him to also effectively address questions connected with statistically tracking police reform on communities of color. Again, he resisted myopic solutions:

I feel like graduation rates [are] a great way to track outcomes. Are more of our young people graduating? Are less of our young people in prison? . . . Are the suspension rates going down? These are trackable ways of seeing if improvement is really happening in our community. Do more people have access to jobs then they did when we started this program? . . . Right now, we can see that people are underemployed, undereducated, overworked, underaccredited with humanity and dignity as a person. So can we track human dignity? No. We cannot, but we can definitely track a community's progression and growth. Are there more institutions that support this community? Are there more banks that give loans to developers that build low-income houses in this community?

This was neither the first time nor the last time that members of Researchers for Fair Policing would draw upon our research to help frame the police reform discussion from the perspective of young people of color. The collective meaning making that emerged from the entire participatory research *process*, not only the actual findings, has proven a valuable and grounded source to draw upon as the members of our team were given opportunities not only in NYC but also at the national level. For example, Jose Lopez, co-principal investigator of the Researchers for Fair Policing project, longtime leader in police reform organizing, and a co-author of this chapter, was one of the 11 members appointed by President Obama's Task Force on Policing. Our collective theorizing and research informed how Jose participated in the task force, and the research team submitted testimony to the president's task force, sharing our research and its implications for national criminal justice reform. The act of doing participatory research and producing collective knowledge is embodied, and each of our team members has found ways to engage our work and our participatory process in our activist, organizing, and political activities.

Ruth Wilson Gilmore (2007) notes, "In scholarly research, answers are only as good as the further questions they provoke, while for activists answers are only as good as the tactics they make possible" (p. 27). Our research held this idea in productive tension, moving between theory and practice, with a commitment to public science for the public good, as defined by young people of color on their own terms. From our research partnership, Adilka and Darian, organizers at Make the Road New York, came to understand how research could inform their activism: "So this research," Darian reflected months after the city council hearing, "is definitely helping to fuel our policy arguments, and that's the biggest takeaway from this research project. . . . I think that is the most important thing." In fact, as Adilka came to realize, "Research and activism go hand in hand. They go hand in hand because these are the folks who are living this, right?"

ACKNOWLEDGMENTS

Special thanks to The Adco Foundation; Antipode Foundation; Graduate Center, CUNY; Institute for Human Geography; John Jay College of Criminal Justice, CUNY; Make the Road New York; Pratt Center for Community Development; Pratt Institute; Public Science Project; Sociological Initiatives Foundation; and the Taconic Fellowship.

NOTE

1. For young people who identified as Latino or Latina, "@" combines both the masculine "o" and feminine "a" for gender-neutrality.

REFERENCES

Appadurai, A. (2006). The right to research. *Globalisation, Societies and Education*, 4(2), 167–177. http://dx.doi.org/10.1080/14767720600750696

Arnstein, S. R. (1969). A ladder of citizen participation. *Journal of the American Institute of Planners*, 35(4), 216–224. http://dx.doi.org/10.1080/01944366908977225

Cacho, L. M. (2012). *Social death: Racialized rightlessness and the criminalization of the unprotected.* New York, NY: NYU Press.

Cahill, C. (2007). Doing research with young people: Participatory research and the rituals of collective work. *Children's Geographies*, 5(3), 297–312. http://dx.doi.org /10.1080/14733280701445895

Cahill, C., Stoudt, B. G., Matles, A., Agostini, D., Belmonte, K., Djokovic, S., . . . Torre, M. E. (forthcoming). The right to the sidewalk: The struggle over broken window policing, young people, and NYC streets. In J. Hou & S. Knierbein (Eds.), *City unsilenced: Urban resistance and public space in the age of shrinking democracy.* London: Routledge.

Cahill, C., & Torre, M. E. (2007). Beyond the journal article: Representations, audience, and the presentation of participatory action research. In S. Kindon, R. Pain, & M. Kesby (Eds.), *Connecting people, participation and place: Participatory action research approaches and methods* (pp. 196–206). London: Routledge.

Cammarota, J., & Fine, M. (Eds.). (2008). *Revolutionizing education: Youth participatory action research in motion.* New York, NY: Routledge.

Chávez, V., & Soep, E. (2005). Youth radio and the pedagogy of collegiality. *Harvard Educational Review, 75*(4), 409–434. http://dx.doi.org/10.17763/haer.75.4.827u 365446030386

Cooke, B., & Kothari, U. (Eds.). (2001). *Participation: The new tyranny?* London: Zed Books.

Fine, M., & Barreras, R. (2004). To be of use. *Analyses of Social Issues and Public Policy, 1*(1), 175–182. http://dx.doi.org/10.1111/1530-2415.00012

Freire, P. (1997). *Pedagogy of the oppressed.* Harmondsworth, Middlesex: Penguin Books.

Gilmore, R. W. (2007). *Golden gulag: Prisons, surplus, crisis, and opposition in globalizing California.* Berkeley, CA: University of California Press.

Ginwright, S., & James, T. (2002). From assets to agents of change: Social justice, organizing, and youth development [Special issue]. *New Directions for Youth Development, 2002*(96), 27–46. http://dx.doi.org/10.1002/yd.25

Giuliani, R. W., & Bratton, W. J. (1994). *Police strategy no. 5: Reclaiming the public spaces of New York.* New York, NY: New York Police Department.

Hall, B. L. (1992). From margins to center? The development and purpose of participatory research. *American Sociologist, 23*(4), 15–28. http://dx.doi.org/10.1007/BF02691928

Harcourt, B. E. (2001). *Illusion of order: The false promise of broken windows policing.* Cambridge, MA: Harvard University Press.

Harding, S. (1993). Rethinking standpoint epistemology: What is "strong objectivity"? In L. Alcoff & E. Potter (Eds.), *Feminist epistemologies* (pp. 49–82). New York, NY: Routledge.

Harris, A., Carney, S., & Fine, M. (2001). Counter work: Introduction to "Under the covers: Theorising the politics of counter stories." In M. Fine & A. M. Harris (Eds), *Under the covers: Theorising the politics of counter stories* (pp. 6–18). London: Lawrence & Wishart.

Lefebvre, H. (1996). *The right to the city.* Oxford: Blackwell.

Lorde, A. (2003). The master's tools will never dismantle the master's house. In R. Lewis & S. Mills (Eds.), *Feminist postcolonial theory: A reader* (pp. 25–28). New York, NY: Routledge.

Pratt, M. L. (1992). *Imperial eyes: Travel writing and transculturation.* London: Routledge.

Shabazz, R. (2015). *Spatializing blackness: Architectures of confinement and black masculinity in Chicago*. Urbana, IL: University of Illinois Press.

Staeheli, L. A., & Mitchell, D. (2005). The complex politics of relevance in geography. *Annals of the Association of American Geographers, 95*(2), 357–372. http://dx.doi.org/10.1111/j.1467-8306.2005.00464.x

Stoudt, B. G. (2016). Conversations on the margins: Using data entry to explore the qualitative potential of survey marginalia. *Qualitative Psychology*. Retrieved from http://www.apa.org/pubs/journals/qua/

Stoudt, B. G., Cahill, C., Lopez, J., Torre, M. E., Pimentel, A., Matles, A., . . . Djokovic, S. (forthcoming). *A young person's guide to broken windows policing: The punishments, insecurities and contradictions of growing up policed in NYC*. New York, NY: Public Science Project and Make the Road New York.

Stoudt, B., Fine, M., & Fox, M. (2011). Growing up policed. *NY Law School Law Review, 56*, 1331–1370. Retrieved from http://www.nylslawreview.com/

Stoudt, B., & Torre, M. (2014). The Morris Justice Project: Participatory action research. In *SAGE Research Methods Cases*. London: SAGE Publications. http://dx.doi.org/10.4135/978144627305014535358

Torre, M. E. (2005). The alchemy of integrated spaces: Youth participation in research collectives of difference. In L. Weis & M. Fine (Eds.), *Beyond silenced voices* (pp. 251–266). Albany, NY: State University of New York Press.

Torre, M. E., & Fine, M. (2006). Researching and resisting: Democratic policy research by and for youth. In S. Ginwright, P. Noguera, & J. Cammarota (Eds.), *Beyond resistance! Youth activism and community change: New democratic possibilities for practice and policy for America's youth*. New York, NY: Routledge.

Torre, M. E., Fine, M., Stoudt, B. G., & Fox, M. (2012). Critical participatory action research as public science. In H. Cooper, P. M. Camic, D. L. Long, A. T. Panter, D. Rindskopf, & K. J. Sher (Eds.), *APA handbook of research methods in psychology, Vol 2: Research designs: Quantitative, qualitative, neuropsychological, and biological* (pp. 171–184). Washington, DC: American Psychological Association.

Wacquant, L. (2009). *Punishing the poor: The neoliberal government of social insecurity*. Durham, NC: Duke University Press.

West, C. (2008). *Hope on a tightrope: Words and wisdom*. Carlsbad, CA: Hay House.

Wilson, J. Q., & Kelling, G. L. (1982). Broken windows. *Atlantic Monthly, 249*(3), 29–38. Retrieved from http://www.theatlantic.com/doc/198203/broken-windows

18

In Defense of Education Justice: Postsecondary Institutional Decision Making for American Indian Programs and Services

Jessica Ann Solyom

American Indian enrollment in higher education has more than tripled over the past 35 years—from 76,100 in 1976 (Freeman & Fox, 2005) to 252,314 in 2011 (Ginder & Kelly-Reid, 2013). Despite an increase in the number of associate's, bachelor's, and master's degrees conferred, American Indians remain the least likely group to be enrolled in colleges or universities and simultaneously experience the lowest graduation rates from postsecondary institutions (Brayboy, Fann, Castagno, & Solyom, 2012). In *Official Encouragement, Institutional Discouragement: Minorities in Academe*, William Tierney (1992) suggests low enrollment can be explained, in part, by an attitude of official encouragement and institutional discouragement. In other words, although universities position themselves as supporters of diversity and diverse perspectives, they remain inhospitable to the needs and desires of Native[1] students and their communities. This chapter presents the findings of a qualitative case study of American Indian student activists at a public four-year university who opposed institutional processes that reduced access to Native student programs and services.[2] The students' experiences illustrate how institutional claims to welcome diverse students and their perspectives are negated when objections to internal processes and decisions are raised.

In the spring of 2007 student concerns began to arise when a popular Native professor of Indigenous education resigned without replacement. That same semester, course advertisements that relied on racist and stereotypical messaging to promote courses in the Ethnic Studies program were circulated while the residence halls, in a similar vein, advertised a "Cowboys & Indians" themed mixer. This, the activists argued, marked the beginning of a reduction in services and personnel as well as a campus climate that felt unwelcoming to Native peoples.

In the following fall semester, the university was awarded two federal grants totaling more than $2.1 million to continue running its nationally acclaimed Native Teacher Preparation Program (NTPP). Almost immediately, rumors began circulating that administrators would return the monies and terminate the program, which prepared Native students to teach in Indian-serving communities and schools. To make matters worse, the sole Native American academic adviser responsible for serving Native students resigned, leaving no staff member available to procure university support for its annual student-hosted community powwow. Sacrificing their study time, the activists came together to advocate for university support for the powwow. Their resulting struggle illustrated how the lack of contingency planning for American Indian–serving personnel imperils community-serving events, programming, and student academic success. The semester ended with increased frustration when the university's historic use of a local tribal name and Indigenous iconography to promote its athletic teams continued to inspire the unabated promotion of racist and offensive messages during NCAA-sanctioned events.

The semester ended with increased frustration when racist and offensive messages referencing Indigenous peoples during an NCAA-sanctioned event went unabated. Although aware that the institution's use of an American Indian mascot can sometimes prompt rival fans to display ignorant and insensitive comments, they were outraged by the university's lack of enforcement of respectful usage. That semester one fan chose to engage in banter by making light of historic injustices by displaying a series of signs at a volleyball game. The first suggested the game was to be a "Trail of Tears Part II," while the second threatened to send the home team "back to the reservation."

The spring of 2008 ushered in another semester without a Native student adviser, leaving students without course advising and without a skilled liaison to guide, advocate, or coordinate services between the students' tribal communities and the institution. That spring the university officially returned the NTPP grant monies, effectively dismantling the program—a decision that angered students who believed it violated the university's demonstrated respect for Native peoples' political and educational rights. First, it was undertaken without consultation with partnering tribal communities. Second, since the grant funding was the result of historic treaty agreements to promote education for Native peoples, the students believed the decision suggested a lack of understanding and respect for Native peoples' guaranteed access to education. To appease growing tensions, administrators hired an Indigenous director for its American Indian Resource Center, the first since

1996, but the director left seven months later, citing lack of institutional and professional support.

Throughout this time, students sought to work with administrators to address each issue separately, but lack of progress and frustration came to a head in the fall of 2008 when the university granted an independent merchant, and university alumnus, a vendor's license to sell products featuring stereotypical and culturally offensive depictions of Native peoples. Citing lack of progress or any demonstration of intentional sustained efforts to ameliorate their concerns, the students staged two public protests to raise public support for their struggles. The remainder of this chapter examines how the institution and local community responded to the protests. Study findings suggest that when Native student voices were subverted in mainstream media, youth found alternative ways to rally support and voice their concerns to the larger public and garner support for their cause. I conclude by discussing the implications of these findings.

STUDY BACKGROUND

Scholarship on the experiences, needs, and desires of Native students in higher education remains small but growing. Researchers are increasingly paying attention, not just to the challenges faced by American Indian/Alaska Native students, but also to the factors and experiences that contribute to their persistence and graduation (Brayboy et al., 2012; Shotton, Lowe, & Waterman, 2013). In order to understand the experiences of Native students, it is important to understand the postsecondary context many face.

Nationally, American Indian students are significantly underrepresented in postsecondary settings and account for only 1.1% of total enrollment in colleges and universities and only 0.5% of faculty members at degree-granting institutions (DeVoe, Darling-Churchill, & Snyder, 2008). In line with national trends, Native students remain the lowest enrolled population at the university featured in this study, which I refer to as Mountain State University (MSU).[3] In the fall of 2013, 145 American Indian students were enrolled, comprising less than 0.5% of the total enrollment population (Office of Budget & Institutional Analysis, 2013). Low student enrollment at MSU means the presence of American Indians on campus is largely reduced to Indigenous iconography, inspired by the institution's mascot, seen on campus flyers, websites, athletic stadiums, and buildings.

In general, American Indian students are also more likely to enroll in public and/or two-year institutions than any other institution type. Of those who attend postsecondary institutions, almost 77% attend public two- and four-year colleges and universities. This is important to note as public institutions like MSU are more likely to utilize American Indian mascots, athletic nicknames, and imagery in an ahistorical, racially hostile, or abusive manner, despite the objections of Indigenous peoples (American Psychological Association, 2005; Brayboy et al., 2012; Hofmann, 2005; National Collegiate Athletic Association, 2005; National Congress of American Indians, 2013).

In order to improve the recruitment, retention, and graduation rates of Native students, it is not only important to understand their academic and institutional context but also their unique needs and experiences. Indigenous students who strongly identify with their communities often report attending higher education in order to give back to their community and/or help address current issues (Brayboy et al., 2012). However, a lack of mentors, advising, resources, and hard funding for Native-serving programs is an often overlooked but commonly reported set of factors influencing persistence (Barnhardt, 1994; Brayboy et al., 2012). Despite the desire to give back, the prevalence of racism and policies inconsistent with the goal of supporting Indigenous students across college campuses influences campus context and interferes with student success (Brayboy et al., 2012).

Activism Begins Behind the Scenes with Civil Discussion Before It Goes Public

Engaging in activism is not uncommon for college students, yet media reporting of American Indian student activism remains scant. However, lack of robust reporting does not mean Native students do not engage in activism. Since the 1960s students have called for culturally relevant and historically accurate courses as well as an end to the use of racially offensive mascots across the country.

This study suggests that one reason why media reporting on Native student protests remains low could be that Native students seek to address their concerns in private, dealing directly with university leaders, before drawing public attention to themselves. The behind-the-scenes activism of students in this study included reaching out to various staff members to discuss their concerns. Citing institutional policy and limitations within their own professional positions, staff members stated they could not help but directed them to university administrators who might. The students then met with members of the central administration who listened briefly but politely but invited them to leave their offices when the conversation became uncomfortable. At this time students began to note an important pattern: when Native students, staff, or faculty questioned campus climate or the various initiatives and decisions that limit the scope of opportunities available to them, university leadership responded with ambivalence or punitive actions.

Feeling their concerns were not being met with genuine interest or empathy, the group began to worry. They knew that as "a minority group, which is directly affected by a policy," they did not have the strength in numbers to influence their own destiny (Hofmann, 2005, p. 166). Thus staging walkouts or demonstrations alone would not help. They needed to increase their number of supporters. In late 2008 they staged two rallies and marched from the American Indian Resource Center, located on the outskirts of campus, to central campus, where the offices of the president and highest administrators are housed (Berry, 2009; Fulton, 2008; Gardiner, 2008; Leonard, 2008; Yurth, 2008).

Days prior to the events, protestors issued a media press release outlining the purpose of the march and the group's overall mission, stating:

> Our march through campus will showcase our urge for institutional support from [Mountain State University] for American Indian Educational Equity. While the university states that its mission is to enrich the educational experiences of the campus community; enable individuals to progress, thrive and succeed without barriers, and; encourage and invite everyone to join in their effort. The actions of the university over the last year and a half, demonstrates that [they have] not upheld this mission when working with American Indian peoples. In fact, it has continually violated the rights and sovereignty of American Indians in multiple ways. Any time an American Indian leader, student or support has resisted or voiced concern/opposition toward university policies—they have been met with hostility and alienation. This tension has built up so much that critical university leaders, faculty, and staff have been forced to leave the institution by both termination and choice.
>
> By marching together we hope to raise awareness of the university's attempts to silence American Indian students, staff, and faculty who protest university policies that ultimately alienate, divide and destroy American Indian communities; urge the university to uphold its commitment to Native communities by creating scholarships and programs that exist, in reality, to support Native students; and, gain community support to lend a voice to these issues and to call for an investigation into the treatment of Native peoples at [MSU].

At the event, they carried signs with examples of how the athletic nickname has been misused by sports fans at university events. Others reinforced the argument that Native students should be better supported if the institution is going to truly "honor" them and improve their enrollment and graduation rates. A few students distributed handouts further outlining the full list of injustices and invited attendees to aid in calling for an investigation into these university decisions and practices.

TRIANGULATING AGENDA SETTING THEORY, CRITICAL RACE THEORY, AND TRIBALCRIT

In this section I examine media coverage of the protests and their public impact, outlining how the students' stories were communicated to the public and how the media, as a filter and facilitator of information, (re)interpreted their concerns and purpose. I also consider how the university and outlying communities understood and framed the students' protests and struggles and, subsequently, responded to them. To accomplish this analysis, I integrate a media-based theory, Agenda Setting Theory, with theories on race and power, TribalCrit and Critical Race Theory.

According to Agenda Setting Theory (AST), the media can influence public opinion and thoughts about particular topics. McCombs and Bell (1996) argue that through day-by-day selection and display of the news, editors and news directors focus attention and influence the public's perceptions of what are the most important issues of the day. Attention is further focused—and pictures of the world shaped and refined—by the way journalists frame news stories (McCombs & Bell, 1996). Agenda Setting Theory examines how media can advance the interests of powerful political and social leaders by promoting or upholding assumptions about a particular group (Griffin, 2003). Although AST research has rarely been used to advance social justice goals, pairing AST's focus on media influence with theories such as Critical Race Theory (CRT) or Tribal Critical Race Theory (TribalCrit) provides for a robust framing and analysis of data within a social justice framework.

CRT challenges mainstream notions of race, racism, and racial power in U.S. society by questioning the neutrality of law and policy. The theory rejects the belief that color-blindness to race will eliminate racism and, instead, situates race at the center of its critique. By gathering and centering the stories and experiences of marginalized peoples, CRT offers an understanding of how race and racism influence the creation of law and policy, which in turn can serve to uphold a structure of inequality for historically oppressed communities. Placing value on experiential knowledge in order to posit that reality is situational and socially constructed (Ladson-Billings, 1998), CRT goes a step farther and calls for action and activism, arguing that social justice will not be achieved without actively working toward the elimination of racial oppression, with the goal of ending all forms of oppression (Bell, 1995; Brayboy, 2005; Donnor, 2005; Matsuda, Lawrence, Delgado, & Crenshaw, 1993).

CRT offers an analytical lens to explore the complex issues of race and power in U.S. society. However, it neither adequately addresses the complicated legal relationship between American Indians and the U.S. federal government, nor does it address the experience of colonization. This is because, according to TribalCrit, policies regarding American Indians are often rooted in material and financial gain, particularly for the benefit of non–American Indians. Exploring the relationship among race, racism, power, and economic practices creates a foundation for understanding why social structures, such as predominantly white universities, enact particular decisions and how those decisions come to subsequently impact students and society at large. Both theories would urge us, for example, to consider why MSU's decisions to terminate Indian-serving programs cannot be viewed in isolation from the way it continues to profit from the tribal name and associated American Indian imagery and symbols. Although not generally focused on media effects, literature from CRT and TribalCrit provide promising practices in analyzing the experiences of Indigenous peoples. For example, they illuminate how the creation of race as a sociohistorical concept has enabled the promotion of inaccurate and disrespectful racist beliefs.

Combining TribalCrit with AST may help explain why, how, and for what purposes stereotypical, inaccurate, hurtful, and/or racist depictions of American Indians in research, education, and the media persist. Since AST argues mass media can influence viewers' perceptions of news media events by creating images of events in their minds, policymakers should be cognizant of those pictures (Lippmann, 1922; McCombs & Bell, 1996). Agenda setting thus is the process whereby the news media lead the public in assigning relative importance to various public issues, and it presents the idea that media do not necessarily shape attitudes about issues; rather, they shape perceptions about which issues are important (McCombs & Bell, 1996; Miller, 2007). In other words, the media do not tell viewers what to think but rather what to think about and how to think about it (McCombs & Shaw, 1993; Shaw, 1979).

All three theories—CRT, TribalCrit, and AST—stress the importance of storytelling, which "remains a powerful direct means of grasping and exposing dominant realities and sharing subordinated ones" (MacKinnon, 2002, p. 72). While CRT seeks counterstories in order to understand the effects of law and policy on the lives of marginalized peoples, AST places its focus on understanding how media stories are presented, what values or associations are being promoted, and critically unpacking the associations promoted by media producers. Together, these theories advance an understanding of the powerful ways in which the media influences the issues facing marginalized communities as well as how power functions to promote the needs, rights, and interests of certain groups over others.

MEDIA COVERAGE OF THE STUDENT PROTESTS

The student protests at MSU were successful in garnering much needed media attention; however, media outlets varied widely in how they reported and framed the story. For example, administrative stories about the protests often revolved around four main themes: denial, defense, minimization, and shifting accountability through victim-blaming and scapegoating. What follows is an analysis contrasting the ways local news sources became a platform for university power holders to silence or invalidate the counterstories of American Indians. On the other hand, Native and, to a much smaller extent, student owned and/or operated news sources had a very different effect. Their stories sought to educate readers on the history and importance of the issues presented. These stories centered on themes of institutional accountability, especially how university actions impact the experiences of students, and emphasized that the stories shared by the students are a collective, rather than individual, concern for tribal communities. Instead of overreliance on university power holders to rationalize the experiences and concerns of Native peoples, these media outlets presented a variety of viewpoints and provided important context for why these struggles are important.

Local News Media

The stories reported in local news outlets revealed several tactics used by university administrators to recenter their majoritarian story. The first was minimization. News stories tended to frame student allegations as "absurd" and downplayed the severity of what happened. They also emphasized a belief that when it comes to validating claims of oppression or mistreatment, numbers matter, not experiences. Moreover, they sought to promote the belief that accurate and reliable information on the issues, and thus how seriously they should be taken, is centrally located in university power holders. Such tactics reflected a depiction of the university as a benevolent and paternal caretaker of American Indians who were, in turn, portrayed as ungrateful and militant against the institution.

University officials contested the oppression voiced by American Indians by placing emphasis upon the fact that the numbers of Native students concerned with these issues were low and that those who were protesting were speaking for themselves and not for the group. Media news reports failed to mention that the low number of student protesters could be related to the overall low enrollment of American Indian students at the university. At the time, approximately 200 of the 33,000 students enrolled at the university identified as American Indian. Stressing the small number of people who felt oppressed served to discount the 600+ signatories, most of whom were American Indian, who had signed a student-circulated petition during the time of protest. The petition, which was circulated both online and in person, voiced the signers' discontent with university practices, including inadequate administrative response to the display of offensive signs, which stated "Back to the reservation for [MSU]" and "Trail of Tears Part II." Officials sought to dismiss the concerns of signatories, as opposed to minimizing or denying them, by stressing that the signs were displayed briefly during the NCAA-sponsored event. In other words, they recognized something had happened, but they did not see it as a problem.

Defense as a tactic was used to deflect the conversation and (re)focus the university's commitment to Native peoples rather than its shortcomings. University officials' narratives in response to the counterstories offered by protesters absolved themselves of responsibility to American Indian students. For example, when asked about the inappropriate, hurtful, and offensive comments displayed at sporting events, the director of athletics for the rival team responded by superficially apologizing. He went on to explain, "The comments of this single fan certainly do not represent the views of [our] athletic department, nor of the university. I apologize for the distress that her remarks, *displayed however briefly*, have caused you and any others" (Cohoe-Tebe, 2008, para. 15, emphasis added). This statement points to the singular nature of the event and offers a qualification to the apology that seems to suggest the amount of distress experienced should be in proportion to the brevity with which the comments were displayed. Ultimately it serves as a tactic of defense as well as to minimize the concern the institution has for Native students.

When asked to comment on the protest and specific instances of injustice outlined by Native students at the protest, MSU administrators minimized the validity of the claims by pointing to the low number of students in attendance at the protest. One administrator responsible for diversity and equity efforts on campus stated that the group's actions caught him by surprise. Although he claimed that he worked individually with students to alleviate their concerns, he was unable to provide examples of the steps taken to redress their concerns (Leonard, 2008)—a response that downplays the collective nature of the student concerns. In the same interview, the administrator claimed, "The allegations of disrespect and dishonor that several students say they're experiencing, however, 'are completely absurd'" (Leonard, 2008, para. 2), deftly dismissing the pain endured by students and failing to acknowledge concern for their well-being. Such administrative claims were challenged in another news report published in a tribally owned and operated newspaper. According to this news story, MSU's president refused to meet with students, electing to pass them on to the associate vice president for diversity, who refused to meet with the entire group. Instead, the vice president permitted only two students to enter his office where he listened to their grievances for a short while before scolding them for having "a bad attitude" and raising their voices (Yurth, 2008). The meeting ended prematurely when the administrator silenced students by inviting them to leave his office.

The institution and its leadership sought to defend itself by shifting accountability, subverting, and silencing the voices and experiences of Native students. First, administrators disregarded them and systematically pointed to Native university faculty and staff who had left as responsible for the growing decline in programs and services available to students. Second, they targeted an individual student they believed was leading the student protest efforts, using this student as a scapegoat to dismiss the group's concerns. Administrators accused the student, whom they framed as a rogue troublemaker, of spreading misinformation (Yurth, 2008). This response sought, again, to minimize the collective student concerns and implied their experiences did not matter since the number of dissenters was low. It also erased the pain endured by the group, reframing their efforts as reflecting the experiences of only a small number of people. Here the tactic of denial purports that, even if something has happened, no harm was caused. This perceived absence of harm allowed administrators to present student concerns as a nonissue from the university's perspective and dismiss them from their purview.

When not pointing to the low number of Native students involved with the protest efforts, administrators responded by contradicting, diminishing, and nullifying their claims. One popular method of accomplishing this was by offering the illusion of assumed institutional responsibility over actual institutional inaction. For example, the director of athletics agreed with students that the racist remarks displayed by the fan were inappropriate and offensive but claimed staff intervened as soon as they saw them, telling the fan they must be erased (Cohoe-Tebe, 2008). However, the veracity of this statement remains questionable as the fan was photographed displaying not one, but two offensive signs during the event. The director creates a mixed message by initially claiming the university had no knowledge of the incident prior to receiving the petition and letter from Native students expressing their outrage. Then he points to the brevity with which the signs were displayed. Finally, he states that staff did intervene. The narrative changes from one of personal and institutional unawareness ("I/we didn't know about this") to a story of minimization of the importance of the act ("the signs were displayed briefly") to a story of assumed institutional responsibility ("the staff intervened"). By suggesting the student was reprimanded and/or asked to erase the racist messages, the administrator constructs a story of institutional accountability, suggesting the school really did care about maintaining a respectful atmosphere. However, the insistence on emphasizing the brevity of the display and subsequent reminder that he would have been "happy" to explain to the Native students how the university responded *before* they initiated a petition drive serves to illustrate that it is administrators, not students, who are in possession of the full story. In this instance the institution controls the terms of the debate and uses popular media to do so.

Finally, accountability shifting was accomplished through victim blaming and scapegoating. This tactic not only framed Native students as lone dissenters, but also sought to frame them as responsible for their own problems and the decline in services available to them. For example, in the early spring of 2008, a mid-level administrator circulated a letter to the staff of the NTPP explaining the leadership's decision to return the grant monies. The top university administrators had decided returning the grants was necessary due to the lack of matching funding from the university and the loss of two key staff members who oversaw the program(s), including the program creator/director (Bulkeley, 2008). The mid-level administrator ended by stating the decision was difficult but reflective of the institution's desire to fund its own programs without depending on federal monies. In short, it was to be a "new era" for American Indian education at the school.

The irony of administrators claiming commitment to Native peoples while rescinding federal treaty–based grants did not escape the attention of news reporters. After its decision became public, the university quickly moved to rededicate the American Indian Resource Center, which had been previously dedicated but had remained without a director since 1996 (Florez, 2008, 2009; Norlen, 2008). During the ceremony in April 2008, the university formally introduced the newest American Indian staff member to assume the directorship of the center. And although MSU's president did not attend the ceremony, his office later released a statement claiming the rededication represented a "commitment" to enhance the success of American Indian students, faculty, and staff (Bulkeley, 2008). However, once media attention died down seven months later, the university deviated from fulfilling this "commitment" by firing the director (Florez, 2009). Unfortunately, this institutional exercise of power went largely unnoticed by the press, and the university failed to appoint a new director until December 2010.

Native and Student-Driven Media

While local mainstream news outlets allowed university administrators to recenter their own majoritarian stories by drawing attention away from student counterstories, Native-owned and student-led news sources did not. Neither did they privilege the voices and opinions of university power holders by allowing their quotes to dominate news stories. Instead they presented the perspectives of administrators while also interrogating the institution's commitment to Native peoples by examining the concerns presented by the students. These stories presented additional information to educate readers on the history and importance of the issues presented and the policies used to justify university decisions. Finally, they emphasized student experiences as a shared collective, not individual, concern for tribal communities and asserted that the university as an entity should be continually monitored and held accountable for its statements and actions.

Rather than relying on university power holders to rationalize the treatment of Natives, these news stories offered the viewpoints of both administrators and students while also weaving information on traditional teachings, Native viewpoints, and contextual and historical details. This combination led to the creation of news stories that offered a fuller understanding of the importance and implications of the issues raised and presented them as a larger concern for Indian country. For example, one story explained the significance of the reservation system and the "trail of tears" and why they were inappropriate references to display at a sporting event. Others explained the cultural significance and taboo depicted in the products promoted by the MSU alum. Many of these stories contested the statements provided by university administrators.

In addition to providing historical and institutional context, they included the voices of other Native community members. For example, stories published in a tribally owned periodical mentioned the reactions and support for student efforts from tribal leaders and members of their Native community. By including details—such as the number of signatures collected for the petition regarding the sporting event incident, which Native communities had signed the petition, and which leaders were supporting the student-led initiatives— Native journalists did the opposite of what local media news reporters had done. Instead of minimizing the experiences and voices of Native peoples, they provided a more nuanced story. They explained that although many of the signatories for the petition were not students at MSU, these issues unite Native communities because the comments and reduction in services affect and implicate them all. Pain and suffering were thus not limited to individual students, as university administrators and mainstream publications would have the public believe. Rather, they were a shared experience for all Native communities.

Additionally, Native-owned media did not shy away from the perspectives of students. Rather than relying on the rationalizations of administrators, Native media presented student experiences as legitimate concerns that needed to be addressed in their own right. One media source provided findings from independent research about how the American Indian athletic trademark invited ridicule and disrespect from fellow students. It offered examples unique from those of the students that demonstrated the ways iconography is used to breed mockery and racism at athletic events. These publications often outlined the ways the university benefits financially from the exploitation of American Indian imagery through trademarks of sacred symbols (like a drum and feather). They argued that the (ab)use of Indigenous symbols and a tribal name impacts all Native peoples, not just the ones who have given the university permission to use their tribal name. Therefore, perceived harm was not limited to members of the tribal namesake.

Differences in Framing

Although Native media honored the stories and experiences of students, they also provided the perspectives of university administrators. Unfortunately, these media are not widely distributed among state residents; most draw their opinions and conclusions about issues based on stories published in local mainstream periodicals. Such sources feature stories that privilege the rationalization and response of university administrators, significantly reducing if not omitting the voices and experiences of Native protesters. These stories rarely outline the long-standing history of university inaction that leads to exploitation, stereotyping, and the continued violation of Native students' cultural and community beliefs. Nor did administrators or news reporters in mainstream new stories consider what the institution could have done to preempt the protests. Addressing or preempting the stated incidents would have allowed university administrators to restore the university's commitment to its students. Instead, a few MSU leaders signed the student petition to address the racist, hostile, and abusive messages written about Native communities at the sporting event, but neither created nor addressed policy to mitigate these occurrences. This left Native students alone to deal with the rival institution's athletic director, who chastised them for raising concerns after the university had allegedly dealt with it.

Referring to Native students' collective concerns as the concerns of a few "individual" students allowed MSU to neutralize or minimize the sense of moral panic initiated by student protest and mitigated the impression that MSU was in any way threatening or endangering the rights and interests of Native peoples. By placing itself in the role of victim, MSU appealed to public sympathy and redirected discussion to suggest the only thing to fear is students who are ill-informed about university practices. At the same time, administrators sought to make public statements against the students, suggesting their naiveté in understanding administrative policies and practices insulted the good work of the administrators.

University officials ultimately relied on discrediting Native staff, faculty, and students, suggesting that knowledge and, thereby, credibility resided in the hands of university power holders. By refusing to acknowledge responsibility in any of the identified incidents, administrators (re)shifted blame onto the shoulders of American Indians and the Native administrator, faculty, and staff who had resigned. This suggested that even American Indians (i.e., protesters) could not get it right when it came to figuring out who was responsible for the university's inability to fulfill its commitment to Natives. It was the Native peoples themselves!

The Importance of Context in Protest

University administrators would have readers believe that numbers are more important than experiences and, thereby, treat the number of counter-stories as the single most defining factor determining the effectiveness of counterstorytelling. Using this logic, one might ask exactly how many coun-terstories are needed to establish a mass critical enough to warrant respect and attention. However, it would be misguided to entertain such a question, as it shifts focus from the real issues at hand. Instead, we should ask: when counterstories are shared, how exactly does one preserve the voices of people of color such that the voices of power holders are not immediately reintro-duced and privileged?

Both CRT and TribalCrit recognize personal narratives and stories as valid forms of evidence. Personal narratives challenge the "numbers only" approach to documenting inequity or discrimination that tends to certify dis-crimination from a quantitative rather than qualitative perspective (Dixson & Rousseau, 2005). Administrators pointed to the low numbers of Natives at the protest in an attempt to minimize the significance of student concerns. This raises the question, what does connecting physical presence with the legitimacy of concerns presented during moments of public dissent tell us about administrative values?

The focus on a numbers-only approach to understanding oppression sug-gests MSU administrators were experiencing a case of what Bourdieu and Passeron (1990) refer to as genesis amnesia. Genesis amnesia refers to the act of literally forgetting history to the extent that recent fabrications pass into the subconscious and make current practices and conditions seem natural and self-evident. The administrators' insistence on the presumably small number of Native students concerned with the incidents raised suggests they have forgotten that American Indians were forcibly removed from their homelands by the threat of annihilation. Such comments ignore the series of political agreements entered into by the federal government, which made the acquisition of land—including the land upon which the university is cur-rently built—possible. These agreements forced many tribes to relocate to reservations far away from where the current university stands. Administra-tive lack of American Indian historical and social understanding becomes prevalent when university leaders disregard the support of the 600+ petition signatories. These signers, many who reside in tribal communities far from campus, had chosen to symbolically support the protest through signatures and associated messages when they physically could not.

Taking the historical and social context of American Indians into consideration, administrators might have also remembered that Native communities are among the most economically disenfranchised. Although they insisted that the validity of student concerns stood in direct proportion to the number of bodies physically present at the protest, physically attending the protest for the petition signatories residing in reservation communities was simply out of the question. Not only might they have been located in the outskirts of the city/state, but also they might have lacked the necessary resources to get there. This imposition of a requirement for legitimacy that cannot be met perpetuates yet another violent act on an already marginalized community. Disregarding the distance that many Native peoples would have had to travel, the cost incurred, and the fact that some may have lacked modes of transportation or personal resources (let alone time), administrators imposed their own standards of protest onto a community that shares neither their history nor their socioeconomic mobility.

MSU's rhetoric regarding its commitment to honoring American Indians is difficult to believe given the examples listed above. The institution's treatment of Native peoples is what led students to protest in the first place. The campus treatment of Indigenous peoples in relation to the everyday use and exploitation of its tribal nickname was simply too much for some students. They questioned the university's systematic removal of Indian-serving programs and leaders. They questioned the university's overwhelming inaction during instances in which the history and experiences of American Indians were taken up and used to wield racist and offensive messages. And they appealed to the outlying community for support.

CONCLUDING THOUGHTS

This chapter examined the role of institutional policies and climate for American Indian students' success at a predominantly white institution in the mountain west. The presence of a tribal athletic mascot is important to this study as it serves as a reflection of how American Indians are depicted on campus, rendered both visible and invisible in the milieu of higher education (Solyom, 2014). The nickname influences institutional climate and serves as a reminder of how MSU and its alumni profit from a practice that interferes with the health and success of students.

Not always mentioned in discussions of transformational resistance in higher education are the tolls associated with activism. This study suggests feelings of isolation, loneliness, and not belonging become pervasive for those enrolled in institutions utilizing Indigenous mascots, nicknames, or imagery. Engaging in activism can lead to feelings of fear and paranoia, having one's personal safety jeopardized, persistent feeling of being in physical danger, of possibly losing one's job (for those students who were also staff members at the university), and an overall sense of not being able to freely express them-selves without incurring some type of institutional form of retaliation. Family concerns that participation in activist efforts would inspire the university to refrain from conferring their degree also weighed heavily. All activists indi-cated experiencing a constant tension between feeling fear and rage. "It makes you suicidal or homicidal," one explained. Many experienced weight gain, relational distress, difficulty sleeping, feelings of depression and exhaus-tion, and overall lethargy.

Rather than quit activism or exit the university, students chose to voice their concerns to administrators, hoping to ameliorate feelings of isolation and the symbolic violence they experienced on campus. This study suggests the power of Native voices cannot be stifled. Although they are a minority in higher education, Native students/youth, whose voices are not typically val-ued by the university, chose to speak out anyway. When quiet behind-the-scenes activism did not yield desired results, youth banded together and got creative. For example, when meetings with administrators were not produc-tive, the students in this study galvanized media. When their voices were subverted in mainstream media, they found alternative ways to voice their concerns to the larger public and garner support for their cause. They created their own blog, circulated petitions in Indigenous communities, and worked with Native-owned media outlets to get their message out.

The fact that these activist efforts were driven by Native *youth* remains important. Youth status is important for several reasons. First, the efforts in this study were driven by a desire not to preserve programs and personnel for individual students' success but out of a desire to protect treaty-protected rights and programs for future generations. In other words, youth were advo-cating for the rights of youth who would come after them. Second, the univer-sity's desire to scapegoat students publicly may have been intended to silence or minimize their objections, but ultimately the ostracization and/or exhaus-tion associated with protest can leave young dissenters feeling pushed out. In these cases, students may exit the university prematurely, which may allow the institution to preserve the status quo, though it affects their Native stu-dent graduation rates. However, even when they exit prematurely, the broader study of which this study is a part finds that Native youth activists go on to pursue opportunities elsewhere, where they can serve the needs of diverse and/or Indigenous peoples (Solyom, 2014). Still, pushing out activist youth means the institution loses important agents of justice and change. If students exit but go on to serve as leaders in other places—if they refuse to work with the university in the future—can the university really claim to be preparing the leaders of tomorrow? This question becomes especially poignant consider-ing the university cannot seem to hold on to the leaders of today.

Finally, this study suggests that the heart of activism remains strong and that protecting collective education rights as well as educating others help activists persist. The youth in this study are not just college social justice advocates; they are advocates for life. They recognize institutions can and do chew them up, but they are like their ancestors: people who would not die, who are committed to the perpetuation of the health, well-being, and strength of their nations.

ACKNOWLEDGMENTS

The author wishes to thank Jerusha Conner, Sonia Rosen, Sundy Watanabe, and Kristin Searle for their feedback and support on this project.

NOTES

1. Although the students prefer to individually identify by their tribal names, I use American Indian and Native (American) interchangeably to capture the diverse ways the students described themselves as a group. These terms refer to the first inhabitants of what is now considered to comprise the contiguous United States of America.

2. This study took place at a flagship institution in the mountain west region of the United States. Data profiling five American Indian student activists were gathered over a seven-year period (2007–2014) and included in-depth, semistructured interviews. Data collection also included participant observation of public protests and activists' planning sessions for community and media outreach. Finally, archival research was used to gather internal documents and emails that outline administrative decision-making rationale and intentions.

3. To protect the identity of research participants, I have chosen to use pseudonyms for all people and places.

REFERENCES

American Psychological Association. (2005). APA resolution recommending the immediate retirement of American Indian mascots, symbols, images, and personalities by schools, colleges, universities, athletic teams, and organizations. Retrieved from https://www.apa.org/about/policy/mascots.pdf

Barnhardt, C. (1994). Life on the other side: Native student survival in a university world. *Peabody Journal of Education, 69*(2), 115–139. http://dx.doi.org/10.1080/01619569409538768

Bell, D. A. (1995). Who's afraid of critical race theory? *University of Illinois Law Review,* 893–910.

Berry, C. (2009, February 4). Native student protest has diverse roots and reasons. *Indian Country Today.* Retrieved from http://indiancountrytodaymedianetwork.com

Bourdieu, P., & Passeron, J. C. (1990). *Reproduction in education, society and culture* (2nd ed.). London: Sage.

Brayboy, B. M. J. (2005). Toward a tribal critical race theory in education. *Urban Review, 37*(5), 425–446. http://dx.doi.org/10.1007/s11256-005-0018-y

Brayboy, B. M. J., Fann, A. J., Castagno, A. E., & Solyom, J. A. (2012). *Postsecondary education for American Indian and Alaska Natives: Higher education for nation building and self-determination*. San Francisco: ASHE Higher Education Report.

Bulkeley, D. (2008, April 10). University of Utah turns back about $2 million in grants. *Deseret News.* Retrieved from http://www.deseretnews.com/

Cohoe-Tebe, C. (2008, August 7). Petitioners seek BYU apology for racist incident. *Navajo Times.* Retrieved from http://indianz.com

DeVoe, J. F., Darling-Churchill, K. E., & Snyder, T. D. (2008, September). Status and trends in the education of American Indians and Alaska Natives: 2008. NCES 2008-084. *National Center for Education Statistics.* Retrieved from nces.ed.gov

Dixson, A. D., & Rousseau, C. K. (2005). And we are still not saved: Critical race theory in education ten years later. *Race and Ethnicity in Education, 8*(1), 7–27. http://dx.doi.org/10.1080/1361332052000340971

Donnor, J. K. (2005). Towards an interest-convergence in the education of African American football student athletes in major college sports. *Race, Ethnicity and Education, 8*(1), 45–67. http://dx.doi.org/10.1080/1361332052000340999

Florez, J. (2008, May 12). University should not let Indian-education die. *Deseret News.* Retrieved from http://www.deseretnews.com/

Florez, J. (2009, June 8). University needs to support American Indian teachers. *Deseret News.* Retrieved from http://www.deseretnews.com/

Freeman, C., & Fox, M. A. (2005). Status and trends in the education of American Indians and Alaska Natives. NCES 2005-108. *National Center for Education Statistics.* Retrieved from http://nces.ed.gov/

Fulton, B. (2008, December 6). Students protest, say Ute nickname breeding racism. *Salt Lake Tribune.* Retrieved from www.sltrib.com

Gardiner, D. (2008, December 4). American Indians protest unfair treatment. *Daily Utah Chronicle.* Retrieved from http://www.dailyutahchronicle.com.

Ginder, S. A., & Kelly-Reid, J. E. (2013). Enrollment in postsecondary institutions, fall 2012; financial statistics, fiscal year 2012; graduation rates, selected cohorts, 2004–09; and employees in postsecondary institutions, fall 2012: First look (provisional data). NCES 2013-183. *National Center for Education Statistics.* Retrieved from http://nces.ed.gov/

Griffin, E. (2003). *A first look at communication theory* (5th ed.). Boston, MA: McGraw-Hill.

Hofmann, S. (2005). The elimination of Indigenous mascots, logos, and nicknames: Organizing on college campuses. *American Indian Quarterly, 29*(1), 156–177. http://dx.doi.org/10.1353/aiq.2005.0051

Ladson-Billings, G. (1998). Just what is critical race theory and what's it doing in a nice field like education? *International Journal of Qualitative Studies in Education, 11*(1), 7–24. http://dx.doi.org/10.1080/095183998236863

Leonard, W. (2008, December 5). University mascot, policies protested. *Deseret News.* Salt Lake City, Utah. Retrieved from http://www.deseretnews.com

Lippmann, W. (1922). *Public opinion*. New York: Harcourt, Brace.

MacKinnon, C. A. (2002). Keeping it real: On anti-"essentialism." In F. Valdes, J. M. Culp, & A. P. Harris (Eds.), *Crossroads, directions, and a new critical race theory* (pp. 71–83). Philadelphia, PA: Temple University Press.

Matsuda, M. J., Lawrence, C. R., Delgado, R., & Crenshaw, C. W. (1993). *Words that wound: Critical race theory, assaultive speech, and the First Amendment*. Boulder, CO: Westview.

McCombs, M., & Bell, T. (1996). The agenda-setting role of mass communication. In M. B. Salwen & D. W. Stacks (Eds.), *An integrated approach to communication theory and research* (pp. 93–110). Mahwah, NJ: Lawrence Erlbaum Associates.

McCombs, M. E., & Shaw, D. L. (1993). The evolution of agenda-setting research: Twenty-five years in the marketplace of ideas. *Journal of Communication, 43*(2), 58–67. http://dx.doi.org/10.1111/j.1460-2466.1993.tb01262.x

Miller, J. M. (2007). Examining the mediators of agenda setting: A new experimental paradigm reveals the role of emotions. *Political Psychology, 28*(6), 689–717. http://dx.doi.org/10.1111/j.1467-9221.2007.00600.x

National Collegiate Athletic Association. (2005). NCAA news release: NCAA executive committee issues guidelines for use of Native American mascots at championship events. Retrieved from http://fs.ncaa.org

National Congress of American Indians. (2013). Ending the legacy of racism in sports & the era of harmful "Indian" sports mascots. Washington, DC. Retrieved from http://www.ncai.org/proudtobe

Norlen, C. (2008, April 14). American Indian grants returned. *Daily Utah Chronicle*. Retrieved from http://dailyutahchronicle.com/

Shaw, E. F. (1979). Agenda-setting and mass communication theory. *International Communication Gazette, 25*(2), 96–105. http://dx.doi.org/10.1177/001654927902500203

Shotton, H. J., Lowe, S. C., & Waterman, S. J. (Eds.). (2013). *Beyond the asterisk: Understanding Native students in higher education*. Sterling, VA: Stylus.

Solyom, J. A. (2014). *The (in)visibility paradox: A case study of American Indian iconography and student resistance in higher education* (Unpublished doctoral dissertation). Arizona State University, Tempe, AZ.

Tierney, W. (1992). Official encouragement, institutional discouragement: Minorities in academe—the Native American experience. In G. W. Noblit & W. T. Pink (Series Eds.), *Interpretive perspectives on education*. Norwood, NJ: Ablex.

Yurth, C. (2008, December 18). Navajo "Ute" not running from fight. *Navajo Times*. Retrieved from http://navajotimes.com

19

Injustice Is Not an Investment: Student Activism, Climate Justice, and the Fossil Fuel Divestment Campaign

Joe Curnow and Allyson Gross

On March 19, 2015, the student club Swarthmore Mountain Justice (MJ) began an occupation of Swarthmore College's administration building that would last for 32 days. As students, alumni, and supporters gathered outside of the college's finance and investment offices, the spotlight of the fossil fuel divestment campaign turned toward the very place the campaign began four years prior. In a spin on the classic labor song, "Which Side Are You On?" MJ student occupiers sat and sang, "Oh students can you stand it? / Oh tell me how you can. / Will you let the world burn / or will you take a stand?" By occupying the administrative building, the students posed a clear dilemma to Swarthmore's Board of Managers: "Make history or be vilified by it" (Swarthmore Mountain Justice, 2015, para. 8).

The sit-ins spread across the United States, as students called on their universities to divest their endowments from the fossil fuel industry. Mountain Justice was just the first of a coordinated series of actions across the United States, from northeast schools like Yale and Harvard, to southern schools such as Tulane and the University of Mary Washington. The next month and a half would find seven sit-ins, dozens of escalated actions, and 22 arrests for civil disobedience from student campaigns around the country. The wave of escalation marked a turning point for the fossil fuel divestment campaign. "For months," noted Julia, a sit-in organizer at Bowdoin College, "our Board of Trustees ignored our concerns. The only way to move forward was to take matters into our own hands, and show them our collective power." Students were organized, and if their universities wouldn't take action, they would.

With an unprecedented number of wins for the divestment campaign in the first half of 2015, the string of sit-ins represented merely the tip of the iceberg for fossil fuel divestment and youth climate organizing. While at its most visible in such moments of escalation and success, student mobilization around climate change has grown exponentially over the last decade. In 2005, a small number of student organizations were working on climate issues. Today, the scene is dramatically transformed, with large networks of campaigns that support more than 400 campuses across the United States and Canada (Fossil Free USA, 2016).

Fossil Fuel Divestment is the most common campaign to address the climate crisis in North America. The campaign works with college and university students on their campuses as they encourage their governing councils, boards of trustees, and other leadership bodies to divest their endowments from the 200 fossil fuel companies with the largest reserves. These campaigns have experienced mixed results, with many rejections by university administrations. Recently, though, they have achieved significant wins, including Syracuse University and the University of California system's divestment from coal and tar sands, reaching a total of $2.6 trillion divested by September 2015.

In this chapter we ask what impact divestment campaigns have. We explore the potential of divestment, but also look beyond the tactic to explore the learning and political development that divestment campaigns can foster. Reflecting on a spring of sit-ins and direct actions in the United States, followed by a wave of weeks of action in Canada, we examine the state of youth climate organizing and explore the divestment campaign's potential to create change. The student activists engaged in fossil fuel divestment are taking a powerful stand—not just against the world burning, but against what they argue is a fundamentally unjust system that disproportionately impacts frontline communities.

YOUTH ACTIVISM AND STUDENT CAMPAIGNS

Youth activism is thoroughly established as an important site of learning and development, and many academic researchers are involved in this work politically and professionally. Ginwright, Noguera, and Cammarota's (2006) edited volume has served as a cornerstone for this work, as has work by Fine (Cammarota & Fine, 2010; Fine, 1991) and Calabrese Barton (Calabrese Barton, 1998; Calabrese Barton & Tan, 2010). These authors have worked to illustrate and support youth activism related to schooling and learning, extending the traditional boundaries of the classroom and insisting that youths' experiences of activism are indeed critical spaces for identity development and resistance. Many researchers have documented the ways that youth participatory action research can be used as an activist strategy in classrooms, expanding approaches to critical pedagogy and looking beyond the classroom, to include discussions of civic engagement, school reform, and the myriad ways youth engage in politics (Booker, 2010; Checkoway & Gutierrez, 2006; Conner, 2011; Kirshner, 2008, 2015; Kwon, 2008; Rogers, Morrell, & Enyedy, 2007). The field is expanding rapidly and brings value to discussions of schooling, learning, and civic development and creates space to explore systemic oppression and the work youth are doing to resist and re-create those systems in local and global ways.

Within this field, though, there is less work on student campaigns, despite the fact that in the last 15 years, the campaign has become one of the most common forms of activist action on college and university campuses. Student campaigns ask that students take action on issues outside of their immediate self-interest or role as students. Examples of student campaigns include students against sweatshops and the student fair trade campaign, where students use their institutional position as students on the issues of fair labor practices, international trade policy, development, and other areas (Cravey, 2004; Featherstone & United Students Against Sweatshops, 2002; Silvey, 2004; Wilson & Curnow, 2013). These campaigns are often coordinated in conjunction with larger nongovernmental organizations (NGOs), reflecting the NGOization of activism today (Choudry, 2010; Kwon, 2013), and tend to use guidebooks circulated by NGOs to launch affiliates or chapters of the campaigns across the country. Affiliates take up the same types of actions across time and place, following the steps of the guidebooks to achieve their wins. There is variety among the campaigns, where different types of political action are asked of students, from raising funds to raising awareness to raising hell.

Surprisingly little has been written on youth climate campaigns. The academic work on student environmental issues tends to center on campus-specific work to change individual and institutional behaviors, including implementing campus recycling programs, promoting energy efficiency, and managing green initiatives on campus (Helferty & Clarke, 2009; Stephens, Hernandez, Román, Graham, & Scholz, 2008). For high school student organizing around climate change, even less is documented, though important curricula have been developed as part of youth participatory research projects that bridge the climate crisis and science curriculum to encourage youth projects to address climate change (Calabrese Barton & Tan, 2010; Niemeyer, Garcia, & Naima, 2009). These studies reflect a long-running theme in some parts of the environmental movement to focus on individual environmentally friendly behaviors rather than look systemically (Grady-Benson, 2014). As climate change has become the big environmental and political discussion over the past years, the individualization of responses has begun to shift, as both scientists and activists have called for international policy change as the most fundamentally necessary intervention to prevent devastating climate change. As this discursive and strategic shift has occurred, campus-based activists like Sam at the University of Toronto have sought campaigns that move beyond the recycling and energy-efficiency strategies, quipping, "We need to change policy, not lightbulbs."

Situating Ourselves

Drawing on the contributions of Indigenous researchers (Absolon, 2011; Wilson, 2008) and feminist researchers (Bloom, 1998; Hill-Collins, 2002), we locate ourselves within the context of the fossil fuel divestment campaign and our research. Indigenous researchers have emphasized the importance of relational accountability and context (Wilson, 2008) in allowing readers and research participants to fully understand why we commit ourselves to certain questions and how the lessons we learn from the research fit into a broader theory of change that will benefit the communities we are accountable to. These scholars argue that who we are as researchers matters for what we investigate and how we do our work and that making our standpoints and political commitments known is foundational to making sense of our relationships to our participants and our research questions.

Joe has been involved in the fossil free divestment campaign at the University of Toronto for two years, primarily as a researcher, and also as a participant. She spent five years as a student organizer in the fair trade movement and as an anti-oppression trainer for multiple student-led campaigns, including environmental and global justice movements. Allyson has been involved in the movement for fossil fuel divestment since January 2014 as a student leader and organizer with Bowdoin Climate Action and the Divestment Student Network (DSN). Since joining, Allyson has helped develop national escalation strategy with 350.org and worked to develop the regional network structures and long-term strategy of the DSN. Our engagement in the fossil fuel divestment campaign across North America positions us to offer an insider's account of how youth are engaging in climate activism. It allows us to articulate the dominant frames of the campaign, as well as to contextualize the challenges the campaign faces as the student climate movement attempts to stretch the frames and extend the political analysis that structures our tactics and materials. Our relationships with participants foster accountability to the movement and a reliable accounting of the state of the fossil fuel divestment campaign.

Our chapter draws primarily from ethnographic data. We draw from our firsthand experiences of campus campaigns, regional and national conferences, national planning and alignment meetings, and marches documented with ethnographic field notes, as well as our personal emails, tweets, and Facebook timelines. We also analyze primary documents, including the kits and materials produced by 350.org, the Divestment Student Network, the Responsible Endowments Coalition, and the Canadian Youth Climate Coalition.

From the Divestment Student Network, we draw on seven interviews with members of the organization's Coordinating Committee and representatives from their national working groups. Interview data were coded based upon participants' involvement with the DSN. Additionally, at the University of Toronto we draw from semistructured interviews of eight focal participants and video data of most meetings and actions over the course of the campaign. These data were collected over eight months using multiple camera angles for each event. Once data were captured they were content logged and thematically coded for areas including the dominant frames of the divestment campaign; instances of climate justice, solidarity, anticolonialism, and decolonization being discussed; questions of race, class, and gender; and other content areas. These preliminary codes were developed based on the initial research question and were refined through iterative rounds of coding, which reflected the data and participants' use of the terms. This thematic coding was supplemented with the field notes and primary sources in order to clarify significant themes across all the data.

Our analysis focuses on widespread themes across the divestment campaign in both the United States and Canada and identifies the potential and limitations of divestment as a tactic and a tool for politicization. To connect the U.S. and Canadian contexts, we compared and contrasted the dominant themes that emerged, looking for places of convergence as well as divergence. We often built off each other's experiences and supplemented each other's analyses with data from the other context. Initial drafts of this chapter were shared with several willing participants, and their feedback is gratefully integrated into our analysis.

FINDINGS

Fossil Fuel Divestment on Campus

The Fossil Fuel Divestment campaign represents the greatest focus of the youth climate movement on campuses right now, yet almost nothing has been written about this topic in academic spaces. Grady-Benson and Sarathy (2016) outline the divestment tactic and the logic of fossil fuel divestment and provide case studies of campuses that have been successful at their bids for divestment, as well as some that have not. Such documentation is an important first step in establishing fossil fuel divestment as a significant student campaign that deserves attention. We build on the foundation laid by Grady-Benson and Sarathy (2016), but draw on multiple contexts to extend their discussion and complicate it by looking at what people learn and are wrestling with at the different levels of the campaigns. As part of this extension, we focus on students as political actors, look at how students' political praxis shifts through their engagement, and ask what significance those shifts hold for student and youth activism today.

The first fossil fuel divestment campaign originated at Swarthmore College in early spring of 2011, as Mountain Justice—originally intent on fighting mountaintop removal for coal extraction—decided upon divestment as a way not only to support those on the Appalachian front lines, but also to engage with their school's complicity in the crisis and attempt to build a student movement against the fossil fuel industry.

Swarthmore was joined over the following 18 months by a handful of campus groups campaigning for coal divestment, united around the Divest Coal coalition in the fall of 2011 (Grady-Benson, 2014). Less a movement than a loosely connected conglomeration of campaigns and organizations, it was not until 350.org's *Do the Math* tour in November 2012 that mass action for divestment gained traction across the country. The tour, headlined by environmentalist Bill McKibben and a rotating panel of movement celebrities from author/ activist Naomi Klein to Archbishop Desmond Tutu, advocated a mathematical logic to the growing necessity to stop the fossil fuel industry—"Unless we rise up to stop them," they argued (350.org, 2016, para. 2), the industry would burn the 2,795 gigatons of carbon dioxide in its reserves—far more than the planet can handle—and push global temperatures above the 2°C recommended by scientists and into climate catastrophe (350.org, 2016).

Do the Math (Nyks & Scott, 2013) not only laid out the facts against the fossil fuel industry, but also called for its audiences to join together in the creation of a mass movement to combat their destructive practices. Through promoting a neatly packaged "ask" and easily replicable pathways toward starting a local campaign on the resource website GoFossilFree.org, campaigns for fossil fuel divestment flourished across the country. By April 2014—just three years after Swarthmore's first calls for divestment—the campaign had grown to more than 300 campus campaigns, and more than 560 worldwide (Grady-Benson, 2014). Today, the numbers have grown to more than 400 student groups, with 33 commitments from colleges and universities to divest as of February 2016 (Fossil Free USA, 2016).

In Canada there has been explosive growth around the divestment campaign as well. Twenty-five schools have launched campaigns since 2013. At the time of this writing, three schools—Dalhousie, McGill, and the University of British Columbia—have seen high-profile rejections of their divestment proposals from administration decision makers; others have quietly rejected student proposals, including Trent and the University of Calgary. However, Queen's University has established a committee to evaluate the moral and fiduciary responsibility that the institution has vis-à-vis climate change and fossil fuel investments (CYCC, 2015). At the University of Toronto, the president's ad hoc committee has recommended divestment and student activists are hopeful, awaiting a final decision.

Do the Math: Framing the Divestment Campaign

Do the Math (Nyks & Scott, 2013) introduced the idea of divestment to many involved in or running fossil fuel divestment campaigns from 2012 to today. As such, its rhetoric has influenced the primary frames of the original phase of the campaign. The first frame, the numerical logic of divestment, focused less on the human impacts of climate change than it did the hard facts of its numerical implications. The "simple math" of the tour's numbers—2,795 gigatons of CO_2 in reserve, and 565 gigatons of CO_2 available to burn to stay under 2°C—established an understanding of the need to divest as a logical action based upon rational facts (350.org, 2016). Many campaigns adopted such numerical rhetoric further into their arguments in support of the finances of divestment. A 2011 white paper published by corporate responsibility organization As You Sow introduced the financial concepts of "stranded assets" and "carbon risk" associated with long-term investments in the fossil fuel industry (Lowe & Sanzillo, 2011). On top of the numbers supporting the need to target the fossil fuel industry popularized by McKibben, the financial language disseminated by As You Sow further solidified the rhetoric of the movement. Based in monetary returns, assets, and financial risk, to divest from fossil fuels became a logical course of action for the rational institution.

The second frame promoted on the tour and further popularized throughout the campaign is that of the impact of industry stigmatization, which served to justify the rationale behind the tactic of divestment itself. McKibben argued that "[the fossil fuel] industry has behaved so recklessly that they should lose their social license, their veneer of respectability" (Stephenson, 2012, para. 4). To divest, then, was to act upon the simple mathematical reality of the growing climate crisis, and publicly point the finger at the fossil fuel industry as culprit. Ben, an organizer at Ryerson University, explains this logic, saying:

> Divestment is about the stigmatization and the movement building. That's what will carry things forward. The idea is that we take away the social license—so, like, the entire thing is about taking [fossil fuels] and turning those into toxic investments.

Through divesting the endowments of institutions across the country, the campaign seeks to hold the fossil fuel industry accountable for its actions and shift public support out from under its wide range of influence. For Sara, alumna and organizer of Swarthmore's MJ, stigmatizing the fossil fuel industry means that "people in their daily lives are coming to terms with the fact that this industry does not have our stake at heart in any way," and serves to highlight producers of fossil fuels as part of a "noncompliant, irresponsible, rogue industry." The stigmatization found through divestment ultimately attempts, McKibben argues, to "tarnish [the] brand" of the fossil fuel industry (350.org, 2016).

Just how the campaign seeks to accomplish such stigmatization is accounted for in the several hundred campaigns on college campuses across the continent and around the world. Following the *Do the Math* tour, where attendees were encouraged to join the campaign by starting their own divestment campaign, the campaign ballooned through the easy-access kits and resources made available by 350.org to provide a template for the campaign format. Templates found on the resource websites GoFossilFree.org (United States) and GoFossilFree.ca (Canada) ask students to form a team and create a petition outlining the standardized demands of the campaign. The petition asks universities to "freeze new fossil fuel investments and drawdown current holdings over the next five years" (Fossil Free, n.d., p. 15), leading students across Canada to cheekily adopt the chant, "What do we want? Divestment! When do we want it? Gradually over five years!" These petitions intend to gain access to decision makers and gather support across campus. Alongside a series of actions used to put pressure on campus targets and engage the campaign's base of support, this format is the standard for U.S. and Canadian fossil fuel divestment campaigns, with variations based upon campus context.

At the University of Toronto (UofT), for example, the campaign is coordinated by a group of undergraduate and graduate students who have worked to develop an extensive brief on the issue of divestment and climate change. They collected the necessary signatures to trigger the university's divestment process, which established an ad hoc committee to advise the president and governing council on whether or not to divest the endowment. The students involved in the campaign organize their work within three subcommittees: outreach to the Governing Council and ad hoc committee, including developing the brief and providing arguments and information for the official bodies; outreach to the university community, including alumni, faculty, and student groups; and member outreach that seeks to educate and mobilize students to get more involved in the campaign. In the last 18 months, the committee has grown to around 25 regular members and scores of peripherally involved students. They have met with and advised the ad hoc committee members appointed by the university president. Additionally, they held a divestment meme party, Divestment Action Week, including outreach events like the signature drive, which they called "Cookies for Climate Change," a panel of environmental and financial experts, and marches of more than 200 students through central campus to the doors of the office of the president to submit signatures of community members demanding that UofT divest. The campaign follows the guidebook's step-by-step instructions and coordinates with other campaigns across Canada and the United States to align strategies and show solidarity with other campaigns. Their coordinated actions are shaped by the materials and the dominant frames of the larger fossil fuel divestment campaign, focusing on building a rational and well-argued case to present to decision makers and building support on campus to push those decision makers should they balk.

Shifting Frames: "Divestment Is the Tactic. Climate Justice Is the Goal."

While divestment is a tactic primarily based in financial and media strategy that argues that pulling institutional resources will make a bold statement against the fossil fuel industry to stop the worst of the extraction and emissions, participants in the divestment campaign have been quick to extend that frame. Through the introduction and incorporation of a climate justice analysis and an intersectional framework, the divestment campaign has sought to broaden the dominant frame beyond the mathematical and financial. According to Amil, an organizer at the University of Toronto, "When we talk about climate justice, we're not only talking about climate change as a problem; we're hoping to have our actions challenge the systems that cause climate change and makes certain communities more vulnerable than others to the impacts of climate change." This climate justice frame attempts to expand upon the notion of removing the "social license" of the fossil fuel industry and shifting such public support toward the front lines of extraction, burning, extreme weather, and other climate change–related impacts. The climate justice frame works against the notion that divestment is a purely economic strategy, in part acknowledging the limited scope of power that campus divestment holds economically, but also resituating the terms of the debate. Instead, this frame intentionally integrates an analysis of race, colonialism, and capitalism into the divestment talking points and centers the experiences of frontline communities. As Joanna, an organizer at UofT, explained it, "Climate issues do not exist as an island; they are intersectional. They interact with different social constructs and power relations, such as race, gender, and class." As the divestment campaign is focused on changing public discourse around fossil fuels and removing the "social license," they also insist on integrating a climate justice frame into divestment. This has the potential to shape a generation of activists to be more attentive to the racialized, classed, and gendered impacts of climate change, as well as the ways that racialization, colonialism, class, and gender influence the ways we do activism, the strategies we choose, the voices we hear and amplify, and the fights that we invest in.

Students organizing for fossil fuel divestment in the United States have also worked to incorporate an analysis of climate justice into campaign rhetoric and action. Distinctly departing from a strictly financial or mathematical perspective, the incorporation of climate justice into the campaign has sought to highlight the disproportionate impacts of the fossil fuel industry on low-income communities and communities of color. As the first campaign at Swarthmore was originally formed as a means of solidarity organizing with those on the front lines of mountaintop removal in Appalachia, such rhetoric has worked to reincorporate and reinfuse such a purpose back into the campaign's narrative. As noted by organizer Jess Grady-Benson, "[Divestment] is not about carbon—it's about humans." Focusing on the human impacts of the fossil fuel industry has allowed for a departure from the original framing of the Do the Math tour's numerical analysis, as demonstrated at campaign convergences in the United States and Canada and in the burgeoning reinvestment projects of the Divestment Student Network and Climate Justice Alliance.

The first national convergence, or conference, of the fossil fuel divestment campaign, held in February 2013 at Swarthmore College, sought to infuse a climate justice analysis within campaigns by highlighting frontline narratives throughout its programming, principles, and goals for gathering. The organizing principles put forth by the planning team included a commitment to an "environmental/economic justice framework" that recognized divestment as "a form of solidarity organizing—a way to be an ally with frontline organizations" (Power Up!, 2013, p. 5). The agenda for the weekend specifically sought to elevate frontline voices over the traditional leaders of the environmental movement, as Crystal Lameman, an Indigenous leader from the Beaver Lake Cree Nation, delivered the keynote address on the transition from divestment to climate justice. She shared stories of how her community has been impacted by tar sands development and drew on treaty rights to connect Indigenous land struggles to the fight against climate change. According to convergence organizer and DSN Coordinating Committee member William Lawrence, "Bill [McKibben] had been in the spotlight so much that year from the Do the Math tour, and we thought that there were other perspectives that students ought to be hearing." The intentionality behind inviting Lameman rather than McKibben to speak and the general focus of the agenda on climate justice frameworks exemplify the shift in the student movement away from a mathematical analysis and toward an intersectional perspective of the impacts of the industry. By presenting more diverse perspectives, the DSN sought to exemplify the diversity of the climate movement. Convergence planner and DSN organizer Sachie noted how they

> tried very hard to build a program for that convergence that was almost entirely speakers of color. I really felt the significance as a person of

color in centering communities of color in the climate movement and grassroots struggles, and also just generally making broader narrative interventions around the whiteness of the movement and lifting up the amazing organizing that was happening in these communities.

For the DSN, divestment without centering those most impacted by the climate crisis was inadequate. With such goals in mind, the oft-used campaign phrase "divestment is the tactic, and climate justice is the goal," coined at the convergence, has proliferated throughout the campaign.

In Canada, this step toward intersectionality and solidarity has occurred concurrently but manifests differently. The attention paid to Indigenous solidarity fits within the broader context of social justice organizing in Canada, where far more attention is paid to Indigenous solidarity than in the United States. Interestingly, the only differences between the divestment toolkits in the United States and Canada is that the Canadian guide explicitly addresses (briefly) Indigenous land rights, settler solidarity, and the tar sands being on stolen Indigenous land (Fossil Free Canada, 2016, p. 9). Joanna, a Canadian organizer, described the importance of climate justice, saying, "Indigenous peoples and marginalized communities are often at the front lines of climate impacts because of the legacy of colonialism, racism, sexism, and other -isms, so it is important that we keep that in mind when we are doing climate organizing."

At the Canadian Youth Climate Coalition convergence in 2014, Indigenous solidarity featured centrally in all discussions of divestment because of the Canadian Youth Climate Coalition's partnership with Indigenous organizers (Canadian Youth Climate Coalition, 2015). The keynote speeches were delivered by Indigenous women activists fighting extractive industries in their communities and a settler woman working with Indigenous communities. The main plenary featured Indigenous organizers, making the case for why it is important for settler students campaigning for divestment to take Indigenous land struggles seriously. They made arguments for why campaigns should take up the practice of territorial acknowledgment, relationship building, and substantive solidarity in the face of the Canadian government's aggressive policy agenda that devastates the environment and undermines Indigenous sovereignty and land claims. They stressed that the divestment campaign needed to build and sustain relationships with Indigenous communities.

On the third day of the convergence, one of the three breakout groups focused on Indigenous solidarity. The group's task was to operationalize ways for campaigns to act in solidarity with Indigenous peoples. While the group of all settler-identified students from different campuses worked together for two hours, participants struggled. There were two campus campaigns where the language of Indigenous solidarity was already entrenched in their practices, but the students from the other seven campuses felt challenged to find ways to do the work. Many student activists were afraid of messing up, didn't know how to start a relationship with Indigenous people whose territories they occupied, wrestled with settler guilt, and overall found it hard to find space within the day-to-day campaign work to fit Indigenous solidarity. One organizer from Mount Allison was concerned about how to approach and engage Indigenous Elders. Hannah, a student organizer from Quebec, worried that territorial acknowledgments were inadequate and could become rote and stale. Others struggled to understand the language of colonialism at all, since it was completely new material for them. Riley stressed how important it had been for her to hear from impacted Indigenous people, saying, "This was my first exposure to these ideas." When University of Toronto students discussed it afterward, some group members resisted, suggesting it was a "distraction from the actual campaign." Melina responded:

> We were there and we heard these people talk, right? And that's why I think I am having such a hard time, like understanding—I mean, I do understand where you are coming from—but—like—hearing them talk—Y'know what I mean? Hearing them explain it, you were like, "Oh that makes sense!", right? And I just want other people to hear it the same way too. I don't think, like, it should be something that we just don't do, just because it might . . . like . . . because it's really important.

Though she didn't have a clear idea of how to act on the ideas of Indigenous solidarity yet, she felt strongly that it was a priority that the group should commit to.

This move to grapple with the complexity of climate justice is one of the biggest contributions youth are making to the climate movement. Doing the work of bringing anti-oppression conversations into a space that otherwise may not enable or encourage engagement with these issues, especially in the parts of the environmental movement that historically have been white, settler, and upper/middle class, is significant. In many ways, students' attempts to bridge the dominant frames of divestment and climate justice demonstrate the hard work facing the climate movement today and indicate how underequipped settler students are to take on anticolonial and decolonizing work as part of the environmental movement. Yet despite the challenges, student activists do seem to have a sense that this is the right direction to take, and they are fighting hard to reframe the campaign. Climate justice is moving from being the mantra to becoming the raison d'être for the divestment campaign. Sam, a University of Toronto organizer, said:

Oppression and race and injustice are the whole reason I am involved in climate change. Because, um, I mean, I love the polar bears, and the trees and the fish, but that's not the reason that I do this. It's because it's so fundamentally unfair, based on race, gender, age. Basically all the people who have decision-making power on climate change are not the ones getting the short end of the stick when it comes to the effects. It's time we stop framing this as an environmental issue and start framing it as an issue of justice and oppression.

This shift to embrace climate justice also shows us some of the limitations of the divestment strategy, where divestment does not require attention to justice issues. As campus groups follow the set of steps laid out in the guidebooks, it is possible, and arguably much easier, to proceed without attention to the ways that race, colonialism, and capitalism shape questions of climate change and activism. However, students are reshaping how they understand divestment and working to integrate deeper forms of solidarity throughout.

Toward a Deeper Solidarity

The rallying cry of the student divestment campaign speaks volumes about the direction in which the campaign is heading. We find this turn to integrate climate justice hopeful and radically necessary for addressing climate change meaningfully. However, from our research and our engagement in the campaign, we recognize the limits and potential of divestment as a climate justice tactic. Divestment is not inherently a tool for advancing climate justice, but many students are working to situate divestment within broader conversations about colonialism, institutional racism, and the limits of capitalism. There is much to be done to take climate justice from a recently introduced frame to a deeply integrated strategic and tactical set of actions. We know from our research that this work is slow, and that while in some spaces, discussions of climate justice, intersectionality, and solidarity are central, in many spaces they remain nascent, sometimes dormant, complicated, sometimes fraught. There is significant potential within campaigns for the language and political analysis of intersectionality and solidarity to take off and become inextricably linked, but there is more to be done in order to make sure all divestment activists understand a political analysis that ties climate change to race and colonialism explicitly.

Reinvestment is an emergent conversation that is coming up in more and more campaigns and has the potential of bridging some of the gaps between the climate movement and the environmental justice movement. Where youth activists have felt that divestment may not necessarily give them a way to work in solidarity, reinvestment makes explicit direct ties to community-driven development projects that seek to create the backbone of a just transition. Alexandra, a reinvestment partner of the campaign, described the shift to more solidarity driven work, saying, "Over the past couple of years of building the fossil fuel divestment movement, we've realized that it's not just important where our money isn't going, but it's also equally if not more important where our money is going. So we have an obligation to push our universities to invest their money in the right places as well."

Reinvestment attempts to move campus investments away from the carbon economy and redirect them to grassroots climate justice organizations working on alternative energy development. Students are working with grassroots climate justice organizations and larger NGOs to develop strategies to reinvest portions of funds divested from the fossil fuel industry into the "just transition" of affected communities. As this initiative develops, divestment organizers are hopeful that attempts to include a climate justice analysis in the campaign will have the potential to be grounded in real solutions over symbolic rhetoric. DSN organizer Sachie said:

> I really believe that where the movement is heading is towards a focus on community reinvestment and to frontline-led solutions. I think that's both vital in terms of lifting up real solutions, in terms of shifting power to communities who have been most disenfranchised in the extractive economy, and to the DSN's mission of movement building and actually building shared power beyond campus with the broader grassroots climate justice movement.

For many, reinvestment offers divestment campaigns and their institutions an opportunity to put their money where their mouths are, and serves to anchor the climate justice framework in real solutions for affected communities.

CONCLUSION

The fossil fuel divestment campaign is important activism at an important historical and ecological moment. Students are leading a campaign that fits into a much broader movement to stop climate change, and in so doing they are developing a political analysis that has the potential to greatly expand the discourse of a generation of activists and the environmental movement. Through their campaigns, divestment organizers are working to bring solidarity, anti-oppression, and climate justice to the fore for the next/current generation of leaders of the environmental movement. They link the histories and continuities of colonialism to climate change and understand that the root causes are shared. Ben explained:

We're not going to actually deal with climate change until we, like, address, like systemic issues around race and class and gender. In a sense, all I mean, really is that, like, climate change is the by-product of colonialism—those structures have led to climate change and are what make it difficult to address. The fact that some lives don't matter and some voices are, like, immediately discounted from political power is a big reason why what should be an obvious issue is not at all politically salient.

Tracing the shifts over the last years allows us to see how this political analysis is becoming more present in the campaign and how relationships are growing, usually tied to local campaigns and rooted in trust and accountability. We can also see it across the national campaigns, as the convergences have centered Indigenous activists' voices and challenged students to find ways to bridge land and sovereignty struggles with the campus campaigns. As activists and scholars, we are hopeful that the shifts we see occurring in the environmental movement are representative of larger transformations in youth-led activism, where anti-oppression, intersectionality, and justice are being integrated into the core work more centrally. We are optimistic about the alliances being built between racial justice organizations, Indigenous struggles for sovereignty, and environmentalists, and hope that it signals a dramatic shift. Amil, an organizer at the University of Toronto, often argues that this shift toward climate justice is fundamentally necessary for the youth climate campaign, saying, "This is the way most of the world frames environmental issues, and without this understanding we cannot build a movement." We want to stress his concept here. In youth organizing today, the logic of movement building is deeply tied to the antiracist and anticolonial approaches. Though making connections is difficult work, student organizers we work with are clear that this is the work. About integrating intersectionality into the campaign, Lila said, "It's not just divesting. If we divest and that's it, we've failed. We have to build something bigger." This is one of the great opportunities and challenges youth organizers offer social movements today.

ACKNOWLEDGMENTS

Many thanks to our participants, the talented and committed students pushing for fossil fuel divestment. Additional thanks to the Divestment Student Network Coordinating Committee, Anjali Helferty, Ben Donato-Woodger, and Andrew Kohan for their edits and feedback on the draft. This was written with the generous support of the Vanier Canada Graduate Scholarship, the New College Doctoral Fellowship, and the Mellon Mays Undergraduate Fellowship.

REFERENCES

Absolon, K. E. (2011). *Kaandosswin: How We Come to Know.* Winnipeg, CA: Fernwood Publishing.

Bloom, L. R. (1998). *Under the sign of hope: Feminist methodology and narrative interpretation.* Albany, NY: State University of New York Press.

Booker, A. (2010). Framing youth civic participation: Technical, pragmatic, and political learning. In L. Lin, H. Varenne, & E. W. Gordon (Eds.), *Educating comprehensively: Varieties of educational experiences* (pp. 209–231). Lewiston, NY: Edwin Mellen Press.

Calabrese Barton, A. (1998). Teaching science with homeless children: Pedagogy, representation, and identity. *Journal of Research in Science Teaching, 35*(4), 379–394. http://dx.doi.org/10.1002/(SICI)1098-2736(199804)35:4<379::AID-TEA8>3.0.CO;2-N

Calabrese Barton, A., & Tan, E. (2010). We be burnin'! Agency, identity, and science learning. *Journal of the Learning Sciences, 19*(2), 187–229. http://dx.doi.org/10.1080/10508400903530044

Cammarota, J., & Fine, M. (Eds.). (2010). *Revolutionizing education: Youth participatory action research in motion.* New York, NY: Routledge.

Canadian Youth Climate Coalition. (2015). Retrieved from www.ourclimate.ca

Checkoway, B., & Gutierrez, L. M. (2006). Youth participation and community change. *Journal of Community Practice, 14*(1), 1–9. http://dx.doi.org/10.1300/J125v14n01_01

Choudry, A. (2010). Global justice? Contesting NGOization: Knowledge politics and containment in anti-globalization networks. In A. Choudry & D. Kapoor (Eds.), *Learning from the ground up: Global perspectives on knowledge production in social movements* (pp. 17–34). New York, NY: Palgrave Macmillan.

Conner, J. O. (2011). Youth organizers as young adults: Their commitments and contributions. *Journal of Research on Adolescence, 21*(4), 923–942. http://dx.doi.org/10.1111/j.15327795.2011.00766.x

Cravey, A. J. (2004). Students and the anti-sweatshop movement. *Antipode, 36*(2), 203–208. http://dx.doi.org/10.1111/j.1467-8330.2004.00400.x

Featherstone, L., & United Students Against Sweatshops. (2002). *Students against sweatshops.* London: Verso.

Fine, M. (1991). *Framing dropouts: Notes on the politics of an urban high school.* New York, NY: State University of New York Press.

Fossil Free. (n.d.). Fossil free: A campus guide to fossil fuel divestment. Retrieved from www.gofossilfree.org

Fossil Free Canada. (2016). About. *Fossil Free.* Retrieved from www.gofossilfree.ca

Fossil Free USA. (2016). About. *Fossil Free.* Retrieved from www.gofossilfree.org

Ginwright, S. A., Noguera, P., & Cammarota, J. (Eds.). (2006). *Beyond resistance!: Youth activism and community change: New democratic possibilities for practice and policy for America's youth.* New York, NY: Routledge.

Grady-Benson, J. (2014). *Fossil fuel divestment: The power and promise of a student movement for climate justice* (Unpublished undergraduate thesis). Pitzer College, California.

Grady-Benson, J., & Sarathy, B. (2016). Fossil fuel divestment in U.S. higher education: Student-led organising for climate justice. *Local Environment, 21*(6):661–681. http://dx.doi.org/10.1080/13549839.2015.1009825

Helferty, A., & Clarke, A. (2009). Student-led campus climate change initiatives in Canada. *International Journal of Sustainability in Higher Education, 10*(3), 287–300. http://dx.doi.org/10.1108/14676370910972594

Hill-Collins, P. (2002). *Black feminist thought: Knowledge, consciousness, and the politics of empowerment.* Abingdon, UK: Routledge.

Kirshner, B. (2008). Guided participation in three youth activism organizations: Facilitation, apprenticeship, and joint work. *Journal of the Learning Sciences, 17*(1), 60–101. http://dx.doi.org/10.1080/10508400701793190

Kirshner, B. (2015). *Youth activism in an era of education inequality.* New York, NY: New York University Press.

Kwon, S. A. (2008). Moving from complaints to action: Oppositional consciousness and collective action in a political community. *Anthropology & Education Quarterly, 39*(1), 59–76. http://dx.doi.org/10.1111/j.1548-1492.2008.00005.x

Kwon, S. A. (2013). *Uncivil youth: Race, activism, and affirmative governmentality.* Durham, NC: Duke University Press.

Lowe, L., & Sanzillo, T. (2011). White paper: Financial risks of investments in coal. *As You Sow.* Retrieved from http://www.asyousow.org/ays_report/white-paper-financial-risks-of-investments-in-coal/

Niemeyer, G., Garcia, A., & Naima, R. (2009). Black cloud: Patterns towards da future. *Proceedings of the 17th ACM International Conference on Multimedia, USA,* 1073–1082. http://dx.doi.org/10.1145/1631272.1631514

Nyks, K. (Director), & Scott, J. P. (Producer). (2013). *Do the math* [Motion picture]. United States: PF Pictures.

Power Up! (2013). Power Up! Student Convergence. *Divestment Student Network.* Unpublished convergence program.

Rogers, J., Morrell, E., & Enyedy, N. (2007). Studying the struggle: Contexts for learning and identity development for urban youth. *American Behavioral Scientist, 51*(3), 419–443. http://dx.doi.org/10.1177/0002764207306069

Silvey, R. (2004). A wrench in the global works: Anti-sweatshop activism on campus. *Antipode, 36*(2), 191–197. http://dx.doi.org/10.1111/j.1467-8330.2004.00398.x

Stephens, J. C., Hernandez, M. E., Román, M., Graham, A. C., & Scholz, R. W. (2008). Higher education as a change agent for sustainability in different cultures and contexts. *International Journal of Sustainability in Higher Education, 9*(3), 317–338. http://dx.doi.org/10.1108/14676370810885916

Stephenson, W. (2012, October 18). Cue the math: McKibben's roadshow takes aim at Big Oil. *Grist.* Retrieved from grist.org

Swarthmore Mountain Justice. (2015, March 19). Breaking: 37 Swarthmore students and 6 alumni begin sit-in in finance and investments office for divestment. Retrieved from swatmj.org

350.org. (2016). *Do the math* tour. Retrieved from www.math.350.org.

Wilson, S. (2008). *Research is ceremony: Indigenous research methods.* Black Point, NS: Fernwood Publishing.

Wilson, B. R., & Curnow, J. (2013). Solidarity™: Student activism, affective labor, and the fair trade campaign in the United States. *Antipode, 45*(3), 565–583. http://dx.doi.org/10.1111/j.14678330.2012.01051.x

Part IV

Conclusion

20

Conclusion

Jerusha Conner and Sonia M. Rosen

It has been 10 years since the release of the seminal work *Beyond Resistance: Youth Activism and Community Change* (Ginwright, Noguera, & Cammarota, 2006) and the comprehensive two-volume *Youth Activism: An International Encyclopedia* (Sherrod, Flanagan, Kassimir, & Syvertsen, 2006), and during that time, both the field of youth activism and U.S. society have changed in key ways. Over the course of the last decade, new social problems have developed, while existing problems have become both more entrenched and more urgent. At the same time, youth activist groups that take on these problems have matured and become more sophisticated in their approaches, even as new sets of actors, coalitions, and forms of activism have emerged. It is important that research keep pace with these fast-moving developments not only to document their rise and impact, but also to identify the implications of this work and to extract key lessons about how social change happens, how conceptualizations of social justice can be broadened and shared, and what roles youth can play in advancing these causes and transforming society.

In this book, we frame the social problems that have arisen or worsened in recent years as a function of the neoliberal state. The neoliberal state refers to a model of governance that favors the unregulated expansion of free markets and a reduced role for government in the provision of social services and safety nets. It is also a context in which the exercise of agency is equated with consumer choice and individuals favor protecting their own self-interest over adhering to any notion of the common good or shared public interest (Au & Ferrare, 2015). The term "neoliberalism" does not feature prominently in most of the chapters in this book; however, the authors use related language, such as "privatization" and "privatized spaces" (e.g., Gallay, Lupinacci, Sarmiento, Flanagan, & Lowenstein, this volume), "state violence" (e.g., Dohrn & Ayers, this volume), "state-sanctioned violence" (e.g., Stoudt et al., this volume), and "interlocking systems of oppression" (e.g., Daniel & Valladares, this volume) to describe the conditions and contexts against which contemporary youth activists rail. These conditions are marked by reckless environmental policies that accelerate climate change (Curnow & Gross, this volume; Gallay et al., this volume); the breaking apart of families through detention and deportation policies and the denial of access to higher education for undocumented youth (Negrón-Gonzales, this volume); aggressive policing practices that disproportionately impact Black and Brown bodies (Dohrn & Ayers, this volume; Stoudt et al., this volume); harsh school discipline policies that push youth of color out of school (Fernandez, Kirshner, & Lewis, this volume); educational policies and practices that sanction or perpetuate discrimination against and violence toward indigenous youth (Solyom, this volume), recent immigrants, English language learners (Yee, this volume), and victims of sexual assault (Brodsky, this volume); and media narratives that frame youth as problems to be feared or solved, rather than as capable civic actors (Ferman & Smirnov, this volume.) Each of these issues is in some way connected to neoliberalism, either through a market-based profit motive (whether that motive is held by the businesses that seek to avoid regulation, oversight, and taxes for pollution, the private detention centers that generate revenue from taxpayer money, or the media corporations that favor slick and sensationalized stories to nuanced, complicated portraits) or through the neoliberal worldview that sees victims of violence as having either invented their plight or invited such acts upon themselves through their poor life choices.

The contributors to this book show how the work of contemporary youth activists presents fundamental challenges to the logic of neoliberalism. Collectively, the 18 chapters make a clear case that even as contemporary youth activists draw on the legacies of prior struggles and social movements, they work at the cutting edge of today's issues, responding to changing conditions in social structures, contesting new forms of injustice, anticipating future challenges, and championing more inclusive and democratic alternatives. In so doing, they have brought to the fore a number of issues and strategies that were not previously in the public eye. They force the difficult conversations, they present new complex analyses, and they demand alternatives. The chapters show that through the course of this work, not only do the young people derive great benefits, but so does society. As contemporary youth activists push back against neoliberal social, economic, and political structures, they both alter their own positionality as neoliberal subjects and open doors for broader civic involvement by other groups, thereby creating the conditions for a more just and equitable society. In what follows, we look across the 18 chapters in this book to draw three broad lessons about the roles young people can and do play in contesting neoliberalism and advancing social justice.

WHAT WE CAN LEARN FROM CONTEMPORARY YOUTH ACTIVISTS

Although contemporary youth activism takes many different forms (Braxton, this volume), three common features stand out across the various studies and cases included in this book. Here, we argue that today's youth activists are building an effective resistance movement by working with, around, and at intersections; using counternarratives to exercise agency and self-determination; and standing with and for youth. We describe each of these features further below, while showing how they enable contemporary youth activists to mount a powerful challenge to neoliberal solutions and enact alternatives to a neoliberal worldview.

Working at the Intersections

The authors in this volume demonstrate the many ways contemporary youth activists work at intersections. All three sections of this volume point to the places where various issues, social identities and interest groups, geographic regions, and time periods intersect. Youth activists recognize the strategic value of crossing geographic boundaries, connecting issue-based struggles, and forming alliances with adults and other youth activists. In these ways, they demonstrate an expanded conception of what kinds of organizing work are in their own interests, understanding oppression as intersectional and viewing different types of progressive activism as interconnected.

Several authors write about how youth activists have dealt explicitly with the notion of intersectionality. The groups featured in Chapter 7 framed environmental justice as an intersectional issue—a melding of environmental degradation and social injustices such as racism and classism—that disproportionately impacts the most marginalized communities. In response to policies and practices that have poisoned, privatized, and laid waste to public resources in low-income Black and Brown communities, youth have organized to reclaim the commons by mobilizing specific social identities to gain public support for their work. For instance, concerned about the detrimental environmental and health effects of an incinerator on their communities, youth activists in Detroit pointed to the intersecting issues that framed this problem, including economic and racial injustice and widespread environmental harm. These youth then worked alongside adults to mobilize their peers and communities to demand policy changes aimed at shutting down the incinerator and taking other measures toward achieving a zero-waste city (Gallay et al., this volume). Eric Braxton points out that young adult organizers are also quick to identify intersectional oppressions, lifting up the leadership of people who have been marginalized in past social justice struggles (such as women in the struggle for racial justice), understanding how multiple oppressions reinforce one another (such as racism and sexism), and . . . building an analysis that recognizes that in order to end one form of oppression, all oppression must be ended.

This acknowledgment of intersectionality is thus a central feature of and driving force in contemporary youth activists' organizing work.

In addition to showing how various social identities intersect in the work of contemporary youth activists, the cases in this book illustrate the moments when youth activists strategize to capitalize on the convergence of different groups' interests. Rachel Gunther tells the story of Youth on Board's (YOB) campaign to improve the feedback loop between students and teachers by introducing a system in which students could regularly offer their teachers constructive feedback. Recognizing that teachers may be reticent about the idea of being evaluated by their students, YOB members organized a meeting with the Boston Teachers' Union (BTU) in which they successfully demonstrated to union members that their plan would serve the interests of both students and teachers.

Youth activists also find ways to transcend the local by connecting across geographic boundaries, a trend that is particularly apparent in Chapter 19. In this chapter, Joe Curnow and Allyson Gross detail university students' initiation of a continent-wide fossil fuel divestment campaign. The students featured in this chapter planned a nationwide convening of youth activists, hoping to prompt cross-country collaboration and encourage activists across the United States and Canada to view their work from an "environmental/economic justice framework." Similarly, Mark Warren and Luke Aubry Kupscznk point to the Alliance for Educational Justice (AEJ) as a space for youth organizing groups to coordinate nationwide campaigns and share organizing strategies related to education reform. In connecting with one another through AEJ, youth are traversing geographic boundaries that might otherwise limit the scope of their organizing work.

Though these activists are adept at crossing boundaries, campaign development frequently begins with young people's personal experiences with oppressive power structures (explored in more depth in the following section), which they then broaden and connect to their peers' experiences as well. In these situations, young people also commonly find themselves making connections to the past and future, as was the case for the activists featured in Chapter 18. Solyom explains,

The efforts in this study were driven by a desire not to preserve programs and personnel for individual students' success but out of a desire to protect treaty-protected rights and programs for future generations. In other words, youth were advocating for the rights of youth who would come after them.

This focus on the future allows youth activists to engage in what is called "prefigurative politics," or the enactment of relationships within organizations and movements that characterize the kind of world they are attempting to create together (Yates, 2014). Collectively, these acts of connecting through and across time, space, and social identities allow youth activists to strategically position themselves as influential change agents in an often divisive social context.

Using Counternarratives to Exercise Agency and Self-Determination

Young organizers navigate these intersections bearing their own very human stories and experiences. Many of the chapters in this book explore the ways youth produce counternarratives, which facilitate internal, individual transformation and simultaneously have the power to change broader discourse about particular issues or policies. These counternarratives are, in essence, forms of discursive resistance that push back against the oppressive systems that obscure the voices of marginalized peoples, either pathologizing those groups or rendering them invisible (Fernández et al., this volume; Solyom, this volume; Stoudt et al., this volume).

The authors in this volume demonstrate that counternarratives emerge when youth voice testimonies that employ personal experience to contradict dominant discourse or point to the presence of injustice in systems and institutions. For instance, in Chapters 6 and 17, Jesica Fernández and her colleagues and Brett Stoudt and his colleagues demonstrate the power youth asserted when they used public testimony to name the ways they and their peers were being systematically criminalized. In these cases, the youth activists told the stories of their and others' personal encounters with either the police or harsh school discipline policies, situating those stories in a broader analysis of how specific policies and institutional practices function to dehumanize low-income Black and Brown youth and funnel them into the criminal justice system. In both cases, testifying was part of a larger organizing strategy, and it put a human face on the analysis the youth activists had constructed.

For the Y-MAC youth in San Francisco, the oral testimonies they presented in their community-wide public event were the starting point for a series of other strategies that involved connecting with more students and community members through flyers, websites, and planned face-to-face encounters. Testifying became a strategy for changing public perception and mobilizing other youth to join the struggle to disrupt the school-to-prison nexus (Fernández et al., this volume). For the youth in Researchers for Fair Policing, who testified in New York City council hearings in support of passing the Right to Know Act, the expertise they had gained from their extensive research into Broken Windows policing allowed them to speak directly to the people with the power to shift policy. In this case, their use of testimony was layered, since their findings were, in large part, based on the systematic collection of youth narratives that they interpreted and combined with statistical data in order to produce a cohesive narrative that would sound compelling to lawmakers (Stoudt et al., this volume). For both groups, testifying was also a means of altering the public's perception of a problem that primarily affects youth and offering up creative solutions for persistent problems.

Across the chapters in this volume, we saw many examples of youth using their testimonies to position themselves as experts around issues that shape their lives. In Philadelphia, Asian immigrant high school students' careful records of violent incidents at their school became instrumental in mounting a legal case against the district. Their testimonies in a public, citywide forum were central to establishing solidarity with youth across racial and ethnic groups, forming a counternarrative that allowed them to challenge the district's framing of the issue as stemming from unresolvable racial divides (Yee, this volume). At the university level, students fighting to end campus gender violence at Yale University mobilized the testimonies of victims to support a case against the university with the Department of Education's Office for Civil Rights. Ultimately, the use of testimony as counternarrative became a widespread strategy that students across the nation used to "call out" their universities (Brodsky, this volume).

The power of youth testimony is equally apparent in Rachel Gunther's discussion (this volume) of Youth on Board's campaign to transform teacher-student relationships by introducing a system to capture and communicate students' constructive feedback. In this example, youth activists testified about their experiences in the classroom to a gathering of teachers in the BTU as a means of garnering support for their constructive feedback system. By producing a counternarrative that showcased their expertise and contradicted teachers' assumptions about the need for and value of student feedback, these youth successfully gained the support of the BTU in order to move forward with their districtwide plan.

The cases above illustrate the power of targeting specific audiences with youth testimony. However, youth testimonies are equally powerful in establishing counternarratives when they are geared toward more general audiences, as in the case of youth from the Philadelphia-based University Community Collaborative, who produced their own television news show, called POPPYN. In the media-making process, youth drew on their own stories as a basis for interpreting, explaining, and resisting the oppressions that impacted their communities. Pairing these stories with their own critical analysis in the programming they created, then, was a key strategy for changing public discourse. In this way, their testimonies—the personal stories with which they began—served as an entry for youth and their audiences to develop a deeper understanding of a range of important social issues (Ferman & Smirnov, this volume). Native American university students used a similar media production strategy in order to counter inaccurate and problematic mainstream accounts of their multifaceted struggle to make the university a more welcoming and inclusive space for Native Americans. By engaging with Native journalists and utilizing student-led media sources, these students were able to ensure that their stories, which were being misrepresented in mainstream media outlets, were communicated accurately and adequately contextualized as part of the history of the Native American genocide. As such, they created counternarratives that contradicted the university's attempts either to diminish the severity of the issues that the Native student activists were raising or to dismiss them altogether (Solyom, this volume).

The stories presented in this volume also demonstrate that when young people testify to one another, they produce counternarratives that can shift the internal social dynamics of an organization or movement. In Chapter 9, Kira Baker-Doyle deconstructs how youth activists used testimonials about their own organizing experiences to inspire nonorganizer youth. As part of PEPP-UTLP, program participants had the chance to meet with youth activists from several different nearby organizations. The stories these activists told about their organizations, their campaigns, and their victories served as a counternarrative that contradicted the widely held belief that young people do not have any significant social and political power. Program participants left these meetings with an expanded sense of possibility and a belief that they too could effect change. One participant said,

[The youth organizers' presentations] opened my eyes to how big of a role I can play and how much of a leader I am. Now I'm trying and going to make a difference in my community and in society. . . . We are going to build a foundation for a brighter future.

Here, a counternarrative about the power of young people's organizing helped high school students resist their own internalized oppression, inspiring young people to view themselves as part of a bigger movement for change.

These testimonies can also challenge problematic movement dynamics that further the marginalization of particular movement actors. In Chapter 11, Julia Daniel and Michelle Renée Valladares present an account of Black women and Black gender-queer individuals who created explicit collective space to relate their experiences being victimized and marginalized both within and outside of their movement work. This opportunity to collectively construct intersectional race- and gender-related counternarratives empowered activists to influence the direction of the movement and gave them a chance to support one another's healing.

Though counternarratives are powerful as a strategy for producing systemic change and as a means of confronting difficult internal movement dynamics, using testimony as the basis for these counternarratives can itself be challenging. Testifying—telling personal stories of suffering and relating them to collective narratives of systemic oppression—is risky, especially for youth who are already marginalized because of their age, gender, residency status, race/ethnicity, socioeconomic status, or sexual orientation. This was a dilemma for many of the youth described in this book. For instance, for undocumented youth, merely revealing their status can put them in danger of detention and eventual deportation (Negrón-Gonzales, this volume). Similarly, activists experiencing gender-based violence may be perceived as threatening and yet again become targets of the perpetrators of such violence (Brodsky, this volume; Daniel & Valladares, this volume). Youth who are speaking out against unfair educational practices can become the targets of teachers and administrators (Astorga-Ramos, this volume). In these cases, activists may find themselves in precisely the dangerous situations that they are seeking to end. Further, though the act of naming and telling the story of one's oppression can precipitate healing, reliving horrific experiences (and potentially opening oneself up to new attacks) can be traumatizing as well (Brodsky, this volume; Ballard & Ozer, this volume; Daniel & Valladares, this volume; Negrón-Gonzales, this volume). In circulating these counternarratives, youth activists are empowered by their decision to be publicly vulnerable, yet they also risk becoming even more vulnerable precisely because of the powerful stances they are taking.

Moreover, when activists share their stories in an effort to produce counternarratives, they leave these narratives up to public interpretation. Alexandra Brodsky captures the frustration of feeling constrained by these interpretations as a radio producer prepared her for an interview:

I explained to the producer that I planned to speak about the policy change I had championed, not my personal backstory. Shortly thereafter, I was disinvited. "We already have an expert, so we need a survivor," the producer explained, as though one could not be both at the same time.

In effect, the producer was positioning her in a way that was antithetical to how she wanted to be perceived, and, in doing so, this individual undermined the structure and message of the campaign.

Yet youth activists also employ strategies that can mitigate the risks associated with sharing a counternarrative. For instance, presenting stories collectively rather than individually emphasizes the pervasiveness of the problems youth encounter. In the examples offered in Chapters 5, 10, and 15, the authors point to ways that youth activists have gathered and curated many individual stories—whether of police violence in Black communities, experiences with disabilities and mental health, or violent incidents in a high school—and used media or the legal system to communicate these stories as collective, rather than purely individual, narratives (Dohrn & Ayers, this volume; Ferman & Smirnov, this volume; Yee, this volume).

Another strategy some youth activists use to mitigate the risks they assume in telling their stories is to collaborate or work in coalition with adult allies, who publicly affirm these counternarratives and offer emotional and intellectual support for their actions (Baker-Doyle, this volume; Braxton, this volume; Ferman & Smirnov, this volume; Gunther, this volume; Warren & Kupscznk, this volume). For example, in Chapter 15 Yee explains that although many of the youth activists in her study initially "lacked confidence to speak out, adult advocates and allies taught them about [past] community victories." Yee argues that the lessons imparted from "the longtime community activists were crucial in educating the youth, raising their political consciousness, providing a strong sense of self determination and agency, and connecting them to networks of support." In Chapter 6, Fernández et al. (this volume) provide one small example of the power of adult support for youth whose activism has made them vulnerable. Using an excerpt from their field notes, the authors recount a poignant moment when a youth activist who was testifying at a campaign event about the impact of zero tolerance policies on her sense of self broke down in tears. An adult ally from her organizing group called out, "Deep breath, [Itzel]! You got this!" This simple exhortation seemed to embolden Itzel, and she continued her testimony in stronger tones. Certainly, activism can involve hardship, elicit pain, and require taking personal risks; however, when these risks are taken and these challenges are met in the context of supportive relationships with adults as well as other youth, they can lay the groundwork for powerful individual as well as societal transformation.

Standing with and for Youth

A central argument of this book is that contemporary youth activism benefits society. Part 3 contains a number of examples documenting how youth activists have spurred changes to policy and practice, influenced decision-making processes, and shaped public opinion. While all these approaches represent important means of bringing about a more just and responsive society, here we argue that another way in which contemporary youth activists improve society is by supporting one another. When youth express love and concern for one another, and especially when that love extends to youth who have been otherwise marginalized or scorned by society, they create a powerful space for belonging. In these spaces, not only are individual life trajectories possibly altered in some fundamental ways (as suggested by Rogers and Terriquez's finding that youth organizing alumni are far more likely than comparable peers to enroll in four-year colleges and universities and engage in various civic activities in early adulthood), but also a new generation is enacting and prefiguring the kind of society they wish to bring about for their peers and future generations (Yates, 2014). The themes of support and care by youth and for youth surfaced in multiple chapters across all sections of this book.

Many chapters in this book profile organizations or groups in which a culture of care, created and maintained by youth, is on full display. In some cases, this culture is demonstrated through the expression of care from one individual youth to another. For example, in Chapter 4, a veteran student organizer with the Philadelphia Student Union, Mike, spent hours patiently supporting a newer member, Terrance, in conducting the necessary background research to produce a successful radio segment on the Campaign for Nonviolent Schools. In her chapter on a youth participatory action research collective, Kira Baker-Doyle describes how a sense of mutual responsibility and care came to pervade the entire group and characterize the youths' interactions with one another:

> Participants began to push each other to be leaders—to speak up and use their talents. They developed a shared respect for one another, and a sense of caring. Participant Michelle described this emerging sense of trust and passion in terms of "*la familia*" in her journal, noting, "We are a *familia por la vida siempre!* (We are a family for the rest of our lives!)."

While Baker-Doyle's case study involved in-person interactions among youth, a culture of care could also develop in virtual contexts, as we learned in Chapter 13. Here, Brodsky recounts how the activists who grew the movement to end sexual assault on college campuses "coalesced on email chains and Facebook groups to share tips and ask for advice." She writes, "Soon we had an organic, rapidly growing community of student and young alumni organizers determined to change their campuses and support one another." In these cases, as well as in others, youth contributed to one another's socio-political development as researchers, media producers, leaders, and social change agents.

The importance of establishing safe, loving spaces in which youth care for one another and process, heal from, and respond to the injustices and violence perpetrated against them was also apparent in several chapters. In Chapter 11, Daniel and Valladares describe how one member, Logan, was inspired to "create a mobile safe space that is inclusive for youth of color across the gender spectrum at S.O.U.L. Sister" and how this space became a resource for others to "access their authentic humanity, heal from their pain," and come together to support one another. Similarly, Yee documents in Chapter 15 the horrific conditions that led first-generation Asian immigrant youth to form the Asian Student Association of Philadelphia (ASAP), "an autonomous youth organization, youth-run and youth-led." This organization, Yee argues, afforded youth "the space to be heard, explore, learn, and grow . . . to gain new knowledge and skills, develop their critical consciousness, and exercise their collective strength." Throughout this book, we see many examples of youth deliberately carving out these more inclusive, affirmative, and transformative spaces for themselves and one another.

Nowhere, though, were the themes of love and the desire to stand with and for other youth more prominent than in the three essays contributed to this volume by youth activists themselves. Beatrice Galdamez succinctly explains, "As an activist, I don't just fight for myself—I fight for everyone who wants to be able to live their full selves." Jamia Brown recalls the words of Assata Shakur:

> "It is our duty to fight for freedom. It is our duty to win. We must love and support each other. We have nothing to lose but our chains." . . . Even in my toughest times and when I feel that it isn't worth it, I remember these words, keeping in mind that I need to show solidarity with the people with whom I share the same risks. I think that this is the most beautiful part of the duty and the process of dismantling systems and institutions of oppression.

She concludes her essay, "This is for all the colored girls. 'It is our duty to fight for freedom!'" And Janelle Ramos echoes, "We will not give up. This isn't just for us; it's also for our brothers, sisters, and cousins, all of whom deserve a high-quality education." These youths' voices resonate with the unwavering sense of commitment to their peers and to future generations that is so characteristic of the many contemporary youth activists profiled in this book.

The centrality of love and commitment to others in activism work is neither new nor specific to youth activism. For example, Freire (2000) insisted that "true solidarity is found only in the plenitude of this act of love" (p. 50). Similarly, the Reverend Dr. Martin Luther King Jr. called for a "love that does justice" as fundamental to social change (Edwards, 2014). Research, too, has long noted links between activism and love (Conner, 2014; Ginwright, 2010; Su, 2009; Warren, 2010). In uplifting the salience of contemporary youth activists' concern and care for one another, we do not wish to dismiss or downplay the importance of adult allies joining with and conveying love and care for youth activists. The role of adults was described powerfully in chapters by Braxton, Baker-Doyle, Warren and Kupscznk, and Yee, among others. Nonetheless, we do believe that there is something particularly salient about young people expressing care and concern for one another, standing with and for one another, as they work to advance social justice. Janelle Ramos envisions a "generational effect which will eventually change society." Contemporary youth activists set this generational effect in motion as they contribute to one another's well-being and personal growth and refashion the world in which they live consistent with their vision for an inclusive, just, and sustainable society.

DIRECTIONS FOR FUTURE RESEARCH

Collectively, the contributors to this volume make the case that even as contemporary youth activism continues a rich historical tradition of youth engagement in the United States, it charts new territory, pioneering new forms of activism, deploying new tools, responding to new emergent issues and challenges, and bringing new perspectives and analytic frames to bear. Some have argued that today's student activism is also marked by a newfound sophistication and maturity (Johnston, 2015). In 2016, we may well be witnessing the cresting of a new wave of contemporary youth activism; however, research is needed to validate such claims and to continue to track the magnitude of the wave and its implications both for the youth involved, as they age, and for the systems and structures they have targeted. Many new questions surface, as this new wave swells and gains power and force. For how long will it build? What is the nature of the winds at its back? When will it crest? What will it succeed in wiping out and what will be left in its wake?

Speaking less metaphorically, the contributors in this volume identify several avenues for future research. For example, Ballard and Ozer (this volume) call for more research on how involvement in activism affects the well-being of individuals from various social identity groups. Rogers and Terriquez (this volume) suggest the need to study how differences across youth organizing groups, such as their longevity, shape their ability to promote educational and civic outcomes. Turning from questions about the effects on individuals to societal effects, Warren and Kupscznk (this volume) ask, "What will be the relationship of the youth movement to other social movements?" Similarly Fernández and colleagues (this volume) wonder about possible connections between those involved in organizing to end the school-to-prison pipeline and those involved in the Black Lives Matter movement. We would add to these calls for future research the need to study how policymakers and adults in positions of power respond to youth-led research and youth testimony. Under what conditions do youths' personal accounts, research, and analyses lead to change in decision-making processes and outcomes? Other important questions for the field include: What roles do and should adults play in advancing youth activism? What networking and organizing strategies do youth activists need to employ as part of the broader movement to counter neoliberal social policies? Finally, as the field continues to mature, it becomes possible to conduct more longitudinal research like Rogers and Terriquez's large-scale study of California youth in Chapter 8. Research that tracks the long-term effects of youth activism not just on the young people themselves but also on their organizations and communities could enrich the field and contribute important new understandings. Robust research on youth activism and its processes and impacts is needed if we are to take seriously the concerns raised by Braxton (this volume), Brodsky (this volume), Daniel and Valladares (this volume), and Rogers and Terriquez (this volume) about the lack of sustainable funding for youth activists and the need to convince philanthropic and governmental agencies to invest in youth-led solutions to the economic, social, and environmental problems they identify as most pressing.

CONCLUSION

In 2016, the United States remains the only country out of 197 nation states to have signed but not ratified the 1989 UN Convention on the Rights of the Child (UNCRC), "the most widely and rapidly ratified human rights treaty in history" (UNICEF, 2016). This Convention prohibits the imposition of life sentences without parole and the death penalty for youth under the age of 18. It protects children from exploitation and violence. And it clearly articulates children's rights to participate in decision making that affects them, commensurate with their maturity. Article 12 of the Convention reads:

> Parties shall assure to the child who is capable of forming his or her own views the right to express those views freely in all matters affecting the child, the views of the child being given due weight in accordance with the age and maturity of the child. (UNICEF, 2016)

Various groups in the United States stand in opposition to the ratification of this treaty, including parent-rights groups who worry that their parental authority will be curbed, conservative Republicans who want to safeguard states' rights to allow corporal punishment in schools, and law enforcement officials who favor harsh sentencing options for youth under the age of 18, which they fear this treaty would prohibit. Furthermore, as explained by *The*

Economist ("Why won't America ratify the UN convention on children's rights?," 2013), "fear that the social and economic rights established by the treaty could provoke lawsuits demanding that the government pay for these things" has led to a profound lack of political will among elected officials responsible for treaty ratification. As the case of the UNCRC treaty makes clear, in the United States, powerful neoliberal forces have converged to undermine (some would say attack) youths' agency and autonomy.

Nonetheless, contemporary youth activists are not waiting for adults to recognize their rights to have a say in the matters that affect them, their friends, their younger siblings, or future generations. They are rising up and staking their claims to the commons, defined so beautifully by Gallay and colleagues (this volume) as

> the natural areas and systems that we all share and for which we are all responsible, including the environmental systems and areas on which life depends; the public spaces and settings where we gather and negotiate how we want to live together; and the culture, values, and beliefs that hold a people or a polity together.

As they lay their claims to the commons, contemporary youth activists intentionally assert their own rights to these spaces and invoke the rights of others with whom they stand in solidarity and the "rights of the youth who [will] come after them" (Solyom, this volume).

We hope that this volume can serve as a call to action, a call to recognize, support, and celebrate the work of contemporary youth activists. In mounting this call, we wish neither to romanticize nor fetishize their efforts, and so this volume includes cases of real struggle, defeat, and heartache, as well as cases of success; however, it is our hope, too, that this collection helps readers to understand the vital role contemporary youth activists are playing in the larger struggle to reclaim and revitalize the public good in a neoliberal era.

REFERENCES

Au, W., & Ferrare, J. J. (2015). Introduction: Neoliberalism, social networks, and the new governance of education. In W. Au & J. J. Ferrare (Eds.), *Mapping corporate education reform* (pp. 1–22). New York, NY: Routledge.

Conner, J. (2014). Lessons that last: Former youth organizers' reflections on what and how they learned. *Journal of the Learning Sciences, 23*, 447–484. http://dx.doi.org /10.1080/10508406.2014.928213

Edwards, M. (2014). *Civil society* (3rd ed.). Hoboken, NJ: Wiley.

Freire, P. (2000). *Pedagogy of the oppressed* (30th Anniversary Edition). New York, NY: Continuum.

Ginwright, S. (2010). *Black youth rising: Activism and radical healing in urban America*. New York, NY: Teachers College Press.

Ginwright, S., Noguera, P., & Cammarota, J. (Eds.). (2006). *Beyond resistance!: Youth activism and community change: New democratic possibilities for practice and policy for America's youth*. New York, NY: Routledge Taylor and Francis Group.

Johnston, A. (2015, December 18). Student protests, then and now. *Chronicle of Higher Education*, pp. B6–7.

Sherrod, L. R., Flanagan, C. A., Kassimir, R., & Syvertsen, A. K. (Eds.). (2006). *Youth activism: An international encyclopedia*. Westport, CT: Greenwood Press.

Su, C. (2009). *Streetwise for booksmarts: Grassroots organizing and education reform in the Bronx*. New York, NY: Cornell University Press.

UNICEF. (2016). Convention on the rights of the child. Retrieved from http://www.unicef.org/crc/

Warren, M. (2010). *Fire in the heart: How White activists embrace social justice*. New York, NY: Oxford University Press.

Why won't America ratify the UN convention on children's rights? (2013, October 6). *The Economist*. Retrieved from http://www.economist.com/blogs/economist-explains/2013/10/economist-explains-2

Yates, L. (2014). Rethinking prefiguration: Alternatives, micropolitics and goals in social movements. *Social Movement Studies: Journal of Social, Cultural and Political Protest, 14*(1), 1–21. http://dx.doi.org/10.1080/14742837.2013.870883

Index

intergenerational strategies to claim,
124–126; intersectional effects of
restricting, 119–121; mobilizing for,
118–119, 123–124; resisting
enclosure of, 121–122; theory of
youth activism for, 126–130
Environmental discrimination, 116–118
Environmental justice movement,
116–118, 265, 267, 370–371
Environmental movement: race and
class in, 116–118; social justice and,
114–118
Environmental oppression, 119–121
Environmental stewardship, 113–130
Enyedy, N., 368–369
Epifano, Angie, 251
Erikson, E. H., 224
Essed, P., 208
Ethnic Studies: preservation of, 273;
stereotyping in, 347–348
Evans, M., 166
Expert validity, 335
Expertise transparency, 178, 179
Extrainstitutional movements, 43
Eye to Eye, 189–190

Fair policing, 330–331
Faith-based organizing networks, 49
Fan, R., 227, 231
Fanelli, S., 150
Fann, A. J., 347
Fast-food/restaurant workers, 34–35
Featherstone, L., 369
Feeley, T. H., 229
Feminist activism, 26; of Black women,
207–208; boot camp for, 256;
"slutwalk" movement and, 42;
storytelling in, 205
Femme-identified nonbinary people,
205–206
Fenning, P., 94
Ferguson, Missouri, 11, 80;
demonstrations in, 89–90; media
coverage of, 230; youth-organized
uprising in, 35

Ferguson Action, 80
Ferman, Barbara, 14, 185–198, 199n.9,
388, 393, 395
Fernández, Jesica Siham, 2, 8, 13, 30,
45, 46, 93–109, 388, 391–392, 395,
398
Ferrare, J. J., 4, 6, 12, 387
Fifteenth Amendment, 85
Fight for Fifteen, 35
Fine, M., 48, 49, 164, 294, 327, 329,
331, 333, 340, 368
Finkel, H., 296–297
First Nations, genocide of, 86
Fisher, J., 249
Fisher, R., 43
Fitoussi, J. P., 233
Flanagan, Constance A., 4, 13,
113–130, 165, 224, 231, 235, 387
Fletcher, A., 44
Flores Carmona, J., 102
Flores-González, N., 42
Florez, I., 123–124
Florez, J., 357
Floyd, et al. v. City of New York, 340
Folkman, S., 226
Food justice, 174–175
Forman, James, 83
Fossil Fuel Divestment campaign, 15,
367–381; on campus, 371–373;
framing, 373–379; intersectionality
and solidarity in, 376–380
Foster-Fishman, P. G., 230, 236
Fox, M., 327, 329, 347
Franklin, J. H., 84
Franklin, S., 39
Free Minds, Free People conference, 11
Free MUNI for Youth program, 234
Free rider mentality, 126
Free the Children, 9
Freelon, R., 150
Freeman, C., 347
Freire, P., 100, 102, 293–294, 304, 329,
341–342, 397
Frustration, 103–104, 236, 348–349
Frye, N., 120

About the Editors and Contributors

EDITORS

JERUSHA CONNER, PhD, is an associate professor of education at Villanova University. In 2015, she co-edited a National Society for the Study of Education yearbook, *Speak Up and Speak Out: Student Voice in American Educational Policy*.

SONIA M. ROSEN, PhD, is an assistant professor of education at Arcadia University and a member of the Philadelphia Student Union Board of Directors. Her research focuses on youth activism, exploring key themes such as youth identity development, youth leadership, youth civic dispositions, and young people's impact on policy.

CONTRIBUTORS

JANELLE ASTORGA-RAMOS has been a youth advocate since she was 14 years old and is a student at the University of New Mexico. She is studying Political Science and Chicano Studies.

WILLIAM AYERS is the author of *A Kind and Just Parent; Teaching toward Freedom; To Teach: The Journey in Comics*, and several other books on teaching and youth.

KIRA J. BAKER-DOYLE, PhD, is an associate professor of education at Arcadia University School of education in Glenside, PA. She is the author of *The Networked Teacher: How New Teachers Build Social Networks for Professional Support* and a forthcoming book with Harvard Education Press about teachers organizing for educational change.

PARISSA J. BALLARD is a developmental psychologist and research scientist at the University of California, Berkeley School of Public Health.

KIMBERLY BELMONTE is a doctoral student in the Critical Social/Personality Psychology program at the CUNY Graduate Center and a researcher with the Public Science Project.

ERIC BRAXTON is the executive director of the Funders' Collaborative on Youth Organizing, a national association of grantmakers and youth organizers committed to advancing youth-led social change. He is a founder and former executive director of the Philadelphia Student Union.

ALEXANDRA BRODSKY is a student at Yale Law School, senior editor at Feministing.com, and the co-founder, former co-director, and board chair of Know Your IX. She is the co-editor of *The Feminist Utopia Project: 57 Visions of a Wildly Better Future.*

JAMIA BROWN is a poet and a freshman at Ben Franklin High School. A native New Orleanian, she has been a member of Rethink since 2013. She is the Co-Facilitator of the Rethink Organizing Collective (theROC) and a 2015 and 2016 member of Rethink's Ujima Collective.

CAITLIN CAHILL, PhD, is Assistant Professor of Urban Geography & Politics, Pratt Institute, Brooklyn, NY. Her work has been published widely in journals and edited collections in feminist and urban geography, youth studies, and qualitative research.

JOE CURNOW is a PhD candidate at the Ontario Institute for Studies in Education at the University of Toronto. Joe previously worked as a student organizer and community organizer.

JULIA DANIEL is a PhD student at the University of Colorado, Boulder, with a background in community organizing around issues of racial, gender, and economic justice, focused on ending the schoolhouse-to-jailhouse pipeline.

SELMA DJOKOVIC is a Research Associate at the Public Science Project. She received her BA in Forensic Psychology from John Jay College of Criminal Justice.

BERNARDINE DOHRN is the founder and former director of the Children and Family Justice Center at the Bluhm Legal Clinic of Northwestern University School of Law. She writes and advocates for abolishing extreme sentences for children, for applying international human rights here at home, and for ending the institutionalized violence against, and the incarceration of, youth of color.

BARBARA FERMAN, PhD, is a professor of Political Science at Temple University and founder and Executive Director of the University Community Collaborative, a social justice initiative that provides media-based leadership development programming for high school and college students. She is the author of three books and numerous articles on urban politics and policy, community development, housing, racial integration, and pedagogy.

JESICA SIHAM FERNÁNDEZ, PhD, is an adjunct faculty member in the Ethnic Studies Program at Santa Clara University. She is a fellow of the Research Justice at the Intersections (RJI) scholars program at Mills College.

CONSTANCE A. FLANAGAN is the Associate Dean in the School of Human Ecology at the University of Wisconsin–Madison. She is the author of the book *Teenage Citizens: The Political Theories of the Young.*

BEATRICE GALDAMEZ is a 19-year-old youth organizer with the Youth Organizing Institute who is completing her freshman year at Peace College in Raleigh, NC.

ERIN GALLAY is a practitioner and researcher of youth environmental civic engagement. She studies youth environmental commons activism at the University of Wisconsin–Madison.

ALLYSON GROSS received her undergraduate degree at Bowdoin College and ran Bowdoin Climate Action's fossil fuel divestment campaign. Allyson is in the national leadership of the Divestment Student Network.

RACHEL GUNTHER, MSW, is the Associate Director of Youth on Board in Somerville, MA. In addition to her leadership role at Youth on Board, she has written numerous publications and provides consultation, training, and curriculum development for organizations regionally and nationally.

BEN KIRSHNER, PhD, is an Associate Professor of Education at the University of Colorado, Boulder, and Faculty Director of CU Engage: Center for Community-Based Learning and Research. He is the author of *Youth Activism in an Era of Education Inequality* (2015).

LUKE AUBRY KUPSCZNK is a doctoral candidate in Public Policy at the University of Massachusetts, Boston. In addition to his research on school accountability, education policy, and youth activism, he currently teaches high school in Orlando, Florida.

DEANA G. LEWIS is a doctoral student in educational policy studies with a concentration in gender and women's studies at the University of Illinois at Chicago.

JOSE LOPEZ is the Lead Organizer at Make the Road New York. He received a BA from Hofstra University. He was appointed as a member of the President's Task Force on 21st Century Policing.

ETHAN LOWENSTEIN, PhD, is a professor of teacher education at Eastern Michigan University and the Director of the Southeast Michigan Stewardship Coalition (www.semiscoalition.org), a hub of the Great Lakes Stewardship Initiative (www.glstewardship.org).

JOHN LUPINACCI is an assistant professor at Washington State University in the College of Education. His work as a former high school math teacher and experience with adult learning and place-based education contribute to his work in examining environmental education and sustainability through an interdisciplinary approach to cultural studies and social thought in education.

AMANDA MATLES is a geographer, filmmaker, artist, and activist. She is currently a doctoral student in the Earth and Environmental Science Department, Geography specialization and the Women's Studies Certificate Program at the CUNY Graduate Center.

GENEVIEVE NEGRÓN-GONZALES, PhD, is an assistant professor of education at the University of San Francisco. She is co-author of *Encountering Poverty: Thinking and Acting in an Unequal World*.

EMILY J. OZER, PhD, is a clinical/community psychologist and professor of community health and human development at the University of California, Berkeley School of Public Health.

ADILKA PIMENTEL is the Police Accountability Organizer at Make the Road New York. She works to politicize Black and Brown youth ages 14–24 using political education, leadership development, and the arts.

JOHN ROGERS is a professor of education at UCLA where he serves as the director of UCLA's Institute for Democracy, Education, and Access, and the faculty director of Center X.

CAROLINA S. SARMIENTO is an assistant professor at the University of Wisconsin–Madison in the Department of Civil Society and Community Studies. Sarmiento's research and practice focuses on learning from the grassroots and building sustainable and creative alternatives that help address inequality and injustice.

NATALIA SMIRNOV is a PhD candidate in Learning Sciences at Northwestern University. Her work focuses on civic learning in the context of digital and networked technologies, and the design of learning environments and infrastructures that support collaboration, cultural production, and democratic practice.

JESSICA ANN SOLYOM, PhD, is a postdoctoral research fellow at Arizona State University, Tempe, AZ. She is co-author of *Postsecondary Education for*

American Indian and Alaska Natives: Higher Education for Nation Building and Self-Determination.

BRETT G. STOUDT, PhD, is an assistant professor in the Psychology Department with a joint appointment in the Gender Studies Program at John Jay College of Criminal Justice and the Environmental Psychology Doctoral Program at the Graduate Center.

VERONICA TERRIQUEZ is an associate professor of Sociology at the University California, Santa Cruz. Her research focuses on civic engagement, educational inequality, and youth transitions to adulthood.

MARÍA ELENA TORRE, PhD, is the founding Director of the Public Science Project and faculty member in Critical Psychology at the Graduate Center of the City University of New York.

MICHELLE RENÉE VALLADARES is the Associate Director of the National Education Policy Center at the University of Colorado, Boulder. She has a PhD in education from the University of California, Los Angeles. Her work focuses on education equity, research use, youth and community organizing, and systemic school improvement.

MARK R. WARREN is an associate professor of Public Policy and Public Affairs at the University of Massachusetts, Boston, a John Simon Guggenheim Memorial Foundation Fellow, and a Fellow of the Hutchins Center for African & African American Research at Harvard University. He is the author of *A Match on Dry Grass: Community Organizing as a Catalyst for School Reform* and *Fire in the Heart: How White Activists Embrace Racial Justice.*

DARIAN X is a Youth Leader and Board Representative at Make the Road New York. He is dedicated to community organizing and forwarding public policy in New York City around both education and policing reform.

MARY YEE is a doctoral candidate at the University of Pennsylvania Graduate School of Education in the Reading/Writing/Literacy Program. Her interests are educational issues in immigrant communities, community and youth activism, and the intersection of health and educational disparities.